*The American
Immigration Collection*

Our Slavic Fellow Citizens

EMILY GREENE BALCH

Arno Press and The New York Times

NEW YORK 1969

OUR SLAVIC
FELLOW CITIZENS

A "SLAV INVADER"

The picture is of a young woman of Bohemian parentage, a graduate of a university of the Middle West. She was asked to pose in peasant costume to help interpret her people to America.

OUR SLAVIC
FELLOW CITIZENS

EMILY GREENE BALCH
Associate Professor of Economics, Wellesley College

NEW YORK
CHARITIES PUBLICATION COMMITTEE
1910

PRESS OF WM. F. FELL CO.
PHILADELPHIA

PREFACE

No critic, perhaps, will be so alive to the defects of this study as is the author, yet it is hoped that the book may have a value of its own. It is at least based upon first hand inquiry both in Europe and in America; and both are necessary. Acquaintance with any immigrant people in America only is not enough. The naturalist might as well study the habits of a lion in a menagerie or of a wild bird in a cage. To understand the immigrant we should know him in the conditions which have shaped him, and which he has shaped, in his own village and among his own people; we should study the culture of which he is a living part, but which he is for the most part powerless to transport with him to his new home. He must, however, be known also as he develops in America in an environment curiously and intricately blended of old and new elements.

Convinced of this, I spent the greater part of the year 1905 in Austria-Hungary, studying emigration on the spot, and over a year in visiting Slavic colonies in the United States, ranging from New York to Colorado, and from the Upper Peninsula of Michigan to Galveston. California was unfortunately not reached. One autumn was spent as a boarder in the family of a Bohemian workingman in New York City. Everywhere in Europe and this country, whether or not furnished with letters of introduction, I found Slavs of all classes and kinds ready to show me kindness and lend me intelligent and cordial assistance.

While this work has been in progress two most interesting books by Dr. Edward A. Steiner have appeared which deal with the same subject with an insider's close knowledge of conditions. Furthermore, the historical study of immigration which Professor Walter F. Willcox is conducting for the Carnegie Institute has been proceeding, and it is to be hoped that this will ultimately give us an adequate account of immigration from all the Slavic countries, as well as a history of Irish immigration,—which should have been written long ago, while the men of the famine era were still available as sources of information,—and an account of German, Scandinavian and Canadian immigration, of all of which there is crying need. The Italian and Jewish movements, having fallen in a more socially self-conscious period and at a time when the pressure of foreign colonies in our cities was a source of acute public concern, have been more written of. Students of immigration are also eagerly awaiting the completion of the work of the Commission on Immigration appointed by President Roosevelt.

The point of view from which my study was made is that of interest in the social character and consequences of the emigration in question. This is obviously a matter which, in the nature of the case, cannot be exhaustively studied, and in which the personal equation must play a considerable part. Certain aspects of the subject are left outside the program of this study,—among others, the question of routes and of conditions of transportation, and of Austrian and Hungarian legislation controlling emigration.

An important subject which has not been considered is the amount of pauperism and crime among Slavic immigrants. Such data as exist are commonly classified by country of birth and are therefore entirely unusable for our purposes. What inquiries I was able to make were quite inadequate and it was clear that to get trustworthy results (and untrustworthy ones are far worse than none), would require a long and laborious special investigation.

Among points that would repay a fuller study than

has been possible here are the relation of emigration to birth rates and over-population, to subdivision of property, and to other migration movements (especially to internal migrations), and to relative wages and costs of living.

The matter for this book was originally prepared as a series of magazine articles, which appeared in *Charities and the Commons* during 1906 and 1907. It has, however, been revised throughout, brought up to date so far as practicable, and increased by the addition of the first three chapters which are almost wholly new, of considerable statistical and bibliographical material, and of a reprint of the *True Story of a Bohemian Pioneer*. Having tried to make the book available to general readers, and especially to busy social workers, and at the same time useful to students, I sometimes fear that in consequence it will fit the taste of neither class. In more cheerful moments, on the contrary, I cherish the hope that the lighter and the heavier parts will mutually strengthen one another.

The subject seems to naturally classify itself in three ways—geographically, racially and by topics. For the European end of the story the first two classifications, the geographical and racial, coincide fairly well, and the subject is taken up province by province and at the same time race by race. Various topics,—causes of emigration, effects of emigration and so on,—naturally recur in each account. In the study of the Slavs in the United States, on the other hand, it seemed best not to take up separately either the different racial groups or the different sections of the country, but to consider the whole situation, topic by topic, with such incidental recognition of geographical and racial differentia as appeared practicable or necessary.

In conclusion I wish to thank the many persons, friends, correspondents and students, Slavs and Americans, in Europe and in this country, who have helped me to gather information and to prepare it for the press.

Their names are literally too many to include, but I
must at least make special mention of my obligations
to the unselfish traveling comrade who accompanied me
through Austria-Hungary.

EMILY GREENE BALCH

WELLESLEY COLLEGE
     March, 1910

TABLE OF CONTENTS

PART I

SLAVIC EMIGRATION AT ITS SOURCE

CHAPTER I

CHAPTER II

CHAPTER III

CHAPTER IV

CHAPTER V

CHAPTER VI

CHAPTER VII

CHAPTER VIII

CHAPTER IX

LIST OF ILLUSTRATIONS

LIST OF MAPS

LIST OF CHARTS

LIST OF TABLES

APPENDIX TABLES

PART I

SLAVIC EMIGRATION AT ITS SOURCE

Über den Bergen sind auch Leute

CHAPTER I

INTRODUCTORY*

The importance of American immigration is something that it is easy to underrate, just as it is easy not to see the forest for the trees. As a matter of fact, has history anything of equal importance to show since the great folk migrations which marked the breakdown of classic culture and the birth of the new Europe?

Significance of immigration to America

The era of exploration and colonization of the fifteenth and succeeding centuries opened up to Europe vast new regions in every quarter of the globe, but of these the American continents offered incomparably the most important opportunities for the spread and development of European civilization. The paramount question of the eighteenth century was not whether mediævalism was to yield its last strongholds to modernism,—a foregone conclusion only ratified by the French Revolution,—but rather, who was to hold the body of the North American continent. This was determined externally and apparently by wars and treaties, but more truly by the character of the migration to the new territory. Soldiers, missionaries, traders and trappers necessarily yielded to expanding colonies of permanent settlers.

Contest for the new world

The fate of nations was such that England acquired, as we know, the control both cultural and political over this region. The American Revolution broke, for the most important section of the continent, the political tie to England, but only to leave the United States to continue its independent development on the old foundations of English culture. The new world of

English control

* In the Bibliography will be found complete references to all writings mentioned in the text or in the foot-notes.

3

the Republic was substantially a renovated and modernized England.

Other constituents

But with all the English predominance in speech, institutions and views, there were always present considerable non-English elements; and culture, and to a less degree speech, was from the beginning modified and streaked with other national factors. How important the non-English contributions were is shown in Professor Commons' chapter on Colonial Race Elements.*

Immigration to 1880 English-speaking or Teutonic

Since that time, moreover, the country has received an almost continuous inflow which, at first made up of people either English or English-speaking, has gradually come to be of a composition more and more alien to the English in blood, speech and ideas. From the forties to the eighties, Irish and Germans were the chief immigrants. That is, until 1880 the bulk of the new additions to the population were either English in speech or, as Teutons, fairly near in blood to the English.

The new immigration

But with the eighties, roughly speaking, began a new wave of immigration, greater in numbers than any previous influx, differently constituted racially, different in economic character. The thirty years 1880–1909 brought us over seventeen million immigrants as against less than ten million in the preceding forty years. Not only did numbers thus increase, but during this period three new elements have been coming to be of main importance among our immigrants; namely, Italians, Jews, and Slavs. It is not until 1899 that it is possible to get the necessary data, but in the eleven years since then these three groups have made nearly six out of every ten immigrants, Italians being about a quarter and *Slavs over one-fifth of our total immigrant body* for that period.

The figures for the eleven years are: Total immigration, 8,514,103; Slavs, 1,849,139 (22 per cent); Italians, 2,061,148 (24 per cent); Hebrews, 990,182 (12 per cent).

The change in economic character referred to, con-

*Commons, John R.: "Races and Immigrants in America."

sisted in a lessened proportion of immigrants coming to settle (especially of those coming to settle as farmers), and an increased proportion of laborers and of men coming without their families with no intention of remaining. In all these characteristics Slavic immigration shares.

Necessarily this large influx of immigrants permanently affects the substance of the population of the United States. In 1900 only a little over half (53.8 per cent) of the population were what are commonly understood by the term "Americans"; that is, white people of native parentage on both sides.* The colored population of native parentage accounts for not quite one-eighth (11.9 per cent), and persons with one or both parents foreign make up the remainder of over one-third (34.3 per cent). Even of the "American" half, an indefinite number are descendants of foreign grandparents and of slightly more remote foreign ancestors.

To measure what all this means we must remember that back of all political developments, of all social institutions, lie the two great fundamental facts of human history—land and men. The innate qualities of these two determine all the rest. Thus, the character of the continent and the character of immigration have determined and are determining the quality of the civilization of this country, perhaps the greatest seat of the white race. *The two factors of history—population and environment*

There is much alarmist writing about our immigrants, and especially about those who come from the southeast of Europe. Whether or not sharing in the alarm, must we not recognize the movement as one of transcendent importance, and certainly one which it behooves us to understand as far as we can? *Immigration determines the first*

Yet the facts are realized by comparatively few. Many people are quite unaware that the Slavs have grown to be not merely a very large part of the total immigration, but an important element in our permanent *Slavs becoming an important element*

* If we add white persons with one parent native born the percentage rises to 60.5.

population. Indeed, as we shall şee, reliable estimates show that there are some four to six million now in the United States. We are unaware of these facts partly because the movement is so recent; partly, too, because the Slavs are less conspicuous among us than the Italians and Jews. They are less massed in the great cities; they are not constantly under the eyes of the ready writer and the reformer. A caricature of an Italian or a Jew on a vaudeville stage would be as readily recognized as that of an Irishman. Is this true of any Slavic type?

Slavic history unfamiliar

Furthermore, the Slavic group of peoples, whether in Europe or in America, is much less well known to most of us than are any of the Germanic or Latin peoples, or the Jews. Italian and Hebrew immigrants stand against a background of familiar history; we know something of their homes, their literature and their racial characteristics. This is much less true of the Slavs.

To educated people, of course, certain Slavic countries are fairly well known, notably Russia, Poland and Bohemia; but even to most of them I suspect southeastern Europe is in something of a snarl. Few perhaps would find it easy to locate precisely the Austrian provinces of the Bukowina or Carniola, or define the status of Bosnia, or even bound Servia or Bulgaria.

Complexity of Slavic national groups

Not only this, but there is no such person as a Slav any more than there is such a person as a Teuton or a Celt. All Slavs are primarily members of some distinct nationality; they are Russians, Poles, or what not, as the Teuton is a German or a Swede or an Englishman. With all but the chief of these Slavic nationalities we are so little acquainted that even their names are often unknown to us. In those places in America where Slavs are most numerous, in mining settlements and the industrial centres formed about great foundries or steel works, there is naturally even less knowledge of obscure groups of foreigners than in more academic circles. The Americans, Irish and others who have to

SLOVAK PEASANT DRESS. (See page 91)

Three types of cloak are shown, a woman's sheepskin coat with wool inside, a man's sheepskin jacket, and a man's cloak of white felt or "hunia," trimmed with braiding and embroidery. Boots of white felt are also shown. The embroidery of the women's dress, often so beautiful, is not conspicuous here.

do with them, whether as employers or as fellow workmen
or as neighbors, generally neither know nor care enough
to attempt any distinctions.

Frequently some one name is hit upon, and by that
all foreigners of a less familiar sort are called. In some
places Slav or Slavish serves to cover all but English-
speaking and German people,—even Italians, who are
no more Slavs than they are Irishmen. Dr. Warne, in
his excellent study of the situation in the coal regions,
"The Slav Invasion and the Mine Workers," uses the
term in this sense, as it seems to me most unfortunately.
In another place all may be called Hungarians, Huns or
Hunkies, whether or not they ever saw or heard of
Hungary; or they may all be Poles or Polanders or
Polacks, whether the name has any application or not.
The term Austrians, when used with an attempt at
precision, seems generally to designate either Italians
from the Austrian Tyrol, or the Slovenes from Carniola
and neighboring Austrian provinces.

Unfortunately, the unavoidable complexity of Slavic
classification is increased by the confusion and multi-
plicity of the English nomenclature as found in official
or semi-official reports and in current literature. To
designate the group as a whole, we have the words Slav,
Slavic, Slavonic, Slavonian, and sometimes Slavish,
—by some authors spelled Sclav, Sclavonic and so forth.
These commonly all mean the same thing, but Slavonian
may mean specifically "from Slavonia" (the eastern
part of Croatia-Slavonia), and Slavonian and Slavonic
are sometimes used to mean Slovak.

As regards the names of the different Slavic nationalities, there are in almost every case a shorter and a longer
form, as follows:

Russ	Russian	Croat	Croatian
Ruthene	Ruthenian	Serb	Servian or Serbian
Slovak	Slovakian		
Slovene	Slovenian	Bulgar	Bulgarian
	Czech or Chekh	Bohemian	

Confused nomenclature

The Pole alone has no variant of his name in good usage, though Polander and Polack are commonly heard. It is interesting to notice that though there is now no authority for this latter form of the name (which is apparently borrowed directly from the Polish word *Polak*, plural *Polaci*) it is found in Hamlet: "and meet the sledded Polacks on the ice."

I have tried in each case to use the more familiar form which, except for the Slovaks, appeared to me to be the longer one. The Bohemian word Čech I have represented by its English equivalent Chekh rather than by the more usual spelling Czech, which is Polish and has nothing to justify its adoption as the English form.

Eight groups of Slavic immigrants

Of the thirty-nine groups recognized in the classification of the Immigration Department eight are Slav; namely (in order of numerical importance as immigrants), (1) Polish, (2) Slovak, (3) Croatian and Slovenian, (4) Ruthenian or Russniak, (5) Bohemian and Moravian, (6) Bulgarian, Servian and Montenegrin, (7) Russian, (8) Dalmatian, Bosnian and Herzegovinian.* This does not exhaust the Slav nationalities, as we shall see, but it is enough to thoroughly bewilder most Americans.

Distinct though undistinguished

As a matter of fact, it is often impossible in America to distinguish these national groups, the Slovak, the Slovenians, and so on, especially as the men themselves, ignorant of English, can give little help. Yet the differences are there. The various Slavic nationalities are separated by distinctions of speech, historical experience, national self-consciousness, political aims, and often of religion. In American communities they have different churches, societies, newspapers and a separate social life. Too often the lines of cleavage are marked by antipathies and old animosities. The Pole wastes no love on the Russian, nor the Ruthenian on the Pole, and a person who acts in ignorance of these facts, a missionary for instance, or a political boss, or a trade-union organizer, may find himself in the position of a host who should

* For discussion of this classification see page 247.

innocently invite a Fenian from County Cork to hobnob with an Ulster Orangeman on the ground that both were Irish.

This great group of the Slavs must therefore be studied not merely as a whole in which all lesser outlines are blurred, but separately, each nationality by itself. This is even more true with respect to their conditions in Europe than in this country. Moreover, as has been said, it is only in relation to their European background that they can be understood here. And the study of the Slavic world is full of fascination.

CHAPTER II

THE SLAVIC NATIONALITIES IN EUROPE

Nationality has three factors

So much of the following account hinges upon questions relating to the racial and political conditions of the Slavs that it may be a convenience to some readers to have a certain small measure of preliminary information brought together to form a background.

First, as to the question of Slavic nationality. The idea of nationality is itself a complex one. It is far from being identical with that of the political unit (the state or nation), or with the purely physical conception of race. Three factors at least enter into it: community of blood evidenced by physical likeness, community of language, and community of culture and ideals.*

(1) Physical kinship

The first of these, racial kinship in the strict sense, involves anthropological questions too intricate for discussion here. All of the so-called races of Europe are clearly much mixed. Nevertheless, each of them generally has certain minor facial and other characteristics which, though not of scientific value, and far from universal, yet seem to constitute a type in a popular sense. So too with the Slavs. Although Professor Ripley in his "Races of Europe" calls them "physically an offshoot of the great Alpine race of central Europe," of which we may take the southern Frenchman or the northern Italian as the type, they are far from a pure or uniform race. Deniker indeed says that it is as useless to seek a Slav type as a Latin or Teutonic one.† Dolichocephalic and brachycephalic, tall and short, light and

---

* An interesting discussion of this will be found in the first chapter of Professor Auerbach's "Les Races et les Nationalités en l'Autriche-Hongrie."

† Deniker, "The Races of Man," page 345.

dark, all varieties are present. Their intermixture goes back indefinitely far into the mists of prehistoric eras, but in historical times also the inheritance of the Slavs has been complicated by exchange of blood with their various neighbors. Thus they have contributed a large though unmeasurable amount to German stock, and have themselves received in turn considerable contributions from Germans and others.

Yet amid all these complicated variations there gradu- The Slavic
ally forms in the mind of the observer what is felt to be type
a type, much as a composite photograph is made up by the merging of many impressions on the sensitive plate. This type, as it has shaped itself in my mind, is short, thick-set and stocky, rather than the reverse; not graceful nor light in motion. The face is broad, with wide-set eyes and marked cheek-bones; the nose broad and snub rather than chiseled or aquiline, the forehead rather lowering, the expression ranging from sullen to serene but seldom animated or genial. The eyes are of a distinctive shade, grey inclining to blue. One often sees these honest grey eyes in the dark-faced, dark-haired Croatians or Bosnians, as well as in the blonder northerners. The hair, in my typical Slav, is light in childhood, though never the pure flaxen of the Scandinavian; with added years it turns to a deep brown, darkening gradually through successive ash-brown shades. The whole suggestion is of strength, trustworthiness, and a certain stolidity, until excitement or emotion lights up the naturally rather unexpressive features. This picture is based upon personal opportunities for observation, which have included little acquaintance with Russians. It seems to me to agree fairly well with that of other observers.*

* My attempt at a portrait may be compared with Professor Steiner's, in the twelfth chapter of his interesting book, "On the Trail of the Immigrant," and with the excellent photographs by Mr. Lewis Hine, reproduced herewith. There are some excellent types in the pictures accompanying Miss Grace Abbott's article on the Bulgarians of Chicago in *Charities and the Commons*, Jan. 9, 1909.

(2) Community of language   Turning to the second point, community of language, we find the situation simpler. The Slavic languages form a well-marked family, clearly related to one another. The people who speak these languages consider themselves and are considered by others as Slavs; those who do not speak them cannot easily find any other test either to prove or in some cases to disprove Slavic affiliations. A common language implies, first, local proximity either past or present; second, some degree at least of common history; and third, it means a continuing possibility of intercourse—in modern times, of intercourse even apart from all except literary contact. It is likely, at least, to imply also a considerable measure of community of ideas and ideals. Furthermore, it facilitates intermarriage, if the prime necessity of proximity be present, and so constantly works toward fusion and physical uniformity.

Speech as a criterion of nationality   Thus, language is generally, for all practical purposes, the best and sufficient criterion of nationality; a rule, however, to which the Jews form an interesting exception. In Austria and Hungary, with their heterogeneous population, it is for the most part regarded as the test, and national feeling so rages that it invades even the domain of the census inquiry as to language. In Austria, the *Umgangsprache*, or language of ordinary intercourse, is asked for. This form of the question tends to swamp out small minorities, unless where now and then national zeal overleaps the barriers and, for instance, causes an individual to register himself as the only person in a locality using a given language in ordinary intercourse! One must suppose he talks a great deal to himself.

In Hungary the form of the question is altered, and the "mother tongue" is asked for, but as it is expressly provided that a man may select what tongue he chooses, and as heavy pressure is exerted upon every one to count himself a Magyar, the results doubtless underrate all non-Magyar elements. In any case the data as to lan-

A BOSNIAN VILLAGE

Except for the little mosque in the foreground and the costumes of the men, the scene is typical also of Croatia.

guage do not reveal the strength of the Hebrew element, which feels itself and is felt to be a markedly distinct group.   Here the rubric Israelite, in the data as to religious confession, gives the desired information except for baptized Jews.   How confused is the situation, is suggested by the answer to a census inquiry quoted by Boeckh, "My mother tongue is Polish, also Hebrew, also German, as happens to be required."*

The Slavic languages belong to the great Indo-Germanic or Aryan linguistic family.   If we divide this family into nine groups, as follows: (1) Indian (Hindi, etc.), (2) Iranian (Persian, etc.), (3) Armenian, (4) Hellenic (Greek, etc.), (5) Illyrian (Albanian, etc.), (6) Italic (Latin, modern Romance languages, Roumanian, etc.), (7) Keltic (Welsh, Irish, Gaelic, Breton, etc.), (8) Slavo-Baltic, (9) Germanic (Scandinavian languages, German, Dutch, English, etc.), the Slavic belong to the eighth. This includes the Lettic or Baltic languages as well as the Slavic.   Within the Slavic division the existing languages are many, even if we do not count dead languages like the Church Slavonic now used only in church rituals.

The Slavic languages

Their degrees of relationship do not correspond to the present geographical situation of the different peoples; on the contrary, one great linguistic group includes the languages of the Russians and of the three South Slav nationalities—Bulgarians, Servo-Croatians and Slovenians, while another contains those of the Bohemians, the Slovaks and the Poles, who, although neighbors of the Russians, are less nearly related to them in speech than are the distant Slovenians.†

Their relationships

* Compare Boeckh: "Die statistische Bedeutung der Volkssprache als Kennzeichen der Nationalität."   Berlin, 1866.

† A table showing relationships of Aryan languages may be found in Edmonds' "Introduction to Comparative Philology for Classical Students." See also Morfill: "Slavonic Literature," page 264, and Šafařik: "Geschichte der Slavischen Sprache und Literatur nach Allen Mundarten," pages 4 and 5.

The chief Slavic languages are:

The chief
Slavic lan-
guages

I.
1. Russian:
   a. Great Russian
   b. Little Russian
      (Ruthenian, Ukrainian)
   c. White Russian
2. Bulgarian
3. Servo-Croatian
4. Slovenian

II. 5. Polish
6. Bohemian
7. Slovak

Richness of grammatical forms

There are many dialectic groups within those named, but all that are given in the table doubtless deserve to rank as languages. All of these languages are elaborate, highly inflected tongues, even more so than Greek and Latin, which they resemble in many ways. Some of them even retain quantity as well as accent, which makes them especially fitted for singing or for quantitative verse like the classic.* As regards declensional forms Bulgarian is an exception in having almost entirely lost its cases. Bohemian, with seven cases, three numbers (the dual being by no means wholly absent), and three grammatical genders (besides in some cases different forms for animate and inanimate objects), is certainly not simple. The adjective is declined, as well as the noun, and takes a different form if in the predicate. The verbs too are very difficult, having elaborate iterative, frequentative and similar variations. On the other hand the spelling is absolutely logical, and an unerring guide to the pronunciation, and the accent falls uniformly on the first syllable. Russian, on the contrary, has a varying accentuation, impossible to predict, and a complicated orthography.

Alphabets and spelling

Slavic languages are made to seem much more remote from us than they really are, by the fact that some of them, namely Russian, Servian and Bulgarian, are

* Cf. Šafařik, page 39.

written in a different alphabet, while others, like the Bohemian, use so-called diacritical marks, or, like the Polish, employ different combinations of letters than ours to represent certain sounds. *Cz* is a no more unreasonable sign than *ch* to express the same sound; but like any convention, it needs to be explained to be understood. Another puzzling characteristic of spelling is the frequent omission of the vague vowel sound which goes with a liquid in such words as *trn* (thorn), *srb* (serb). The Croatian singer Trnina has recognized this by spelling her name for our benefit with an *e*.

This unfamiliar look of many Slavic words is due in part, as has been said, merely to unfamiliar systems of spelling, but it is not that only. It is a Slavic peculiarity to prefer to have a compound consonantal sound precede rather than follow the vowel—to say *brada* instead of the cognate *barba*, *mleka* rather than *milk* or *milch*, *lgati* rather than *lügen*, while we prefer the contrary.* But besides this, the Slavic tongue easily combines consonants which we cannot manage together, just as we can say sixths and not think it difficult, while to almost any other nationality it is literally inspeakable.

I am convinced that this unpronounceable appearance of many Slavic words, and especially of proper names, really sets up no small barrier to acquaintance. It has an actual psychological effect on many minds, awaking a sense not only of strangeness but of impatient rejection, as if choking food were offered one. The Pole or Ruthenian in America has more difficulty than the Italian or Jew in handing on his name unaltered to his children, especially if it be a long or difficult one, and not only employers but sometimes even teachers are guilty of the barbarism of arbitrarily making over or replacing a name that strikes them as uncouth or troublesome. *Difficulty of pronunciation a barrier*

As to the third element in nationality, community of culture and ideals, the question will be discussed later in connection with the question of so-called panslavism. *(3) Community of culture*

* Cf. Šafařik, page 37.

Estimate of
numbers
If the main living Slavic languages are some ten in number, how widespread is their use? In other words, what are the numbers and location of the main Slavic nationalities? It is not possible to give a perfectly precise answer, but Komarow, a Russian authority, offers interesting estimates (see Table 1) as to the numbers of Slavs in different national groups and in different geographical divisions.

This table shows a total of nearly 98,500,000 Slavs in Europe (out of a total European population in 1900 of some 398,000,000), and a grand total for all parts of the world, of 101,724,000 Slavs. The Slavs are thus almost a quarter of the total population of Europe, and if we consider not numbers but area their relative importance is still greater, as may readily be seen on Map I. If a line be drawn north from the head of the Adriatic they occupy most of the territory lying to the east of it.

The early
settlement
of the Slavs
in Europe
The Slavs are not only a numerous and widespread but an ancient European population. From an unknown date they have been moving westward in Europe, often in the wake of more aggressive and warlike peoples.* Early in the fifth century they seem to have reached the Elbe to the north, and the country near the head of the Adriatic to the south. In the sixth century they penetrated into Italy and, further east, settled in Greece and the Balkan country. By the end of the seventh century we hear of them in Bavaria, Thuringia, Mecklenburg, Brandenburg and Pomerania.†

Subsequent
loss of
territory
The Slavs indeed in early times occupied much territory which they afterward lost. Slavic tongues were spoken at Kiel, Lübeck, Magdeburg, Halle, Berlin, Dresden, Salzburg, Vienna. Slavs were in Oldenburg, Mecklenburg and Holstein to the north, almost as far

---

* Cf. Leger's "History of Austria-Hungary from the Earliest Time to the year 1889," pages 25, 26, 32.
† Pomerania still preserves a form of its Slavic name (*po*, upon, *more*, the sea). Cf. Latin *mare*. It is interesting to note the related name of Pomorski today given to the Slavs of the Adriatic shore.

TABLE 1.—NUMBERS AND LOCATION OF THE MAIN SLAVIC NATIONALITIES*

LOCATION	RUSSIANS INCLUDING LITTLE RUSSIANS	BULGARIANS	SERVIANS AND CROATIANS	SLOVENES	BOHEMIANS AND SLOVAKS	SORBS (WENDS)	POLES INCLUDING KASSUBS	TOTAL
European Russia	66,388,000	122,000	8,000	..	20,000	..	5,912,000	72,450,000
Germany	15,000	..	..	..	60,000	136,000	2,604,000	2,815,000
Austria-Hungary	3,096,000	30,000	2,960,000	1,260,000	7,007,000	..	2,645,000	16,998,000
France	3,000	..	..	..	..	..	8,000	11,000
England	1,000	..	..	..	..	..	5,000	6,000
Italy	..	..	1,000	30,000	..	..	..	31,000
Sweden and Norway	1,000	..	..	..	..	..	..	1,000
Roumania	16,000	30,000	45,000	..	..	..	..	91,000
Turkey	..	1,000,000	..	..	..	..	..	1,000,000
Bulgaria including East Roumelia	1,000	1,920,000	2,000	..	1,000	..	..	1,924,000
Servia	..	10,000	1,646,000	..	1,000	..	..	1,657,000
Bosnia and Herzegovina	..	..	1,197,000	..	..	..	..	1,197,000
Montenegro	..	..	260,000	..	..	..	..	260,000
All Europe	69,521,000	3,112,000	6,119,000	1,290,000	7,089,000	136,000	11,174,000	98,441,000
Asia	3,000,000	..	..	..	..	..	..	3,000,000
America	18,000	..	10,000	..	250,000	..	5,000	283,000
Total	72,539,000	3,112,000	6,129,000	1,290,000	7,339,000	136,000	11,179,000	101,724,000

*Komarow: "Karta Slavjanskich Narodnostej." (Chart of Slavic Nations.) St. Petersburg, 1890; as quoted in article "Slawen" in Meyer's Conversations Lexicon.

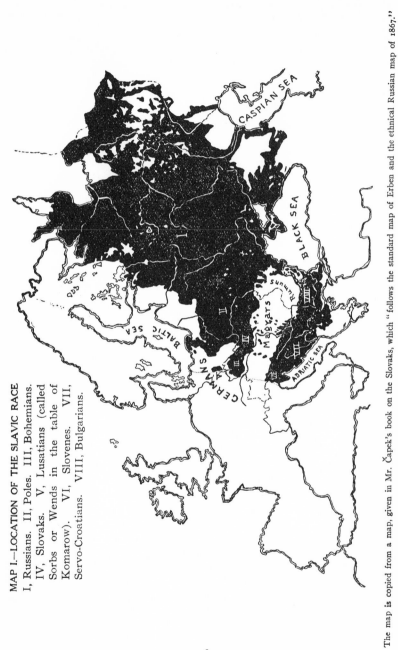

MAP I.—LOCATION OF THE SLAVIC RACE
I, Russians. II, Poles. III, Bohemians.
IV, Slovaks. V, Lusatians (called
Sorbs or Wends in the table of
Komarow). VI, Slovenes. VII,
Servo-Croatians. VIII, Bulgarians.

18

The map is copied from a map, given in Mr. Čapek's book on the Slovaks, which "follows the standard map of Erben and the ethnical Russian map of 1867."

as the Rhine on the west, and in Bavaria in the south. Leipzig takes its name from *Lipa*, the Slavic name for lime or linden, the national sacred tree. Place names in *itz, zig, a* (as for instance Jena), *dam* (like Potsdam) are Slavic.* In Germany proper all that is now visible of the Slavic population which once occupied nearly the whole of North Germany is (outside of the conquered Polish territory) names of places, family names, and little islands of Slavic folk like the Wends or Sorbs of the Lausitz† (Lusatia), whom Komarow estimates at 136,000. The Polabish people who once dwelt on the Elbe‡ have vanished, speech and all, though the speech was not entirely extinct in the early nineteenth century. The Germans, expanding eastward, killed out, forced back or overlaid the old Slavic population, and a process of intentional Germanization was begun which is perhaps at its height today in the efforts to depolonize the German territory which once was Poland.

Nowhere do the Germans, whose rôle in history is for the most part so noble, appear in such a sorry light as in their contact with their Slavic neighbors, whether we think of the Teutonic Knights in Slavic Prussia,§ of the persecutors of the Bohemian Hussites, or of the present policy of Prussia in whipping Polish school children for saying the Lord's Prayer in their own language.‖ Wherever Slav and Teuton have been in contact there has been friction, and the softer Slav has as a rule been the sufferer.

Teutonic-Slavic friction

Since the Slavs are and so long have been thus numerous and widespread in Europe, the question suggests

---

* Cf. Ripley: "Races of Europe," page 239; Morfill: "Slavonic Literature," page 3.
† The name is derived from a Slavic word for marsh. Cf. Morfill, pages 34, 35, 247 ff.
‡ The Slavic name for this river is *Labe*. The name means dwellers on the Elbe.
§ For a Polish version of this period see Sienkiewicz's spirited novel, "The Knights of the Cross."
‖ See the *Press*, organ of the Polish Newspaper Association of America, Milwaukee, April 1, 1907.

itself, why then have they played in history a part so much less prominent than the Latin and Teutonic peoples?

Slavic national character

Part of the answer may be, as has just been suggested, Slavic national character. I feel a profound scepticism, however, as to the value of generalizations in regard to the character of nations or races, more especially if it is assumed that such characters are inherited and unchangeable. Group types are perhaps quite as much products of social development and imitation, determined by historical causes economic and other, as they are the expression of innate qualities. Moreover, generalizations as to Slavs are particularly dangerous, in that they relate not to any single national unit but to a vast group defined largely by kinship of speech. As in discussions of the Teuton, they have their place, but too often the person making statements as to Slavs has in mind some special group with which he is best acquainted, or which is in point for the moment. I frequently find that by "the Slav" is meant the Russian. Now generalizations about Russians are themselves sufficiently hazardous at best; certainly they should not be lightheartedly applied to all Slavs, from most of whom Russians in some ways diverge widely.

Lack of aggressiveness

In any case, it appears to be true that Slavic peoples have not been fitted to play a conspicuous part in the era of bloody struggle which Europe has passed through, during the feudal period and since. In spite of the personal bravery which has made Slavs famous fighters, from the Polish Legion to the Cossacks of the Ukraine or the Croats of the military confines, they seem to lack some element of aggressiveness, something of the instinct to retaliate. The phrase "Das Tauben-blut der Slaven" (the dove blood of the Slav), which apparently originated with the poet Kollár, owes its currency to its element of truth.

Lack of cohesion

With the exception of the steady expansion of the Russian empire and the extension of Poland in its era

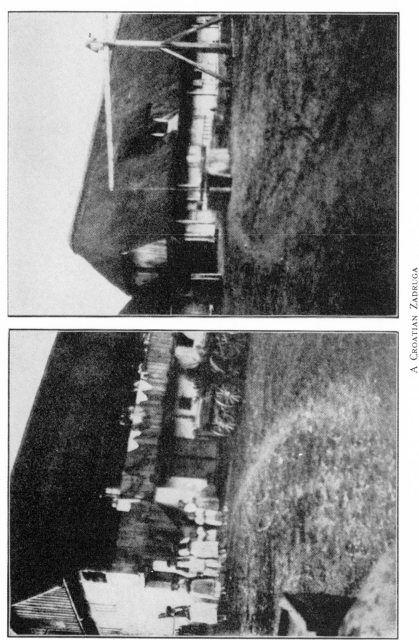

A Croatian Zadruga

1. The main dwelling house, where sixty persons were living as one family with property held in common. Some of the young men were in America. 2. One of the farm buildings built about the central yard.

of political greatness, the Slavs have not shown much gift for state-building. They appear to be deficient in the faculty for cohesion and leadership. Only within the smallest social unit has Slavic political genius evolved stable forms of organization and mutual social control. The Russian communal village or *mir*, the South Slav *zadruga*, or communal household, and *bratstvo* (literally brotherhood), or clan, are developments of the very greatest interest.* But the various early agglomerations of territory and power under Slavic rulers like Samo or Svatopluk or Boleslav of Bohemia, which for a time seemed to promise a Slavic empire, soon fell to pieces of themselves, or were overpowered, or else were absorbed by the chances of dynastic inheritance. Historians are full of references to the lack of Slavic cohesion. Seton-Watson,† for instance, says "Suffice it to say that the Slavs have throughout history shown a fissile and centrifugal tendency, and thus the mysterious figures of Samo and Svatopluk are the only Slav empire builders till we reach the days of Peter the Great. Ottocar of Bohemia and Ivan the Terrible are possible exceptions."

But quite apart from any supposed national characteristics, there have been three powerful reasons for backwardness and disunion in Slavic lands. *External causes of division*

For one thing, the Slavic peoples are, as may readily be seen on Map I (page 18), separated into two groups by a strip of non-Slavic population forced between the Russians, Poles and Bohemians to the north, and the Slovenians, Servo-Croatians and Bulgarians to the south. This non-Slavic wedge is German in the west, extending in a solid mass through the Austrian provinces of the Tyrol, Styria, Carinthia, Upper and Lower Austria and across into Hungary as far as Pressburg (Poszony). Austria is, indeed, the Eastern Empire (Oester Reich) of the Teuton. Where the German population ends the *(1) The Slavs split into a northern and southern group*

* For the zadruga see page 161; for the bratstvo see the book by Krauss on the customs of the South Slavs, or Mijatovich's books on Servia.

† Seton-Watson: "Racial Problems in Hungary," page 15.

Magyar begins, and to the east of the Magyars lie the
Roumanians, extending across to the Black Sea. The
Slavs, thus held apart, have been by this fact alone
shut off from the possibility of forming a single whole,
or of wielding an influence comparable to their numbers.

But to this have been added two far more important
historical causes which have tended to keep Slavs apart
from one another and also outside of the main current
of European life.

(2) The
schism be-
tween East
and West

The moral watershed between East and West ran
through the Slavic countries, and the greater part of the
Slavs found themselves on the eastern side, looking to
Byzantium for light, as those of the West looked to Rome.
To this day Russians, Bulgarians and Servians are, taking
them as a whole, Greek Orthodox, while on the other hand
Poles, Bohemians and Croatians are Roman Catholics.
Šafařik, writing forty or fifty years ago, counted about
35,500,000 Greek Orthodox, 18,500,000 Roman Catholic,
and 1,250,000 Protestant. The strength of the *odium
theologicum* is notorious, and this difference in ecclesiastical allegiance has been a cause of contention and mutual
aversion throughout Slavic history.

Political
and literary
results of
religious
divergence

Moreover, this inclusion of the major part of the Slavs
in the Eastern sphere of influence had political and
literary as well as religious results. Byzantium as a
centre of the world of ideas meant something very different from Rome; something much less vitalizing and
significant for the future. The mere fact that the
Orthodox Slavs used the Cyrillic or Russian alphabet
meant a real barrier between them and the West, a
serious obstacle to the interchange of ideas with Catholic
Slavs, and to knowledge of one another's literatures.
The Roman Catholic Slavs used either the Latin characters as we do or the German ones. The latter are still
employed by the Sorbs in Germany and till about 1830
were used by the Bohemians also. Polish and Bohemian
books intended for the lowest class are still occasionally
so printed, and one runs across old Bohemians who can-

not read Bohemian except in German print and script. Moreover, the Western and Catholic nationalities were in touch with Frenchmen and Germans, and, along the Adriatic coast, with Italians, and were constantly involved in the politics of Western Europe. Thus in a second way the Slavic unit was split in two,—north and south by an alien body of population, east and west by differences of religious, political and literary affiliation.

A third and most important factor which kept the Slavic peoples off the European stage and delayed their political and cultural development was the Tatar and Turkish invasions against which their countries served as a set of buffer states. They were indeed, with Hungary, the heroic bulwark of Christendom, and in the tremendous struggle great bodies of them were submerged for longer or shorter periods. Russia was not freed till 1489 from a subjection to the Tatars which had lasted two and a half centuries. Turkish misrule came later and lasted longer. The Balkan Slavs suffered under it until 1878, when certain provinces were freed, Servia being made an independent kingdom, Bulgaria a practically independent principality, and Montenegro an independent principality, while Bosnia and Herzegovina were given to Austria-Hungary to administer. Thus ended, except for the Slavs of Macedonia, some three centuries of Turkish control which, so far as opportunity for progress goes, might almost be eliminated from Slavic history.

Even countries which were not subjugated were almost equally handicapped by incessant border warfare. Poland spent much of her best blood repulsing the Tatars and Turks, and as late as 1681, under her gallant king Sobieski, was delivering Vienna from its Turkish besiegers. Croatia in all its border parts was organized as the so-called "Military Confines," and its people were withdrawn from normal civil life. This situation was not put a final end to until 1881.

In almost every case there was an exhausting drain

(3) Conflict with Tatars and Turks

on the vital forces of the Slavic peoples, and a most demoralizing degree of uncertainty. A farmer does not need to have his barns burned every harvest time in order to lose his interest in expensive improvements. It is interesting to note how the figure of the raiding Turk pervades the different folk literatures, even the Slovak. All this border warfare and political confusion militated against the growth of capital and the development of architecture and city life, and in general against the evolution of modern societies, non-feudal, industrial and enlightened. Meanwhile, sheltered behind the living barrier of Slavs and Magyars, the rest of Eúrope was developing and progressing.

Slavic unity

Not only have Slavic peoples suffered from conflict with external oppressors; they have also been at various points in bitter conflict one with another. The Poles have suffered at the hands of Russians, the Ruthenians at the hands of both Russians and Poles. Croatians and Servians have rubbed. Yet on the whole there has been, to a rather surprising degree, a sense of a certain unity among the different Slavic nationalities. Long before modern ideas of nationalism had awakened there were evidences of some measure of this "consciousness of kind," and early Slavic history has some interesting examples, already alluded to, of more or less successful efforts toward political union, under Samo, "King of the Slavs," in the seventh century, Svatopluk, King of "Great Moravia," in the ninth century, and in the tenth century under Boleslav the Great of Poland as king of the Slavs.*

Rise of nationalism

But it was with the close of the eighteenth century that national feeling in its modern form awakened under the stimulus of the ruthless way in which national demarcations were disregarded and national organisms cut up or forced under the rule of hated and alien powers. Germany, stirred by Fichte to rise against Napoleon; Greece and Italy achieving their independence;

* Leger: "History of Austria-Hungary," pages 28-29, 45-49.

—these are the stock examples. But Poland, when her peasants with their poor scythes went out under Kosciuszko against her invaders in 1794, is an earlier instance.

The claims of national feeling grew more insistent with the passage of time, and the revolutionary year 1848 brought to vivid expression not only demands for the constitutional rights of states but passionate yearnings for the deeper rights of nationalities. There was a renascence of languages that had been relegated to the peasant hut and the nursery; an outburst of national literatures. Along with a revival of the Bohemian, Slovak, and Illyrian (or South Slav) languages came also the desire for a Slavic *rapprochement*, the so-called panslav movement, the way for which had been prepared by poets and thinkers for years previous. It is interesting to note that even as early as 1713 the philosopher Leibnitz said to Peter the Great, "We are both of Slavic ancestry. You have wrested the world's mightiest powers from barbarism, and I have founded a realm of equal extent. The originators of a new epoch, we are both descendants of that race whose fortunes none can foretell."* This sounds like an anticipation of Herder's prophecy, in his "Ideas on the Philosophy of a History of Mankind," that a great future lay before the Slavic peoples, an era of territorial expansion and of peaceful devotion to arts and economic progress.

Linguistic revivals and Slavic rapprochements

In 1848, as already said, the growing enthusiasm for these ideas found expression. A Slav congress met in Prague, which, to the vast amusement of its enemies, found it necessary to confer in German as the only language understood by all. At that date Russia was the only independent Slavic state, for Poland was divided under three masters, Bohemia was under the heel of Austria, and the other Slavic nationalities under one or another alien rule. Russia was thus given an overpowering prestige which she employed to turn the move-

The Slav Congresses and Russian hegemony

*Quoted in Čapek's "The Slovaks of Hungary," page 23.

ment to her own advantage. She has been glad to assume the title and rôle of "Protector of the Slavs," and was lauded as such by different Slavic deputations at the Ethnographical Congress at Moscow in 1867. Especially in Balkan affairs this has strengthened her influence.

Panslavism   The panslavic trend has thus become to a greater or less degree confused with a tendency to look to Russia as the head of the Slavic family, and a desire for political affiliation. For this reason the Poles have held markedly aloof from it, and governments with a Slavic minority among their people have made it a bogey, and often a very convenient one. Thus the Magyars choose to represent all nationalistic efforts of the Slovaks as panslavic agitation and treason. Unfortunately some color was lent to this view by the events of 1848, when the Slovaks welcomed the Russian invaders of Hungary whom Austria had called in against the Magyars under Kossuth,—a policy since bitterly regretted by Slovaks themselves, who now recognize that their lot is indissolubly bound up with that of Hungary, and who ask only for the just treatment of all citizens at the hands of the ruling race, the Magyars.

Russo-phobia   The Magyar fear of Russian conspiracy often leads to laughable results. I had just heard that it was only by an accident that my girl traveling companion and I had escaped being arrested as Russian spies, when I was amused to find in a book of travels, "Across the Carpathians," published some fifty years before, an account of the actual imprisonment on the same charge of two equally innocent English lady tourists.

Panslavism as a non-political ideal   In reality, so-called panslavism, as voiced, for instance, by its great apostle, the poet Kollár, is a striving for a non-political and purely spiritual union. In an essay written in 1837 he says, "For the first time in many centuries, the scattered Slavs regard themselves once more as one great people......The Slav nation strives to return to its original unity." But the common bond "does not consist in a political union of all Slavs, nor in demagogic agitation against the various governments and rulers, since this could only produce confusion and misfortune. Literary reciprocity can subsist in the case of a nation which is under more than one sceptre and is divided into several states. Reciprocity is also possible in the case of a nation which has several religions and confessions, and where differences of writing, of climate and territory, of manners and customs prevail. It is not dangerous to the temporal authorities and rulers, since it leaves frontiers and territories undisturbed, is content with the existing order of things, and adapts itself to all forms of government and to all grades of civil life."....."Under alien non-Slav rulers, so long as they are tolerant, the weaker Slav races find better guarantees and security for the independence and survival of their language, which under the rule of some more powerful Slav race would, according to the laws of attraction, be entirely absorbed, or would at least commingle and finally vanish away."*

Kollár's program, as stated by Mr. Seton-Watson, was: book depots in the various capitals, free public libraries, chairs of Slav languages and literatures, a general Slav literary review, the reform of Slav spelling, comparative grammars and dictionaries, collections of songs, proverbs and folklore.

In some such shape as this the idea lives in the minds of many Slavs to-day. Again, it takes political form and is a powerful force cautiously reckoned with by continental diplomacy. The Balkans, Servia, Montenegro, Bosnia, Croatia, all Slavic Hungary, all Slavic Austria, Poland, Russia are more or less permeated by it. It is a current which often complicates economic and constitutional movements and groupings in all these regions, and the happy direction of its energy is one of the great problems of European statesmanship.†

Political panslavism

* Kollár, J.: "Über die literarische Wechselseitigkeit," quoted by Seton-Watson, page 55.
† See Panslavism in the Bibliography.

CHAPTER III

CONDITIONS IN AUSTRIA-HUNGARY

Importance of Austria-Hungary for Slavic immigration
For the study of Slavic immigration to the United States, the centre of interest is Austria-Hungary, not Russia as might be supposed, although only 17 or 18 per cent of all Slavs are subjects of Emperor Francis Joseph, while over 70 per cent are subjects of the Czar. The former country sends us the great bulk of our Slavic immigrants. During the decade 1899–1908 nearly seventy out of a hundred of them came to us from Austria-Hungary and only twenty-five in a hundred from the Russian empire.

Not only this, but the different Slavic nationalities are so placed that all of them except Bulgarians and Russians are to be found within the boundaries of Austria-Hungary. Poles, Ruthenians, Slovaks, Croatians, Servians, as well as Bohemians are subjects of the dual monarchy. A study of the stream that comes to us thence is therefore a study of a part at least of every Slavic immigrant group except two,—and those of minor numerical importance,—and an investigation of Slavic emigration from Austria-Hungary should give us a fair basis for the discussion of the Slavic movement to America. The remainder of the first part of this book is confined substantially to that part of the Slavic world.

Geographical conditions
Geographically as well as politically, Austria, to consider her first, is very complicated.* With no natural centre or frontier, she is made up of a stretch of adjoining

---

* Physical features are shown on Map IV, opposite page 35. See also the Bibliography under the titles Austria-Hungary, Austria, and Hungary.

territories lying like a wreath almost three-quarters of the way around Hungary, which, with Croatia and Bosnia, is set like a kernel within this embrace. All of the northeastern provinces of Austria,—Moravia, Silesia, Galicia, Bukowina,—are bounded to the south by the arc of the Carpathian range, which separates them from Hungary. The Carpathians are great rounded green hills rather than mountains, except in one place where the peaks of the High Tatra, with their romantic crags and lakes, attract pleasure seekers from both the Hungarian and the Polish (Galician) sides.

From Vienna, south and west, the country is broken by complicated Alpine ranges which run into the Swiss Alps to the west and merge to the south in the Balkans, while the Julian and Dinaric Alps parallel the Adriatic shore. Bohemia and Galicia alone of the Austrian crownlands have any considerable stretch of open, level land.

Hungary on the contrary, apart from mountainous Transylvania and the slopes and foothills of the Carpathians which bar it from the Austrian provinces to the north, is a great fertile plain watered by the Danube and the Theiss which flow across it. *Of Hungary*

Politically, the dual monarchy is nothing short of a monstrosity. The relation between Austria and Hungary created by the *Ausgleich* of 1867 is much slighter and more formal than is perhaps always realized. The same ruler is emperor of the one country and king of the other. To speak of Emperor Francis Joseph at Budapest is to give bitter offence: there he is king only. The two countries have in common an army and navy, a tariff, a system of weights, measures and coinage, and three ministers (for war, foreign affairs and finance), and their "delegations" meet to arrange common affairs. Outside of these matters they stand apart; they have not even a legislature in common, nor the same money nor post-office system. *Political organization of the monarchy*

Austria herself is an accidental dynastic agglomeration of kingdoms, archduchies, duchies, margravates and so

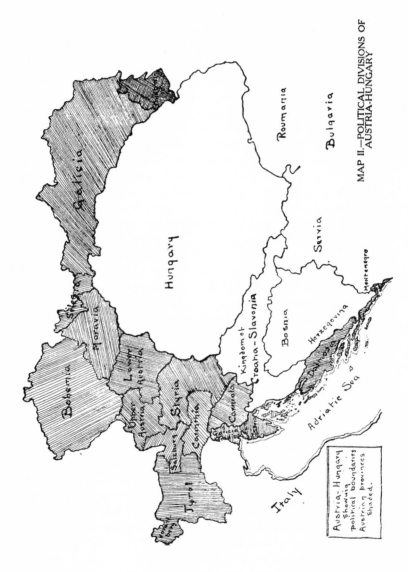

MAP II.—POLITICAL DIVISIONS OF
AUSTRIA-HUNGARY

Galicia

Hungary

Roumania

Bulgaria

Silesia

Moravia

Lower Austria

Upper Austria

Bohemia

Styria

Carinthia

Carniola

Kingdom of
Croatia-Slavonia

Bosnia

Herzegovina

Servia

Montenegro

Tirol

Adriatic Sea

Italy

Austria-Hungary.
Showing
Political boundaries.
Austrian provinces
shaded.

forth, seventeen "crownlands" in all, which the house of Habsburg has brought together as an inheritance. *Tu felix Austria nube.*

Hungary proper is less confusing, since the only distinct divisions are the former principality of Transylvania or Siebenbürgen (and even this is now an integral part of the country), and the important Adriatic port of Fiume which, though separated from her other territory by the whole width of Croatia, belongs to Hungary, and gives her her only outlet by sea. The "autonomous kingdom" of Croatia-Slavonia, under an elective Ban or Governor, is united to Hungary proper somewhat as Hungary itself is united to Austria. Together these constitute "the lands of the crown of Saint Stephen," or the Kingdom of Hungary.

Add to all this the provinces of Bosnia and Herzegovina, which, until they were annexed in 1908, were still nominally under Turkish sovereignty.

(The geographical and political confusion of the dual monarchy is insignificant compared with the confusion of tongues, and the racial or national conflicts and animosities which divide it, for the most part cutting across all political and administrative lines.)In Bohemia, where the national conflict is perhaps as acute as anywhere in Austria, it is Bohemians (Chekhs) against Germans. To the east in Galicia (Austrian Poland) there is a triple tangle with Poles, Ruthenians and Jews. Further east still in the Bukowina, the large Roumanian element adds to the complexity. In the northwest there is the Italian Tyrol, and an actively agitating Italian element in Istria, and along the Dalmatian shore, and above all in Trieste. The Slovenes, who form the bulk of the population in Carniola, and a considerable minority at least in Styria, Carinthia and the Coast Lands, are everywhere in conflict with the German element, whether as upper or under dog, and in Trieste with the Italians as well.

In Hungary the situation is even worse than in Austria, in proportion as more pressure from above creates an

Friction between nationalities

MAP III.—NATIONALITIES OF AUSTRIA-HUNGARY AND THE BALKAN STATES, AS INDICATED BY LANGUAGE SPOKEN

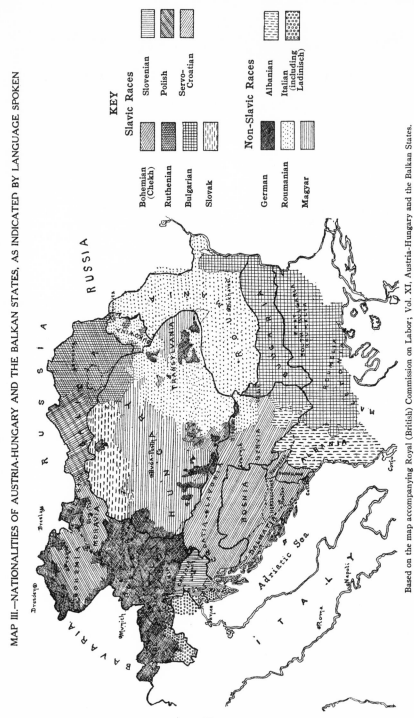

KEY

Slavic Races

Bohemian (Chekh)
Ruthenian
Bulgarian
Slovak

Slovenian
Polish
Servo-Croatian

Non-Slavic Races

German
Roumanian
Magyar

Albanian
Italian (including Ladinisch)

Based on the map accompanying Royal (British) Commission on Labor; Vol. XI, Austria-Hungary and the Balkan States.

intenser national reaction.   The almost 3,000,000 Roumanians in and about Transylvania, the 2,000,000 Slovaks in the Carpathian highlands, and the scattered German populations amounting in all to over 2,000,000, are all utterly discontented with Magyar treatment, which too often amounts to arbitrary and cruel persecution.

In Croatia, with a population racially fairly homogeneous, religious differences and diverse political aspirations sometimes make trouble between Croatians and Servians in spite of their common blood and common language, and all Croatia is in a constant state of tension as regards Magyar policy and practices.   These mutual jealousies and antagonisms would seem enough without being further complicated by external attractions and repulsions—by the "All-Deutsch" movement in Austria and outside, by the cry of "Italia Irredenta," by the panslav tendencies already discussed, by Russian and Servian ambitions, and by the whole Balkan problem and the dream of a federated Slavic state to include all the South Slavs.*

We in the United States have little conception of what such conflicts mean.   Our racial problems may be worse; at any rate they are quite different.   In Austria and Hungary these are struggles of different cultures, languages (and of political states back of them), to win adherents and power.   Men indignantly repudiate the use of languages which they understand perfectly well, and questions of the language of school instruction engage the most impassioned feelings.   Blood has been shed, not so long since, in riots caused by the determination of the Germans that the Italians should not have a university at Innsbrück, nor the Chekhs one in Brünn. Even questions which should be purely scientific are troubled by these prepossessions and aims.

The awakening of nationalistic feeling has done im-

Effects of nationalistic feeling

* Some statistical data as to the nationalities of Austria and Hungary are given in Appendix I, page 429.

3

mense good, but it also does immense harm. The good human energy wasted, for instance, by Germans and Bohemians in merely blocking one another is pitiable. All this not only narrows and embitters, it greatly retards progress. It must be said, however, that these questions chiefly interest the class which is designated throughout these countries as "die Intelligenz"; and those absorbed in these questions range from the sort of politicians who love to fish in troubled waters, to the purest and most disinterested idealists. The simple people in the country places, however, who are for the most part the people that come to us, are at home comparatively little concerned with such matters. They are mainly "conscious of kind" in a much narrower range. (Each little village is a tiny world in itself, with its own traditions and ways, its own dress, perhaps even its own dialect. The neighbor from the next town, even, is an outsider. In a Bohemian market-place I saw a sign, which might have come out of the guild-merchant period of English history, forbidding "foreigners" to sell to dealers before ten o'clock.

It is an interesting question how the transition to the new world affects these racial relations.

How emigration affects racial relations   In the first place, among some peoples and at some points emigration has as a consequence a growth of racial feeling. The man whose sense of social solidarity had been limited to his hamlet or parish wakens to a wider group consciousness. The Slovak finds other Slovaks quite intelligible even if of another town, nay even if of another county, and he thus matures for political-racial interests. Political leaders take advantage of this heightened racial feeling and of the freedom of the new world to teach their people patriotism as they understand it. For instance, in America, Polish leaders indoctrinate their people with Polish enthusiasm and hopes of a future free Poland, as they could not do in Europe; and the Slovak is taught by his national guides to interest himself in the struggle for national

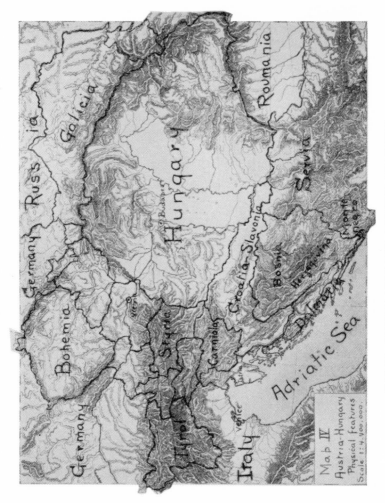

MAP IV.—AUSTRIA-HUNGARY. PHYSICAL FEATURES

Germany

Russia

Galicia

Roumania

Bohemia

Hungary

Servia

Germany

O Budapest

Vienna O

Styria

Croatia-Slavonia

Bosnia

Herzegovina

Monte negro

Carniola

Dalmatia

Tirol

Venice

Italy

Adriatic Sea

Map IV
Austria-Hungary
Physical features
Scale 1:4,400,000

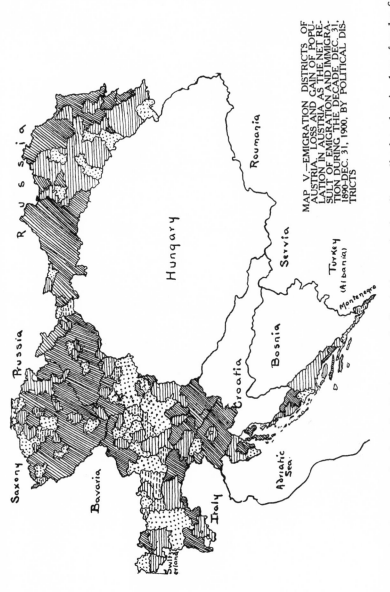

Districts showing net gain, dotted; districts practically stationary, broken lines; districts showing loss of under five per cent, horizontal lines; districts showing loss of five per cent or more, oblique lines.

For the figures by provinces see Table 3, page 48. For the corresponding data for Hungary and Croatia see Map VII, page 105. For the figures for the Slovak Counties of Hungary, see Table 7, page 102.

MAP V.—EMIGRATION DISTRICTS OF AUSTRIA. LOSS AND GAIN OF POPULATION IN AUSTRIA AS THE NET RESULT OF EMIGRATION AND IMMIGRATION DURING THE DECADE DEC. 31, 1890–DEC. 31, 1900, BY POLITICAL DISTRICTS

existence in Hungary. In the same way not only Slavs
but of old the Irish, and later the Syrians, Armenians
and other oppressed and burdened peoples have found
in America, where liberty and prosperity give them room,
a national recruiting ground for patriots.

But the secondary effect and the more universal one
is in the opposite direction. The widening process
continues. The Slovak, for instance, comes naturally to
find himself classed, both by himself and by others, with
Poles, Ruthenians, even Croatians; he feels that he is
nearer to them than to Germans, Irish or Yankees.
But panslavic feeling is a frail plant in America; the
contrast of practical concern is that between "foreigners"
and "Americans," between the green outsider and the
insider who alone has a chance at whatever plums
there may be. The children above all are apt to be
profoundly bored by national questions over which
their parents become so strangely agitated. Thus' the
old national passions tend to die away, partly checked
by personal and material concerns and the desire to
"get on," partly replaced by new interest in questions
of wider import, or at least of more immediate application.

CHAPTER IV

GENERAL CHARACTER OF SLAVIC EMIGRATION FROM AUSTRIA-HUNGARY *

While it is true that each Slavic national group, each Slavic territory, must be studied separately to be understood, there are certain features which occur in all, and which in spite of some repetition, may to advantage be discussed in a preliminary way in their general bearings. ^{— removed}

One of the most important general facts about our Slavic immigrants is that apart from the early Bohemian movement they for the most part represent the peasant class. There is, I think, much misunderstanding in America as to what this means. A peasant seems to be understood as a synonym for a member of the lowest possible social class; a being devoid of all claims to respect who takes a great step up when he becomes a factory employe. Such views rest on a serious misconception. The peasant is a landholder, more nearly comparable to the American farmer than to any other class among us, and at home is far from being at the bottom of the social ladder. The old peasant life, the substratum of all European history, is known to us as Americans only through literature, history and travel, for America has never had a peasantry, and in England, from which we derive, agriculture has been carried on for centuries, not by peasant proprietors, but by landless laborers. Yet the system which still largely subsists in Austria and Hungary was once universal throughout feudal Europe, passing away in some countries earlier, in others later.

Common features in Slavic emigration

Some misconceptions as to peasants

* The development and amount of Slavic emigration is considered province by province in the following chapters of Part I. An account of sources of statistical information (apart from the American data) is given in Appendix V, page 433.

37

In Austria, up to 1848, mediæval conditions were comparatively little changed. Actual serfdom, in the sense of absence of all personal rights, had indeed disappeared in the fifteenth century. But up to 1848 the legal ownership of land was still all vested in the lords or landed class; the peasants had only so-called *unterdominium* in their holdings, which were of two main classes, those which were inherited and those held for life only.

The peasant's status in Austria The peasant holding involved very definite duties and rights. In return for his land the peasant had to do a certain amount of work for his lord, and these labor dues (Bohemian, *robota*) were often very oppressive. At certain seasons, as Christmas or Easter, he had to pay special dues in kind, such as poultry or eggs. Besides all this, the lord still retained many of the old privileges, such as hunting rights and the monopoly of milling, brewing and of selling drinks. The peasant could not sell or mortgage his land except on certain conditions nor without permission, and he could not throw up the land at will, nor withdraw from it without supplying a responsible substitute,—his son, for instance. Above all, he could not divide it. On the other hand, he had carefully defined privileges as to the use of wood, pasturage, and so on.

His holding The regular peasant holding differed in size according to locality. In general, it comprised probably 50 or 60 yokes of arable land (35 to 42 acres). Below the "full peasant" were poorer classes, the half peasant and the quarter peasant with correspondingly smaller holdings; and below these, lower classes still,—cottiers, laborers and so on. In the time of Maria Theresa the man with an eighth of a peasant holding counted as a cottier merely.

Serfdom in Austria-Hungary abolished, 1848 In 1848 serfdom, in the sense in which it still existed, was abolished in Austria, and also in Hungary where the conditions had been similar to those in Austria. The peasant became a free peasant proprietor, repaying gradually to the state the redemption money which the

After the painting by Jaroslav Špillar

FEUDAL LABOR DUES IN BOHEMIA.   ABOLISHED 1848

EMBROIDERED BODICE OF A SLOVAK PEASANT

state had advanced to the landlords. The payment was practically completed in Austria by 1872.

In many parts of Austria it was not till the sixties that the peasant was given the right to subdivide his land. In 1867–1869 the right was made general, except for the Tyrol and in certain excepted cases. This liberty has produced very different results in different provinces. In the German Alpine territory custom has, in general, preserved the size of the holdings, and in many cases a prosperous and substantial peasantry has maintained itself. In other districts, on the contrary, where it has not been the custom to leave the land to one heir, but to divide it equally among the children, extreme subdivision has resulted in increasing indebtedness, frequent foreclosures and general impoverishment. *Subdivision of land*

While it is nearly two generations since the old agrarian system, resting on an unfree peasant class, was legally abolished, its results are by no means a thing of the past. In a Hungarian village which I visited there was an old man who still remembered being beaten as a boy by the lord's steward for some trivial fault in connection with the feudal field work. One even hears of the old feudal dues being paid by ignorant peasants in out-of-the-way spots, just as in our South unpaid labor was for some time given by negroes who did not know that they were free. In some places in Hungary there are still actually unfree tenants called Zeliary, who are kept bound to the soil by a sort of peonage system. They are under a debt for their land which they are never allowed to work off, so that they are not at liberty to leave the place and try to do better elsewhere. Consequently the landlord is at liberty to make his own terms. The hideous poverty resulting in one such village is something which I can never forget. *Survivals of old conditions*

Shocking as such conditions of acute misery are, they are less serious than the hampering effects of certain widespread remnants of the mediæval system. The holding of a peasant in Austria, as in mediæval England, *Land held in strips and open field farming* was not one compact area like an American farm; instead it consisted of a number of scattered strips. If a man held 30 acres, he had perhaps 60 half-acre strips, not contiguous, but lying interwoven with those of others as designated shares of great open fields. The different holdings being thus interlocked, all had to follow the same plan of farming and sow and harvest at the same date and, what is involved in this, raise practically the same crops. The complex division of the land holdings of a village, and the way in which a man's acreage is cut up and scattered, is shown in the survey of a Moravian village printed as Map VI.

The three-field system

This subdivision of the land, with all its consequences, survives in much of Austria and Hungary today, and makes it almost impossible to break away from the antiquated "three-field" system of agriculture which, in the absence of sufficient fertilizer or scientific rotation of crops, kept one-third of the soil fallow each year, one-third in autumn-sown crops and one-third in spring-sown.

Among the Slovaks one can see now Langland's "fair field full of folk," and for the same reason. I have counted thirty men ploughing at the same time, each working his share of the same big, unbroken field,—open, for each man's share is marked, not by hedge, fence or wall, but only by a furrow some thirty centimeters (or about a foot) wide, which must not be planted. It is said, and I believe the case has actually occurred, that the strips are sometimes so narrow that a man must walk on his neighbor's land to lead the plough-horse on his own. You may follow such a strip with the eye, over hollow and swell, till it disappears over the last ridge in sight. When land is divided, for instance among sons, each strip is generally split lengthwise to insure equality. Otherwise one might get the sunny slope and the rich hollow, another the cold slope and a poor bit of sandy soil. Thus the strips get ever narrower. This system is wasteful in every way. First, it is wasteful

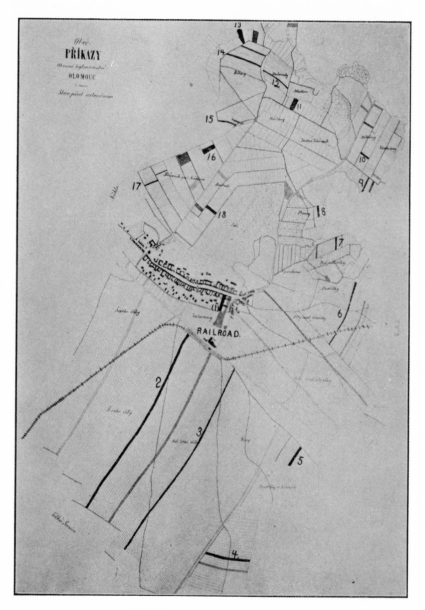

MAP VI.—VILLAGE MAP, MORAVIA

MAP VI.—A MORAVIAN VILLAGE WITH LAND IN OPEN FIELDS AND PROPERTY HELD IN STRIPS.

The holdings of one man, scattered in eighteen different places, are numbered to show their location.

The inhabitants of this village of Přikazy, near Olmütz in Moravia, having decided to reapportion their land had a survey made from which this map was taken. The village is a rich one and therefore not wholly typical of those which send many emigrants to America but some details in regard to it may be interesting.

The houses stand in a row on each side of the street which is lined with a solid facing of housefronts and high yard walls or gates. The houses stretch back from the street with quarters for married servants, perhaps a room for cooking food for the high-bred cattle and swine, store-houses and so forth. There may be a silo pit in the yard for beet-root feed, besides sheds, barns, stalls, pig-pens and so on, and from the yard a farm road leading back to the fields.

In the old days this village owed its prosperity in part to the comparative freedom of Moravia from the wars and persecutions which devastated Bohemia, and in especial to the fact that it had no lay overlord but was under the lighter rule of the Chapter of Olmütz and exempt from labor dues.

If I understood my informant correctly this village has no "whole peasants," nothing above a "half peasant," but about fifty-six homesteads with holdings of about fifty acres each. There are beside "small peasants" (*chalupnice*) with some ten yokes (14.2 acres) apiece, and cottiers (*domkaře*) with a third of a yoke of land (or none if of more recent origin). They may hire land from peasants who do not work their land. Thirty-five families own no house. They hire a dwelling or live with their employers. Some of these men work in the beet sugar factories near by

A peasant in this village commonly owns three horses and a peasant's social standing is largely measured by his stock. A "horse peasant" so outranks an "ox peasant," I was told elsewhere, that a man often keeps a pair of horses at an economic loss for the sake of the prestige. More horses were formerly kept in Přikazy than now and horses were bred there. Now grassland previously held in common has been converted into arable at a great profit and subdivided pro rata. The profit on the draining of some wet land thus converted was put at $80,000.

The dowry of a peasant's daughter in this village is from five thousand to twelve thousand dollars and a wedding festivity would, not long ago, last the greater part of a week with much drinking, dancing and feasting. A coöperative town bank has $320,000 in deposits.

41

of land. Where the holdings are in strips only seven meters wide, the boundary furrows take up nearly a tenth of the land (8.6 per cent). Moreover, the strips being straight, if a field happens not to be rectangular, awkward corners are left which must be laboriously worked by hand. It is wasteful of time, for a man has to travel all over the crazy-quilt of the township to work his many scattered bits of land.

Reform difficult

This system, though thoroughly superannuated, is hard to change. The process of "commassation," by which all the land is thrown together and redivided in equivalent lump lots is hard to carry out fairly, and impossible to carry out to the satisfaction of all concerned. Simpler, though less adequate, is a readjustment which forms lots of more reasonable shapes, and relocates them so that their owners have access to their pieces freely, instead of having to get at them across their neighbors' lots, and so only under severe restrictions, as is necessarily the case with the intermixed strip holdings.

Social standing of peasant

A peasant is thus something quite distinct from anything that we know in America. On the one hand, he is a link in a chain of family inheritance and tradition that may run back for centuries, with a name, a reputation, and a posterity. On the other hand, he is confessedly and consciously an inferior. It is part of his world that there should be a God in heaven, and masters (*Herrschaften, Pani*) on the earth.

His superiors

When the peasant's holding became his own property, a large part of the land in the village probably remained in the hands of the lord. The typical village has one considerable gentleman's estate and a number of small properties. So the peasant takes off his cap to those dressed like gentlefolk, known or unknown. He bears himself toward them with an inherited respect. At the same time there is a sense of profound and hardly bridgeable difference between, himself and gentlemen, a feeling which may be friendly, but is sometimes colored by distrust or intense antagonism.

On the other hand, if the peasant has his superiors, he also has recognized inferiors, and in many places three classes of them.   First is the cottager or cottier, (German *Haüsler*, Bohemian *chalupnik*), the man who, with a house and bit of field, has yet no pretensions to getting his living off his land.   Cottagers may eke out their living with trades, as shoemakers or smiths or weavers, for example, or they may hire themselves to work for other landowners in their free time.   In a satire of the Bohemian writer Havliček's he is describing how, in an interregnum in heaven, everything nevertheless went on in the old way:

> "Všecky řeky byly mokré
> A kameni tvrdé:
> Chalupnice hubovaly
> Že jsou selky hrdé."

> "All the rivers still were wet,
> The stones they still were hard,
> And the cottagers' wives complained
> That peasants are (too) proud."

Secondly, there are the day laborers, who often live in cottages belonging to their employer, and may be paid partly in cash, partly in kind.

Thirdly, there are the "farm servants," not servants in the American sense, but rather what we should call "farm hands."   These are both men and girls, and are generally hired by the year, and boarded by their employer.   You will often find peasants living so wretchedly that we should consider them on the brink of misery, who yet are worlds above their servants housed more like animals than people.   On the other hand, in a well-to-do Moravian village there were often comfortable one or two-room homes in the back part of the main house, where married farm servants kept house in privacy and comfort.

In his circumstances the peasant may be not only prosperous but rich,*—very rich, even, if one takes his

* See the account of a rich Hungarian peasant in Baroness Orczy's "A Son of the Soil"; or in Appendix II, page 431.

way of living and aspirations into account. But he is more likely to be hard pressed with work, with care, perhaps with debt. His roof may leak, his meal chest show the bottom, his crop be sold to the usurer before it is sown,—he is still a property owner, a tax payer, a permanent constituent of an old social order, known to and knowing all his associates, and enjoying a respect nicely adjusted to his acres and family.

His son's marriage, his daughter's dowry, the pensioning of his superannuated parents, the paying off the portions of his brothers and sisters, all are questions of property consideration; one might almost say that they have a dynastic character.

Contrast with the industrial workman

The peasant is an entirely different type from the workingman. He has not the workingman's quickness, nor all that he has gained in intelligence and self-reliance through competition, frequent change of place, and the trituration of city and factory life. On the other hand, he has the conservatism, the solidity, the shrewdness, the self-respect that go with property, independence, and an assured social position. He is likely to be hard and niggardly; this is perhaps the ugliest side. He and his are likely to be in some degree coarse, with the coarseness of those that have to deal with nature not mainly as the source of aesthetic emotions but of a good litter of pigs and a proper production of manure.

Tradition and arts

Yet along with all this, and seemingly contradicting it, the Slavic peasant has created a world of fancy, of song, of tradition, a whole code of dress, manners, morals. The family living is apt to be what is to our minds a curious combination of frugality carried to the verge of want with luxury of a very solid and expensive sort. If you wish to respect the peasant's purse, try to buy clothes or furniture like his. If you wish to respect his disregard of money, try to buy them of him. It is amusing to see how incomprehensible this latter characteristic is to a commercial-minded Jew. "Silly geese," said a shopkeeper, as some women refused his offers on our behalf for some embroidered caps that they were wearing. "Silly!"—They were refusing to sell when a buyer was ready to pay more than market value,—something explicable to him only by lack of sense.

Now import a man like this peasant into America. The courtesy which rested on acceptance of a fixed class station disappears as he realizes that he is not expected to regard himself as an inferior. On the other hand, he loses that standing which largely gave him his old form of self-respect and self-consciousness. Again, there is nothing in his sensitiveness to make him revolt at coarseness and roughness, which here, in our cities, have different connotations and consequences from country plainness. But at the same time his endurance, persistence, toughness of fibre and ingrained loyalties will in many cases pull him through and put him at last in a situation which will open new possibilities to his children, if not to himself, especially if he settles in America. *Effect of America on the peasant*

I do not of course mean to imply that those who emigrate are all peasants, in the strict sense; that laborers and landless men do not also come. But the Austrian census figures given in Table 2 show in the first place how large a proportion of the population is agricultural, in the second place how large a part of those in agriculture (in the provinces with which we are most concerned, well over one-half) are members of independent agricultural families. *Emigrants now largely peasants*

As a matter of fact, many who appear in the table as employes are to all intents and purposes of the same class as the self-employed, being sons and daughters of relatives and neighbors whose land does not occupy all the family energy. The figures therefore corroborate the fact that is clear on any first-hand knowledge of the situation, that the bulk of the emigration with which we are dealing represents the experience and point of view of peasants and of agricultural laborers who are not far removed from peasants. For Hungary we do not have to rely on indirect indications as the occupations of

TABLE 2.—PERSONS OCCUPIED IN AGRICULTURE. AUSTRIAN CENSUS OF 1890*

	Bohemia	Galicia	Carniola	Dalmatia
Percentage of population whose chief occupation is agriculture and forestry	41.0	77.0	72.0	86.0
(1) Independent self-employed (Selbständige)	292,945	842,275	55,787	68,709
(2) Dependents (Angehörige) without other main occupation of their own	924,713	1,903,285	128,042	165,204
(3) Persons working for themselves or for their own families (i.e., classes 1 & 2 together)	1,217,658	2,745,560	183,829	233,913
(4) House servants	6,981	14,941	617	81
(5) Day laborers (Taglöhner)	213,142	201,726	14,396	1,514
(6) Workingmen (Arbeiter)	930,437	2,144,466	159,766	218,646
(7) Salaried (Angestellte)	6,928	6,677	175	60
(8) Employes (i. e., 4, 5, 6, & 7 together)	1,157,488	2,367,810	174,954	220,301

* V. Schullern-Schrattenhofen: "Die Oesterreichische Landwirthschaft in ihren sozialen Beziehungen," pages 4 and 6.

persons known to have emigrated are reported and about two-thirds of them come from agricultural occupations.*

The old peasant economy was almost self-sufficing. *Peasant economy self-sufficing* House industry eked out the farm production. The earthenware for cooking and the pretty flowered crockery, the wooden utensils for stall and house, the farm tools— fork and rake and plough,— the products of spinning-wheel and loom and needle and dye-pot, all were home-made, and few were the articles that must be bought for money.

This old self-sufficient household economy was, how-ever, gradually broken in upon from many sides as *Industry revolution-izes the old system* industry developed at the expense of agriculture. Even in places where no industry arose the effect of that which was growing up in other countries, afar or nearby, made itself powerfully felt. As a "money econ-omy," with purchase and sale, extended, the dependence on household production diminished. Money was needed for taxes. The obvious economy of cheap factory textiles, the superiority of iron pots to earthen ones, indeed the temptation of novel wares of various kinds at low prices, all made new demands for money. With these changes went a rise in standards of living; new goods were available and new desires were contagious.

* See Appendix V, page 433, or the further figures for Croatia in Appendix XIII, page 452.

The American immigration statistics in regard to the occu-pation of immigrants, which ought to give complete data on the point in question, are unfortunately worse than use-less. For instance, although Ruthenians are generally en-gaged in agriculture, of 1400 Ruthenians arriving in 1899, only 3 are reported to have been farmers, 76 farm laborers. Of 16,170 Slovaks in 1908, 20 are given as farmers, 6,733 as farm laborers. In 1907, Hungary reported 27,915 Slovaks emi-grating to all destinations, of whom 17,334 were engaged in agriculture, 4587 of them on their own account. In the year begun July 1, 1907, the United States authorities reported 23,573 Slovak immigrants, of whom 558 were in agriculture, 52 of them on their own account (as "farmers"). The unreliability of these figures is not hard to understand when an agent who makes them out for all his emigrant clients remarks that he puts down not the past occupation of an emigrant *but what will be his occupation in America*. (See page 137, note.)

At the same time with this rise in demands, growth of population without growth of industry made an increased pressure on the land.

The following table is interesting, showing as it does the net loss or gain by emigration and immigration, in connection with the excess of births over deaths, and the density per square kilometer. If the figures were given for arable land instead of for total area they would be more significant; as it is, the greater densities reflect sometimes urban populations and industrial districts, sometimes agricultural over-population.

TABLE 3.— POPULATION OF AUSTRIA; MOVEMENT AND DENSITY.*

AUSTRIAN CROWN LANDS	Net Loss or Gain Per Thousand of Population During the Decade 1891–1900			Density per Square Kilometer in 1900
	By Births and Deaths	By Migration †	Total	
Bohemia.............	+ 10.22	— 2.08	+ 8.14	121
Moravia.............	+ 10.39	— 3.32	+ 7.07	110
Silesia..............	+ 12.44	— 0.09	+ 12.35	132
Galicia..............	+ 15.30	— 4.58	+ 10.72	93
Bukowina...........	+ 15.04	— 2.11	+ 12.93	70
Carniola............	+ 8.35	— 6.51	+ 1.84	51
Carinthia...........	+ 6.07	— 4.32	+ 1.75	35
Styria..............	+ 6.19	— 0.44	+ 5.75	60
Goricia and Gradisca..	+ 9.39	— 3.68	+ 5.71	80
Istria..............	+ 11.02	— 2.38	+ 8.64	69
Dalmatia...........	+ 14.95	— 2.37	+ 12.58	46
Trieste and its district.	+ 2.71	+ 10.74	+ 13.43	1880
Tyrol..............	+ 4.67	+ 0.25	+ 4.92	32
Vorarlberg..........	+ 6.91	+ 4.43	+ 11.34	49
Salzburg............	+ 5.47	+ 5.64	+ 11.11	27
Upper Austria........	+ 5.91	— 2.80	+ 3.11	67
Lower Austria........ (includes Vienna)	+ 9.52	+ 6.97	+ 16.49	156
All Austria	+ 11.11	— 1.67	+ 9.44	87

* "Die Summarischen Ergebnisse der Volkszählung," 1900, pages xvi and xix.

† For a graphic representation of these data by districts see Map V, page 35.

The old peasant economy had represented a fairly stable economic equilibrium. Population was kept more or less at a level by it, since only one son could take his father's place, and consequently it was difficult for more than one to establish a family, unless, indeed, he went away "to seek his fortune." It was the expectation that everything should go on as it had done. That is the essence of custom, and the peasant world is the world of custom. *Old peasant economy stable*

The results of the breakup of the old system of land holding were often disastrous. The peasant being free to divide his land and feeling that his children all had equal claims, cut up land which was only sufficient to support one household among a number of descendants. The landholder unable to support himself from his own plot sought to eke out his living by working for wages in a population where few could afford to hire labor. In some districts debts, contracted under circumstances which put the borrower at the mercy of a Jewish creditor, worked havoc. *Broken up by subdivision*

Thus the peasant with mortgage payments which he could not meet or with children for whom he could not provide an adequate patrimony, saw himself face to face with an intolerable decline of social status for himself or for his children; namely, reduction to the position of a propertyless day laborer. This is the sting which induces many a man among the Slovaks, the Poles, the Ruthenians, to fare over seas or to send out his son to the new land from which men come back with savings. *Peasant emigrates to avoid decline in status*

In some cases the country-side had never supported its population; there had always been an exodus, permanent or seasonal, of some of the men and boys, as for instance in some Slovak counties. As the dislocation of the old economy became more serious, and as mobility of population increased, there was further overflow,—to Germany for the summer farm work, to the cities, to less closely settled districts, (e. g. to Southern

4

Hungary), to Russia, to Brazil, to the United States. Quicker transportation, and above all, knowledge of the facts, opened the way across the sea, and all the requisites for a heavy emigration movement were present. Sometimes the head of a family goes to retrieve the family fortunes, sometimes he sends the most promising son. Or a brother goes hoping to earn enough to pay off the inheritance of his co-heirs and buy the sole right to the land which cannot support more than one family.

Not settled poverty but a disturbance of the budget a cause

While the grounds of emigration are in the main economic, it is a mistake to suppose that poverty is its cause in the sense that the greater the poverty of a man or district, the greater the impulse to emigration. Poverty, especially a settled poverty to which people have adjusted themselves, and which finds expression in a low standard of living and perhaps in physical deterioration, is not an initiating force. Rather, it means stagnation and lack of any margin of energy for new undertakings.

It is when the habitual balance of family budgets is disturbed that a sense of poverty incites to emigration. The misadjustment may be due to a cutting down of income by some disaster, or it may be due to an increase of wants. The result is the same. And this awakening of new wants is a characteristic of our time, affecting one backward and lethargic region after another. It is extremely contagious, and the news that it is anywhere possible to earn more and to live better calls slumbering forces of energy and unrest into sudden life. Emigration will then result if there is any opening which promises improved circumstances.

Emigrating on credit

That is, it will result if there are means to meet the expenses. A district like upper Arva county in Hungary may be too poor to provide emigrants. The emigrant himself, however, need not have the ready cash for the journey, and in a very large proportion of cases he has not. But if he or his family have land, he can readily borrow, and lacking this, many an emigrant borrows on his personal credit merely.

Co-operating with the general economic cause—an agrarian economy of a primitive type, dislocated by the competition of modern industry—are, of course, many more special causes.   One of these is the excessive burden of taxes,* which sometimes fall with crushing force on those least able to bear them.   A striking story of the visit of a tax collector to a poor Ruthenian family will be found in the *Ruthenische Revue*, 1904. Special causes: Taxation

Military service is another direct and continuing cause of emigration.   Every man in Austria and Hungary, with certain exceptions, must serve his three years, and he is forbidden to marry till after his liability to this service is past.   Undoubtedly the interruption of work caused by the time in the army is in many cases felt as a grievous burden, and many emigrate to escape it, either while they are still under age, or with more or less secrecy during the period of *Stellungspflicht*. One constantly runs across cases of men who have emigrated that their boys, one after another, might not be made to serve, or in order to escape their own duty.   Nevertheless, it is my impression that the influence of this factor is apt to be exaggerated, and for corroboration I would call attention to the figures for Carniola in Appendix XII, page 451.   Previous to 1863–4, when the time of military service was longer, the desire to avoid the army is said to have been more important as a cause of emigration than it has been since. Army service

Another complicating cause is political unrest.   Many of our Slavic immigrants come from groups which are more or less in the position of the under dog.   This is most notable in the case of the Slovaks, but even with other nationalities political discontent and the growing-pains of a yet undeveloped democracy often play a part.   I was told, for instance, that emigrants from the rich eastern counties of Croatia-Slavonia, who seem to have no economic reason for leaving home, when asked why they go, say, "Mi ideme traẑeti ima li još pravice Political unrest

* See Appendix III, page 432.

na svieto" (We go to see if there is still justice in the world).   Generally, however, I think that the effect of such conditions is less to initiate emigration than to cause the emigrant who returns to his old home to feel himself a misfit there, and to decide to take up his permanent residence in America.   (See page 118.)

Stimulation by agents   Another "cause" of emigration is the advertising and solicitation of transportation agencies.   My impression is that the less direct and concrete knowledge of the matter a man has, the more weight he lays on this factor. To ascribe immigration to the steamship companies is a rhetorical commonplace of the kind of speaker who tells us that "the immensity of the problem palls upon the patriot who confronts it."   (The quotation is a literal one.)

In the old days the agent was doubtless active, while on the other hand the government gendarmes were arresting would-be emigrants who had no passes and turning them back.   Today emigration is free, except for certain provisions to insure the performance of military service, and passes are generally little more than a form; and, on the other hand, advertising and solicitation are carefully regulated.   Doubtless even today, however, much soliciting is done secretly.

New routes   The opening up of new routes and ports of embarkation has made emigration easier.   Havre and Marseilles, Antwerp and Genoa, besides Dutch and Belgian ports, get part of the lucrative business of shipping emigrants. Of late both Austria and Hungary have been seized with a desire to keep all this profit in the country, and also keep a closer control of emigration conditions, by inducing emigrants to embark at the home ports.   That is, Austria would like to see her emigrants sail from Trieste by the Austro-American line and Hungary wishes hers to go by the Cunard line *via* Fiume.

Hungarian emigration policy   In 1903 there was great excitement in the United States about the contract between the Hungarian government and the Cunard Company, by which the former was said to have guaranteed a fixed number of passengers a year, with a forfeit for all the deficit below that number. This arrangement, if it ever existed, was canceled, at any rate apparently, but for some time the Hungarian government went to the most unwarrantable extremes, not, I believe, to increase emigration, but to force intending emigrants to embark at Fiume. This whole matter of the policy and practice of the Austrian and Hungarian governments in regard to emigration is a complicated one, to which I can only allude.*

In the advertisement and pushing of emigration facilities many classes of agents are concerned—agents of various of our states which maintain or have maintained officials to stimulate immigration; agents of steamship lines from the central office to the pettiest sub-agent or peddler of tickets; agents of railroads; agents of land companies; emissaries (in the old days at least) of employers, individual and corporate. But whether private or governmental, open or illicit, such stimulation can at most signify little more than greasing the wheels. Where the circumstances are such as to produce emigration men will learn the facts and act on them in the course of time, even if advertising be absolutely excluded. The importance of the emigration agent is in opening up new regions which are ripe for emigration and in setting the ball rolling. He hastens the starting and makes smooth the course of the avalanche; he is not responsible for more than this. *[sidenote: Agents facilitate rather than cause emigration]*

Emigrants, though in many senses ignorant, are men taught shrewdness by hard lives, and they are venturing upon a very costly experiment. They know much better what they are about than Americans generally suppose. The first to go from a given locality at home, the first to try a new district here, report their experiences directly or indirectly. All but a comparatively few pioneers are acting on advice from their forerunners. *[sidenote: Emigration not at random]*

Look at our immigration figures (quoted in Appendix IV, page 433) showing whether or not immigrants are coming

* For reference see Bibliography under Legislation.

to join relatives or friends.   Even the Bulgarian, Servian
and Russian immigration, so largely still in a pioneer
stage, shows only ten in a hundred who are not coming
to join relatives or friends already here.   Among the
older immigrant nationalities the number falls to between two and three in a hundred.   This is a condition
not, I think, generally realized.   To read all that is
written about directing the flow of immigrants, distributing it to better advantage and so forth, one would
suppose that not two in a hundred, but all, were coming
with no known reason for selecting one destination rather
than another.

The rôle of
accidents

The general causes at work are intensified at given
places and at given times, by all sorts of occurrences.   A
flood, a conflagration, a new American tariff, an outbreak
of phylloxera in the vineyards, or a treaty admitting
Italian wine at a lower rate—all these have been actual
stimulants of Slavic inflow.

Personal
motives

As in any mass movement, the individual is more
conscious of the purely personal and special motives
which have moved him than of the general causes at
work.   Men emigrate to avoid family friction, to escape
a scandal, to see new scenes, to join relatives, because
others have gone, and for a thousand other unclassifiable
reasons.   It still remains true that these causes play
on the surface of the stream and do not give it its bulk
of energy nor its direction.

The true
cause—dif-
ferences in
earning
power

I have spoken of the dislocation of the old agrarian
economy as the cause of emigration.   But this, after all,
is only a part of the story.   The *causa causarum* is a
broader one.   The fundamental problem of all economics
is how much labor will produce a given product, how
much product a given output of labor will produce.
In emigration districts things are relatively dear in terms
of labor.   In America, labor is relatively dear in terms
of things.   Given an open sluiceway, and men are
bound to pour to the place where land, grain, and meat
cost least in terms of hours of human energy.

PRIMITIVE METHODS OF PRODUCTION IN SLOVENSKO

1. Breaking hemp. This woman had been in America. 2. Herding swine. 3. Dye house with wooden elbows under the eaves for drying cloth. 4. Making shingles by hand.

That they do cost less in America is due to three main facts. First, America has a vast wealth of comparatively undrained natural resources including above all agricultural land and, of only less importance, metals, minerals, timber and oil. Second, it has an organization of production which is beyond any known to history until the present era, and which is today equaled perhaps by Germany alone. This rests on the liberal use of machinery, on specialization of skill, and on elaborate business organization, all of which are impossible in industrially backward countries. Third, citizens of the United States have the immense advantage of practically feeling no military burden; they have no compulsory service, and in the general prosperity the taxation for military affairs, met as it is by indirect taxes, though absolutely large, is scarcely noticed.

Causes of American productivity

The whole situation is suggested by a passage that I ran across in an article on forestry in an Austrian encyclopedia. The author complained of the shocking waste of woods going on in some places. This sometimes went so far, he said, that the inhabitants used wood to build fences, simply to save the trouble of having the cows herded. What should we think of the unthrift of an American farmer who should pay an able-bodied person to watch one or two cows day after day, to save building a fence? The instance epitomizes the whole situation, —relatively cheap labor against relatively cheap raw material.

Cost of things in terms of labor

What is patent and obvious is, of course, the money expression of these facts. Wages are higher in the United States than in Bohemia or Galicia or Dalmatia. Precisely how much higher, it is impossible to say. Complicated forms of payment, with receipts in kind, rights to the use of land, free milk, or fodder, etc., confuse it at one end, and the difference in the cost of living at the other. Table 4 is given for what it is worth. Whatever the amount of the difference is, there is no question of the fact that it is an important one.

Money wages

TABLE 4.—AVERAGE DAILY WAGES OF AGRICULTURAL LABORERS, 1891

COUNTRY	WITH BOARD	ADDITIONAL WHEN NO BOARD GIVEN
Bohemia......................	0.25	0.4
Moravia......................	0.14	0.10
Silesia.......................	0.14	0.13
Galicia.......................	0.12	0.12
Bukowina.....................	0.15	0.9
Carniola......................	0.21	0.12
Carinthia.....................	0.16	0.19
Styria........................	0.18	0.17
Goricia and Gradisca		
Istria	0.20	0.15
Trieste and District...........		
Dalmatia.....................	0.26	0.22
Tyrol and Vorarlberg..........	0.27	0.17
Salzburg.....................	0.21	0.20
Upper Austria................	0.22	0.19
Lower Austria................	0.26	0.22

Austria-Hungary and the Balkan States.   Report of Royal British Commission on Labor, 1894, Vol XI, page 75.

Price of land   The other chief money expression of the economic ratios of the countries is the price of land, and here again precise comparison is impossible.   But it is not only the price of land; it is its availability, its plenty.   It is hard for us to reproduce to ourselves the impression which America makes on the European; the sense of space, of opportunity, of a very clamor of the earth to men to come and use it.   Our talk of congestion, of being overfilled with hordes of foreigners, strikes a Polish priest, let us say, in a country parish, who does not know the East Side of New York which perhaps dominates the mind of the writer, as not so much ludicrous as hypocritical.

Is emigration a good thing for the emigrant?   When the question is asked whether the emigration movement is to be regarded as a blessing or a curse, one must first distinguish—a blessing or the reverse to whom? And if one begins with the emigrants themselves, one immediately finds himself trying to measure incommensurables; to weigh the relative values of things which every one will estimate variously, and which the same person will estimate differently in different moods.

The old village life may not always be sanitary or clean or moral, but it is harmonious, complete, self consistent. Lying aside from beaten routes of travel, many Slavic districts retain to an amazing extent an old-world aspect which gives them unspeakable charm.   The beautiful costumes, fixed by tradition but differing from village to village, ornamented with exquisite embroidery, hand lace, rich braiding or leather work, are still in many country places the ordinary and general dress.   They are seen at their best at the weekly market, in the crowded church during mass, or at a wedding or a dance on the green. *Advantages and disadvantages of the old*

The gift of the Slav for color and for music touches the whole life with poetry.   Every occasion and act, every wood and hill and stream, has its adornment of custom, superstition or legend which, with its glamour, veils to the sentimental traveler at least, the hard and sordid side of lives often close to actual want.   And indeed, the primitive and natural labors of plowman and reaper, of spinner and weaver, of raftsman and shepherd, need no adornment to be beautiful.

Sometimes this beauty and harmony of the simple, long-adjusted conditions seem of supreme value; sometimes narrowness, suffering and degradation seem to outweigh their advantages tenfold; just as on the other side, the American side, one sometimes realizes only the bright features, and again only the shadows of our tenement and industrial life.   But beautiful or degraded, the primitive life is doomed.   As household arts come into contact with the world of competition and factory production, they are either blighted, or deformed into sweated house-industries.   All the old-world relations of the village are changing as modern agriculture with capitalistic methods gradually replaces the old and technically wretched peasant farming.   Education is gradually drying up the superstition, and with it the poetry. *In any case the past is gone or going*

Yet, at the cost of what is picturesque, comfort, intelligence and morality increase.

The change is under way, and the emigration to America is one of its accompaniments.   It is also in turn an accelerating cause of the change.   Immigration is thus a part of that great leveling and fusing activity which is one side of the historical process.   It owes its ease if not its possibility to the cheapness and speed of modern transportation and communication, and it co-operates with them in wiping out local differences, spreading among distant peoples the reciprocal knowledge of one another, and evening up their levels.   As Tarde has said, civilization of the prevailing type is becoming planetary; it has gone round the globe and back again. The tendency, as he shows, is to differentiate individuals more sharply as individuals, while lessening the distinctive differences that used to mark country from country, class from class, even village from village.   Dress is a symbol of the change.   Instead of a costume, uniform for all persons in one locality, but unlike that of the next, we have one and the same fashion from Paris to Fiji, and yet no two persons dressed alike, but each, within the limits of the mode, individually and according to personal circumstances and taste.

If we turn to simpler aspects of the question and ask, "Does the individual emigrant gain?" we have to deal with less vast if still elusive factors.   In the first place, emigration always involves pain; pain to those who go, and, above all, pain to those who are left behind. One thing that Americans might with grace remember is that immigrants are inevitably to some extent exiles, separated from the old familiar scenes for which every one sometimes yearns, and divided, even if the more immediate family has all been brought together, from some of those near and dear to them.   I traveled from Vienna to Bremen with a group of emigrants, and I shall never forget the suffering of one little woman who was going to join husband and children, but who had just said goodby for life to her mother.   Where husband and wife, parents and children are separated, it is harder yet.

Life among our immigrants is full of such incidents as one told by Miss Byington:

" As we waited in one of the little railway stations of Homestead, a Slovak came in and sat down beside a woman with a two-year-old child.   He made shy advances to the baby, coaxing her in a voice of heartbreaking loneliness.   She would not come to him, and finally the mother took her away.   As they went, the Slovak turned sadly to the rest of the company, taking us all into his confidence, and said simply, " Me wife, me babe, Hungar."   But were his family in America, it would mean death for one baby in three; it would mean hard work in a little dirty, unsanitary house for the mother; it would mean sickness and evil.   With them in Hungary, it means for him isolation, and loneliness, and the abnormal life of the crowded lodging house."*

What it means to be in a country where one cannot speak the language is, as many a traveler can testify, a feeling that must be experienced to be understood. With me, a sort of inhibition of all expression sets in; it seems as useless to gesticulate or smile as to speak. It is almost as if one could not even think, so pervasive and numbing is the sense that the channels of communication are blocked.

I get the impression that the women are more apt to be homesick than the men, and that in consequence wives often make their husbands return against their wishes. As a matter of fact, I think the women both lose more and gain less by the change than the men.†   They do not like the iron stoves, which do not bake such sweet bread as their old ovens.   They miss, I think, the variety of work, — Women find the change hard

*Byington, Margaret F.: "The Mill Town Courts and Their Lodgers."   *Charities and the Commons*, XXI, page 922 (Feb. 6, 1909).
† Mr. Steiner in "The Immigrant Tide" brings, on the other hand, much evidence to show the special gain of the women in America as regards their personal position.

employment within doors alternating with field work in sociable companionship with husband or lover and neighbors; the garden with its row of tall sunflowers or poppies; the care of the chickens and ducks and geese, the pig and the calf; and most of all the familiar, sociable village life where every one knows every one else, and there are no uncomfortable superior Yankees to abash one, and where the children do not grow up to be alien and contemptuous.

The men live more out in the world. They get more from America and perhaps had less to lose in the old conditions. In spite of the undemocratic treatment of immigrants which is too common in the United States, and which sometimes makes one's blood boil, they do get in America a sense of being more regarded, of being equals, that is new and very dear to them. To the men it often means expansion.

Emigrants returning to Croatia say of America, "There is no sun there like ours, but there is freedom and justice." They comment on the fact that employers and officials treat them like fellow men, not patronizing them nor treating them as if rebellious. So in this country a Croatian informant who could not say hard things enough about the experiences of his fellow countrymen in Pennsylvania, yet said to me with brightening eyes, "But they *love* their American employers. The owner will come in of a morning, perhaps, and say 'How are you Mike? How is your wife?'" So far does a little consideration go.

The personality that the emigrant develops in America is, I believe, in successful cases something higher, and (at least I wish to believe so) finer than the old. But the change that takes place reminds me of the process by which the individual grows from the grace and simple unconsciousness, the imperfect perfection of childhood, from its dependence and trustfulness and creative fancy, through the ugly period of the shedding of teeth and curls, into the hobbledehoy period of conflicting condi-

The men feel the touch of democracy

The hobbledehoy stage

tions—self-assertion and helplessness, rationality and ignorance—into the transitional awkwardness of self-consciousness and uneven development. Thus the emigrant, or emigrant's son or daughter, who is half "Americanized," is often in a disagreeable phase.

This is often the case with the emigrant who returns to the old country. He is less docile, less contented, perhaps less religious, often self-assertive and rough in manner. Sometimes he gives himself airs as an "American," displays the silver dollar that adorns his watch-fob, and turns the heads of the boys with his big talk. I was asked in Croatia why it was that men who came back from America refused to take off their hats in the bureau of an official. Some of the old neighbors are impressed by such displays of lack of deference; others, especially superiors, are scandalized. *The returned emigrant*

Often the returned emigrant is spoiled for hard work, either by overstrain in America or by a change in his views, but he is also likely to be more enterprising and ambitious—qualities greatly needed in most Slavic villages. These peasants of Austria and Hungary, and above all of Russia, are not in the least accustomed to initiating anything themselves. "Why do you people not mend that hole in the road where everyone has broken down regularly for years?" said a traveler in a Croatian village (so runs the story). "No one told us to do it, sir." Again take Miss Dowie's story of a Ruthenian who was asked what he would charge to shingle a roof. He was dismayed at the idea of undertaking such a contract, and refused to make any estimate. A Jew was then given the contract, and he came to the same man and offered him a fixed sum, which was accepted, for shingles and shingling, making of course his own profit on the business.

The fact is, many Slavs are really living largely in the pre-commercial age, where there is no fixed scale of values, and where every possession has its own incommensurable worth to its owner, who has never bought or *Slavs, pre-commercial and commercialized* sold it, or thought of doing so.   American life is a whole business college to men from such an environment, but not always an ennobling one.

Effects on the prop-ertied class

The ruling classes, especially the landlords, dislike the emigration movement, not only because the returned emigrant is less docile, but because they suffer by the diminution of the labor supply and the consequent rise of wages.   Indeed, the large land-owner who farms for profit is caught between the upper and nether mill-stone.   Grain from America, North and South, has lowered prices, and wages have increased.   Too often the aristocratic landlord is unbusinesslike and self-indul-gent, a poor manager.   The consequence is that large estates frequently come into the market through bank-ruptcy, and are bought up by peasants in small lots with American money.*

America's responsi-bility

The question of how this emigration affects America is the subject of the second part of this study, but one point that may well be emphasized both there and here is that the cost of the emigrant's education need not be so great.   Even if, in spite of the change sometimes making itself felt in childish and disagreeable forms, his gain in the happier cases outweighs his loss, yet the loss is apt to be great and, at least in many cases, quite unnecessarily great.   It is not a law of nature that the transition should involve so much that is brutalizing and demoralizing as it does in our slums and our mills. Never did I feel that the function and the opportunity of the social settlement were so great as in meeting these people, at once so ready and able to learn of Americans, and in America so seldom having an opportunity to come into touch with what is best in America.

* For instances see page 144.   Interesting pictures of the difficulties of gentleman farmers in Poland, Hungary and Ger-many respectively will be found in three remarkable novels: Freytag's "Debit and Credit," Baroness Orczy's "A Son of the Soil," and Fritz Reuter's "Ut Mine Stromtid" (translated under various titles as "Seed Time and Harvest" or as "An Old Story of My Farming Days").

CHAPTER V

BOHEMIAN EMIGRATION

On a brilliant autumn day, with white clouds chasing A walk in Bohemia through the splendid blue above, and the stream beside us running as gayly as the blood in our veins, we started out for a tramp in the neighborhood of Strakonice, in Southern Bohemia, to learn what we could of emigration from that vicinity.

With us went an old workingman who was to take us to visit various families who had been in America themselves or who had members there. He not only knew the neighborhood and its people, but was much interested in our errand—for he had six children in the United States.

As we left the orchard path beside the brook, and struck across by field tracks to the nearest village, we had to ask our way now and again of a man doing his fall ploughing, or a woman at work among her cabbages. The countryside was widespread and rolling, with a wooded hill dark on the horizon, and everywhere about us open fields, now bare of crops. The village itself, characteristically clustered about an irregular open space, was given a forlorn appearance by the traces of a recent fire such as are all too common in these close-built settlements, but the low houses with their farm-yards and outbuildings looked pleasant and homelike.

We found the one we wanted and were hospitably Families of emigrants welcomed by a friendly elderly peasant woman, kerchief on head. As we drank the great mugs of cream which she set before us, and ate her good rye bread, we heard all about the daughter settled in New York, and saw pictures of her, first in her pre-American stage as a heavy-faced, ill-dressed girl; then in America with her husband (a band-master) and her child, all three with faces intelligent and refined as well as good; and finally, as a widow in a position of some responsibility in a hotel.

This was one of the most marked cases that I have met, where the pictures seemed to indicate a great personal advance. Too often, when one contrasts a photograph of relatives in America with the home surroundings that it is supposed to adorn, the impression left is that while there is plenty of gain in comfort and in the standard of expenditure, the advantages as regards grace of bearing, real beauty of dress, and personal dignity, are all in favor of the peasant stay-at-homes.

At another house we found a woman threshing beside her brother-in-law. She had left her husband and two daughters in Nebraska, and returned to look after her old mother, but expected soon to rejoin her husband in the United States.

Another house was the home of a family decidedly better off, with the ample barns which are the sign of successful farming the world over. Our time was getting short and we had only a talk at the doorway with the housemother. Her youngest daughter was going to America the next week to join an elder sister, traveling with a girl friend from the next village. "Was there any chance that they could go with us?" we were asked.

Our guide   All of this was interesting to us, but what we enjoyed most in the day was our guide. His talk, in the more or less imperfect German which even quite "uneducated" Bohemians generally command, was racy and delightful, partly from its curious blending of elements, partly from his entertaining and kindly personality.

Now he gave us the story of his uncle who went to America in 1852, one of those who made up the first large wave of over-sea emigration from Bohemia. A shoemaker by trade, he sold his house and went out with his wife and two children. According to our guide's account he had various affairs with the Indians as he traveled westward in his prairie schooner, including, if I remember rightly, a gift from him of one of the precious chickens which he carried with him in a cage, and a return gift from the Indians of a nugget of gold done up in a cover of pitch. He became a farmer, but later, after an exciting career during the Civil War selling provisions and carrying pay to the Confederates, he met his death—by hanging, as is supposed.

Intermixed with these pictures of Western life were stories of ghosts and devils, told with all the appearance of the most naïve belief. Whether this was the art that conceals art or not, we were never sure. The legend of the Strakonice bagpiper who piped to Satan and his companions is one of the best known bits of Bohemian folklore. I preferred the account of the girl who, coming home one evening by the very path that we were then on, suddenly felt a hobgoblin leap upon her shoulders, and found herself obliged to attend personally to the founding of three chapels (duly pointed out to us), in order that the soul of a blind man, who had been unjustly hanged for a church robbery, might find rest. The event had such an air of actuality that it might have been chronicled in yesterday's *Abendblatt*.

Our guide was a Socialist, and quite of the twentieth century in his politics. Nevertheless, as an old soldier, he had never shaken off his admiration of the emperor, which was evident as he told us of various occasions on which he had seen him, as well as in the greeting which he sent us after our departure—a postal card with a picture of His Majesty on horseback.

On the long home tramp he talked to us again of his relatives in America. There are twelve of them there, six of them his own children, and he has a whole box of letters from them.

One nephew, who is a little "leichtsinnig," fought in the Philippines. One sister has a pension on account

A father of emigrants

of her husband's service in the Civil War. A son is a
turner by trade and lives in Minnesota, as do various
other members of the family. The rest are in
"Nevyork."

Apparently all are doing well in the world; the
tragedy is on the personal side—in the parting felt to
be almost as hopeless as death itself. One married
daughter in the West had ceased to write. About the
youngest girl, evidently rather flighty even at home,
he was heartsore and anxious. He showed us a letter
in English, written by her, which he asked us to read to
him. It had been mailed to him by mistake, being
intended for a young man, making an appointment to
meet at a street corner on the East Side. Our guide had
surmised as much for himself.

We had naturally supposed, when he took a day's
leave from his regular work to tramp the country-side
with us, that it was to be a business arrangement. But
no, he would not hear of such a thing. He could hardly
bid us goodby. "It seems to me in a sort of way as if
you came from my girls in America," he said; and,
with a catch in his old voice, "It is hard to lose six
children all at once."

Bohemian
emigration
of early date

I have been tempted to tell this episode at length
because it stands for so many similar experiences and
talks. One point in which it is characteristic of Bohemian emigration is in reaching back into a comparatively
distant past. Of all Slavic emigration to America (as
well as of all from Austria whether Slavic or not), that
from Bohemia was the first to be of importance, and in
the fifties, the day of the uncle of this tale, it was already
very considerable.

In colonial
America

There had, indeed, been stray Bohemian colonists in
America from almost the earliest times.* And while
these men are interesting mainly to the antiquarian, it

* Further accounts of Bohemian emigrants, in connection
with their settlements in the United States, will be found in
Chapters XI, XII, and XIII.

AUGUSTINE HEŘMAN

Portrait of Augustine Heřman said to be drawn by himself. Reproduced from
Čapek's "Památky Česky Emigrantů v Americe."

is worth while to bear in mind that "the fathers" were not all English; that even the French, Dutch, Spanish and Swedish settlers by no means completely exhaust our colonial genealogy.

Moreover these men, although of no actual historical importance to America, are picturesque figures linking the stories of old-world countries and new.* The defeat of the Battle of the White Mountain in 1620, at which German Catholicism triumphed over the Chekh Reformers, subjected Bohemia for more than two centuries to a régime of persecution and oppression. The old Bohemian nobility, executed or exiled for their Hussite faith, were ruthlessly rooted out, and replaced by a carpet-bag foreign nobility who received practically all the great landed estates of the nation as a return for services in court or camp. Thousands of valuable volumes were burned by Jesuit fanatics, the profession of any religion but the Roman Catholic was effectually repressed, and 36,000 families, of which 185 were of the nobility or gentry, emigrated, many of them to Holland.

Of these exiles from Bohemia and Moravia the most famous was the great Comenius or Komenský, who came near being president of Harvard College. Cotton Mather writes in his "Ecclesiastical History of New England" (page 128), "That brave old man, Johannes Amos Comenius, the fame of whose worth hath been Trumpetted as far as more than Three Languages (Whereof every one is endebted unto his Janua) could carry it, was agreed withal by our Mr. Winthrop, in his travels through the Low Countries, to come over into New England and Illuminate this Colledge and Country in the quality of President: But the Solicitations of the Swedish ambas-

Harvard's invitation to Comenius

---

* The details of the lives of all these early Bohemian-Americans have been carefully worked out by Mr. Thomas Čapek of New York in a little volume written, unfortunately for us, in Bohemian: "Památky Českých Emigrantů v Americe." 1907. A number of references drawn from this book are included in the Bibliography under Bohemians in the U. S.

sador, diverting him another way, that Incomparable Moravian became not an American."*

Augustine Heřman

In all probability, too, Augustine Heřman of Prague, who came to "New Amsterdam" in 1633, was one of this group. A surveyor, he was present at the purchase of the site of Philadelphia from the Indians, and in return for his services in making for Lord Baltimore the first map of Maryland he was given a patent for an estate of some twenty thousand acres, partly in Maryland, partly in Delaware, the celebrated Bohemia Manor. Other estates he called Little Bohemia and Three Bohemian Sisters. The rivers on which they lie are still called by the names he gave them, Big Bohemia River and Little Bohemia River. He was connected with the West India Company, and claimed to be the "founder of the tobacco business in Virginia." His tobacco warehouse was in New York at what is now 33–35 Pearl Street. He and his descendants were connected by marriage or descent with the most prominent families, the Bayards, the Virginia Randolphs, and many others.

Frederick Phillips

About twenty-five years later than Heřman came Bedřich Filip (Anglicized as Frederick Phillips). John Jay, the first supreme justice of the United States, whose wife Sara Livingstone was descended from Phillips, wrote: "The first ancestor of this family who settled in this country was Frederick Flypson, a native of Bohemia, where his family being Protestants were persecuted. His mother becoming a widow was constrained to quit Bohemia with him and her other children. She fled to Holland with what little property she could save from the wreck of their estate. The amount of that little not admitting her to provide better for Frederick, she bound him to a carpenter, and he became an excellent workman. He emigrated to New York, which was then under the Dutch government."† In America he became rich, being called "the

* Quoted by Čapek, page 3.   † Quoted by Čapek, page 67.

Bohemian merchant prince." He married Catherine van Cortland and built two fine colonial mansions, one the so-called "Castle Phillipse" at Phillipsburgh, and one which the city of Yonkers later bought and used as the City Hall. His descendant, the beautiful Marie Phillips who refused the hand of George Washington, is the heroine of Fenimore Cooper's "The Spy." With the Tory proclivities of the family in the Revolution its importance in the male line ceased, though its blood flows in many distinguished families.

The Moravian brethren who went as missionaries to America in 1736, while they represent a spiritual inheritance from that which is most central in Bohemian experience, the Hussite movement, went from Germany, and were themselves largely either German or Germanized. Matej Stach, however, the first missionary to Greenland, who died among the Brethren in South Carolina in 1787, was born in Moravia.* Moravian mission-aries

Memory has been preserved of a few other stray emigrants to America in the early nineteenth century: a Bohemian associate of John Jacob Astor; Dr. Dignovity of San Antonio, Texas, physician and author (arrived New York, 1832); and Professor Hruby, of Oxford University, Ohio (arrived Baltimore, 1834).†

In spite of stray emigrants there was nothing that could be called an emigration movement from Bohemia till the revolutionary years 1848–9. At this time there was a triple ferment in Bohemia: first, a desire for political independence; second, a resurrection of national self-consciousness symbolized by the revival of the Bohemian language, the use of which among cultivated people had been abandoned for German; and third, a spirit of religious questioning and vehement challenge of current Christianity, largely due to reaction against the corrupt and benighted influence of Austrian clericalism. Effects of the Revolution of 1848

* For further details of this movement see page 208.
† Čapek, pages 98–112.

These years brought from Bohemia, as from other countries, political refugees, some of them choice spirits. One of the most influential, not in America, but in Bohemia, was Vojta Náprstek, who, after ten years in the United States, returned to Prague to devote his life to the spread of enlightenment and liberty, in which he felt that America had much to teach. His main visible monuments are an industrial museum and a library, both in Prague, carried on by his widow in the spirit of international hospitality until her recent death. The Bohemian poet Zeyer wrote for his urn this beautiful inscription: "What remains of the body can be easily put into a small vessel, yet his great heart carried in itself the whole world."*

Abolition of serfdom Emigration at this time may have been quickened by two other influences besides those of the revolutionary activity of the period. The first of these was the abolition in 1848 of serfdom and labor dues in Bohemia, which, for the first time, gave the peasant his personal freedom. The effect of this on emigration was, however, probably slight, as the law did not yet grant the right to emigrate at will. This was first conceded in 1867, and then subject to requirements of military service and of passports.

Gold discovery The second possible influence was the discovery of gold in California in 1849, which is said to have brought Bohemian gold seekers and to have stimulated the activity of ship agents. The census of 1850 mentions 87 natives of Austria (out of 946 in the United States), as then in California; these were probably Bohemians.

Movement of the fifties and sixties Throughout the fifties and early sixties there was a pretty steady outflow from Bohemia; most of this was directed to the United States, though in the early sixties many tried for a time going to Russia, apparently not with very happy results. In the ten years 1850–1860, the United States census showed a gain of nearly 25,000

*Cf. Humpal-Zeman, Josefa: "Bohemia: a Stir of Its Social Conscience." *The Commons*, July, 1904.

natives of Austria, which practically, at this time, means Bohemians.*

In the home districts the early emigration is by no means forgotten, as we have seen, and pioneer relatives are all the more remembered because the proverbial uncle in America is a better source of hopeful dreams than any castle in Spain. In Domažlice, in 1905, we were given a very interesting account of the movement by a man who was semi-professionally acquainted with the circumstances:

"The earliest went from here in 1845 in a sailing ship and were many weeks at sea. Forty or fifty years ago it was an epidemic. Then the whole family went at once, while now the son commonly goes first, then the daughter, then the parents. Most older people who emigrate now are going out to join their children. The first to emigrate were *handwerker*, [which would mean carpenters, tailors, shoemakers, butchers, smiths, weavers, etc.] Peasants, [or as we should say, farmers,] at first would not hear of America; they only began to go in the sixties. The early emigrants generally settled in the country, while now they go to the cities. It was a hard business then. There were no relatives to go to as there are now. But the children learned the language, 'und sie haben's gut g'habt.'" The grandson of one early emigrant who had recently returned on a visit was evidently a shining example of this good fortune.

In general the earlier emigration now seems remote, and indeed, it never had much reaction on the home country. For instance one man who went out about 1855 has sons in the state of Washington, but the family do not write home to Bohemia any more. All their ties with the old country are broken; they have never been back and would know no one if they came.

Another informant was a tailor, one of the last of

As is shown by Buzek, in "Das Auswanderungsproblem und die Regelung des Auswanderungswesen in Österreich," pages 445–448.

Stories of pioneer emigrants

those who know how to make the pretty peasant costumes of this region about Domažlice, where almost alone in Bohemia the old dress has not become obsolete. He was a quaint and attractive figure, bending with his big spectacles over his gay silk embroidery, or raising his intelligent, deeply lined face to talk of the old days or of his son, now a priest in America.

In 1854 went the first five families from his place, all to Ohio; in 1866 went three families, also to Ohio; the next year three families and four lads, one to Ohio. One has a brewery, the rest farms. In 1880 three more families went to Ohio. This represents the contribution, or part of it, of one little neighborhood.

The Bohemian emigrated to settle

While one must beware of accepting the experience of individuals as the criterion for a whole mass of facts, the impression here given that Bohemian emigration, and especially the early emigration, has been a movement of settlers, whole families going together, is borne out by all that we know, and notably by the large proportion of women, children and old persons that has always characterized Bohemian immigration to the United States.

For the epidemic character of the earlier movement there is also other evidence, and it is interesting to note that the government tried to check the movement by having it preached against from the pulpit—naturally without effect.

Emigration after the Prussian War

With 1867 came a fresh impulse to emigration. Besides the newly granted right to leave the country freely, the disastrous war with Prussia in 1866 gave added reasons for going, while in the United States the Civil War was over and everything invited the settler. For the fourteen years before 1867 the Austrian emigration figures averaged something over 2,000 a year, in 1867 they rose to over 7,000, and for the fourteen years 1867 to 1880 they averaged over 4,000. The real increase was doubtless greater than the figures show, since the registers,—the so-called

Emigrations Tabellen*—kept by the Austrian authorities, became much less complete after the freedom of movement granted in 1867 and were abandoned as useless in 1884.

These figures are for Bohemian emigration to all countries, and as already said, emigration in the early sixties was largely directed to Russia. The figures for the ports of embarkation do not give data for Bohemians separately.

The American census first gives figures for natives of Bohemia in 1870; at that time over 40,000 were already in the United States. According to the same census figures, the decade 1870–1880 added 45,000, 1880–1890 not quite 33,000, and the last decade not quite 38,000, with a total of nearly 157,000 Bohemians in this country in 1900. It will be seen that the decade 1870 to 1880 brought the largest contingent. *(American Census data 1870–1900)*

Although Bohemia appears in the census schedules in 1870, it is not till 1882 that the figures of the United States immigration authorities distinguish Bohemia among the countries of origin of immigrants, so that American data begin just before the Austrian data fail us. The annual emigration from Bohemia into the United States fluctuates from under 7,000 in 1882 to nearly 12,000 in 1891, and 8000 in 1892. Then came the panic of 1893, which seems to have made itself increasingly felt till 1897, when the numbers had declined to under 2,000. *(Statistics of American immigration authorities)*

In 1898 a new change was made in the statistics of the immigration authorities. Beginning with 1899, the number of immigrants coming from Bohemia is no longer given, but there is instead a careful classification by races and nationalities. This includes a group, "Bohemians and Moravians."

This brings us to the difficulty involved in the word Bohemian. Of the population of over 6,000,000 inhabiting Bohemia, not quite two-thirds are Bohemians or *(Who is a Bohemian?)*

* See Appendix V, page 433.

Chekhs by race, or more properly by language. On the other hand, the Chekhs of Bohemia are only a part of the fairly homogeneous Slavic population which makes up the population of most of Moravia and western Silesia, as well as of Bohemia (see Map III, page 32).

This situation makes great confusion, and the term Bohemian covers quite a different whole, according as it refers to a territorial or to a racial and linguistic group. The classification " Bohemians and Moravians " made in our immigration reports means the latter group. That is, it includes practically all persons speaking the Bohemian or Chekh language, or choosing to be reckoned with them; most of these come from Bohemia and Moravia. It does not include Germans, Jews and other non-Bohemians coming to us from Bohemia. These appear under the appropriate headings.

Bohemians
not Gipsies

Perhaps attention should also be called to the curious fate of words, which has given the name Bohemian to the gipsies who, coming to France across Bohemia, came to be known there as Bohemians. Anything less Bohemian in the French sense than the conservative and retiring home life of the Chekh can hardly be imagined.

The figures for Bohemian and Moravian immigrants to the United States from the time the new classification was made are as follows:

TABLE 5.—BOHEMIAN AND MORAVIAN IMMIGRANT ALIENS ADMITTED TO THE UNITED STATES, 1899–1909.*

Year ended June 30,	No. of Immigrants
1899	2,526
1900	3,060
1901	3,766
1902	5,590
1903	9,591
1904	11,911
1905	11,757
1906	12,958
1907	13,554
1908	10,164
1909	6,850

* Note the steady rise, from two and a half thousand in 1899 up to thirteen and a half thousand in 1907 the year of the last depression, and the progressive decline since.

BOHEMIAN TOWN SCENES

1. Domažlice, showing tower famous in local history and old town-gate roof at end of vista of modern arcaded shops. 2. Market place, Budweis. 3. The roofs of Tabor, the old stronghold of the Heussetes. 4. Náprstek Library and Industrial Museum. Bethlehem Place, Prague. The low building with tiled double roof is the old family home which holds the library; the tall building behind it is the museum. Both were the outcome of Mr. Náprstek's stay in the United States.

Geographically, Bohemia is made up of a central The country plain surrounded by ranges of mountains or hills. It may be noted on Map III that the German settlements, which go back to the early thirteenth century at least, are mainly along the frontiers where also the greater part of the industry and a large part of the mines are to be found.   In a general way the land slopes downward toward the north, which is not only lower but warmer and more fertile than the southern parts of the country, the mountains protecting it from the cold winds to which the latter are exposed.*

It is mainly from the little-favored southern dis- Geography of Bohemian emigration tricts that emigrants come, and have come from the beginning.† In 1853 and 1854 nearly three-quarters came from about Pilsen and Budweis; and the same region, together with that about Tabor and Pisek and Kuttenberg and Časlau, seems still to send the bulk of the emigration.   That is, it comes mainly from districts which are Chekh rather than German, agricultural rather than industrial, and notoriously infertile. Milčin, a town a little to the north of Tabor, is supposed to be the coldest spot in the country, and is called the "Bohemian Siberia." In the district about Pisek one sees wide stretches of apparently unusable land, and indeed, *pisek* is the Bohemian word for sand.

The causes of Bohemian emigration are not far to Causes economic seek, at least in a general way.   While, as we have seen, political factors have played a part at times, this move-

* In area Bohemia is somewhat less than half as large as Ohio, or more than twice as large as Massachusetts (Massachusetts, 22,133 square kilometers; Bohemia, 51,967; Ohio, 106,-240), in population more than equal to Pennsylvania and not far from equal to New York (figures for 1900, Pennsylvania, 6,302,115; Bohemia, 6,318,697; New York, 7,268,894). This makes it more dense than any American state except Massachusetts and Rhode Island, which exceed it. (Inhabitants to a square kilometer: Bohemia, 122; Massachusetts, 127; Rhode Island, 133; Belgium, 237.)

† Map V (page 35), shows the local distribution of recent Bohemian emigration. With this may be compared Map III, (page 32), showing Chekh and German population, and Map IV (opp. page 35), showing topographical character of the country.

ment, like Slavic emigration in general, has been essentially an economic one. At first the great inducement was the opportunity to get land in America free, or at least for small sums, and the settlement in the United States was characteristically agricultural, in spite of the fact that, as has been said, Bohemian peasants rarely emigrated in the early days. For a movement of this sort no further grounds are necessary than those already discussed, at home political unrest, in America promising openings, and the opportunity—and the knowledge of the opportunity—of getting here.

As the movement progressed, the industrial element as contrasted with the agricultural has come more to the fore. In America the best of the openings for homesteaders have long been exhausted, and the general trend toward city life and the vast expansion of industrial opportunities have naturally turned immigration in this direction.

Emigration related to economic changes in Bohemia

Bohemia at the same time has been making the fateful transition from a mainly agricultural to a mainly industrial country, and this change has been accompanied by the usual shifting of population from country to city, from agricultural to industrial districts. Of the whole population only about one-half are living where they were born,* and doubtless a chance to earn more has been the cause of the move in most cases. While in 1869 agriculture and forestry occupied 54.44 per cent of the population, in 1900 the proportion had sunk to 41.12 per cent.†

Character of movement

Naturally, therefore, the later Bohemian immigration has been of a somewhat different character from the earlier; more industrial, more urban. Large city colonies began to form among American Bohemians, the Chicago and New York colonies becoming important apparently in the seventies.

* Rauchberg, Dr. Heinrich: "Der Nationale Besitzstand in Böhmen," I, page 229.
† Ibid., page 459.

The fact is that Bohemia sends a large proportion of men with skilled trades. According to our immigration figures for 1908 their proportion for all immigrants was 16 per cent of those with occupations; among South Italians it was 11 per cent; among the Irish 14 per cent; among Bohemians it was 25 per cent. The most numerous trades were, in this order, tailors, miners, carpenters and joiners, shoemakers, locksmiths, butchers, clerks and accountants, bakers and masons. Except among the miners, a large part of these are probably country people, many of whom would at home have owned their bit of land and combined farming with their trade. Many, if not most, would however have had careful training as apprentices, as well as good ordinary schooling. Cultural and industrial equipment of immigrants

The small trade or handicraft, organized under Austrian law as a more or less modernized guild, is a very widespread form of production in Bohemia. One of the quaintest sights that I saw there was the funeral procession of a butcher, in which the masters of the trade in costume and with great axes as symbols of the craft, proudly led the way, followed by journeymen and apprentices. It was like getting back into the Middle Ages. With all that is mediæval in this system it supplies men with a many-sided skill, an industrial intelligence, and a fitness for individual work which our specialized machine-ridden factories do not produce, but which our employers have often been very glad to make use of.

To turn again to the immigration statistics of 1908, it is interesting to note that the proportion of the laborers is among the Bohemian immigrants only about one-sixth what it is among immigrants in general (3 per cent and 18 per cent). The farming class is also relatively small (11 per cent where the proportion for all immigrants is 19 per cent). Statistics of occupations

On the other hand the proportion of servants among Bohemian immigrants is rather high (16 per cent as compared with 11 per cent of all immigrants). This is connected doubtless with the large proportion of women immigrants. A study of the occupations in America, as shown by the census, of Bohemians as compared with various other classes, will be found in Chapter XIV. It is notable that the Bohemian has so largely maintained in the new world his more highly skilled and more individualized work. He may work on his farm, in a sweat shop at tailoring or cigar making, in his own work shop, or in an office. He is not to be found apparently in the massed bodies of factory labor nor in the mines.

Literacy   As regards literacy, I fancy the figures may be a surprise to many. Taking the American immigration figures for 1900, we find that of all immigrants of fourteen years and over, those not able to both read and write were 24.2 per cent; among the Germans 5.8 per cent; *among the Bohemians and Moravians only 3.0 per cent;* among Scandinavians, under 0.8 per cent. Certainly to supply only about one-half as many illiterates per hundred as the Germans is a notable record.*

All of this is quite borne out by the impression one gets of Bohemians both in the United States and in Bohemia. The fact is that in development and conditions they rank with the immigrant from northwest Europe. The struggle with the Germans is in a sense the master-thread in their whole history, and this contact, even though inimical, has meant interpenetration and rapprochement. No other Slavic nationality is more self-conscious and patriotic, not to say chauvinistic, in its national feeling, and at the same time none begins to be so permeated with general European culture and so advanced economically.

Local and special causes   Besides the general causes of Bohemian emigration, already mentioned, special causes also have been present, both temporary local conditions or misfortunes, and special circumstances of individual lives.

Results of American tariff   An interesting example of emigration due to specific disasters is that caused by the ruin spread by the

* For further comparisons see Appendix XXVII, page 479.

McKinley bill. Take for instance the making of pearl buttons, the forced transfer of which to the United States was so much vaunted. Not only was the industry moved, but the workers, against whom there is no tariff, had to come too. At Neuhaus in Southern Bohemia we heard of a whole neighborhood of these people that had emigrated; and among those still clinging to their homes we found men earning $2.40 a week making pearl buttons, who before the Act got $6.00 or even $10.

A frequent special local cause of emigration is a strike. Strikes The Bohemian colony in New York apparently grew out of a strike in the Government tobacco factory at Kuttenberg (Kutna Hora) in the seventies.* In Kladno, a coal-mining town rather out of the usual emigration district, we found in 1905 that emigration on a large scale had recently set in locally as a result of an unsuccessful strike and a fall of wages.

In Pilsen I was told that many coal mines had been given up or were being worked with less men, and that as a consequence many miners, unused to agriculture and wanting better wages, had gone to Germany and to America.

As to purely individual causes, they are naturally Individual most varied. One man emigrates because his family causes do not approve of his chosen bride; another, because he loves change; another because his accounts are short or because his family think that he may do better in new surroundings. Occasionally I found the feeling that to go to America was a fact that needed explanation, one that rather implied failure of some sort at home. Occasionally, too, I heard it said that those who emigrated believed that they were going to an easy life in a land of gold. It happened that I heard both these ideas expressed in a place where a considerable emigration had only recently set in, and they are, I think, commonly confined to this early phase. As a general

* See below, page 357.

thing, I found people amazingly well informed as to conditions in America, and deeply convinced that work there was harder than at home, and that there was nothing but hunger for the man who did not work. On the whole, too, I found surprisingly few cases of emigrating ne'er-do-wells, and in nearly ten months' investigation I could hear of only one case of assisted emigration.

Steamship agents

As to the steamship agent as a cause of emigration, his importance, as I have already said, is in the early days of an emigration movement. The old tailor already mentioned told how in the first days of the movement agents came from Bremen and traveled about and urged and promised. This sort of thing is not done now-a-days, and what solicitation there is seems to be sporadic and occasional. An instance, however, came under our notice in a peasant house not many miles away from Domažlice, where we found a poster of a well-known Bremen firm urging emigration to the southern states, and especially to Texas, with letters from settlers there, and the pleasant assurance that the examination for entrance to the country was less strict in Galveston than in New York.

But the importance of these particular exciting causes tends to be greatly exaggerated. The occasional person who goes away under a cloud,.or lured by promises or baseless hopes, is a drop in the bucket compared to the great number who go for the legitimate reason that they see a better opportunity in America, and who are acting on the advice of relatives and friends who are conversant with the situation on both sides.

Emigration vs. domestic migration

It should not be overlooked in studying Bohemian (or any other) emigration, that emigration to America is directly related to available opportunities nearer home. As a general thing, a smaller gain in a neighboring district or country will be preferred to the risks and expenses of going over seas, though this tendency may be modified by all sorts of cross currents of habits, hopes

BOHEMIAN AND MORAVIAN SCENES

1. Moravian peasant woman coming home from market. 2. Homes of thatch and stucco in Moravia. 3. Pilgrimage to shrine of the Virgin at Hostein near the Hungarian border. A recent outbreak of typhoid was due to drinking holy water at this shrine. 4. Gossips near town well, market place of Domažlice in Bohemia.

and affinities which may make America seem more
desirable or easier to move to than nearer places.   Thus
many Bohemians leave their homes to go to Germany
or to other parts of Austria, notably to Vienna, and
especially to the industrial centres of Bohemia itself.

For instance, the district about Neuhaus, which formerly sent emigrants to America, is now within the sphere
of influence of the Austrian capital, and overflows in
that direction.   In Vienna wages are much higher *
but so is cost of living, and there is said to be small
margin for saving, so that little or nothing is brought
home.   The migration to nearby places is naturally
often seasonal or temporary.   The house may be simply
shut up and left for the time being, with the windows
shuttered or boarded up.   Those who go to New York
sell their property.

Emigration is thus a product of two variables—conditions at home and conditions abroad.   The falling off
of Bohemian emigration in the nineties was due not
only to business depression in America, but to a high
tide in the iron and coal industries of Germany and
Austria.

In regard to the effect of emigration on the old coun- Few Bohe-
try, the fact that Bohemian emigration is generally mian emi-
a permanent withdrawal of entire families means that return
the reaction of America on Bohemia is, as already said,
comparatively slight.   There are neither large numbers
of returned "Americans" with a leaven of new ideas and
habits, nor any very considerable influx of remittances.
Doubtless many old persons are supported by children
in America, but generally the children make every
effort to reunite the broken family, either by bringing
over the parents or by returning to them.   Some
doubtless retire on a competence to the old country.
One interesting case that I ran across was a teacher

* Daily wage: masons, Neuhaus, 48 cents; Vienna, 80 cents;
common laborers, Neuhaus, 24 cents; Vienna, 40 cents.   These
wages are those stated by a local informant as current in 1905.

6

who, finding himself declassed at home by a besetting temptation to drink, emigrated to America and worked in the Carnegie steel works, keeping his social class and education hidden.   The facts became known, however, and he was given work as a bookkeeper.   He is now living in Bohemia on a small Carnegie pension.

Such money as is either remitted to friends in Bohemia or carried home by returned emigrants, is not enough to have any perceptible effect on the general economy, and Bohemia receives no flow of money available as capital, such as has produced very interesting results, as we shall see, in Croatia, Galicia and the Slovak districts of Hungary.

Emigration a modernizing force

So far as American emigration has any cultural effects, it probably goes to enhance the tendency of the civilization of our times to wipe out all distinctive traits.   The nineteenth century brought indeed a great renascence of Bohemian, or Chekh, the national language, which is one of the richest and most highly developed of the Slav linguistic family, and the organ of a noble literature; but most of the old-world ways, that is, the specifically Bohemian ways, which once gave the country a more special flavor, are gone or going fast.

The wane of picturesque Bohemia

The towns afford indeed picturesque and charming bits; perhaps a cluster of steep red roofs on a slope or in a dip of the hills beside a pond or a stream, and over all a church with the odd, bulbous belfry so characteristic of these parts; or a castle, or a bastion remaining from the former town walls.   But, except in parts of Moravia and in the historic district around Domažlice, the original peasant dress is mainly obsolete.   Yet even in the Budweis market, how pretty were scarlet stockings and low slippers under the short petticoats; and everywhere among the women working in the fields, what flashes of the clear bright reds which all Slavs seem naturally to seek and instinctively to know how to use with rare effect.

The legends and superstitions, too, the ballads and pretty poetical customs, are becoming more and more matter for the student of folklore, if not for the antiquarian.

And in this connection let me recommend that A Bohe-charming little classic, "The Grandmother," into which mian idyll the author, Božena Nemec, one of the best-beloved of Bohemian writers, weaves reminiscences of her childhood (she was born in 1820), giving us a succession of pictures—the pilgrimage, the wedding, the ordinary events of farm life—which are not only a mine for the student of comparative custom, but the best possible introduction to Bohemian spirit and ways. Over and over again in our little travels my companion and I pointed out to one another this or that—"Don't you remember, Grandmother always did that, too," or "Grandmother explained this so."

That not all the old lore perishes even in America, Traditions at least in the first generation, I had a chance to ob-in America serve in a stay of some months in the family of a Bohemian workingman in New York. I never could hear often enough an old song, sung properly at Twelfth Night, when the boys go about the village masquerading as the Three Kings, one, of course, as a blackamoor. Then there were ballads and nursery rhymes in plenty, some of which are given in Appendix VI. I was especially struck with the way in which the latter paralleled ours while yet they were quite distinct. There were variants of "Knock at the door, peep in" and of "Pat-a-cake"; there was a combination of "Creep mouse" and of "This little pig went to market," and an amusing string of verses that suggested "This is the house that Jack built," besides others, quite fresh, often with charming melodies.

Speaking from the practical point of view, the Community fact that Bohemia is less picturesque than it once of culture was means that the chasm between them and America is less wide.

In the household that I speak of, after the first strangeness on both sides had worn off, and the barriers of the intense shyness and reserve of Bohemians had given way, I had peculiarly little sense of being an alien in the family, and this was due to our fundamentally similar outlook on life, to our having a culture, education, religion fundamentally similar in spite of differences of race, class and sect.

CHAPTER VI

SLOVAK EMIGRATION

The Home of the Slovaks

One of the most attractive of the Slavic nationalities is the little group of the Slovaks of Hungary, though they have no independent history, little fame, and are the very step-children of fortune.

They live for the most part in the district which they themselves call Slovensko, along the southern slopes of the Carpathians, which make the boundary of Hungary to the north. It is a lovely but infertile hill country with clear, quick streams and a now diminishing wealth of woods. The Slovak peasants own mainly the poorest parts of the soil of this poor region.*

Below them to the south is the rich *alföld* or plain which makes up central Hungary, and is the home of the Magyars, or Hungarians proper, a brilliant, masterful race. Here in the plain are the famous *pusztas* with wide-sweeping wheat fields and immense herds of horses or of cream-colored, wide-horned cattle. This endless expanse shimmers in the hot sun, the level lines cut only by a stiff well-sweep here and there, while on the horizon the fairy Délibáb (the mirage) shows illusive groves and pools. Here the Slovaks sometimes betake themselves to get work, but their homes, with the exception of some scattered colonies, are in the hill country to the north.

---

*A charming illustrated description of the Slovak district which deserves translation is Kálal's "Na Krasnem Slovensku." But the most delightful presentation of this picturesque and winning people is the portfolio of reproductions in color of Joža Uprka's paintings of his countrymen, the Slovaks of Moravia. Mr. Seton-Watson's book, "Racial Problems in Hungary," also has excellent illustrations, some of them in color, and contains besides an essay on "Slovak Popular Art," by Jurkovič Dušan.

Numbers

The total number of Slovaks is probably 2,500,000 to 3,000,000. In Hungary proper they have (even according to the Hungarian census, which the non-Magyar nationalities claim underestimates their strength) nearly 2,000,000 souls, or nearly 12 per cent of the population. Of this 2,000,000 much the greater part is massed in fifteen northern counties of Hungary, the hill country already mentioned, and in a small adjacent district in Moravia, across the border to the west, where dwell perhaps some 75,000. Smaller numbers are scattered through other parts of Hungary, and in Croatia-Slavonia are 17,000 more. There are probably about 500,000 in the United States.*

The Slovak
tongue

Both in language and, presumably, in blood, the Slovaks are very close to the Chekhs, so close that Protestant Slovaks use the old Bohemian translation of the Bible, made in 1613 by the followers of Huss. Indeed, till after 1850, when the first Slovak grammar was written, authors of Slovak birth, including the poet Kollár and the scholar Šafařik, wrote in Bohemian, regarding that as the literary form of their own tongue. Nowadays newspapers, poetry, novels and other works are published in Slovak, but a person who knows Bohemian can read them probably more readily than an Englishman reads Burns.

The Slovaks claim that their vernacular, as compared with the Chekh, is purer from contamination with foreign idioms, racier, richer in old words that are obsolete or unknown in Bohemia, and above all more musical and euphonious. Admittedly, the Slovaks are singularly rich in folk-songs—like most primitive songs, frequently in a minor key—and in beautiful popular melodies.† The county of Trencsén is especially noted

---

* For Slovak population of Hungary see Appendices I and VII, (pages 429 and 445). For numbers in the United States, see page 266.
† See Lichard and Kolísek " Slovak Popular Melodies " and Vajansky "Slovak Popular Poetry "—two delightful essays in Mr. Seton-Watson's "Racial Problems in Hungary."

for the custom of its peasants of singing in parts. As I recall hearing this music ringing from the roadside as the workers walked together to their fields, I seem to see again how splendidly the women carried themselves, how freely and finely they moved in their short petticoats.

As has been said, the Slovaks have no independent history, though the part of the country which makes their home has been the scene of many wars and romantic episodes, and the Slovaks have made sturdy fighters on many a bitter field. The capital of the ninth century kingdom of Great Moravia was the Slovak town of Nyitra. The Slovaks have endured successively Polish rule, Magyar rule, Tatar invasions, peaceful incursions of German settlers, Hussite raids, and dynastic wars of Hungary. The most striking episode, however, is the semi-independence in the fourteenth century of Matthew of Trencsén, "Lord of the Waag and the Tatra," who with some thirty fortified castles defied king and pope.* Slovak history

All this has left its impress both on the face of the country and in folklore. On almost every crag in some districts stands a ruined castle, all that the most romantic could desire in site and story. Sometimes the legend seems to be purely mythical, as at Beczkó, where a faithless lord is supposed to have been stung in the ear by an adder and to have jumped in a frenzy over the cliff; sometimes it is a mixture of reality and fable, as at Trencsén, where a well, hewn nearly six hundred feet into the solid rock, is explained by a story which tells how the captive daughter of a Turkish pasha was held for ransom, the ransom to be a water supply for the castle which stands high on the rocks above the lovely river Waag, and how this water supply was furnished by the Turkish prisoners who earned their liberty and their lady's by hewing down to water level. Sometimes the legend is actually historical, like the terrible one of Ruins and legends

*Cf. Čapek: "The Slovaks of Hungary," page 103; also Seton-Watson: "Racial Problems in Hungary," page 23.

Csejte, where the Countess Báthory is said to have had three hundred young girls murdered in order to restore her beauty by bathing in their blood.   After a terrible *cause celèbre*, in which her guilt was proved, an old woman, her accomplice, was executed, while she was thrown into prison, where she died in 1610.   An idea of the way in which war raged all through this now smiling country, and how it centered about the siege of these castles, may be gained from Jokai's novel translated into German as "Geliebt bis zum Schaffot."

Not only in legends but in song the memory of "old unhappy far off things and battles long ago" survives. Especially are the ballads full of reminiscences of the sufferings from the Turks.

Village life of today

But of more interest than romantic ruins and traditions is the living variety of the people today.   The villages, while sometimes dreary, are often full of life and charm.   As a quiet pond is a common feature of a South Bohemian village, characteristic of a Slovak village is a brook running through its midst.   It is peopled by geese, now plump and sleek, now newly plucked and dismal, by playing children and by women knee-deep in the cold water pounding their linen on little wooden stands.   Willows and a foot bridge, and a wagoner watering his horse before he drives through the shallow ford, perhaps complete the picture.

If it is a town and not a village, there may be a church, occasionally of some architectural pretensions, and perhaps a good deal else of historical interest, such as the remains of the old wall that kept out the Turks in their day, with a stone cannon ball embedded in its side; the former gallows hill; and an old linden which now shades the image of a Christian saint but under which a heathen god may once have been worshipped (for the linden is the sacred tree of the Slavs).

Gipsies

Just outside some of the towns will be seen a gipsy settlement, all dirt, naked children and beggary.   One man is squatting over a fire forging a chain, for the

SLOVAK SCENES

1. In Rosenberg, in Liptó county, home of Father Hlinka. 2. Shingle roofs with ornamented gable ends. Zólyom county. 3. "American" houses in Liptó county, built by returned emigrants. 4. Carrying home hemp. Thatch roofed houses in Zemplén county. 5. A Zólyom mother who wanted to send a picture to her husband in America.

gipsies are clever iron workers. In a grass-roofed hovel, where the air is dense with smoke, a violin hangs on the wall. The boy who owns it may some day be earning gold and glory as a member of one of the gipsy bands which afford the Magyar such extravagant delight, but a gipsy he will remain in every fibre.

The return from such a settlement to the Slovak town or village is a return to another world. Here are long, low houses, neat and clean, ranged with their gable roofs end to end in an even row, flush with the street, the eaves just above the door. The roofs are apt to be of hand-made shingles, for thatch means plenty of grain to supply the straw, and not much grain grows here. The houses are generally either of brick, frequently merely sun dried, or of wood. Often the ends of cross-laid logs or great squared beams show clearly at the corners. But whatever the material, it is generally covered with plaster or raw clay, and either whitewashed or painted some pale shade of buff, blue or green. The houses are generally perfectly plain in their design, though some have pretty woodwork at the gable ends, or patterns painted on the walls or about the windows—a kind of work which is a specialty of the women, who are said to do it freehand.* ^{Slovak houses}

Of course, conditions vary with localities and with individual housewives, but my general impression is of interiors tidy and homelike, however deep the mud in the village street. Even an earthen floor may be made to suggest cleanliness. I remember especially a call at a house where the daughter had recently gone to America to get work. The mother who welcomed us led us through the entry, where a girl was washing, into the living room and offered us the traditional "bread and salt"—that is, as a matter of fact, a loaf of rye bread and a knife that we might serve ^{Interiors}

* For specimens of Slovak architecture and wall decoration, including a wall painting reproduced in color, see Seton-Watson, pages 88, 204, 320, 352, 354, 356, 358 362

ourselves unstinted.   We honored the pretty old custom, and I wished that I had cut off a bigger piece, it tasted so good.

The room was low, but scrupulously neat.   On the wall hung gay flowered crockery, products of an old home art, specimens of which collectors highly prize. There were double windows, opening casement fashion, and, in the space between, pots of wallflowers.   On the bed were piles of square feather pillows, the pride and visible assets of the thrifty housewife.   Each has a bright undercover (among rich city people this would be of satin,—yellow, pink, blue or what not), over which is drawn a case of handspun linen, with ends of lace insertion, also handmade, through which the color peeps prettily.   It takes some sixteen geese to supply one feather bed.   There was a sewing machine and a table on which lay a copy of a Sokol magazine (that is, the organ of one of the universal patriotic athletic associations).   On the wall were pictures of sacred subjects. These often, even in much poorer homes, make a sort of frieze about the top of the room.   Often, too, there hangs over the table a curious little ornament made of a blown eggshell, with tail and wings of pleated paper.   This represents a dove and symbolizes the Holy Ghost.

Spinning bees

In many houses there was a loom, but I think we never saw a spinning wheel, for the spinning season was over.   It is only in winter that the famous spinning bees take place, where young and old gather in separate groups to sing, tell legends and, in the case of the girls, receive their lovers who drop in toward the end of the evening.   Clothes are kept for the most part in chests which are sometimes painted with rude designs of flowers on a red, blue or green background, and which the bride must bring to her husband well replenished.

Costume

It is difficult to describe the dress, it varies so from place to place.   Every little village has its own peculiarities, so that its people are distinguishable to the initiated, and this doubtless helps to give a strong sense of local solidarity. Within the village there is the most scrupulous adherence to custom. The kerchief knotted under the chin, apparently carelessly, is in reality arranged in certain folds and at a certain angle, precisely as prescribed by local usage and in a way that is different from that of the next place.

The colors are generally harmonious and brilliant, *Coloring* though in some districts a wonderful effectiveness is gained by heavy embroidery of black on white, with no color. In many places bright-patterned stuffs, usually in large flowered designs, are attractively used for skirt, bodice or apron. The latter is generally the show piece in a woman's holiday costume. I was interested to note the same curious and beautiful combinations of color, most unlike those that we are accustomed to choose, which had struck me years ago on a visit to the settlement of Slavs (Vends) which survives in the Spreewald, near Dresden.

The great beauty of these costumes is the embroidery *Embroidery* which is indeed, with song, the chief art of the Slovak. The women do this work mainly in winter, when their fingers are sufficiently soft again after the field work. They are said to often embroider their patterns without first drawing them, and they work so neatly that the under side is almost as perfect as the upper. The variety of stitches is great, and embroidery is combined with pillow lace and drawn work. The feeling for style is admirable. The designs are conventional and the motives, generally from plant life, are roses, poppy heads, tulips, cornflowers, and so forth. One animal motif, the cock, is also commonly introduced, but perhaps the commonest single figure is the heart-shape. Special units of design often have special names, like the quilting patterns of our grandmothers. Many of these seem to be quite fanciful—the "lover's eye" or the "little window" may have no visible resemblance to the object named.

Girls and married women are generally distinguished, the former as a rule by their long braids, the latter by their caps, which are usually hidden, however, under the universal kerchief. Otherwise the dress is the same from childhood to old age; if the skirts of the district are full and short, they are short for the grandmother, and if long, they are long even for the toddler of three or four.

In many places the women wear very short skirts and leather boots to the knees, like a man's. At first these boots strike a stranger as clumsy and unfeminine, but an experience of what mud can be here soon converts one to their good sense, and as to grace they give a new impression when one has an opportunity to see the quick, graceful dancing of the girls, the high heels of their trim-ankled boots clicking the measure. In Transylvania one sees these tall boots made of soft scarlet morocco leather with patterns in gilt nail-heads on the heels. Sometimes, instead of boots, low moccasin-like shoes called *Krpce* are worn, bound with leather thongs about the ankle. These, too, are worn by either sex.

One of the prettiest forms of dress is a low square-cut bodice, over a chemise of white linen with full short sleeves, with a wide ruffle above the elbow and a broad band of embroidery—perhaps in orange and canary-yellow silks—across the sleeve just below the shoulder.*

Men's dress
The men, especially the young fellows, are often great dandies. Sometimes they wear jackets and trousers of cadet-blue cloth, fitted like a glove and braided with black in looping designs. Sometimes they are dressed in white linen, with wide fringed trousers and a narrow, dark-blue apron. It is astonishing how both men and women dig and delve in white linen and still look clean.

Especially archaic are the wide-brimmed black felt

* Embroidery in this style is pictured in color in Seton-Watson, opposite page 368.

SLOVAK PEASANT GIRLS

The girl at the door has just come from church with her prayer book under her arm. Note the tall leather boots and pretty head dress. The other girls are also in holiday dress. The white kerchief covers a lace cap beneath, the little embroidered border of which shows over the forehead. The apron, sleeves and floating cap ends are richly embroidered.

hats, looking almost like the old-fashioned cocked hat, worn by the men in some districts, and the enormous leather belts. Sometimes these appear to be a good foot and a half wide; they are studded with brass trimmings and serve as pouches for all the necessaries, especially tobacco.

A very important article of dress for both men and women is the sheepskin garment, made with the wool inside and the leather out, or sometimes reversible according to weather. It may be quite plain or much adorned,—dyed, embroidered, trimmed with appliqué leather or with brass work, or with borders of wool of a contrasting color. These garments take many forms; in some places they appear as close-fitting, sleeveless jackets, very pretty and very comfortable; in other places, as long-sleeved coats. Sometimes this coat is made not of sheepskin, but of the heavy home-made felt called *hunia*. This may be dark brown or blue, but is oftener white and is also used instead of leather for tall boots, which can be kept white and clean by washing.

It interested me very much to note how certain characteristic articles of dress—such as the moccasin-like shoe, the leather coat, the belt, the kerchief or shawl —appear here and there among all the different Slav nationalities that I have had an opportunity to observe, running through a whole gamut of modifications. Nowhere could the student of the natural history of costume find richer fields.

The Slovaks seemed to me comely and sweet-faced, rather than beautiful, though there are of course excep- tions. Among the elders one sees the best sort of beauty in the strongly marked lines of character and experience; here "the old, plain men have rosy faces and the young fair maidens quiet eyes." One seems to distinguish two markedly contrasting facial types. There is the round, full face with short nose, high cheek bones and widely separated grey-blue eyes. In

Facial characteristics and physique

other places this is replaced by a strongly marked facial contour, with straight, long, sharpset nose and long lantern jaw.

Physically they are often splendid creatures, powerful without being heavy, and full of the grace that goes with health and varied activity and the bearing of burdens. Nothing seems too heavy for the women to carry. A child of two or three will be slung comfortably on the back in a linen cloth, and apparently regarded as scarcely an addition to other burdens. The women marry young, bear a child a year—"always either bearing or nursing," is the saying,—and perhaps in consequence grow old fast.

Both men and women seem insensible to heat and cold. In summer they will dance gaily under an almost unbearable sun in their sheepskin or wool coats, which represent full dress; in winter the men, I am told, labor in the woods in their shirts without any sort of vest or jacket. They are very hard workers. In the season when field operations are pressing there are often weeks when a man sleeps only four or five hours, and snatches his food as he can. I was told of a peasant who was hired to thresh for a man whose crop was not so large but that he might have done his own work. The comment of the thresher was, "Er muss doch ein Schwein sein der nur acht Stunden arbeiten will."

The darker side

All these good qualities are handicapped by various unfortunate circumstances acting on the weaker sides of the Slovaks, on their passiveness and lack of initiative and their proneness to drink. Apart from the natural infertility of the soil, intensified as this is by conditions of landholding and tillage, the great curses of the country seem to be three: political conditions, intemperance and financial exploitation (the last two very closely related). To the first of these, political conditions, I will recur later.

Intemperance

As to intemperance, all the powers that be seem to favor rather than to restrain drinking. The large

landowner, who is the local great personage, is interested
in marketing the products of his distillery. The Jew
who pays for the exclusive right of sale and keeps the
drinking shop where the rank potato brandy of the
countryside is sold, is often the only intelligent man in
the little community, the only one who can help in a
money difficulty, translate a legal document (always in
Magyar), or assist with advice in an emergency. He
often controls not only the drink traffic but practically
all the retail trade, and is the only man who can supply
goods or buy produce. For all these reasons it is essential to stand well with him, and his goodwill must be
won by buying his wares, especially his liquor.

The government also, I am told, is opposed to temperance agitation as likely to lower revenues, and some
years ago actually put a stop to a series of mission services that the Redemptorist fathers were proposing to
hold throughout the Slovak counties in the interest of
temperance. The local priest is not likely to be a
total abstainer, and too often has neither the desire
nor the courage to take a decided stand on the question,
though there are honorable exceptions. Public opinion,
while not so low as in eighteenth century England, or
colonial New England, is much below what it is at
present in the more advanced countries. One of the
most frequent comments of returned emigrants, in regard to the United States, is in the first place that beer
is cheap and abundant in America, and in the second
place that men are arrested there for being drunk.
"And rich men as well as poor ones; that could not
happen here."

As to financial exploitation, the local reputation
of the Jews seems to vary with the credit situation.
Where credit institutions have been established,
lending money at 5½ or 6 per cent instead of at the
Jewish rate of 8 or 12 per cent or more, the Jews are
often respected and not disliked; but in too many
places, where the simple, drink-loving peasants are

Indebted-
ness

wholly at their mercy, the Jews are accused of getting them into debt, often through tavern bills. There is especial complaint of the way they contrive to get control of the woods, which are the only valuable asset of the region, and which are being recklessly cut down by speculators. On these steep chalky hillsides this means destruction of the soil, floods and general disaster. Where there has been a movement to America, the peasants, educated by experience, are said to know how to keep out of the hands of designing individuals.*

Illiteracy

Among our Slavic immigrants the Slovaks rank second in education—next, but far below, the Bohemians. Our immigration figures for 1900 for those fourteen years of age and over show that of Bohemians, 3 per cent are illiterate; Slovaks, 28 per cent. It is worth noticing, as bearing out my view that we get the pick of the Slovak population, that this is decidedly better than the proportion at home. The Slovak counties range from Gömör, with 28 per cent of the population illiterate, to Ung, with over 67 per cent. Twelve of the Slovak counties are worse than the general Hungarian average (50.6 per cent) of illiteracy, four are better.†

Co-oper-ation

One of the promising things I noted is a thriving co-operative movement, in which the priests seem to lead. The co-operative store, served by the members, the co-operative dairy and sometimes the co-operative hall for dancing, co-operative banks,‡ amateur theatricals and entertainments, all these things furnish the best possible sort of training in business and in organization, apart from more direct benefits.

Agriculture

For livelihood the main dependence is agriculture. This, in spite of the presence of some other kinds of

---

* Terrible stories of Jewish treachery and exploitation are told in detail in a series of articles by Karl Kálal in the Prague monthly *Osvěta*, 1900, Nos. 3, 4 and 5.

† For further immigration data on illiteracy see Appendix XXVII, page 479.

‡ Data as to thirty-two Slovak banks, with a total capital of over 5,000,000 crowns, will be found in Seton-Watson, page 469.

work, is the main occupation—agriculture, that is, including stock raising, but all on a very small scale.

As in Russia, the mechanics and factory hands and the wandering peddlers and workers are in most cases simply peasants temporarily employed otherwise than in their fields. The thickly settled village, which to American eyes suggests town life, is surrounded by land belonging to the houses and employing men and women alike. Population is not dense absolutely, but take into consideration the character of the soil, the amount of land held in large estates (and this is apt to be the best situated), the amount that is in woodland or otherwise unfit for tillage, the degree of subdivision of property, the primitive methods and the frequent indebtedness, and it is not hard to understand why, as Hurban Vayansky's pathetic song of the wandering Slovak says, "Our native village does not give bread to her children."

As a general thing, agriculture alone is not a sufficient source of income and must be eked out in other ways. Some of the men have trades, are blacksmiths, shoemakers, tanners, dyers, and so forth; some are woodsmen and raftsmen, leading a hard and dangerous life, at work in ice-cold water or piloting their floats past rocks and rapids. Some are shepherds, spending the summer at a mountain pasture preparing the famous Liptó cheese, which is exported even to New York.

Some, especially in certain poor districts which *Wandering* have long been unable to support their population, have *trades* for generations been accustomed to set out on foot either to follow a wandering trade or to sell certain wares, sometimes handmade, sometimes bought abroad. Most characteristic of these wanderers was the *Drotar*, or as the Germans say, *Drahtbinder*, who made all sorts of things of wire, sometimes very elaborate and artistic things, but whose commonest task was the mending of broken earthen pots with a skilful wire network. If

7

the pot rang like a bell when done the work was good. As metal pots replaced earthenware the demand for this service grew less, and the selling of all sorts of wire and tin goods and the like partly took its place. Unfortunately, in some instances small boys are pressed into the business, and one meets them in Prague and elsewhere—wretched little half-beggars working for what an Italian would call a padrone, with the usual story of a beating if they do not bring home a set sum.

In America the wire workers often find employment for their skill in modernized forms of the same craft—making fences, gates and railings, mouse-traps, and small articles, and becoming tinplaters and plumbers.* Mr. Rovnianek reports "In several of the large cities, especially in Philadelphia, New York and Chicago, wire and tinware factories which have been established with Slovak capital and are conducted with Slovak labor, are in a fair way to secure the cream of the trade of this kind in the whole country. A peculiar advantage is derived from the fact that for centuries the tinware of Europe was made largely by the Slovaks. In this country also electrical designs and other skilled work turned out by Slovak plants have obtained a very high position in the markets." † This is interesting as a case where it has been practicable to utilize an old form of skill in the new country.

Specialization of wandering trades

Another famous specialty was glass setting, and the wandering Slovak glazier was eagerly watched for when a window pane or the glass of a holy picture needed replacing. Others again dealt in spices, in oils, in fruit; others in dry goods, especially in linen. In some cases this peddling was built up into large, settled wholesale businesses, and well-known firms in Russia, Bucharest, Warsaw, and elsewhere have been developed in this way. Generally these different types were quite specifically located; the wire men came from

* Wandering Trades in the Bibliography.
† *Charities*, XIII, page 242 (Dec. 3, 1904).

SHEPHERD IN A SLOVAK VALLEY

AN ABODE OF MISERY

The house is the home of Slovak "Zeliary," compelled to work for their landlord at starvation wages. Two families shared the house; in one a man, unable to afford a physician, was dying; in the other a girl had Pott's disease.

Trencsén, the spice dealers from Liptó county, the linen merchants from Túrócz.

Modern conditions have greatly militated against these old Slovak methods of eking out an existence. Russia, Germany and France, which with the near East were among the chief markets, have passed laws or laid taxes which shut out the Drotars and the rest, and cheap factory products have underbid them.

Other employment away from home

More modern forms of temporary employment take men to neighboring districts for harvest and other agricultural work, or to the cities for building or factory labor. In the years when Budapest was making its most rapid growth many masons, carpenters and others went, as they put it, "to build Pest," and the slackening of this work is said to have been one cause of increased emigration to America. Factories about Budapest and Pressburg now give employment to considerable numbers, but unfortunately, in the Slovak counties themselves, in spite of minerals, water power and cheap labor, industry is very little developed. Where it does exist it tends to keep men at home since it supplies the ready money which is so needed and of which agriculture yields so little.

Obviously such a situation as has been described means that many will emigrate if the way only opens. Their own land has never fully supported them, and if America offers opportunities better not only than the wandering trades, which modern conditions are killing out in any case, but better than the possible earnings as hired hands in neighboring districts and countries, then to America men will go if they can.*

Slovak emigration: origin and spread

The movement seems to have begun in the northeastern part of the Slovak district in Zemplén, Sáros, Szepes (German Zips) and Ung. This district is racially very mixed, containing large numbers of Jews, Germans and Ruthenians, besides Slovaks. The Jews have come in largely from Galicia (Austrian Poland) just across

* See Appendix VIII, page 447, for studies of Slovak emigration.

the border, whence many have migrated of late years into the Eastern Slovak counties of Hungary.* They are a cosmopolitan element, alert to find every profitable opening, and have often piloted emigration movements. The Ruthenians also are an overflow from Galicia, a continuation of the Ruthenian settlement in the eastern part of that province. The German population, most numerous in Szepes, goes back to the founding of sixteen free towns by Saxon settlers in the twelfth century.

Early emigrants

The Jews and Germans may easily have been the means of infecting the Slovaks with the emigration fever, or it may have begun in other untraceable ways. In any case it began much later than the Bohemian and Polish movements. One hears of sporadic cases of emigration to America from 1864 on; in the late seventies the exodus was already well marked, and by 1882 it was sufficiently important to be investigated by order of the Minister of the Interior and repressed by gendarmes posted on the frontier.

American immigration figures

The American immigration figures indicate the first important Slovak influx in 1873, when 1300 immigrants came from Hungary, and a second in 1880, when 4000 came, rising to nearly 15,000 in 1884.† Mr. Rovnianek says, "Previous to 1882 the immigration had been sporadic, but in that year the people began to come in companies of considerable size, and settled in the mining and industrial regions of Pennsylvania."‡

At Bartfeld, a town in Sáros, we had an interesting talk with one of the earliest emigrants, a hatter who went to the United States about 1880. The account he gave was that a Jew from this town (which swarms with Polish Jews of the most typical sort, side curls,

* See articles by Karl Kálal on this migration of the Jews in *Osvěta*, 1900, Nos. 3, 4 and 5.

† The figures do not give Slovaks separately till 1899, but the earlier immigrants from Hungary may be assumed to be in general Slovaks with some Jews and others.

‡ *Charities*, XIII, page 240 (Dec. 3, 1904). See also below, page 238 ff.

long coats and all) was the first to go. This Jew was a dealer in cloth, but became bankrupt and went to America. He afterward came home, and his account induced others to go, among them the hatter. He went hoping to find work at his own trade, but *he could find no one to tell him where hats were made*, so that he had to take what employment he could get. He worked as a longshoreman, miner, etc. He was first in New York, then in Drifton, Pa., where there was a mine superintendent from Austria, then in Cleveland, and later in Boston, where he did get work at hatmaking. Wages in the mines he found to be $1.25 to $1.30 above ground, and $2.00 under ground. Passage was cheap in those days— $20 from Hamburg going, and under $23 as far as Oderburg (the station on the Hungarian border) returning.

From the counties where emigration first began the movement has spread, affecting both the Ruthenians of Hungary in the counties to the east of the Slovaks, and the Slovak counties to the west of the first emigration district, and quite recently those to the southwest also. Thus in Zólyom we were told that the movement had set in only three years before (i. e., in 1902) largely as a result of bad harvests and cattle diseases causing debt. Zólyom is, in general, a well-to-do district. It is noted, even in this land of almost universally preserved peasant dress, for the archaism of its costumes and customs. In some places the men even wear the tight-braided pigtails, one on each side of the face, which one connects with pictures of Hungarian hussars of the olden time.

Spread of the movement

Emigration from Hungary, far from falling off, has shown, as is proved by the figures of the Hungarian authorities, an almost steady increase, rising from 24,846 in 1896 to 178,170 in 1906. Of this outflow the Slovaks make only a part. The Roumanians, Germans, Ruthenians, and other "nationalities" are also emigrating and the Magyar peasantry itself is seriously affected, which is to Magyar statesmen the gravest aspect of the case.

Since 1899 the American data for immigrants by country of origin have merged emigrants from Hungary in the whole group from Austria-Hungary except in the year 1905. The following tables show the Hungarian totals for emigration, 1896–1906, and both the American and Hungarian tables for 1905:

TABLE 6.—TOTAL EMIGRATION FROM HUNGARY, AS REPORTED BY LOCAL AUTHORITIES IN HUNGARY, 1896–1906.

YEAR	NO. OF EMIGRANTS
1896	24,846
1897	14,310
1898	22,965
1899	43,394
1900	54,767
1901	71,474
1902	91,762
1903	119,944
1904	97,340
1905	170,430
1906	178,170
Total	889,402

TABLE 7.—EMIGRATION AND RE-IMMIGRATION, 1905.*

NATIONALITY	HUNGARIAN FIGURES		AMERICAN FIGURES
	LEFT HUNGARY	RETURNED	IMMIGRANTS ENTERING U. S. FROM HUNGARY
Magyars	43,754	4,575	45,300
Germans	28,303	2,453	25,759
Slovaks	38,770	4,038	51,009
Roumanians	17,747	2,506	7,167
Ruthenians	7,287	1,012	3,268
Croatians	17,523	1,885	22,007†
Servians	10,376	930	2,340‡
Others	2,101	167	6,853
Men	122,059	14,489	
Women	43,802	3,077	
Total	165,861	17,566	163,703

* The figures are not strictly comparable, as the American figures refer to the fiscal year ending June 30, 1905.
† Croatians and Slovenians.
‡ Servians, Bulgarians and Montenegrins.

The American figures for Slovak immigrants since 1899, when they were first printed, are as follows:

TABLE 8.—SLOVAK IMMIGRANT ALIENS ADMITTED TO THE UNITED STATES

Year Ending June 30	Number	Year	Number
1899	15,838	1905	52,368
1900	29,243	1906	38,221
1901	29,343	1907	42,041
1902	36,934	1908	16,170
1903	34,427	1909	22,586
1904	27,940		
Total			345,111

The loss of population by emigration for the two decades preceding 1900 as shown by the census is given for the chief Slovak counties in Table 9.* This table also shows the percentage of Slovaks in the counties where they are most numerous.

Map VII, drawn from the same source, shows the relative intensity of emigration in all parts of Hungary as represented by the percentage of the population of 1900 reported by the local authority as having emigrated in 1899–1901. It will be seen how great is the relative intensity of emigration in the Slovak counties. Szepes, Sáros, Abauj-Torna, Zemplén and Ung, and these counties alone, show a loss of 5 per cent or over of the population in three short years. In Árva and Gömör the loss is 2 to 3 per cent. In Turócz, Liptó and Bereg the loss is 1 to 2 per cent. Even these last figures cannot be paralleled elsewhere in Hungary proper. Only in Croatia do we find in Modruš-Fiume county a loss of 2 to 3 per cent and in Agram (Hungarian Zágráb) county a loss of 1 to 2 per cent.

* Taken from Thirring, Gustav: "Die Auswanderung aus Ungarn." Bulletin de la Société Hongroise de Géographie, vol. XXX (1902), page 8; except the figures for Slovak percentage of population, for which see Niederle, "Národopisna Mapa," page 121. For further data see Appendices V and VII, pages 433 and 445.

TABLE 9.—CHIEF SLOVAK COUNTIES OF HUNGARY. NET LOSS AND GAIN BY EMIGRATION AND IMMIGRATION.

Counties	Slovaks, Per Cent of Total Civil Population 1900	Net Loss and Gain by Emigration and Immigration. Non-urban Population					
		1881–1890		1891–1900		For the period	
		Absolute	Per Cent	Absolute	Per Cent	Absolute	Per Cent
Pozsony (Pressburg)	51	—13,272	—5.1	—14,501	—5.2	—27,773	—10.6
Trencsén	93	—8,239	—3.4	—6,747	—2.6	—14,986	—6.1
Nyitra	73	—13,811	—3.7	—22,063	—5.6	—35,874	—9.7
Bars	58	—5,346	—3.7	—6,030	—3.9	—11,376	—8.0
Hont	40	—2,366	—2.3	—3,146	—2.9	—5,512	—5.5
Árva	95	—4,615	—5.6	—7,268	—8.6	—11,883	—14.6
Liptó	93	—2,958	—4.0	—2,670	—3.5	—5,628	—7.5
Turócz	74	—109	—0.2	—2,860	—5.7	—2,969	—6.5
Zólyom	89	—1,756	—1.7	—2,889	—2.6	—4,645	—4.5
Nógrád	27	+16	+0.0	—1,327	—0.6	—1,311	—0.7
Gömör	41	—6,450	—3.8	—5,951	—3.7	—12,401	—7.3
Abauj-Torna	23	—19,912	—13.1	—14,532	—9.6	—34,444	—22.6
Zemplén	32	—16,458	—5.9	—22,873	—7.6	—39,331	—14.2
Ung	28	—11,256	—8.9	—9,275	—6.7	—20,531	—16.2
Szepes	58	—22,124	—12.8	—11,202	—6.9	—33,326	—19.3
Sáros	66	—21,956	—13.1	—21,402	—12.7	—43,358	—25.8

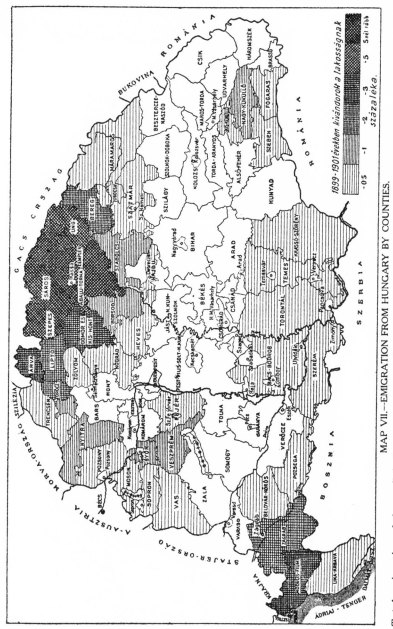

MAP VII.—EMIGRATION FROM HUNGARY BY COUNTIES.

Total emigration of the period 1899–1901, expressed in percentages of the population of 1900. • The scale runs from under 0.5 per cent to 5 per cent or over.

Character
of the emi-
gration

The character of the Slovak emigration has been throughout quite different from the Bohemian. Instead of emigrating to settle, taking his family and property with him, the Slovak merely went to America, instead of to some nearer field, to earn needed money. The wife remained, as before, to care for the house, bring up the children and work the land till he should return.

Successive
phases

Such an emigration movement often runs through quite well-defined phases. First the man goes alone and returns with his earnings, as planned. Then he goes again, and this time decides to settle or at least to remain for some time, and returns and takes out his wife and children.

At a later stage, when the routes are better known and parties are frequently starting, the man often sends for his wife to come and join him, without going himself to get her. She is not always eager to begin life again under strange conditions; often she fears to face the long and difficult journey alone with a family of little children. One woman we met just starting out, waiting at the home railroad station with baby and bundles. Her husband, after vainly urging her to come to him, had finally cut off supplies and sent a prepaid ticket, and willy-nilly she was going. Her brother-in-law, a sturdy young man who was traveling with her, was eager for work however hard, and I judged that she too, now that the wrench was over, was ready enough to go.

Emigration
of unmar-
ried girls

A still later phase is when the unmarried girls begin to go over independently, as the Irish girls have done for so long. And the Slovak girls, like the Irish, go mainly to service. America is to them even more of an Eldorado than to the men. Instead of three or four dollars a month a girl has American wages and almost no expenses. If she secures a good place she is treated with more respect, if not also more kindness, than she is used to; if she is a good maid her industry, cleanliness, honesty and docility are appreciated, and—glory of glories— she wears a hat. A Slovak lady was telling us (as so

many had done) of a former servant who had gone to
America and recently written to her from there. "Tell
me, it can't be true, can it?" she said. "She writes that
she wears a hat. Of course even in America that is
impossible. And she says that the master is so kind,
he bids her good morning before she has spoken to him."
And we tried to explain that in America neither wearing
a hat nor greeting last is a hall-mark of the socially
superior.

Sometimes very young girls go alone; that is, with
a party of comparative strangers. A friend told us of
going to a village in Nyitra county and finding a little
peasant lass, "only fourteen and pretty as a picture,"
dressed, for the first time in her life, not in her short,
full peasant petticoats, but in a long, citified skirt.
When asked why she was so dressed up, she answered,
"Tomorrow I am going to America." She was to join
relatives there, but had only strangers to look to for
protection on the way. I must admit that one seldom
hears of any evil chance resulting from such journeys,
and it is gratifying to note how confident the experienced
emigrant is that conductors will be kind in looking after
the helpless; nevertheless, it is probably a wise provision
of our immigration law of 1907 which gives the authorities
discretionary power to refuse admission to children
under sixteen traveling apart from their families.

One of the most important questions to us, as regards Favorable
any stream of emigrants, is what selective forces are at selective influences
work. Are we getting the failures who cannot succeed
at home—as people say, "the dregs," "the scum"?
Or are we getting the best? Among the Slovaks, the
main selecting traits would seem to be energy, strength
and trustworthiness. The ones who are the most apt
to emigrate are those who are ambitious and those
whose credit is good,—for they commonly go on borrowed money. They are therefore those who are physically strong and who expect (and are expected) to be
able to make "big money" in America by undertaking

what is known to be the very hard work here. I was told at the Tatra Bank in Saint Martin that in all the years during which the bank had been loaning money to emigrants, they had never had a case where the money loaned (generally about 400 crowns, or $80), was not repaid in four months. To my inquiry as to what happened if a man was absolutely unable to pay, in case of sickness or accident, for example, "Then his brother pays," I was told. A peasant is seldom refused a loan on account of lack of character, though he may be because of absolute poverty. Peasants are "good pay," I was told, gentlemen uncertain, and stories were related to illustrate the peasants' fidelity in discharging a debt, even a questionable one.

Of course, there are cases of those who emigrate because they have ruined themselves at home by intemperance, by bad management or through ill-luck, but my conclusion is that, on the whole, we get the pick of the population from which emigration mainly draws, but it does not draw from all strata as we have seen.*

Politics and emigration

While the main causes of emigration are doubtless here also, as among the Slavs generally, economic not political, the political conditions yet play an important part. Aside from desire to avoid military service, and individual cases of persecution,† it is probably not very often that political reasons cause a Slovak peasant to leave the country, but on the other hand these are often a chief cause for his finally remaining permanently in America. A more or less conscious sense of being ill at ease, of being regarded as an inferior,

---

* Cf. Stodola: "Prispevok Ku Statistike Slovenska," page 20, note. "If we today observe Slovak villages from which people stream to America, we see that those who remain at home are not the most healthy, industrious, fit to cope with life, nor the most enterprising."

† Such for instance, as the case of a Slovak Protestant minister, in New York who, as I was informed, was forced to leave Hungary because he refused to preach in Magyar more than two Sundays out of three to a congregation which understood only Slovak.

and on account of his race thwarted in his efforts to progress, makes Hungary unattractive to him. The dark cloud resting over everything in Hungary is the political tension,—not the struggle of Hungary with Austria for advantage in their strange partnership, but internal tension between the different racial elements in the kingdom.*

While one must feel with the Slovaks, who are the injured party, one cannot help also sympathizing with Magyar statesmen in the difficult position in which they find themselves. They desire to strengthen and expand their national life and to develop the peculiar and interesting genius of their own strain; and they find themselves an isolated body of some eight or nine million or so, hemmed in not only by unfriendly states but by a majority belonging to rival nationalities within their own boundaries. Stung by unfriendly prophecies to the effect that the Magyar stock must infallibly be absorbed and perish as a racial entity, they determined at whatever cost to reverse the process and forcibly to assimilate all non-Magyar elements within their borders. The phrase "The Magyar State idea" is on every one's lips for praise or blame,—the idea, that is, that in the state there must be complete unity, or rather uniformity, including uniformity of language. Everything must be Magyar, and Magyar alone. To bring this about in a country where the Magyars are only some 51.4 per cent of the population, and where through whole countrysides their language is absolutely unknown to the mass of the population, is a gigantic and cruel task.

Formerly the language of parliament and of state business generally was Latin. People still living recall this

The Magyar state idea

Forced use of Magyar language

---

* Having seen something at first hand of the shocking oppression of the Slovaks by the Magyars, I am thankful to Mr. Seton-Watson who in his "Racial Problems in Hungary" has given a full account of the too little known conditions prevailing in a country for which the general public feels so much interest and desires to feel so much respect. An account of all this unhappy matter will also be found in Mr. Čapek's book "The Slovaks in Hungary."

era.   Then came the unhappy decision to give a forced monopoly in pulpit, school, courts of justice, and so far as possible in daily life, to the Magyar language.   This is a very difficult non-Aryan tongue of the agglutinative type, akin to Finnic or perhaps to Turkish, and entirely unrelated to Slavic languages.   The Slovaks, who like most Slavs are extremely tenacious, object to this policy on practical as well as on sentimental grounds. Their own language with a little experience practically opens to them the whole Slav world, including Russia (and we have seen what wanderers they are).   German, too, which a large proportion of them can speak, is an important medium of business and culture.   "But what," they say, "does Magyar open to our children? They come out of school, in most cases, not really masters of it and at the same time illiterate in their own tongue, which they have not been allowed to learn to read or write.   This is a cause of an artificial degree of illiteracy among our people.   In America our people learn to read Slovak and come back reading the newspapers."

Other op-
pressive
measures
of the
Magyars

But in Hungary to take a Slovak newspaper or, if an educated man, to speak the Slovak tongue, is to brand oneself in Magyar eyes as a political traitor and to insure every possible obstacle in one's path.   The upper schools (" gymnasiums "), formerly conducted in Slovak and founded and supported by private contributions, have been closed and the funds sequestrated; the Slovak literary association has been dissolved and its building seized.   It is almost impossible for a company of Slovak shareholders to receive the necessary permission to carry on business even, since the undertaking is considered a nationalistic enterprise.*

Educational
interference

Though the State has pledged itself by law to provide instruction up to the university in the mother tongue of

* A cellulose factory at Saint Martin in Túrócz is a well-known instance.   After standing idle for a long time while the Slovak owners vainly endeavored to get a government license to begin work, it was sold to a Jewish company for less than it was worth, and at once was licensed and put in operation.

each of the nationalities, as a matter of fact the government not only fails to do this, but prevents its being
done at private expense, often confiscating school funds
when raised. Even to study for the priesthood a Slovak
must pass through the Magyar seminary, and there any
study of the language of the future flock is treated as
ground for expulsion.*

The natural consequence is that a Slovak who continues his education, religious or secular, beyond the
primary school, necessarily receives a purely Magyar
training, and partly through assimilation, partly through
prudential considerations, generally becomes a "Magyar-
one," and like most converts, *plus royaliste que le roi.*
Thus the Slovaks lose their natural leaders by a constant drafting off of the ablest and most ambitious,
and this fosters the Magyar feeling that *Tót* (Magyar
for Slav), is synonymous with ignorance, dullness and
poverty.   All that is intelligent is assumed to be
Magyar.   This stupid contempt (for all contempt is
stupid), and the desire to appropriate as Magyar all the
specifically Slovak productions, is most exasperating.
In the beautiful ethnological museum at Budapest all
the Slovak treasures of embroidery, costume, etc., appear to be Magyar.   No other nationality is recognized.

Another very trying phase of the Magyarizing process Renaming
is the renaming of places. A Slovak village, for in- of places
stance, will be given a new Magyar name, a forced
translation or a would-be Magyarized form of the im-
memorial word, and this is felt not unnaturally as a great
grievance.   When I have asked Slovaks in America what
place they came from, they have said to me, plaintively,
"I don't know what its name is now; it used to be so-
and-so, but they have changed it."   How is a Slovak who
does not know Magyar to guess, for instance, that
Aranypataka means his old home Zlató?†

The Magyarizing tendency is fostered by the fact that

---

*For a case in point, see Appendix X page 448.
† Cf. Seton-Watson on these subjects, pages 188, 189, 400, 478.

the Magyar language has only one word for the two ideas, Magyar and Hungarian. Hungary is *Magyarország* (that is, Magyar land), and one might almost say that this whole wretched business reduces itself to a poor pun. "A Hungarian" (that is, an inhabitant of Hungary) "must of course speak Hungarian" (that is, Magyar), and if not willingly, then by compulsion.

Evil effects of internal strife   All this bitterness and strife afford many avenues of advance to the unscrupulous, and it is not strange if too often Jews of the type whose only concern in the struggle of nationalities is their own personal advantage become the clever instruments for a great deal of "dirty work" of all sorts. Double honor then to those Jews who, in spite of the bad traditions of a persecuted race and the sinister opportunities afforded by a helpless peasantry, are honorable and just in their dealings. And double honor to those Magyars who unite to love of their own race the magnanimity to appreciate the claims of others, and the wisdom to recognize the folly of a policy which alienates and keeps back millions of their sturdiest citizens. Similarly, double honor to those Slovaks, who in spite of the danger of personal ruin and the daily experience of petty annoyances, which are less heroic but perhaps harder to endure, sacrifice all their prospects in life to loyalty to their own people and to their country as a whole. Meeting such men is one of the greatest pleasures of traveling among the Slovaks. Honor, too, to the quiet and simple people who, except where political inflammation has set in, respect and like all their neighbors, regardless of racial differences. In general there is no antipathy or ill feeling among Slovaks and Magyars. The peasants of both races are generally profoundly unconscious of any reason for hating one another, regard one another as friends, and inter-marry freely.

Effects of emigration on the home country;   I frequently asked in Hungary, "Is this emigration to America an advantage or a disadvantage here?" The answer naturally varied with the answerer.

A Slovak Type

The employer suffers as has been said from the growing scarcity of labor, especially of farm laborers and servants, and from the consequent rise of wages. The value of land is affected, sometimes rising through the demand of returned "Americans," sometimes falling where emigration has been epidemic and has partly depopulated a district. The Magyar dreads the independent spirit and aroused national feeling of those that come back. The thoughtful Slovak passionately regrets the draining away of the lustiest and most energetic of the population; on the side of the fatherland he sees a great physical and moral loss, and on the side of emigrants a pitiful if inevitable exile. He speaks also with bitter regret of the too numerous cases of demoralization of the stay-at-homes. It is very common for a man to marry and install his young wife, and in a very short time, often in a few weeks, go to America. He is loyal and sends her money. For her, with her unwonted liberty and unwonted money, temptation sets in. Too often he returns to find in the home children that are not his, or to lead an unhappy life with a woman who seems to him stupid and dull after his foreign experiences.

One hears, too, the frequent complaint that the home country bears the cost of the rearing of the emigrants through the years when all is outgo, only to see them, as soon as they are in their prime, go to strengthen an industrial competitor; that emigration means the necessity of supporting an undue proportion of the womenfolk, of the aged, the weakly, and the left behind, of those that America refuses to accept and of the unusables generally; and finally, that those who have been to America return, too frequently, either injured by accidents in mines and foundries and on railroads, or worn out with excessive work at a pace to which they are not accustomed and which their diet does not fit them to endure.

However, in considering the balance of advantage to the home country three things must be counted to the good: the providing in some cases for an excess of population over what the country can properly support; the influx of money from America; and the return of emigrants with more awakened personality.

As to the amount of money received, complete figures are not to be had.   An official investigation resulted in an estimate of $17,000,000 sent to Hungary by emigrants through banks alone in 1903.   This money was sent mainly from the United States and doubtless largely by Slovaks.   It does not include what returning emigrants brought with them in cash, nor what was sent by postal orders.   The postal districts of Kassa in the eastern part of the Slovak district, and Pozsony in the west reported that over $4,000,000 was sent into the Slovak district from America in 1899, a time when the numbers in America were much less than they are now.   One banker told me that a Slovak ordinarily sends home $120 a year. Another informant writes me of a place in Zemplén county with 1156 men, which had received $140,000.   He adds: "This gives the best idea of the enormous importance of emigration where the average annual income is hardly over $100 or $120.   And it is not to be wondered at that the public hold emigration to be beneficial.   I have met three men who inaugurated emigration to America in their villages; all were regarded as benefactors of their country, and they were not a little proud of their daring."

As to this flow of money, there is a great deal of thoughtless talk from the side of American interests, as though it represented a loss to America without an equivalent. Granted that it would be better to have the money spent in this country, we may trust the acumen and self-interest of American employers sufficiently to be certain that every dollar of it represents at least a dollar's worth of labor contributed to American production and permanently embodied in our national wealth.

As to the use made of this money in the old country, doubtless some of it is spent foolishly and some of it worse than wasted in drink, both by returned emigrants and by those to whom remittances come from America; but the bulk of it appears to go to pay off debts, while much is invested in farm tools, much is used to buy land, some goes to pay for a higher standard of living, and some is spent for public purposes, religious and political, such as for rebuilding or decorating a church, for metal crosses in a graveyard, or for patriotic funds. My impression is that among a population where so little money is in circulation, this "American money" is on the whole a very great blessing.

On the whole, the effect on the returned emigrant seems to be less than an American would, at first thought, expect, but it must be remembered that not only is the man by every instinct and by all his training conservative, but that many American ways are incapable of being transplanted to conditions so different. Consider for a moment a great American factory or a New York tenement house; what hints can they give as to production or as to house building to a Slovak who has gone back to his native village? *Why America does not teach the emigrant more*

With regard to farming, not only are American methods often inapplicable, but they are seen by few Slovak emigrants,—one might almost say by no emigrants who return. The man who takes to farming in America is generally proposing to stay there.

In considering the amount of effect that America exerts on those who return, we must furthermore note that the emigrant in any case is apt to see less of American ways than we are prone to take for granted. A Slovak comes over with a group of his fellows, goes to a Slovak boarding house, a Slovak church, a Slovak store, a Slovak saloon, and a Slovak bank; knows his "boss," himself very likely a foreigner, only by his orders and oaths, and deals with Americans only as the street car conductor shouts to him, "What do you want, John?" or the boys stone his children and call them "Hunkies."

In spite of this, America does exert an influence. A priest in a Slovak village will show you with interest the *American influence* superior "American" houses in his parish, built in the local fashion but more substantial and better kept, and with American novelties, such as glass tumblers, a nickel clock and other little luxuries.

In America the Slovak is likely to be quickly drawn into a mutual benefit organization of his own nationality, and here he probably gets an education in nationalistic feeling. How far this is really panslav (that is, Russophile), as the Magyars complain, I do not know. At any rate, the Magyars always find panslavism a good cry with which to attack any Slavic activity.

My impression is that the Slovak often does return from America with awakened national self-consciousness, but that he is generally quite unconcerned about distant political Utopias of any sort, and confines his interest to practical local issues, such as education in their mother tongue for his children, and elections to parliament where the Slovaks, with over a tenth of the population, had in 1905 one representative out of 450.

At any rate, I can readily conceive why his Magyar superiors feel that "America has spoiled the Slovak emigrant." He has more money and he is more ambitious. He has often learned to read, if he did not know how before. He takes a newspaper and has political interests and opinions.

Seton-Watson speaks several times of the influence of the Slovaks in America, and of those returned from there:

"The returned Slovak emigrants who have saved money in the United States are steadily acquiring small holdings in Hungary, and helping to propagate ideas of freedom and nationality among their neighbors. The growth of Slovak banks since 1900 has been specially remarkable, and though still trifling compared with the large Jewish and Magyar institutions of North Hungary, they are none the less able to hold their own and extend their business. . . . . .

"During the past generation many thousands of

Slovak peasants have emigrated to the United States, carrying with them feelings of bitterness and resentment towards the authorities of their native land. They speedily learn to profit by the free institutions of their adopted country, and today the 400,000 Slovaks of America possess a national culture and organization which present a striking contrast to the cramped development of their kinsmen in Hungary. There are more Slovak newspapers in America than in Hungary; but the Magyars seek to redress the balance by refusing to deliver these American journals through the Hungarian post office. Everywhere among the emigrants leagues, societies and clubs flourish undisturbed—notably the American Slovak League (Národnie Slovenský Spolok), the Catholic Jednota (Unity) and the women's league, Živena. These societies do all in their power to awaken Slovak sentiment, and contribute materially to the support of the Slovak press in Hungary. The self-confidence and manly independence of the returned emigrants contrast with the pessimism and passivity of the older generation, and they are doing much to leaven the Slovak population with new ideas of liberty and justice. The alarm with which the government views this movement was revealed by its summary action against Francis Pollakovič, a young American citizen, in the autumn of 1907."*

To quote Seton-Watson further:

"Just as the Irish party was financed from America, so the Roumanians of Hungary receive aid from their kinsmen in America, the Serbs from Belgrad, the Slovaks from Bohemia and the United States. The Magyars, instead of treating this as natural and inevitable, indulge in wild charges of treason and bribery. The chief reason, however, that the grapes are sour is that the

Aid to na-tionalist movements

* Seton-Watson, "Racial Problems in Hungary," pages 202–3. A fairly full account of the case of Pollakovič who, though an American citizen, was made to serve a term of imprisonment for "incitement against the Magyar nationality" in 1907, is given by Seton-Watson, page 321 and Appendix xxiv.

Magyars have no kinsmen of their own, outside Hungary, from whom they could under any circumstances receive support, whether financial or military."* . . . . .

"It is interesting to learn that English is occasionally employed by returned Slovak emigrants when they do not wish to be understood by the local officials." (Page 283).

When I have asked what returned emigrants report about America I have been told that they say (in the German phrase in which it was given to me), "Hier ist ein Mann ein Hund; da ist er ein Herr." (Here a man is a dog; in America he is a gentleman.)

The re-turned a misfit
Under the circumstances it is not strange that the returned emigrant chafes. It is hard to exert oneself for twenty or even forty cents a day, after the compara-tively large wages earned in Pittsburgh steel works or Scranton coal mines. It is hard to be sufficiently sub-missive to the pettiest Magyar or Jewish official after an experience of American independence. Naturally, a man who feels thus is looked on with disfavor; his sense of the superiority of American ways does not make him more popular, and the visit to America which was intended to be temporary leads finally to settlement here.

Mr. Koukol says, "I spoke of the powerful call their native bit of earth makes upon so many of the immi-grants. But frequently, when men go back intending to stay, in response to this call, the old country is not strong enough to hold them. Such was the case with this same John Mlinik. It was his ambition to be a well-to-do farmer in Hungary in a few years, and re-cently he and his wife made a preliminary visit to his old home and bought a farm. They remained a few weeks—but those few weeks were quite enough. He came back quite cured. 'Every little clerk in the village looked down on me because I did not speak the official

---

* In Appendix IX, page 448, will be found references to some political memorials published by Slovaks in America.

language, Magyar,' Mlinik said to me. 'He was an official while I was just a peasant. He didn't earn a quarter of what I do, yet I had to bow to him. That made me sore. In America I'm a free man. Besides, I've got a better chance to do well than in the old country. Yes, America is good enough for me.' "*

Often the first visit to America is not final; many men go back and forth a number of times. Of Bohemian immigrants entering the United States in 1905 less than six in a hundred had been in the country previously, of the Slovaks nearly a quarter. It is amazing how easily this race, which is at once so migratory and so firmly rooted, makes the long journey. They will return to see the old parents, to attend to a bit of legal business, to settle an inheritance or sell off a bit of land. Sometimes the wife is sent home to do what is necessary. One such, a simple peasant woman who had gone home on business, knew every detail of the return trip to New York, down to the right street car in Vienna. One boastful gentleman is said to have written home, "As far as Vienna the journey goes well; after that it drags a little." *Migration back and forth*

But after all the coming and going, in the end many stay permanently in the new home. Thus an emigration movement which in its inception seemed to be merely a new phase of the old Slovak wandering industry, a turning to new fields for temporary employment, comes to be in effect a true emigration, which has transferred to America a substantial fraction of the Slovak nationality. *Final settlement in America common*

*Koukol: "A Slav's a Man for a' That." *Charities and the Commons*, XXI, page 594 (Jan. 2, 1909).

CHAPTER VII

EMIGRATION FROM GALICIA: AUSTRIAN POLES AND RUTHENIANS

To many people the word Galicia probably suggests little—if happily it does not vaguely recall the Spanish province of the same name, or even the epistle to the Galatians. Perhaps, if the country is referred to as Austrian Poland instead of as Galicia, it seems more tangible, and Cracow and Lemberg sound as if we knew something about them. But to me at least the names conveyed no idea of the reality until I read, years ago, that inimitable sketch of Miss Dowie's called "A Girl in the Carpathian Mountains," and learned for the first time, among other things, that there are people called Ruthenians, and that they, as well as Poles, inhabit Galicia.

It is the largest of the Austrian lands. In area it is more than half as great as the state of New York, with a more numerous population, giving it a density greater than that of New Jersey. It stretches to the north of the Carpathian arc, from Silesia to the Bukowina, divided from Hungary to the south by the range, but cut off from Russia to the north by merely political boundaries. It consists for the most part of the wide, windswept plains from which Poland took its name,* but the southern part is hilly or mountainous. Zakopane, the well-known and lovely Polish summer resort, lies in a nook of the High Tatra, the only real peaks of the chain.

These mountains were formerly the haunts of brigands who still figure in legend, song, and dance. The tales

---

* *Pole* is the Polish word for field. Bukowina means beech woods and refers to the fine forests of that province.

of Przerwa-Tetmajer, translated into German as "Aus der Tatra," are full of them, and the novel of Emil Franzos, "For the Right," is the story of a Ruthenian peasant driven to revolt and outlawry by his inner insistent demand for righteousness.*

Even where not so rugged, the hill country exposed to the north and cut off from the south is exceedingly unfavorable to agriculture. In high-lying spots the snow sometimes lasts till May and falls again in October, so that even oats do not always ripen, but may have to be cut green to serve merely as fodder. It is not surprising that the living is notoriously poor; rye bread, potatoes, cabbage, "mamaliga," (corn meal porridge), and milk if there is a cow—these are the staples. Meat can usually be afforded only at Christmas and Easter, but there may often be a chicken or duck on the Sunday table.

But a worse drawback than the climate is the economic situation; the lack of industry, capital and markets, the backward agriculture, the excessive subdivision of land, and the excessive population—excessive, that is, in proportion to means of profitably occupying it. Thus without capital or commercial traditions, and in an unfavorable geographical situation, Galicia, to create an industry, would have to compete with the highly developed production of Silesia, Moravia, and Bohemia, which lie just to the west and are within the same customs territory. The home market in Galicia itself is restricted by poverty and inertia, and the country to the eastward,† where Galicia would have a slight advantage of propinquity, is cut off by tariff walls. *Economic situation*

Agriculture in Europe, as in New England, has suffered from the competition of new sources of supply, and

* See also two articles by Wladyslaw T. Benda, illustrated by the author: "Tatra, A Mountain Region between Galicia and Hungary," *The Century*, vol. 72, pages 169–179 (June, 1906); and "Life in a Polish Village," *The Century*, vol. 76, pages 323–332 (July, 1908).

† Except Bukowina, which is in much the same condition as Galicia.

has found it hard to hold its own except in capitalistic and intensive forms like the beet-sugar industry. In a country like Bohemia this not only furnishes employment in field and factory, but supplies the neighboring farmers with fertilizer and extremely valuable feed for their cattle. But Galicia has little of such commercialized agriculture. Mining, except salt mining, is not of any importance, but considerable petroleum is produced. This, however, is largely in the hands of capitalists from outside the country, in some cases of Americans, and brings comparatively little money into Galicia. The Polish district, however, is more advanced industrially than the Ruthenian or eastern part of Galicia.

The population
The population is mainly Polish in the west and Ruthenian in the east. The Roumanian element, which is strong in the neighboring province of the Bukowina, also makes itself felt in the eastern counties of Galicia. There is besides considerable overlapping and intermixture, with puzzles for the ethnologists, like the Górale or mountain folk, and the Huzuls. The mountains, though a political boundary, seem to have been no serious barrier, for the Ruthenians extend across them in a continuous body into Hungary, while further west on the Hungarian side the Slovaks of Upper Arva show the influence of their Polish neighbors across the mountains to the north.

The best criterion of nationality in this part of the world is religion, and by this test the Poles are 46 per cent of the population, the Ruthenians 42 per cent and the Jews 11 per cent according to the Austrian census of 1900. The Ruthenians, though fewer than the Poles, cover considerably more territory, occupying the central as well as the eastern district, and even extending a considerable way westward along the Carpathians, as is shown on Map VIII.

In the case of both Poles and Ruthenians, Galicia is only a part of the territory where they live. Each people occupies a continuous area, of which this province con-

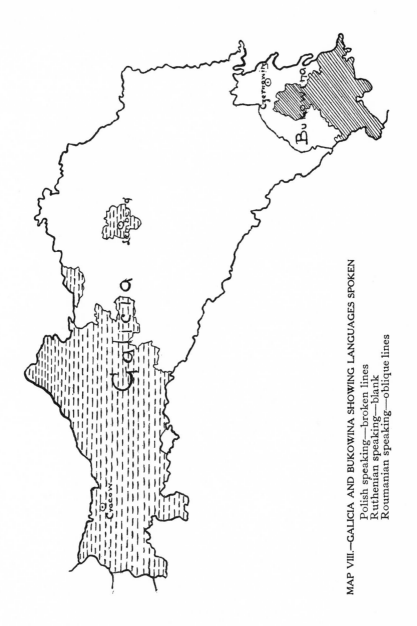

MAP VIII.—GALICIA AND BUKOWINA SHOWING LANGUAGES SPOKEN

Polish speaking—broken lines
Ruthenian speaking—blank
Roumanian speaking—oblique lines

tains a mere slice parted from the rest of the homogeneous population by historical accident and brute force, and the political boundaries which they have drawn.

It is accident, too, and force of circumstances that lead me to treat of the emigration of these two great groups in this geographical fashion. Polish immigration, much the most important branch of the Slavic influx to America, should be studied as a whole, and at the same time with reference to the special characteristics and history of the separate branches from Galicia, Russia and Germany. I can speak only incidentally of any but the former, although the Russian contingent is the most numerous. In the case of the Ruthenians, confining our attention to the contingent from Austria-Hungary is a less serious matter, for though nearly nine-tenths of them live in Russia, and only one-tenth in Austria-Hungary, almost all who come to us are from Austria-Hungary. Each nationality will first be considered separately.

The Poles under three masters

Of the sad history of Poland, ruined at once by its unfortunate internal conditions and by its lack of natural boundaries, every one knows something. Once stretching from the Baltic nearly to the Black Sea, and embracing a territory greater than the present Austria-Hungary, it is now divided between the three neighboring empires. In the rough but graphic phrase of a poor Polish woman in America,* "The Polish flag was bust and Germany, Russia, and Austria each took a little bit." Poland lives as a political entity only in history and in the never-failing hopes of its children. The final adjustment of the prey gave Russia the lion's share, with more than three-quarters of the territory, and two-thirds of the sixteen million or so inhabitants. Austria received only about one-eighth of the territory, but about one-fifth of the Polish population, most of them in

* Quoted by Elizabeth T. White in her article, "Investigation of Slavic Conditions in Jersey City," published for Whittier House, 1907.

POLES FROM ABOUT CRACOW

Galicia, with a smaller body in the neighboring territory of Silesia.

The condition of the Poles under their three sovereigns differs considerably. In Germany, while the Poles have enjoyed order and opportunity for progress along German lines, they have also suffered from the most determined effort to suppress national feeling, to wipe out the Polish language, and of late to forcibly dispossess Polish land-owners in favor of German. *Differing conditions*

In Russian Poland, while there is not the racial contempt for all things Slavic which the German is too apt to feel, the Poles have suffered from oppressive special legislation, as well as from the tyranny and corruption which have been the curse of all parts of Russia, and of late, of course, from the disturbed condition of the empire. On the other hand, the country, especially about Warsaw and Lodz, has become a great industrial centre, protected by Russian tariffs and enjoying the vast Russian home market. Here for the first time in their history the Poles, who have always been either nobles or peasants, have developed a middle class, commercial and industrial.

The Austrian government, in contrast to the Russian and German, has for some time pursued a political policy friendly to the Poles, but nowhere else do they find themselves in so bad an economic plight as in Galicia; the causes for this have already been touched upon.

In religion the Poles, in spite of some episodes of Protestantism and even of Unitarianism in the Reformation period,* are almost universally zealous Roman Catholics. So generally is this the case that Galician agents whose business it is to fill out the manifests which are required by our immigration laws, and on which our immigration statistics are based, write a man down a Pole if he is a Roman Catholic, regardless of any other fact. The zealous character of Roman Catholicism *Religion*

* For references on this subject see the Bibliography under Polish Religious History.

among the Poles, as among the Irish, has political as well as religious roots. To them, too, the political enemy is also the religious opponent. The Russian schismatic, the Tatar heathen, the Turkish Mohammedan, the Swedish Lutheran, were all detestable on patriotic and religious grounds alike.

The Ruthenians: nomenclature

The people who share Galicia with the Poles, and whom I have been speaking of as Ruthenians, have a most confusing variety of names, and the situation is complicated by the fact that the choice of one or another name often implies political preferences. The official Russian term for them is Little Russians (Malo-Russians). Again they are called, from words used by themselves, Russniaks or Russinians. The name Ukraïnian refers to the great Ukraïne district of Southern Russia, and is generally used by those who desire a separate political future for the nationality. Those of a contrary tendency, who wish to ignore differences and to merge with the Great Russian nationality which is predominant in the empire of the Czar, call themselves simply Russians; and those who are called Russians in the United States are in a large proportion of cases properly Little Russians. The classification of our immigration reports has for them the heading "Ruthenians (Russniaks)." I have used the term Ruthenian because it seemed to me to be on the whole the most current. It often is used to refer especially to those of the group who live in Austria and Hungary, and as practically all our immigrants come from these countries, it is the most satisfactory for our purpose.

Number and location

This nationality is closely related to the Russians (Great Russians) though distinct in language and history. They number some 30,000,000, about 26,000,000 of whom live in southern Russia. Thence they extend over eastern Galicia, the western part of the Bukowina, and across the Carpathians, as already said, into northeastern Hungary, occupying in all a continuous territory half as large again as the German empire.

Their history, though less well known than that of the Poles, is also ancient and romantic. Their chief city, Kieff or Kiev, was the capital of the country before Moscow was founded in the middle of the twelfth century. When soon after this the invasions of the Tatars began, the wide open steppes of the Ukraïne lay exposed to their raids, and thus were created the conditions which moulded the wild, roving life of the Zaporogian Cossacks such as Gogol, himself a Little Russian, has painted in his brilliant story "Taras Bulba." Although they had been free as the winds, and had known neither serfdom nor hereditary rulers, they fell later under the domination of Poles and Russians, and found them to be hard masters. Serfdom, especially, though then the general condition of the common people of Europe, was odious to this liberty-loving race, and their bitter resentment of tyranny has been attested not only by the revolt under Chmyelnicki in 1648 (pictured from the Polish point of view by Sienkiewicz in his famous historical romance, "With Fire and Sword"), and by that of a half century later under Mazeppa (known to us mainly by the incident of his youth popularized by Byron and the circus), but also by peasant risings of recent years.*

Not only in history but in literature the Little Russians have an honorable place. They had free printing presses for secular as well as religious literature as early as the sixteenth century, but many of their best writers, including Gogol, have used the Great Russian language even when their themes were Little Russian, much as Sir Walter Scott wrote his Scotch novels in literary English. In 1798 began a renascence of the language as a literary medium, and it has since been employed by authors of international repute, the greatest of whom is the poet Shevchenko. Like Russians and Servians, the Little Russians use the Cyrillic characters. Appar-

* Terrible pictures of oppression by Polish landlords and violent revenge by the Ruthenian peasantry are given in stories of Franzos in his "Aus Halb-Asien, Culturbilder aus Galizien, der Bukowina, Süd-Russland und Rumänien."

ently Great Russians and Little Russians are mutually quite unintelligible and the best authorities seem to agree that the tongue spoken by the latter is not to be considered as a dialect, but as an independent language.

Folksongs   Of all Slavic peoples, perhaps the Little Russians are most celebrated for their profusion of popular lyrics. One collector gathered eight thousand in a single district. These songs are of love and war, of haughty Poles and cruel Tatars and love-sick maidens, and are apt to be mournful and tender.

I am told that here in the United States the Ruthenians continue to produce new songs, but that their American lyrics telling of work in the dark mine and of the hardness of the "boss" are neither so fine nor so free in spirit as the old. But on the wide plains of the Canadian Northwest, as independent landowners, they find a more congenial life. Michael Gowda has not only translated into Little Russian Whittier's "Snow Bound" and much other literature, but has written original verse in his own tongue for his countrymen in Canada.*

Uniates   In religion the Little Russians had always, like the Great Russians, been Greek Orthodox, until in 1595, after various previous attempts, the Jesuits succeeded in bringing large numbers over into the Roman fold. They accepted allegiance to the pope on very favorable terms, however, and were allowed to keep so much of what had always been peculiar to the Orthodox church, that these Uniates, United Catholics, or Greek Catholics, as they are called, are still separated from other Roman Catholics by marked religious differences.†

The married priests with their long beards, the mass in Slavonic instead of in Latin, the arrangement of the church with the great gilt screen—the ikónostas—hiding

---

* A sketch of Gowda's work and an English translation of his poem "To Canada," will be found in Appendix XI, page 449.
† Four very instructive articles, "Our Russian Catholics; The Greek Ruthenian church in America," by A. J. Shipman, will be found in the Jesuit magazine, *The Messenger*, of New York, beginning with the number for Sept., 1904.

RUTHENIANS AND GALICIAN JEWS

1. Ruthenian shepherd lads. Lads like these, piping among their sheep beside a brook or dancing with their sweethearts on the grass, seem to us absolutely Arcadian. On our streets, speaking broken and vulgarized English, dressed in ill-fitting ready-made clothes, bewildered by their strange surroundings, they are too apt to seem to us "stolid," "low," "mere animals." 2 and 4. Galician Jews. The curls before the ears are a necessity to the orthodox. The fur trimmed cap (see 4) and the long coat are typical. 3. Ruthenian peasant with wooden ware, the product of a considerable house industry.

the altar, the communion in both kinds given to the laity, the use of the Eastern form of the cross with three cross-bars the lower one oblique, the calendar thirteen days behind the Roman,—all these things make the Greek Catholics or Uniates strange to the Roman Catholics, in spite of the fact that they are in full communion, members of the same church. Almost the only marks of the severance of the Uniates from the Greek Orthodox and of their Roman connection are the prayer for the pope, which replaces that for the czar as head of the church, and the passage in the creed which affirms the procession of the Holy Ghost from the Son as well as from the Father. By no means all Ruthenians in Austria and Hungary are Greek Catholic or Uniate. A considerable number, mainly of those in the Bukowina, are still Greek Orthodox.

We have many of their churches in America, generally easily distinguished from the Catholic churches by the display of the three-barred cross. In these churches one sees, here and in Europe, the most naïve and touching demonstrations of piety. The head is bared before the crucifix which stands before the church; on entering the building the forehead is touched again and again to the ground; the ikons are kissed with fervor, and the wonderful chanting of the Greek rite, which permits no instrumental music, fills the congregation with religious emotion.

The Ruthenian popas or priests have a very curious status. They long constituted almost a separate caste, recruited from their own ranks, and marrying their daughters to priests' sons only.* They occupy quite a different position from the unmarried Catholic priest of Western Europe, though I should judge a higher one than the Russian village clergy. As to the advantages of

Ruthenian priests

---

* Intimate and interesting pictures of the life of Ruthenian clerical families will be found in stories by "Dorothea Gerard"; namely, "The Supreme Crime," and "The Wrong Man."

celibacy for the priesthood, opinions of course will vary
with belief and experience.   A very intelligent Ruthenian village priest with whom I talked in Galicia held
strongly that the married man is the better priest.   He
thought that unmarried priests are sent by preference
to America to avoid scandal among Roman Catholics
here, unused to a married priesthood, but that these
priests are as a rule morally inferior and much less able
to understand the wants and feelings of their people
than those with families.   I fear that in general it is too
often true that priests and ministers sent to serve emigrant colonies of all sorts, Italian, Hungarian or what-
not, are apt to be unworthy representatives of their
class—either dull, bad, or otherwise below the normal.
On the other hand one meets shining exceptions, and it
happens that I have known a number of Ruthenian
priests in this country, of consecration, intelligence and
energy beyond the ordinary.   One of these was carrying
on an intelligence office for his people.   Of the many-
sided labors of another I have written in a little article,
"A Shepherd of Immigrants," originally published in
Charities.*

Relations
between
Poles and
Ruthenians
In the districts of Eastern Galicia where Polish lords
were set over a Ruthenian peasantry, the subjection
of the latter was embittered by the fact that the Little
Russian had always been a freeman, and by the intol-
erance of the Pole toward a class not only socially inferior,
but alien in speech and above all in religion.   Modern
conditions have not done away with the age-long traditions of hostility.   In Ruthenian organs are printed
tales of incredible cases of barbarity of Poles to Ruthenian dependents.   The Ruthenians claim that Vienna,
in order to keep the political friendship of the Poles,
has given them a free hand in provincial affairs, and that
they use their power to oppress the racial minority and
resort to the most shameless political chicanery to effect
their purposes.   All this, whether true or not, intensifies

* *Charities*, XIII, pages 193–4 (Dec. 3, 1904).

the ill-feeling, and the friction between race and race, added to the friction between Christian and Jew, is one of the curses of this unhappy province.

Much that is inexplicable to Americans in the relations of Slavs in this country is explained by old happenings in Europe. For unfortunately the political and religious tension between Ruthenians and Poles, between Roman Catholics, Greek Orthodox and Uniates is not at once removed by emigration to America. Especially is the Russian state church, which maintains a mission in this country, and counts some fifty Orthodox churches in the United States proper, besides an equal number in Alaska, regarded with great jealousy by Catholics, both Greek and Roman, as proselytizing.

After this brief account of the two Slavic nationalities of Galicia, let us turn to the history of their emigration. Polish emigration is the earlier, and, like the Bohemian, has a long past—even without counting John of Kolno who is said to have commanded Danish ships that rounded the coast of Labrador in 1476, or the various scattered settlers of the colonial period, or dwelling too much on the revolutionary heroes Kosciuszko and Pulaski, or on Niemcewicz, friend and biographer of Washington, who is an important figure in Polish literary history. The political movements in Poland in 1831 and 1848 sent us refugees, and in 1863 a Polish paper was being published in New York and collecting subscriptions for "the January rebellion," including some donations from "Poles of the faith of Moses." In 1854 some three hundred Polish families emigrated from Prussian Silesia to Texas, where they founded a settlement named for the Virgin, Panna Marya.*

Up to 1870, however, the movement was still essentially sporadic, the number of immigrants small. Their quality was such, however, as to give them a significance

*For a fuller history of Polish emigration to America, see Chapter XI.

out of proportion to their numbers, and the record of Polish citizens in the Civil War was a brilliant one.

Origin and spread of emigration   The Polish emigration, where it was an economic mass movement, not a political necessity of individuals, and in so far as it did not originate independently, doubtless spread from Germans to German Poles, from them to the Poles in western Galicia, and from them to the Ruthenians of eastern Galicia and the Bukowina. Like emigration movements in general, it was propagated ever more to the East.

It was in the decade 1870–1880 that Galicia first began to lose population. In the previous decade immigrants had exceeded emigrants by 67,415. In the following decades, on the contrary, emigrants exceeded immigrants as follows: 1870–1880, 1,997; 1881–1890, 81,997; 1891–1900, 340,833.*

In Galicia, as is so often the case, emigration to America was only one part of a wider migratory movement. The Poles had long been going as settlers either to eastern Galicia, the Bukowina, or across the Dnieper into Russia. In the early seventies, when this no longer afforded sufficient outlet, a movement began to the industrial regions of Bohemia, Moravia, Silesia and lower Austria; and also, with varying fates, to different parts of South America, and to some extent to the United States.

American census data   The current once started has flowed on at an accelerating rate, until Polish emigration, drawn as it has been from all three Empires, became of first class importance among immigration movements. While the decade 1870–1880 added nearly 35,000 natives of Poland to the population of the United States as shown by the census, the decade ending in 1880 added nearly 99,000, and the last decade, 1890–1900, nearly 236,000. In 1900 the natives of Poland in the United States were 383,407,† or twenty-six times as many as a generation earlier, in 1870.

---

* See Buzek: "Das Auswanderungs-Problem," page 444.
† The census further distinguishes the parts of Poland. The 1900 figures are Poland (Austrian) 58,503; Poland (German)

The American immigration data do not make it pos- Immigra-
sible to specifically distinguish the Poles and Ruthenians tion data
till 1899. In that year the Polish immigrants were
28,446 out of a total of 311,715, or 9 per cent of the whole.
As shown in the table below, the numbers rose with
some setbacks until they reached over 138,000 in 1907,
or nearly 11 per cent of the immense wave of immigration of that year. The Polish contingent from Germany
is throughout subordinate. Until the last two years
Russia and Austria-Hungary sent about equal numbers
of Poles, sometimes one, sometimes the other leading,
but in 1907 and 1908 Russia sent far the largest contribution.

TABLE 10.—NUMBER OF POLISH AND RUTHENIAN
IMMIGRANT ALIENS ADMITTED TO THE UNITED
STATES, 1899–1909.

| YEAR ended June 30 | POLES FROM | | | | RUTHENIANS FROM ALL COUNTRIES |
	Austria-Hungary	Germany	Russia	All Countries	
1899	11,660	1,271	15,517	28,446	1,400
1900	22,802	1,633	22,500	46,938	2,832
1901	20,288	1,844	21,475	43,617	5,288
1902	32,429	3,313	33,859	69,620	7,533
1903	37,499	5,252	39,548	82,343	9,843
1904	30,243	4,901	32,577	67,757	9,592
1905	50,785 { Austria 50,450 Hungary 335	3,858	47,224	102,437	14,473 { Austria 10,982 Hungary 3,268
1906	48,803	4,108	46,204	95,835	16,257
1907	59,719	3,888	73,122	138,033	24,081
1908	26,423	2,320	37,947	68,105	12,361
1909	36,483	1,320	37,770	77,565	15,808

150,232; Poland (Russian) 154,424; Poland (unknown) 20,436.
These figures include all persons born in the territory which
the census still enters as Poland, and include a very large
though incalculable proportion of Jews, born in German,
Austrian and Russian Poland, as well as Ruthenians and other
non-Polish elements, while on the other hand they exclude the
large numbers who are Polish by extraction and feeling, though
not by birth. For estimates of their numbers see Chapter XIII.

The Ru-
thenian
movement

The Ruthenian emigration, while smaller and later than the Polish, has proportionately grown much faster. While the flood year 1907 brought between four and five times as many Poles as came in 1899, it brought over seventeen times as many Ruthenians. The Ruthenians almost all came from Austria-Hungary, but how many from each is unknown except for the year 1905, when alone the data are given separately. In that year over 75 per cent of the Ruthenians came from Austria (sc. Galicia), over 22 per cent from Hungary, while from the Russian millions not 200 individuals came.

Emigration
areas

The relative intensity of the emigration movement in different parts of Galicia can be seen on Map V. The whole province showed in the decade 1890–1900 a net loss by emigration of nearly 4.58 per cent of its population but this average included various mainly urban districts, which actually gained, as well as many districts which lost only slightly. Some, on the other hand, lost as much as 13 per cent or 14 per cent. By comparing Map V with Map VIII which shows the districts occupied by Poles and Ruthenians respectively, it will be noted that the area which lost 5 per cent or over covers practically all the Polish district (except about Cracow and Lemberg), an adjoining corner of Ruthenian territory along the Carpathians (Lisko and part of Sanok), and most of the Ruthenian districts to the northeast. The place that lost the most was Mielec, near the Tatra and adjoining the Hungarian county of Arva, which lost 14.43 per cent.

It will be noted in Table 3 that Galicia exceeds all other parts of Austria in the excess of births over deaths, which gave it in the decade in question a natural increase of 15.3 per cent. With a loss by migration of 4.58 per cent, the already overburdened province still added nearly 11 per cent to its population in the decade.

"The first
man who
went to
America"

When making inquiries about the history of an emigration movement, one is always hearing rumors about the original emigrant, and in Galicia I drove many rainy miles to see a Ruthenian priest who was said to have known "the first man who went to America." His story was as follows:

"The first emigrant went in 1877 or 1878. It was in this way. The peasants cannot live on their land. It has been subdivided and subdivided until a man has too little to get a living by, even as they live here. In some places they eked it out by weaving cloth on old house looms during the winter, and hawking it about in the summer. Then the railroad was put through, the transversal road that runs south of the old Lemberg-Cracow line, nearer the Carpathians. That was about 1875. This road brought in factory products from Silesia and other places, and ruined weaving and all the old home industries. One of these weavers, a Pole from about Jaslo I think, used to come up this way with his goods, and in Radocyna there was a peasant that he always stayed with when he was there. The last time he came was a few years after the railroad was built, and he said his trade was ruined, and he was thinking of going to America. He had heard across the mountains in Hungary that people were going to the United States, and doing well there.

"At that time the government was doing all in its power to stop emigration. Letters were opened, and if they praised America they were held back. Of course this was illegal, but the Staathalterei gave orders to do it. The weaver promised that when he got to New York he would let his Radocyna friend know how he got on, but instead of writing it all out he arranged to prick the letter through if things in America were not satisfactory.

"After a time the man in Radocyna got a letter from his friend in New York, and it was not pricked. So he went to the priest and told him all about the matter; that he was going to New York, but that he did not want his wife or any one else to know, and he got the priest to promise to keep his secret.

"He reached New York all right, but he had lost the

address of the weaver, he could not speak English nor even German, and his money ran out. He was three days without eating anything. He sat down in the street and cried, and a gentleman coming by stopped and spoke to him in Polish, and asked him if he was not a Ruthenian. He knew him by his clothes.

"The gentleman was a literary man, a Pole or maybe a Polish Jew. At any rate, he took the man home with him and employed him for a while until he got work with a telegraph company, and, later on, with a railroad. Wages were better for emigrants then than they are now. In half a year he sent money home to his wife, and after a time he sent for his family. Other people from the village began to go, and from that on, it spread.

"The government tried to make the priests read a proclamation against going to America. It said that people would die of hunger there, and the priests were to preach about this to their people. But they had a conference and talked it over together. They knew that money came from America, and that people were treated there like human beings, and they promised one another to all ignore the order. That was in 1880. I have destroyed the proclamation that I had. The government used to send gendarmes to the frontier and arrest those who went over. So the emigrants generally went into Prussia on foot, and took the railroad there. There were all sorts of devices for getting through, such as taking wagon-loads of baskets for sale, and so on.

"These peasants have plenty of native wit. One man wrote me that he had finally got through to Bremen all right, but that on the frontier he had been arrested, and as he was being led off he stooped as if to tie up his shoes (moccasin-like affairs, bound about the ankle with thongs), and picked up a great handful of wet mud and threw it in the face of the man who had arrested him. And while the gendarme was working his eyes clear, he got away. Another man, named Michael, bought his ticket only to the border station, so that it would not be supposed that he meant to leave the country. But his wife went with him part way, and she cried so much that it betrayed him, and he was arrested. He got leave from the gendarme to go back for his bundle, and instead of returning with it, got into a second-class compartment of his train. Of course no one dreamed of looking for him there, so he got away too.

"The employers are greatly set against emigration because it carries off farm hands and raises wages. And so are the Jews. The people here were much in debt to the Jews, who had everything, but America has freed them from that."

Such was the story of the beginning of Galician emigration to America, and almost every point in it is typical, as we know by other investigations—the breaking in upon a hardly balanced peasant economy of modern competition in the shape of railroad-borne factory wares, the effect on money-lender and landlord, and their consequent opposition. *Cause of Galician emigration*

The conditions out of which Galician emigration springs are sufficiently obvious in the Austrian census data, which show not only that Galicia is an overwhelmingly agricultural country, but that agriculture is mainly carried on by families doing all the work themselves, and on the smallest possible scale.* *Occupations*

The darkest side of the situation of the Galician peasant is the extreme subdivision of the land. Feudal *Small size of holdings*

---

* As already shown on page 47, one would expect to find Poles and Ruthenians appear in our immigration statistics with an overwhelming proportion of agricultural occupation. But while the United States authorities provide the headings Laborer, Farm laborer, and Farmer, an emigration agent in Galicia, already mentioned, whose business it is to fill out these blanks, told me that if a man has no special trade he enters him as a laborer, even if the man had been a peasant who did no work for wages but farmed his own land independently. He "considered the matter mainly *with reference to what the man would become in America.*" This prophetic method of dealing with the facts naturally vitiates the figures, and makes it impossible to get from them any answer to the important questions as to what proportion are agriculturists, and of these what proportion are independent property owners.

arrangements, as explained in Chapter IV, formerly kept the peasant holdings intact and of regulation size, but since 1868 they have been freely divided between children, and have come to be excessively cut up. Of all the agricultural properties in the country, nearly 80 per cent are "small" (that is, under twelve and a half acres), and *nearly half consist of less than five acres.** The same facts are reflected in the figures which show what a large proportion of those occupied in agriculture are independent producers or members of their families working with them.†

That this excessive subdivision is the main cause of emigration from Galicia is undisputed. When a man has so little land that it can no longer support him, much less provide for his children, he probably gets into debt, and at any rate is in imperative need of money. As already said, for the peasant to lose his land and become a mere laborer is a great step downward socially, for himself and his descendants, and one which he will sacrifice much to avoid. To keep his land, and if it is mortgaged, to pay the interest, he must find paying work. Farm wages, although they have risen, are far from high, and the demand for farm labor has been lessened in three ways: first, by this rise of wages; second, by the increased use of farm machinery; and third, in some places by the breaking up of large estates.

Lack of opportunity to earn

While opportunities to earn money at farm work are so poor, of opportunities for industrial employment there are practically none. Manufacturing, so highly de-

* In the fifty parishes in the political district Skalat, 32 per cent of the "rustical" (sc. peasant) holdings were, in 1882, less than 1½ acres, nearly 60 per cent were under four acres and a half. It is estimated that a man must have fourteen and a fifth acres (10 yokes) to get his living by working his own land and to fully occupy his time. Over 70 per cent have not more than half this, and only about one holding in ten is above this minimum of independent farming.

See Pilat: "Die Auswanderung aus den Podolischen Bezirken nach Russland in Jahre 1892," page 76.

† Cf. Table 2, page 46.

veloped in Russian Poland, has, as already explained, little chance to thrive in Austrian Poland. The consequence is a forced migration in search of work. Every season carries a horde of so-called *Sachsengänger* across the border into Germany, to work on farms during the summer,* but increasing numbers reason, "If we must leave home, why not go further, wherever wages may be highest, and stay until we have earned what we need." So the father goes himself to America, or sends his son, to get money to redeem or to enlarge the farm.

The money for the passage seems very frequently to be borrowed; if from neighbors, then *without any guarantee and without interest*. A Jew takes from 6 to 10 per cent.† Here, as among the Slovaks, we were told that a peasant can always get credit, and never fails to pay; if he is actually unable to do so, his brother assumes the debt. He almost never sells his land (unless going definitely as a colonist), though he may raise money by selling a cow or a couple of pigs or what not. Sometimes the land is leased to a neighbor, the rent being received beforehand at the rate of seven or eight gulden a yoke, or about $2.00 an acre. It is less and less customary to resort to the Jewish lenders for a loan, especially in western Galicia, where the peasants are more prudent; but even among the Ruthenians money is now more often borrowed from credit establishments. *{Passage money}*

The reasons why farming in America is or is not attractive to the immigrant are discussed at some length in Chapter XV. It is of interest to find that among Ruthenian emigrants, those who wish to acquire land in America and settle are apt to go, not to the United *{Ruthenians go to Canada to farm}*

---

* The number of these so-called Sachsengänger, mostly unmarried girls and young men, was estimated for 1900 at 70,000 from Galicia alone. See Buzek: "Das Auswanderungs-Problem," page 483.

† Cf. the very similar account of Bulgarian conditions in Miss Grace Abbott's article, "The Bulgarians of Chicago." *Charities and the Commons*, XXI, pages 653–660 (Jan., 1909).

States, but to Canada, where they can more easily get a farm. The Bukowina has also sent out large numbers of Ruthenian emigrants, but the great bulk of them (up to 1905 at least) were going to Canada, and consequently did not directly concern the United States. In Canada the Ruthenians are said to succeed better than any other nationality, and in losing those of this group who go out to take up farms, we are losing a set of people sturdy and gifted, although backward in culture.*

Women immigrants

A large number of both Polish and Ruthenian immigrants are entered in our immigration tables as servants, and these are doubtless mainly women.† Of late, I was told, many peasant girls go to America to earn money. Very often a girl goes over while her intended is serving his three years in the army, and earns enough to prepay his passage. This is in all cases regarded as a debt, and he always repays the money to her. There is no common property between them till after marriage. I was told of forty girls who had recently gone to Chicago to do embroidery, which they had learned in Cracow, and of some who were "coffee cooks" in hotels.

The drink traffic

Besides the excessive subdivision of land, contributory causes of emigration are doubtless usury and debt, taxes and intemperance, all largely interrelated and all intimately connected with the economic rôle of the Jew. Even more than among the Slovaks, one meets here bitter complaints of Jews, both as usurers and as publicans. Here the old feudal rule which gave the landlords the monopoly of the drink traffic has lasted, at least as regards retail sale, till now, and the usual lessees of this monopoly (called in Polish *propinacja*, in German *propinationsrecht*), are Jews. By a recent law this monopoly expires in 1910, and then, it is said, the United States may expect to receive some ten thousand Jewish liquor

---

* See page 268.

† Taking together the three years 1905, 1906 and 1907, we find that of Polish immigrants 29 per cent were women and girls and 16 per cent servants; of Ruthenian immigrants 24 per cent were women and girls and 17 per cent servants.

GALICIAN TYPES

1 and 2. Galician Polish girls.   3 and 4. Górale, Polish mountaineers of the Tatra.

dealers, no longer able to sell drink at home. Sincerely as one must admire the fine qualities of the Jews, this can hardly seem a bright prospect.

The Galician emigrants being, as we have shown, al- *Illiteracy—* most wholly small peasants with very little land, it is *and growing* *intelligence* not surprising to find them largely illiterate. Our immigration figures for 1900 make the Ruthenians, with 49 per cent illiterate, the lowest among the Slavic groups, though better than Southern Italians, Syrians or Portuguese. Poles (from Germany, Russia and Austria together) make a considerably better showing with only 31.6 per cent illiterate.*

In Galicia one hears much complaint of the lack of schools, which are said to be even scarcer, relative to the population, in the western part of the province than in the eastern. The peasants often combine independently and hire a teacher for themselves for the winter, to teach men, women and children alike. In places where this is done, almost every one can read and write. On the other hand, in a place near Gorlice, the doctor told us that in his district there were only nine schools among thirty villages, and that these schools were so bad that he did not think a quarter of the scholars learned even to read. Sometimes if a teacher complains of truancy he is boycotted, sometimes he is placated with little bribes of eggs and so forth.

But conditions are improving, as is shown by the Austrian census figures of 1900. Among the Poles, while nearly 40 per cent of the older men, those from thirty to fifty years old, could neither read nor write, among lads of from ten to twenty the figure sank below 27 per cent. Among Ruthenians the improvement was much greater, illiteracy declining from nearly 80 per cent to under 37 per cent.

Intelligence is growing also; there is more idea of the world and more desire for education for the children, especially in western Galicia, which forebodes that emi-

* For further comparisons see Appendix XXVII, page 479.

gration will go on increasing, and it seems to be the general opinion that it will increase extensively.

The standard of living
All that has been said of the condition of Galicia connotes necessarily a low standard of comfort. Of course the conditions of life among the peasants differ from place to place, and vary, as they do everywhere else, according to the character of individuals. From what I have heard, however, as well as from what I saw, I should say that in general things were even poorer in Galicia than among the Slovaks. I recall the establishment of a peasant family near Lemberg, better off than many, with a whole series of small farm buildings besides the dwelling house,—granary, barn, wattled bin for Indian corn, cow stall and so forth, grouped about the yard. The old peasant mother, and what we saw of her housekeeping, would have done no credit to any slum, and the farm maid slept in a little, dark, filthy cow-house, where there was no trace of any regard for health or comfort, unless a hole for shoveling out manure on to the heap outside could be called that. One gets a vivid picture of the life of such a maid in Miss Dowie's book, already referred to.

A brighter picture
As I paint this dark picture I think of another village, a Ruthenian one, where the friendly and intelligent priest took us to call in one peasant home after another. The houses were close together, in an irregular settlement, and the visitor had to pick his steps amid pools and barnyard compost heaps to pass from one to another. But in spite of primitive conditions, we saw wholesome, friendly, attractive family scenes. The way in which the priest's hand was kissed as he came in had far more of friendly feeling than of formal respect, and girls, interrupted in the midst of a Sunday toilette in the single family room, were neither abashed nor bold, but quietly and deftly finished the braiding of hair and slipping on of outer garments. These were taken from the little chest which, as the only place for keeping personal articles where closets, wardrobes, bureaus, drawers,

shelves and hooks are alike wanting, is an important piece of furniture. The rooms were low and white-washed; the main objects were always the same,—a big earthenware stove, beds, and possibly a bench along the wall. Perhaps a baby's cradle might be added.

Many of the people had been to America, and the conversation would at once turn to that theme. Some would pass from talking Ruthenian with the priest to talking immigrant's English with us. As they did so, a change of mood, of face, of manner seemed to come with the change of speech. They appeared coarser, commoner, less attractive. This was not the first nor the last time that I have noticed this, and it is puzzling and painful. An element in my impression was doubtless ignorance of their language, which screened me from rough expressions and with this may have gone the glamour of what is strange to one and possibly somewhat idealized. But that is certainly not all. I have talked with a great many of these returned emigrants, and whether in Croatia, Carniola, Hungary, Galicia or Bohemia, they use, even the educated among them, the same singularly disagreeable lingo—an English that is not so much broken as vulgarized. It may be that the Slavic accent in English happens to be disagreeable to me, just as Italian French is specially unpleasing to the French ear. But I do not think this is the case. Had not Modjeska's English a peculiar charm?

It is, I believe, a social effect, a result of being brought into contact in America with the roughest elements of an industrial civilization, and under conditions which mean being ordered about, speeded up to match the unwonted American pace, and cursed at for not understanding directions. Swearing is an integral part of English as they learn it, and not all are conscious of it—as was one returned Croatian laborer who was to be dragged up to speak to us because he knew English, but who refused the interview because he "did not know how to talk in English to *ladies*." Furthermore, their old peasant

Immigrant's English

American experience vulgarizing

courtesy is out of relation with conditions in America. It implies a deference which is not expected and would not be understood, but they, losing this, learn nothing to put in its place.

Sometimes immigrants are themselves regretfully conscious of how little opportunity they have to hear good English, learning it, as they do, mainly from those who know it only a little better than they themselves do. One little Ruthenian woman apologized for her poor English, and told us "most people do not speak it right; the people that speak English best are the colored people." A colored woman, she told us, had taught her to use the sewing machine. She evidently not only liked negroes, but regarded them with special social respect; and while this absence of the prevailing and contagious depreciation of them was refreshing, it spoke volumes as to the social standing and opportunities open to an immigrant. This same woman was about to rejoin her husband and keep boarders for him at Duquesne, near Pittsburgh, and invited me to visit her there. If I would come, I should have anything that I liked to drink; whiskey, rum or—with a hasty remembrance of American prejudices—ginger beer!

Returned emigrants purchase land

An interesting result of the emigration to America, and this not alone in Galicia, is, as has already been said, the breaking up of large estates. The large landowner finds times very unfavorable, and as land comes into the market it is apt to be cut up and sold in small lots. In Galicia 50,000 to 90,000 acres are "parcelliert" in this way annually, and often the money for the purchase comes from America. Interesting instances of this process were related to us among the Ruthenians in Hungary. In one case an estate of some 700 acres was for sale. A hundred or so peasants acting together bought this for $40,000. In another case where some $64,000 was to be paid, a lawyer offered to procure the money for them on easy terms, but they said, "Oh, no, we will send to America for it," and they did so. They paid $24,000 down, and $40,000 more was sent in the course of two years from America to complete the payment. To show how values have risen—this land in Hungary which sold for $64,000, was perhaps a fifth part of an estate which was sold about 1870 for something over $8000.

A curious by-result of Galician emigration is an increased demand for American agricultural machinery. "McCormick, for instance," said my informant, the secretary of an important Chamber of Commerce, "owes his Galician market to the fact that there are workers here who understand how to use his machinery." This is only one instance of what must be in the aggregate a considerable demand for American goods in districts in which returned emigrants spread their use directly or indirectly.

Reëmigration and American exports

One hears interesting accounts of the return of emigrants. In some places they say that the friends of a man who comes back meet him outside the village and bring him his home clothes to put on, that he may not be embarrassed by having to appear in strange American dress. In other places—among the Slovaks—I was told that an "American" would come to church for a few Sundays in his Yankee clothes, but in the village there would be no one to "do up" his starched shirt for him, and he would soon go back to the old village dress.

The transition either to the new life or back to the old is made, on the whole, with surprising ease. I actually did visit afterward in Duquesne, the Ruthenian woman who had offered me her hospitality. I found her established, without boarders, in fairly pleasant and quite well-furnished rooms. She was doing some washing in a clean kitchen where the little girl (who happened to be sick with scarlet fever) sat in a rocking-chair by the resplendent stove with its nickel trimmings. Upstairs were irreproachably made beds, and from bureau drawers she took a few little treasures from home, hand-woven cloth and kerchiefs, to show me.

Transition not difficult

Outside, the whole air was full of rust-colored smoke from the great steel works opposite, where her husband worked. Nearby stood a new and very ornate Ruthenian Church.

What replaces the old pleasures?

In spite of sunny rooms and American plenty, she regretted the change. Perhaps it is only superficially that the transition appears easy. As I have already said, I think the women accustom themselves to America with more difficulty than the men. For one thing perhaps they miss the old customs, pretty or grotesque, which can be only imperfectly kept up in the new country. At home, there are all the traditional observances at Easter and Christmas and midsummer and harvest home, at christenings and weddings. But here the old-world festivity of the wedding, with its prolonged dancing and drinking, and all its quaint symbolic incidents,* is too apt to become, in American eyes at least, a drunken row, and to end in fines and disgrace, if not in the lockup.

The dance

Like all Slavs, both Poles and Ruthenians love dancing, and perhaps one of the best things that could be done for them in this country would be to help them to have decent and attractive gathering places where they could enjoy themselves without recourse to more or less dubious dance halls. At home they dance a great deal out of doors and one of the most picturesque sights

---

*The Countess Françoise Kransinska, in her charming journal, writing of the wedding of her sister Basia in 1759, speaks of the cap ceremony, which still takes place at Polish weddings in America. "At midnight the music stopped, and the cap ceremony was begun. A stool was placed in the middle of the room, the bride sat down, and the bridesmaids began to undo her hair, singing in plaintive voices the old song, Ah, we are losing you, Basia. Then my honored mother removed the rosemary wreath and the Woivodine Malachowska put in its place a big lace cap. . . . . .The cap is very becoming to her, which they say is a sign that her husband will love her very much."

Another curious custom which survives among Poles in this country takes place on Holy Thursday, when the boys chase the girls with little rods, and try to strike them. The girls retaliate by trying to throw water on the boys. This is said to be a corruption of a memorial of the scourging in the Passion.

of my Austrian journey was one such Sunday afternoon dance on the green in a Ruthenian village. The matrons of the place sat on the grass, or on the steps of an old covered well, and held the girls' sheepskin jackets between the dances, or supplied them with a refuge in case of embarrassment. Sometimes the boys and girls danced in whirling couples, like our waltzers, to the fast and furious music of players who stood almost hidden in the thick of the dancing crowd. Sometimes the boys danced by themselves in a ring, with arms outstretched and hands on one another's shoulders. They wore long white linen shirts or tunics almost to their knees, bound about the waist with bright woven girdles; and long, rather wide white linen trousers. The girls, who were very pretty, wore their hair curiously braided from the temple to the nape of the neck, with flowers, dahlias and so on, plastered on behind. Their sheepskin jackets, with the wool inside, were embroidered, and so were the loose straight sleeves of their linen blouses. Their skirts, straight and close, were made by winding a strip of rough dark cloth tightly about their hips. But most striking were the adornments—the peacock's feather tips and the bands of bright bead work, (favors from their fair ones), which ornamented the boys' hats, and the beads and strings of coins round the necks of the girls. These were doubtless heirlooms and indeed one belle who showed us her necklace had a coin with the head of Maria Theresa on it.

Another Sunday afternoon, driving around a bend in the road, we came upon a group of three or four young boys and girls dancing to the music of a fiddle. They had left the cattle that they were tending, in order to enjoy themselves just as the older lads and lasses were doubtless doing in the village behind us. One boy brought us a cap full of milky filberts, and as we drove off into the gathering dusk we felt that we too had been in Arcadia.

CHAPTER VIII

THE SLOVENIANS

"Krainers," or Slovenians

"What kind of people are these Griners?" I was asked in Cleveland, and it did not at first occur to me that the unknown word must be a corruption of Krainer, which is what the Germans call the people of Krain—or, as we say in English, Carniola. As a matter of fact, the term is often used for those not only from Carniola, but from Carinthia and other neighboring territory, and indeed for the whole nationality to which they belong, the Slovenes or Slovenians.*

Their place in history

They are a South Slav group, close cousins of the Croatians, but with a different, though nearly related, language. Like the Bohemians, they have been brought by their situation into intimate relation with German influences, and have been Germanized to a considerable extent.

Conflict with German influences

They seem to have located in and about their present seats in the Eastern Alps in the sixth century, driven before the Avars, and were soon in conflict with their Bavarian neighbors to the west. The conversion of the Slovenes to Christianity by the Germans meant a partial assimilation and absorption by them, the Slavic population of Salzburg and the Tyrol being completely Germanized.

Charlemagne divided the country of the Slovenes into various feudal lordships, and this people has never

* They call themselves Slovinci; an earlier name was Vinds or Wends. In the United States the name "Austrian" is often used specifically, as previously said, to mean Slovenes; though in some places in Pennsylvania I have found it used to mean Italians from the Austrian Tyrol. Information as to the Slovenes, ethnical and historical, will be found in Auerbach's "Races et Nationalités en l'Autriche-Hongrie," pages 65–80; see also, for those in Hungary, pages 298–300.

known a united or an independent political existence. That they were not without political instinct is indicated by the story which Leger tells in his "History of Austria-Hungary," of a curious ancient custom among the Slovenes of Carinthia at the installation of a new prince. 'The ceremony took place near the town of Celovic (Klagenfurt). A peasant mounted on a rock to await the coming of the new prince, who advanced, clothed in rustic garments. The peasant asked, 'Who is this who approaches?' The people answered, 'It is the prince of this land.' The peasant then asked, 'Is he a good judge? Is he the friend of truth?' and, on receiving a reply in the affirmative, the peasant yielded his place to the new comer, who mounted the rock and, brandishing his sword, swore to defend the country of the Slovenes. The people who had imagined it deserved a more brilliant destiny."[*]

In spite of having so little beyond a common language to give them a sense of unity or racial significance, the Slovenes have twice enjoyed a nationalistic revival. The first was at the time of the Reformation, and not only aroused religious zeal (nineteen-twentieths of the population of Carinthia is said to have become Protestant), but also caused a literary awakening of the language, much as the earlier Hussite movement had done in Bohemia, or as Wiclif did in England. At this time a considerable Slovenian literature appeared, including a translation of the Bible, and a grammar. The Counter Reformation, however, brought about the return of Catholicism and of the literary dominance of the German language.

The next Slovenian renascence came as a result of the Napoleonic wars, which for a short time joined most of the Slovenian territory, together with Dalmatia and Croatia, to France as her so-called Illyrian provinces. This led to the "Illyrian movement" in the thirties,

Slovenian revivals [margin note]

[*] Leger, Louis: "A History of Austria-Hungary from the Earliest Time to the Year 1889," pages 51, 52.

under the Slavic enthusiast and author, Louis Gaj, who endeavored to arouse national feeling among all the South Slavs and to inspire them with a sense of their unity and a pride in their language.

A language in process
Slovenian has ever since been cultivated, but as a literary medium it seems to be still, in some degree, in the making. For instance, I asked a Trieste lady what a sign on a theatre door meant. She said she could not understand it. When I asked her further, she said, "Yes, I speak Slovenian, but I learned it as a child in the nursery; I spent my girlhood away from home and was educated in German. When I came back our language had been changed so much that I often do not know what the words mean." The fact seems to be that the language having been for generations mainly an unwritten dialect of the plain people, words must often be borrowed from other Slavic languages, formed by analogy, or built up from existing roots. I could not help being amused to see one of the collaborators in this process himself reduced to asking a waiter to explain to him dishes on a Slovenian menu card.

The folk literature is said to be rich in lyrics and tales, but among the Slovenes one does not get the impression of a living, pulsating national tradition as one does, for instance, among the Slovaks, the Little Russians, or the Croatians. This may be in part because the national costume has almost passed away. Certainly the people appear much more assimilated to the Germans, and so to the general European type.

Numbers and location
The Slovenes number probably in the neighborhood of 1,500,000 only. They are massed in a fairly well-rounded region, but are divided politically by ethnically irrelevant boundaries. The great majority live in Austria, where 1,192,780 Slovenian-speaking persons were counted in 1900, a figure that the Slovenians themselves claim is too low. Across the border in Croatia are 19,875, and in two neighboring counties of Hungary

A SLOVENIAN GIRL

are some 68,000 more. There are also perhaps 50,000 in Italy.* In Austria they are found in southern Styria, southern Carinthia, Carniola, Goricia-Gradisca, northern Istria and in and about Trieste. Of these, nearly 40 per cent are in Carniola where more than nine out of ten of the population speak Slovenian.

The Slovenians are largely a peasant people, and it is noticeable how often cities, even in the midst of Slovenian districts, are mainly German. For instance, in the city of Cilli the Slovenians are only 23 per cent (to the Germans' 77), while in the surrounding country district they are 97 per cent. *City and country*

This relation of city and country population is a very general one in states where Slavs are confronted with Germans, Italians or even Hungarians. They may flock as laborers to commercial and industrial centres, like Vienna, Fiume or Budapest, but they are preponderantly country folk. Laibach, or to call it by its Slavic name, Ljubljana, is, however, an example of a city of Slavs. Of its 37,000 inhabitants, more than eight out of ten speak Slovenian. This beautiful city, with its vistas crowned by a snow-capped Alpine range, is indeed not only the capital of Carniola, but unofficially the capital of the Slovenian nationality.

In places where there is a strong minority of Slovenians, as in Trieste, they make vigorous efforts to come to the top, and everywhere that there is contact with other nationalities there is considerable friction. The Germans are prone to carry things with a high hand, the Italians are equally ambitious, and where the Slavs get into the saddle they are complained of in turn.† So much strength is dissipated in Austria in this national jarring. *Racial friction*

* Auerbach, pages 80 and 299. The figures for Hungary and Italy refer to 1890.
† Cf. Auerbach, pages 78, 79.

Mountains
and Karst

Most of the country where the Slovenians live is mountainous, from the very beautiful Alps of Styria, Carinthia
and upper Carniola, to the Uskok mountains .on the
Croatian border to the southeast; while to the west,
in Istria, stands Monte Maggiore, which gives Abbazia
the shelter that makes it an all-the-year-round resort for
pleasure and health.

Not only is this Slovenian district mountainous, but
much of it is *karst* or limestone waste.   To one who has
first seen what this can be in Croatia and along the
Dalmatian coast, and worst of all in Montenegro, the
karst here seems a mild affair.   Yet this limestone formation gives Carniola its most famous features in the
grottos of Adelsberg and Saint Canzian.

Emigration
districts

Of course, neither mountains nor karst bode any good
to agriculture, and of manufacturing there is little or
none in the districts most affected by emigration.   Of
late years a decline in the iron industry of the Alpine
districts of Carinthia and Styria has sent some miners to
America and more to the Westphalian district of Germany, but so far as I could learn there is no considerable
movement to America from Carinthia or Styria.   Floods
in the narrow Alpine valleys (like that of 1903 in the
Canal Thal of Carinthia) and other local causes, lead men
to emigrate, but these are individual cases hardly con-
stituting an emigration movement.   Nor did my inquiries
on the spot reveal any emigration of the Slovenians from
Goricia-Gradisca, though the Italians from the malarial
and pellagra-smitten coast districts of the province do
emigrate to some extent.

Emigration
from
Carniola

It is only from Carniola that there is any noteworthy
Slovenian current to America, and here there is an emigration fever of marked severity.   The movement attracted local attention in 1893 (when it already had a
few years' start) through the remittances sent home by
emigrants, and the governor of Carniola then ordered an
investigation through the post-office.   The figures, continued since this time, have considerable interest, espe-

cially as our own immigration reports merge the Slovenians with the Croatians; they are given in Appendix XII, page 451.

The Carniolan figures show, for the eleven and a half years represented, a fairly steady increase, culminating in 1903 with over 6500 emigrants. The total for the period was over 30,500, directed mainly to North America. Where not one in fifty is a woman it is obviously not a family movement; and that it is not undertaken with the idea of permanent settlement is shown by the fact that only 145 sold their property while nearly 6000 did not do so. The study of causes is interesting. Out of the whole 30,561, only twenty-seven cases are ascribed to fear of military service, and less than one in sixty to indebtedness, the great majority, over five-sixths, going to earn more money.

The districts of Carniola most affected seem to be Littai (in upper Carniola), Gottschee (a German district), and especially Chernembl, on the Croatian boundary, each of which suffered the enormous net loss by migration of over 12 per cent of its population in the decade 1890–1900, a loss comparable to that of the most severely affected Slovak counties.*

Causes The Chernembl district, which was a wine-growing country, with fine vineyards, had suffered much from the phylloxera. The people, it is said, were used to good living, and instead of retrenching when the blow, fell, ran into debt and finally had to emigrate in consequence.

Some places had depended in part on local house-industries, such as the making of wooden wares and pottery, which the people produced and hawked about. This like the Slovak itinerant trades, was hurt by modern conditions, especially by regulations made in the interests of shopkeepers to restrict peddling. The decline of this source of income was another cause of emigration.

Village life Three days spent in driving through the Gottschee and

* See Table 9, page 104; also for Carniola as a whole, Table 3, page 48.

Chernembl districts gave us a chance to see the homes of the people and to talk with local officials and returned immigrants. On the whole, it seemed a fairly prosperous countryside. My sharpest impressions are first, of a village where we waited to bait our horses,— its little pond, its comfortable looking houses with their stucco walls trellised with grapevines, its big church, and the women in long sleeveless coats, (the only bit of costume I saw in Carniola), hurrying to Mass; and then of the flowery fields, the vineyard slopes with little storehouses for wine shining white on the hillside, the figure of Saint Florian extinguishing a conflagration rudely painted on the houses and apparently taking the place of fire insurance, and the wayside shrines at which our driver would interrupt a skeptical discussion of church doctrines to raise his hat.

Returned
emigrants
    At Gottschee, German gymnastic societies were holding a reunion, to encourage the Germans of the place to hold out against Slovenian influences, and the village was consequently well filled. We were lucky to get a night's lodging and a chance to get information from the Burgomaster. More interesting was a talk with an upholsterer who had returned home for good, after having lived for some time in Brooklyn. "Life and work," he said, "are more *gemütlich* here at home. There is eating and drinking in the middle of the forenoon and again in the afternoon, and not such a sense of hurry. In America, men are driven on with cursing"—which he quoted. "The millionaires exploit the workers. A man is used up after a few years, but there is always a young and strong one ready to take his place, and they say to him 'come on.'"

This is almost the only note of social criticism that I have heard among emigrants. This man, it must be remembered, was a German and from a big city in America. But nowhere, it seemed to me, did I hear so often as in Carniola, that men returned exhausted or injured. Every one seemed to be struck by this. This is probably because the Slovenes work in America largely in the most dangerous trades, in mining and iron works especially.   I think, however, that it is largely the pace that kills, as our upholsterer friend felt.*

Contrasting with his view that America is too strenuous, was that of another man returned after fourteen years in Cleveland.   He stayed at home in Carniola only some six weeks, though he had come back meaning to stay longer.   He saw so much poverty that he could not stand it, he said.   He had given away at least five hundred gulden ($200) since his return home, and was afraid that he would give away everything that he had if he stayed.   In America he owns houses and a "Gast-haus" (probably a saloon), and his wife takes lodgers. If he had not left home, he says, he would be a beggar today.   When he first went to America he shoveled coal and his wife did washing, but gradually they got on.

And the "Krainers" in America do get on.   A man Remittances in Mr. Sakser's bank in New York told me that the firm remits at least a million dollars a year, mainly sent home by Slovenians.   And this is as near as I can come to telling "what kind of people these Griners are."†

---

* I note that Mr. Devine puts first in his statement of the gist of the situation in Pittsburgh, "An altogether incredible amount of overwork by everybody, reaching its extreme in the twelve-hour shift for seven days in the week in the steel mills and railway switch-yards." *Charities and the Commons*, XXI, page 1035 (Mar. 6, 1909).   See for an account of the physical and nervous strain of the steel workers, *ibid.*, pages 1081 ff.

† See chapter on The Household for picture of Krainer factory girls.

CHAPTER IX

EMIGRATION FROM CROATIA

With the Croatians we are in the midst of the world of the South Slavs. Of their three branches, the Bulgarians to the east do not come into this study of emigration from Austria-Hungary; the Slovenians to the west we have just considered, and the most numerous group, the Servo-Croatians, which lies between, must now be taken up.

In blood and speech the Croatians and Servians, as already explained, are one; beliefs and politics divide them. The poetry, legends, and customs, of which they have so rich and important a treasure, are the same among both peoples, or at least shade into one another. As a race they strike the observer as darker, more graceful and more gracious than their northern kinsmen, though fundamentally similar, and their language seems more liquid and southern in character.

As the kingdom of Servia is the chief home and political cynosure of the Servians, that is, of the Orthodox branch of the Servo-Croatian stem, so the kingdom of Croatia-Slavonia, commonly for convenience called Croatia simply, is the centre for the Croatian or Roman Catholic branch. In each case outside the political boundaries are others of the same blood and faith—Servians, notably, in Montenegro, in Novi Bazar across the frontier in Turkey, and in Bosnia and Herzegovina; Croatians along the Adriatic coast in Dalmatia, where they make up most of the population, in Istria, and in smaller groups elsewhere. Croatia-Slavonia itself with a population of nearly 2,500,000 and an area equal to not quite one-third of the state of New York, is a fairly homogeneous country—markedly homogeneous indeed for Austria-

Hungary. Eighty-seven per cent of the population speak "Servian or Croatian" and 71 per cent are Roman Catholic.*

Politically, Croatia-Slavonia is a so-called "autonomous kingdom" bound to Hungary, much as Hungary is bound to Austria, by old dynastic ties and by a modern political contract which fixes the constitutional relations of the two states. Croatia is of course the weaker party and complains bitterly of the illegal and overbearing policy of Hungary and of her financial exploitation. For instance, though Agram lies midway between Budapest and the port of Fiume, the railroad, which is Hungarian, charges more for freight sent to Fiume from Agram than from Budapest. Croatian firms are obliged to do business under Magyar names and to make their headquarters in inland Budapest. Nevertheless, Croatia with local self government and especially with education in her own control is infinitely better off than the non-Magyar nationalities in Hungary proper. {The autonomous kingdom}

Quite apart from unfair treatment at the hands of Hungary, Croatian conditions have been hard enough. "The Croatians look as if they were dying of consumption, but they are tougher than wire," said a doctor of the immigration service, out of his years of experience, and the Croatian has had to face conditions which required him to be tough. For the most part he has had a hard struggle against both nature and man. The counties to the east, which constitute Slavonia, are rich and under-populated, but toward the west there are often more people than the country under present conditions is fitted to support.† Along the Adriatic coast and for some distance inland, including Lika-Krbava county, {Hard natural conditions}

* For the rest, 3 per cent of the population speak other Slavic languages, 3.7 per cent Magyar, and 5.6 per cent German; in religion 25.5 per cent are Orthodox, 5 per cent Greek Catholic, 1.8 per cent Protestant and 8 per cent Israelite.

† In this largely sterile country, dependent on a backward agriculture, the density exceeds that of Pennsylvania or New York state, and is nearly equal to that of little industrial Connecticut.

the land is rugged where not actually mountainous, and largely sterile. Much of it is indeed sheer karst or limestone desert, about as pleasant to try to cultivate as a piece of bare coral. To understand what it means one must drive, day after day, through this country. Even a New Englander, used to fields where "the sheep's noses have to be sharpened so that they can graze between the stones," is appalled at what is here called pasture. Great stretches lie almost bare of any green thing, a mere exposure of broken rock surfaces.

In many places there are depressions in the stony ground, into which soil washes, and one sees such spots, perhaps fifteen feet across, walled around and carefully cultivated. These *dolinas*, as they are called, are characteristic of this limestone region. I counted, I think, forty on one scrubby hillside. The limestone formation also accounts for the wildly romantic character of some of the landscapes in Croatia and adjacent territory; crags, caverns, intermittent waterfalls, rivers that sink into the earth to emerge miles away, or perhaps never more to be seen, and at other places streams that suddenly flow forth full-grown rivers.*

Climate   In the mountainous parts the famous Bora, the dreaded north wind of the eastern Adriatic shore, is very destructive, and the winters are long and severe. "It is a whole fur coat colder here," said our driver as we drove into an attractive valley where a peasant who had been (as we were told) in Missouri, in Wyoming and in Colorado, was doing his spring ploughing. Here the soil was good enough, but the climate was too rigorous for much to grow. Another day our driver mentioned as if it were nothing very extraordinary, being once snowed up for twenty days at the inn where we were lunching. But if the winters are cold, the summer sun of Italy blazing on these whitish rocks is scorching hot.

* The most noted natural beauty of Croatia proper is the lovely group of the Plitvica lakes.

KARST COUNTRY IN CARNIOLA AND CROATIA

1. Birth of a river from underground. 2. A sink hole, "dolina," in the Karst; a little deposit of soil worth cultivating though so small. 3. Laibach, capital of Carniola. 4. The grotto of Saint Canzian in Carniola. 5. An island shore of bare Karst.

This Lika district of Croatia was one of the few places where a local type seemed to be distinguishable. One of the common features of the tall and worn looking men, with their thin, serious faces, was a set of curious horizontal wrinkles across their foreheads, which may have meant sun dazzle and may have meant care. The lined face, together with the "mutton chop" whiskers that he wears, give the Lika peasant as he ploughs his stony field a strange, irrelevant likeness to a British man of business.

As if his natural difficulties were not enough, the Croatian, especially the Croatian of the southern border, has had to face a constant struggle with the Turk. Till 1878 the neighboring territory, Bosnia, was Turkish, and men still living remember the bloody fighting on the Cordon. One occasionally gets a vivid suggestion of what it meant. In a Croatian valley, cultivated from side to side, but without a house among the fields, we noticed that the dwellings were all at the edge of the slopes. "Is the valley subject to floods?" I asked, wondering. "Oh, no," was the reply, "but it was necessary to be able to take refuge quickly in the woods and mountains in case of a raid." *The struggle with the Turk*

Here and there one sees on a hill a castle or fortress built for refugees (Uskoks) and one hears that this or that district has inhabitants who by their dialect are still distinguishable as descendants of unfortunates who formerly fled thither to escape the Turks. Evans, in his most interesting book on Bosnia, has a photograph of a group of such who had taken refuge in Ragusa on the Dalmatian coast.

If a hard outdoor life and constant border warfare toughened the Croatian, there went with these conditions certain institutions which in some degree tended to unfit him for independent life in a system of individual competition. The first of these institutions was that of the "Militär Grenze." This dates back as far as 1564, when to protect the border from the Turks a strip of *Military organization* land along its edge was organized into the Military Confines or Military Frontier. After a period of subjection to the Turks this military organization was renewed. In 1739 the part of the country not under this organization, "Civil Croatia," comprised only the Zeng, Fiume and Modruš districts.* All the rest was divided into so-called regiments, its population being placed on a purely military footing, under military command. All men of military age, that is up to sixty, were soldiers. Though living like peasants they were in the emperor's service, with a regular position in the army, subject to active duty for a part of every year, and liable to be called to the colors at any time. These Croatian regiments, the Likaner and others, were not only made use of in local warfare, but were apt to be sent to the front in the distant wars in which the Austrians have been constantly engaged.

Effects of military conditions

Indeed, the man of the frontier, up to forty or fifty years ago, was more used to fighting than to labor and could not go to his ploughing without his weapons. As is usual under such circumstances, work was then largely left to the women, as it is today in Montenegro where war and hunting still rank, in true barbarian fashion, as the suitable occupations for a man. On this account, it is said, many Croatians have never acquired habits of steady industry, using their great strength energetically for a few days perhaps, and then idling. Not only was work thus interfered with by this military life, but the natural responsibility for self-support was partly lifted by it from the shoulders of the population. As soldiers they were necessary and must be maintained, and their support was eked out with imperial rations and with help in bad seasons.

It was not till 1869 that it was decided to do away with

* "Die Königreiche Kroatien und Slavonien auf der Milenniums-Aufstellung des Königreichs Ungarn in Budapest, 1896." Kgl. Landesdruckerei; Agram, 1896. Historical Sketch, pages 227-235.

the military frontier, gradually abolish the exceptional conditions and restore the inhabitants to civil life, and it was not till August 1, 1881, that the military administration was definitively replaced by a system of civil government.

The other institution referred to as giving a poor preparation for life considered as an economic battle to be fought single-handed, was the famous and much discussed "Zadruga" or communal household of the South Slavs.* The German phrase for it, "House Communion" or "Community" well expresses its nature. Its essence is the custom of owning and carrying on a household and farm, not individually but as a family association. The administration is in the hands of the elected head, generally, though not necessarily, the father or eldest man. The choice depends on character, ability and circumstances. A woman, usually but not always the wife of the head man, is chosen to superintend and direct the women's work and sometimes a woman is made the head of the whole Zadruga.

The Zadruga or communal household

We were in one such communal household not far from Agram, where sixty persons were living in communism. In the main homestead the living rooms opened off a gallery or verandah, raised a story from the ground. One room was set apart for unmarried girls; in the main room was a row of big beds along each side, and at one end stood the table at which all the men eat together. The women eat afterwards. In the yard was a well,

* The Zadruga is of great interest to students of social institutions, and has been the subject of much controversy. Attention was called to it by Sir Henry Sumner Maine in his "Ancient Law" and also in his "Village Communities in the East and West," and by Emile de Laveleye, the Belgian economist, in his "De La Propriété et ses Formes Primitives" (translated and revised by Karl Bücher in 1879 as "Das Ureigenthum"). Maine and de Laveleye interpret the House Communion as a remnant of an early and once widespread communism. Since their time more detailed and critical studies of the subject have been made. The same institution, or one closely similar, exists or has existed among the Slovaks.

For a list of references on the subject of the Zadruga, see the Bibliography under that head.

and about it a variety of farm buildings and also small houses where some of the young married couples live. They eat, however, with the others.

This was quite a wealthy Zadruga, with money in the bank, and the old man at its head was likewise the head official of the village. Three of the sons were away, "two in America and one in 'Spittsburg'" (sc. Pittsburg) and the old man seemed to be seized with a sudden sense of yearning, for he twice smoothed his worn hands down my cheeks and said, "Greet Janko for me if you see him in America."

In Agram I had a very interesting talk with a gentleman, a literary man of cosmopolitan reputation in Slavic countries as a writer and politician, who was brought up in a Zadruga till the age of ten—a Zadruga, as it happened, administered by a woman—and who is a great admirer of the institution. It has, I judge, the good and bad features of communal or semi-communal life in general. There is a lessened appeal to energy and initiative, the lazy man is better off than (in an economic sense at least) he deserves to be, and it is easy to play a rather passive rôle. On the other hand, there is great economy of time, labor and capital and more room for organization of the available forces. One or two women are told off by the elected house mother to do the cooking and household tasks, the others are delegated for field work, herding, and so forth, according to circumstances; and similarly with the men. There are no divisions among heirs, no law suits, no expensive settlements, and the burden of taxation is lighter. It makes possible a varied and highly social household life, and is, moreover, a training in co-operation, tolerance, and more than one beautiful moral quality.

Passing of the Za- druga
The customs of the Zadruga seem to have made progressive concessions to individualism, but not enough to save it. In 1848 in Civil Croatia, and a generation later within the Military Frontier also, the division of Zadrugas, which was not before allowed, was permitted by

law. The old associations began thereupon rapidly to dissolve; so rapidly that statesmen before long took alarm at the resulting subdivision of land, and passed a law more favorable to the old communal groups, and prohibiting division where the portions would be smaller than a certain minimum, fixed at from three to eight yokes (about four and a half to twelve acres) in different districts.*

When a Zadruga is divided, whether by legal process or secretly by mutual consent to avoid legal expenses and increase of taxation, even a prosperous group too often makes a number of poor if not actually insolvent families. Not only is the land cut up, often into small inadequate lots, but the cattle and necessaries of all kinds are divided, and sometimes the old communal dwelling is torn down and divided *beam by beam*. There are not ploughs enough to fit out all the separate undertakings, and they have not sufficient capital and must resort to loans. Moreover, the individual members lack experience and perhaps capacity, as well as capital, for conducting an independent enterprise, and it is said that the disastrous result of the dissolution of Zadrugas is one of the causes which drive the Croatian peasants to emigrate to America.

In general, Croatian living is primitive, with the charm and the drawbacks that that implies. On a house wall in a Croatian village there was pointed out to us a rude drawing, made perhaps by some child, of the epic hero Marko Kralevitch (Marko, the king's son), the subject of some of the most famous Servo-Croatian folksongs. The hero is said to be not dead but sleeping under the beauti- *Primitive conditions survive*

* In spite of the process of dissolution of these communities, which in some districts has swept them away completely, it was shown by an inquiry in 1890 that nearly a fifth of the population was then living in such communal families. Most of these, however, were small—8 per cent having ten members or less—and differed from ordinary families, not in size but in the fact that they held their property like a corporation; no member being at liberty to claim a division or alienate his rights. See Bibliography under Zoričič.

ful snowy heights of the Velebit, ready to return and free
the land when its hour of direst need shall come; and
in the capital of Montenegro we saw a blind gusla player,
with a head like a marble Homer, singing historical epics
in the square. So near are these people to ages which in
Western Europe are far beyond all living memory.

A Croatian house of the poorer sort is often very
pretty, with its steep shingled roof and whitewashed or
stuccoed sides. Frequently there is no chimney, and the
little trap door in the roof is kept closed during the
winter, so that till spring the smoke has no exit. This
is not so bad as it sounds, as the fire is often on a stone
hearth in the centre of the house, while to the right and
left are rooms which are really more like little dwellings
or boxes built inside the house. The smoke rolls through
the space above the planking which ceils these, and this
part of the building is often crusted with the black,
shiny deposit of the soot while the living room is clear of
it within. This room may be heated with a stove of unglazed tiles which is fed from outside the room through
an opening in the wall and which, like all European
stoves of this type, gives no direct fire heat and no ven-
tilation, but radiates warmth from its own surface.
Such a stove is heated like a Dutch oven, with a brisk
fire quickly burned out and usually made only once a
day. These Croatian stoves are often made of what
looks like a series of unglazed flower-pots embedded,
empty, and mouths out, in a mass of clay. This pigeon-
holed exterior gives a great extent of radiating surface,
which is the prime object in all stoves constructed on
this principle, and will sometimes give out warmth for
three days without needing to be re-heated. Around
the stove are rails for drying wet clothes.

In poorer houses, there may be simply a fire of twigs
and branches on the floor and a baby wrapped in rags
lying in the ashes. The family sleep probably in one
room, occasionally on straw covered with the curious

CROATIAN VILLAGE SCENES

1. In "Lipa." Thirty persons from this house alone are in America. 2 and 3. A town that has benefited by American remittances; it has water supply, street lamps and a savings bank. 4. Roofs protected against the Bora. 5. In Otočac.

Croatian blankets which are almost as shaggy as the original sheep, and woven in bright, angular patterns.

The windows are apt to be small. We heard of people Small windows having been burned up because they could not get out through the windows when the house was on fire and the doorway cut off. But this defect is not confined to Croatia. It was among the Slovaks that a priest told us that he preached against windows "so small that it made an eclipse of the sun if a hen flew in," a figure of speech suggestive in more ways than one. It was in Galicia that a woman pointed out a small single pane fixed in the wall to the east so that it might be possible to see the sun rise and know when to get up, and explained to us that there was no window to the north because the north is evil.

The cattle are often accommodated under the same roof Domestic animals with the family, either on the same level, only separated by a partition, or underneath in a sort of basement stall. I frequently heard, and not alone in Croatia, that families had animals living with them more sociably than this, as the Irish used to have both at home and in America, but I never saw a case—except, indeed, hens straying in and out, and once some small pigs who seemed to have the run of the house.

The poor cows, as we saw them emerging after their long winter into the spring sunshine, were pitiable objects, with the dirt so caked on their flanks as to tear the flesh and make sores. One official told us of his efforts to get the people to bring their cattle to market clean. Except in this instance of neglect, however, I have never seen or heard anything in Europe or America to suggest other than kind treatment of animals by Slavs of any nationality; neither do I remember ever having seen a child abused among them.

In the poor western district of Croatia the peasants, though economical, are said to live much better than the inhabitants of the richer eastern counties. Polenta

(corn meal mush) is much eaten, sometimes with sauerkraut.   But there is plenty of meat, too.   No family is
too poor to kill a pig at Christmas which will give pork
for three months, and in spring there are lambs to furnish
fresh meat.   The sheep's. milk cheese is excellent, but
owing to lack of facilities it is not an article of export
as it is among the Slovaks.

The trousseau   The marriage customs are interesting.   A girl is expected, at least in certain districts, to bring a dowry including at the very least a chest and a complete outfit,
from cap to shoes, for the bridegroom as well as for herself.   I am told this is also the way among the Bulgarians, and that the little girl begins on her knitting as
soon as she can be taught to hold the needles, since she
must have ready stockings for herself and her future
husband, enough to last both their lives.   The Croatian
woman is always knitting as she minds her cattle or
goes about her business.   In many places the men wear
big knit garments such as we call sweaters, and heavy
knit socks with a sort of plaid pattern about the ankle.

The man need bring no property to his bride, and
consequently the birth of a boy whose marriage will en-
rich the family is far more desired than that of a girl who
must be portioned off.   A girl who is poor cannot hope
to marry.   This is in the inland counties, and is in striking contrast to the custom on the coast, where a girl
marries without a dowry, except that she must have her
personal ornaments (necklace of coins and what not).
Without these no girl of the coast districts can look for
a lover, but for her other property is not essential.

The making of a match   When a marriage is to be discussed, representatives
of the two sides come together,. generally the girl's parents
and two or three people, very often including a brother,
uncle or aunt, to act for the man.   The bridegroom and
his health are discussed, but his family is a question a
hundred times more important.   What sort of people are
they?   Does his father beat his mother?   What is his
own relation to his brother, his sister?   Is his married

brother a good husband? (and, from the other side—Is the girl's married sister a good wife?) The inquiry may last two or three days or even weeks. The agreement is made simply by passing the word *dobro* (good). The parents then have a meeting at church or elsewhere. After this the next step is taken; the representatives of the two sides come formally together, and an hour or so later comes the prospective bridegroom. He gives an apple to the girl and she gives him a handkerchief. In songs a girl is often likened to an apple, and it seems to be a token at once of comeliness and fruitfulness.

The customs which accompany the celebration of the marriage itself are extremely elaborate. A marriage speech which is handed down by verbal memory takes up eight or ten printed pages. A certain student of folklore would not believe that this was genuine till he found a peasant who convinced him by reciting it entire while he held the book.* *[margin: The wedding]*

It is not surprising that where life in general is still so primitive, education too, at least in the sense of "book learning," is backward. *[margin: Illiteracy]*

The figures of the Croatian census are interesting. They show the following percentages among inhabitants over six years old:

TABLE 11.—CROATIA. PERCENTAGE OF LITERACY AND ILLITERACY.

	1869 PER CENT	1900 PER CENT
Able to read and write:		
Men	23	52.0
Women	11	36.0
Able to read only:		
Men	2	0.75
Women	2	2.0
Able to neither read nor write:		
Men	74	47.25
Women	87	62.0

The American immigration figures unfortunately treat Croatians and Slovenians as one group. The illiteracy

* The above account was given me orally by a Croatian scholar, but for this and much else, see Krauss: "Sitte und Brauch der Süd-Slaven," and also his "Sagen und Märchen der Süd-Slaven."

of this group in 1900 was 37.4 per cent, less than that of the Ruthenians (with 49 per cent) but more than that of any other Slavic group.*

Language and education

Fortunately, Croatia, though in much else she chafes under Hungarian domination in spite of her constitutionally recognized autonomy, has a free hand in education. Consequently the Croatians enjoy the great advantage that teaching, alike in the elementary class and the university, is in the native language, the Croatian. This is one of the most beautiful, or at least the most euphonious, of the Slavic tongues, following the apparent law which gives to southern speech more open vowels, fewer combinations of consonants, and in general more liquidity and grace.

School attendance

School attendance is compulsory from seven to twelve years of age, and from twelve to fourteen "continuation classes" are required. In one such class which I saw I judged that these hours of school were a hardship for poor little apprentice boys who came tired and fagged from the shoemaker's bench or the anvil. It ought to be a good thing to have the school period overlap into the working period, but in practice, under industry conducted for profit, half time systems unless carefully guarded are too likely to mean a double exploitation of a youngster's strength.

The attempt to make school attendance universal is far from successful as yet. In Lika-Krbava I was told that nearly two-thirds of the children do not go to school mainly because their homes are scattered. The parents are said to be generally glad to send their boys to school, but less concerned to have the girls learn. In this county there were 10,601 boys at school and 2,720 girls. Sometimes the children cannot go for lack of school room, but in thirteen years this county had built thirty-five new schools and enlarged twenty more; so there is progress.

Very interesting was a project of Mr. Krshnjavi, a

* See further Appendix XXVII, page 479.

former minister of education.   He had picked from country schools, a few here and a few there, some fifty of the most promising pupils and sent them at government expense to a "gymnasium" to receive a good secondary education fitting them to enter the university.   He was delighted at the progress that they were making, when his retirement from office intervened, and though lacking only one year of graduation, they were all sent back to their narrow peasant homes.

One obstacle to continuous schooling is the excessive number of holidays, where both Catholic and Greek orthodox festivals have to be observed.   In some places the weekly market day is a holiday besides, but in this case it is probably taken instead of the Saturday holiday.

One must remember that illiteracy does not necessarily connote either stupidity or lack of desire to learn, and that it is compatible with all such culture as can be transmitted orally, which is much more according as a society is more primitive.   The printed page was not necessary to the composition of the Iliad and Odyssey, nor to their circulation.   "In every village," I was told in Croatia, "there is a library bought by peasants alone, and in winter they often come together to have some one read to them, not only newspapers but more solid literature, such as translations of Tolstoy, Turgenieff, and Dostoyevsky."   Such glimpses suggest what a different thing illiteracy is under different circumstances. *Other means of culture*

Reading clubs are widespread, and together with an inviting room where the papers subscribed for in common can be read, are a pleasant feature of village life.

Another occasional stimulus is the visit of a troupe of wandering actors.   We were fortunate in happening to see a performance of this kind in the village which I have spoken of under the name of Lipa.   The play was a grandiose historical tragedy and was given on an impromptu stage, lighted by two ordinary oil lamps and so small that the dying hero's head lay in the doorway of one of the side exits while his feet stuck out between *Native drama*

the lamps.   The language was Croatian and quite unintelligible to us.   Yet over all these obstacles the
art of the chief actor triumphed.   I think I have rarely
been stirred in the same way except by Booth.   Duse
and Coquelin I have seen in rôles of such a different
quality that I cannot make comparisons.   Salvini, too,
moved in a different world.   But these are the names
that occur to me in trying to measure the genius of a
strolling player in a Croatian village!   I am hoping that
some good fate may give me another chance to hear
Kostič.

This village boasted, too, among its teachers, a lady
who is said to write very pretty Croatian verse, and who
was kind enough to write for me in German the charming account of emigration as she has seen it, which is
appended to this chapter as "Notes from My Village."

Health and   As regards health and morality, I cannot say that I
morality   heard no criticism of the Croatians.   Especially are the
women of Slavonia, which is much richer than the west-
ern part of the country, said to be excessively addicted
to luxury and beautiful clothes, and in order to gratify
these tastes, to limit their families and to conduct themselves loosely.   It is hard to say how much such rumors
amount to, and they involve a district with which America has little direct concern.   But throughout Croatia,
as in some other emigration districts, one hears a good
deal of sporadic complaint of the injury to morality
through emigration.   Though cases where the husband
has deserted his family appear to be rare, wives left alone
at home sometimes misuse their freedom, and I have
heard it said that infanticide has increased.

The number of illegitimate births is apt to be high in
countries where there are or have been barriers to legal
marriage.   Under the old system of communal families
there was considerable practical restriction on marriage,
and the military regulations still forbid a man's marrying
between eighteen and twenty-three unless he can prove
that there is in the household no woman between sixteen

Agram (Zagráb), Capital of Croatia

and sixty.   The military authorities visit the house to make sure that there really is no able-bodied woman available.   In spite of these facts the illegitimacy rate seems creditable at 70 per 1000 births.   This is worse than in a group of countries including Ireland, Holland, England, Switzerland, Finland, Roumania and Italy (ranging from Ireland with 27 to Italy with 67), but better than Norway, Scotland, France, Germany and Sweden, ranging from 72 to 106 per 1000.

The most serious charge I heard made was that in certain villages the population is honeycombed with—as I understood it—venereal disease, so that officials having occasion to go there carry their own eating utensils with them.   But in this whole matter the most "advanced" populations have nothing to boast of; and any one who knows country life anywhere is likely to be free of the widespread delusion that what is rural is necessarily more innocent than what is urban.*

As regards orderliness and safety, about which travelers returning from any place off the beaten track are often asked, I doubt if one could find a safer country than Croatia.   I remember one late afternoon in Gospič, the county town of Lika-Krbava, where we walked through oak woods, purple with a carpet of spring crocus and lit with the sunset, and through roads along which peasants were returning from the long market day and its following carousals, driving home in tipsy excitement.   Though we were two women without escort we felt no fear, and apparently had no cause for timidity.   In this once wild frontier no case of highway robbery is remembered in forty-five years, and we were asked with incredulity if it could be true, as emigrants reported from America, that they were in danger of being assaulted if they

The population orderly

* It is satisfactory to learn that syphilis appears to be one of the rarest diseases among immigrants.   For instance, of 3427 patients in the immigrant hospital at Ellis Island in the year ending June 30, 1903, only two were found to be suffering from this disease.   See Annual Report of the Surgeon General of Public Health and Marine Hospital Service of the United States for the Fiscal Year 1904, page 194.

walked home alone with their pay along the lonely
stretches of railroad where they worked—that they must
go in groups of ten or twelve and carry revolvers. We
explained that this could be true, if at all, only in wild
and out of the way places. I did not know that Chicago in April, 1906, would report a carnival of highway
murder, nor had I then found myself in the South forbidden to walk anywhere alone on quiet country roads.*

Agram

I have been speaking of the Croatian countryside, but
Croatians are influenced by the life of their national
capital as are none of the other nationalities with which
we are dealing, except the Bohemians. To a Croatian,
to write of his country without speaking of Zagráb
(or as we commonly call it, Agram) would be to give
Hamlet with the Prince of Denmark left out.†

It is a little city with only about 53,000 inhabitants,
but it is a capital in the fullest sense of the word. On
the hill is what remains of the ancient town, with the
residence of the Ban or governor, and curious memorials
of the barbarities of the past. Nearby is the quarter
which formerly was the domain of the cathedral chapter
which of old waged bloody wars with the secular powers.
At the foot of the hill is the market place with Ban
Jellačič on horseback forever waving his bronze sword
in the direction of Hungary. The market scene itself
is like a bed of flowers, the prevailing colors being the
white of linen garments and the orange scarlet of ribbons
and necklaces and dangling garters, of aprons and em-
broideries.‡

The modern
city

But most surprising is the modern city with its boule-
vards and fine residence blocks, and above all its wealth
of institutions of culture. As one follows the avenue

* For the sake of fairness I will add that I have been told in
Pennsylvania of a murder of a paymaster by two Croatians.
† For a sketch of Agram by an inhabitant, see Lucerna, Ca-
milla: "Zagráb," *Agramer Tagblatt*, April 10, 1909, page 9.
‡ Excellent pictures of Agram market scenes and of other
Croatian, Dalmatian and Istrian views will be found in an
article, "In Quaint, Curious Croatia," by F. J. Koch, *National
Geographic Magazine*, pages 809–832 (Dec., 1908).

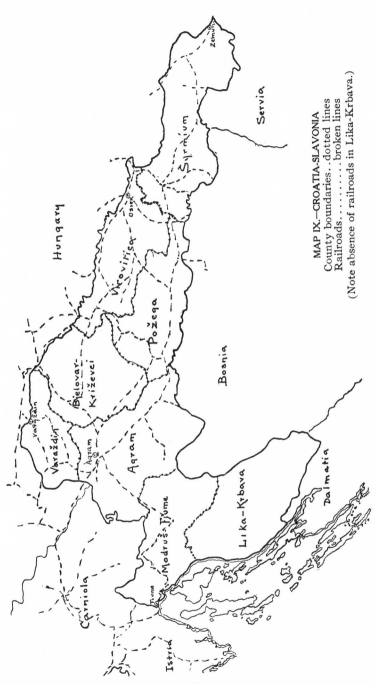

MAP IX.—CROATIA-SLAVONIA
County boundaries..dotted lines
Railroads..........broken lines
(Note absence of railroads in Lika-Krbava.)

Hungary

Servia

Zemun

Syrmium

Osijek

Virovitica

Požega

Bielovar-Križevci

Bosnia

Varaždin

Varaždin

Agram

Agram

Lika-Krbava

Dalmatia

Carniola

Modruš-Fjume

Fiume

Istria

173

north from the railroad station the panorama is for some distance worthy of Paris or Vienna, and in monumental character and absence of any jarring note utterly beyond comparison with anything that I think of in America. The Fine Arts Building, in which yearly exhibitions are held, stands by itself in the first block of the central park space; in the same situation in the next square is the Chemistry Building of the University; then comes an open garden with statues; then the building of the South Slav Academy of Arts and Sciences founded by the patriot Bishop Strossmayer, who died while we were in Croatia, full of years and of honor. This latter building contains a permanent collection of painting and sculpture gathered and given by Bishop Strossmayer, an Archeological Museum, etc.

Further to the west is the public theatre where Croatian dramas are given throughout the season. Nearby is the University with its professional schools (another foundation of Bishop Strossmayer's) and near this again the excellent Art and Industrial School, due, like much else, to the far-seeing plans of the late minister of education, Mr. Krshnjavi, a man who has known how to stimulate and bring forward a whole generation of young artists and authors. To get a little into this atmosphere was like going into the woods in spring, when one feels the new life unfolding on every side.

Causes and course of emigration

To turn now to a more special consideration of Croatian emigration, we may note first that, as regards causes of emigration, Croatia shares with countries like upper Hungary or Galicia the impulse resulting from the abolition of feudal serfdom in 1848, and the invasion of the old self-sufficing peasant economy by modern wares and ways. But Croatia suffers not only from the unstable equilibrium of an economy where modern desires are awaking while there is as yet lack of capital, lack of manufactures, lack of railroads, lack of modern agricultural methods, and in some districts actual lack of sufficient usable soil. Besides all this, certain parts at

least of Croatia suffer from a forced transition, hurrying
the evolution of centuries into a generation—the transition from the subjection and partial support of frontier
soldiery and from the sheltered mutual dependence of
communal family life, to the full responsibility of self-
maintenance on an individual footing in a novel competi-
tive world.

Croatian emigration to America began first among the Earliest
always mobile sea-faring population of Dalmatia and along the coast
seaboard Croatia and the islands which stud the Adriatic
coast, where it occurred sporadically before 1850.   This
population, cut off from the inland by the great limestone
range which runs just back of the shore line, has a character and situation all its own, and though chronologically it
should be considered first, it will, for reasons of convenience, be taken up in the next chapter.   The present one
will deal only with the main body of the Croatians, those
of the inland.

The original occasion of emigration from the back Modruš-
country seems to have been the opening of the first Fiume County:
railroad to the coast, built in 1873 from Karlstadt to Loss of old
Fiume, which started emigration from Modruš-Fiume occupations
county.   Previously freight and passengers had come
over the mountains on wheels or on pack animals, and
this gave occupation to a large part of the mountain
population.   An eighteenth century traveler says that
this traffic then brought $16,000 or $20,000 into circulation, and he tells of women carrying heavy burdens on
their shoulders for a four or five hours' climb up the
mountains, spinning as they went.   When on the opening of the railroad in 1873 this source of earning was cut
off, the people had to look elsewhere, for their lands could
not support them.   In some districts this had always
been the case, and surplus hands had sought a living in
seasonal employment abroad or in peddling, but after
1873 the difficulty became widespread and by the early
eighties people from the northern part of the county were
beginning to go to the United States.   When we were in a

village of this district, which I will call "Lipa," whence people had been emigrating to America since 1885, we were told that of a population of 3,400, 1,800 were in America. So many of their people are in Calumet, Michigan, that they refer to it as "New Lipa." I photographed a house from which I was told thirty persons had gone, and in our little inn the rooms were adorned with pictures of relatives in American finery.

Here, as in all the districts of Croatia where there are forests, the men are famous woodsmen. They are masters of the axe, and a good worker can hew accurately to a line for sixty feet. Accordingly, in the United States they often are woodworkers, stave cutters along the Mississippi or lumbermen in Michigan. An interesting man whom we ran across was a master carpenter who had perfected himself by the old *wanderjahr* plan, going, as he told us, to Germany, Paris and elsewhere, to learn new ways and bring home new ideas. Now, he said, this is not necessary, as there is a good trades school in Agram.

Croatians are said to be clever workmen in general, quick to catch an idea and carry it out. They have a proverb, "What he sees, he makes." I have not happened to learn in America whether they have this reputation here, where they come into comparison with other nationalities.

Agram County: Phylloxera A local cause of emigration which affected the wine-growing districts, especially those about Jaška and Karl-stadt in Agram county, was the phylloxera, which apparently was brought into the neighborhood of Agram in 1872, by a gentleman who imported some American vines from France. It also got into the Varasdin district and spread from there as a centre. It appeared, too, in Syrmium, coming from across the Danube in Hungary, where it had broken out as early as 1870 or 1871. In consequence of this, emigration began fairly early in the district about Karlstadt and Jaška. It is said to have started in 1884 and 1885, but it greatly in-

CROATIAN TYPES, LIKA DISTRICT

creased later, especially in 1900 and 1901. Money has been sent back from America to replant the vineyards with American stocks which are immune to phylloxera, and on which European varieties are afterward grafted. This is an expensive operation, but it is the only way of meeting the evil.

About the middle of the nineties the emigration began from Lika-Krbava. The first men probably went, I was told, as a result of reading about America in the papers. This region not only was formerly the scene of bloody conflicts, as the name denotes, but is largely sterile, stony, and subject to harsh climatic conditions as already described. With a population in 1900 of 208,000 it has only 159,000 yokes of arable land,* which is only about three-quarters of a yoke apiece, and a yoke is reckoned necessary to feed one person. This is actual over-population, for manufacturers are practically nil, and there is no railroad in a region nearly twice as big as Rhode Island, as may be seen on Map IX. *(sidenote: Lika-Krbava County: Lack of land)*

Of course, if culture were intensive it would be a different situation, but the methods are primitive; the plough may be of wood, and the sower, scattering unselected seed, plants weeds with the grain.

The oxen and horses are generally small and poor. A stock joke is that a German tourist wrote, "The Croatians have small, horse-like creatures called *Konje*,"— *konje* being the Croatian word for horses. We saw women ploughing with oxen that came only to their waists. The sheep, too, are poor, and even if a better breed is introduced it is said to degenerate, the wool soon becoming poor and harsh in quality. The government, *(sidenote: Stock-raising)*

* Lika-Krbava County:

Arable land	159,000	yokes
Meadow	89,000	"
Pasture	282,000	"
Woods	464,000	"
Karst	81,000	"
	1,075,000	yokes

A yoke is less than an acre and a half, or more precisely 1.42 acres.

12

however, has agricultural stations for experimentation, breeding and teaching of methods, and is making efforts to improve the stock both of animals and plants; and the public schools often have gardens where the children are taught the care of fruit trees and how to graft them.

The population has sustained a great blow in the government prohibition of keeping goats. They formerly did much damage to woods, and in this limestone region, which so easily becomes denuded, this is a very serious matter. It might have been regulated, however, without cutting off altogether what had been a very important part of the living of the peasant. We were told that the military authorities notice a falling off in physique of the men, ascribed to lack of the wholesome and strengthening goat's milk formerly available.

Varasdin County

Of late years, emigration has been extending north into the Varasdin district, which till comparatively recently remained almost unaffected. It is a poor region, and the most densely populated part of the country, with 209 inhabitants to the square kilometer of agricultural land where Lika-Krbava has 135.* Emigrants do not go from the poorest parts of this district, however.

Slavonia

Another new field for emigration is the eastern counties; that is, Slavonia. Here conditions are just the reverse; the land is rich and thinly populated, with (in Syrmium) only 87 persons to the square kilometer of agricultural land. There have been attempts to colonize this district from Hungary and from the Varasdin district in Croatia, but for some reason population does not seem to flow thither as it might be expected to do.

Growth and grounds of emigration

Figures in regard to Croatian emigration are given in some detail in Appendix XIII. Here we see that while in 1899 only Agram county and Modruš-Fiume county sent over a thousand emigrants to North America (and

---

* The figures are for 1894, see "Die Königreiche Kroatien und Slavonien auf der Milleniums—Landesausstellung * * * in Budapest, 1896," page 33.

neither of them as many as 1500), by 1907 each of the eight counties which compose the country sent over a thousand emigrants and Agram county over 5000, the total rising from 2900 in 1899 to 22,800 in 1907. We see too that the emigrants were mainly young men and most of them engaged in agriculture.

The general census figures, as to occupation and land and size of land holdings, some of which are given in the same Appendix, also throw light on the economic causes of the emigration movement. We see for instance that 82 per cent of the total population of the country depend on agriculture, taking this to include forestry and stockraising, that 87 per cent of those engaged in agriculture are either members of Zadrugas, or individual owners and members of their families, and that almost all the land is held in small or dwarf holdings; indeed, out of over 400,000 properties only 930 (or 2 in a thousand) are of medium size and only 209 are large.

Not only is the land thus subdivided, but the proportion of tillable land is often small; much is in so-called pasture and this is often little more than sheer stony waste land.

A minor cause of trouble in Croatia seems to be, as among the Slovaks and in Galicia, the credit situation. When money has to be borrowed, as it often must be, it is to be had only at usurious rates. The Croatian does not, like the Galician and the Slovak, complain of Jews, who seem to play no rôle in the country; but capital is scarce, and what is available is mainly invested in so-called savings banks, which are really companies for conducting a loan business, and are said to pay enormous dividends to the stockholders. Industrial enterprise, which cannot offer such large returns, is unable to compete, and starves for want of capital. *Loans and usury*

According to an Agram informant the situation is as follows. A peasant must pay 12 per cent for a loan, though a merchant may borrow at 6 per cent. He might get better terms from the local branch of the Mortgage Bank at Budapest, but this makes no loan under about $200, and a peasant is apt to want about $40—for instance, on the occasion of the break-up of a Zadruga, when he must fit himself out for farming his share independently.

Let us suppose, then, a man in this situation wanting $40. He secures a loan from the savings bank on his note, for which he must get two or three endorsements. To each person who obliges him in this way he gives a trifle, if only a glass of wine; this might cost $2.40. Then a discount of $1.80 for the next quarter is deducted at once, so that he starts with $35.80 in hand. At the end of three months he must pay interest, and repay at least 10 per cent of the capital. If the loan was made in the autumn, no money has come in at the end of the three months, and he must secure a new loan, also bearing interest. The process may need to be repeated again at the next quarter. Not till autumn is there any money coming in. The proverb is, "The peasant turns himself once in a year."

This sort of thing sends many to America, but for the journey they must borrow again, so that a man may well owe $200 by the time he arrives. Sometimes the money is advanced by an individual. One man borrowed $40 of an old woman who asked $60 back at the end of three months! She kept her money in a stocking, and it was a mark of confidence that she admitted that she had it, still more that she loaned it. To her there was nothing excessive in the rate that she wanted. It was indeed a *pretium affectionis*. Now Raffeisen banks are coming into being, a very important step forward.

Such is the account of the credit situation in Croatia, given me by an Agram gentleman.

Effects of emigration

Croatian emigration is, in the main points, similar to the Galician and Slovak emigration previously described. The situation of the peasants, the going abroad to earn money, the return of a considerable number (how large

BISHOP STROSSMAYER
The Croatian patriot, saint and patron of art and letters.

a part no one knows), the misfit of the returned emigrant—all of these things recur here.

The man who has been to America, we were told, is easily recognized. "You can tell him as far off as you can see him." He carries himself more independently, he works better, he is more interested in education, but he is unfitted for the old life. One man, for instance, went out a mere laborer and returned a skilled workman, but he was not content to stay. Another story was of a man who was seized with such an uncontrollable longing for America that he got up in the night and ran away, leaving wife and children.

Too many, however, return worn out, though it may be with some money. In America they worked harder than at home, and lived little or no better. They spent themselves to the utmost under the stimulus of the "boss," the climate, and most of all of their own ambition. A Croatian gentleman said to me, sadly, "The Americans know how to save themselves, but our men are not so clever."

The Croatians, too, seem to make much the same report about America that we heard elsewhere. A curious story is, however, quite widely rife in Croatia, and the returned emigrant seems to be responsible for it. It is reported, namely, that in America it is allowable to marry experimentally for a term of years (generally set, I think, at five). Whether this is a *bona fide* impression made by American divorces, or whether it is a mere traveler's tale, or possibly a convenient cover for American experiences of their own, I cannot say.

In Croatia, too, the money that flows in from emigrants is very considerable. I was informed from a most reliable source that in the year 1903 America sent probably $10,000,000 to Croatia-Slavonia. The post office alone transmitted $4,600,000. It is, however, only fair to notice that a part of this inflow is balanced by an outgo; that a considerable part, in fact, goes to repay loans contracted to cover the expense of emigration. Since

Remittances and money drain

Croatian emigrants go mainly to seek temporary employment, not to settle, they carry little capital with them; nevertheless, the actual drain is considerable. In 1905, for instance, according to our immigration reports, 1221 Croatian and Slovenian immigrants brought $50 or more each into the country, or $61,000 at least. If we allow only $15 apiece for thé 31,710 others who brought under $50, it makes $475,650 more, or together well over half a million dollars of cash in hand on entering the country, for this group alone. If to this we add about $50 as expense of journey and outfit for each of the 35,104 arrivals, we get $175,520 more, or over $700,000 in all.

Balance in favor of Europe This outflow of money from Europe through emigration is a fact which is generally ignored by American and exaggerated by European writers, but it is obvious that the balance of this trade is in favor of Europe; that through the emigrants more wealth flows in than they withdraw.

This influx of money naturally makes itself felt. Tile replaces thatch, taxes and debts are paid, field is added to field, better tools and more cattle are bought, phylloxera-smitten vineyards are replaced with immune vine stocks, churches are built and adorned. It is pleasing, too, to hear of cripples supported by contributions from fellow-villagers at work in America. After the riots in Agram some years ago, some of the political prisoners also received aid from the same source.

Standards of peasant life raised Another result is that people live better. The price of poultry has risen because the peasants now eat it themselves. They will pay $8.00 or $10 for a suit of "European clothes." Sewing machines seem to be not uncommon, and are widely advertised. Town improvements are also undertaken. I will instance a specific case. Here in a parish of 4000 souls, $9500 was received in one year from America, besides $100 or so sent to the church. A good town water supply had been put in, not piped to the houses indeed but available at public

hydrants; street lamps had been put up, and a quite imposing building for a savings bank was in process of
erection.

Except to employers the movement is financially a
godsend. Wages rise, and so does the price of land.
The rise in land values is in fact often excessive. In
some parts of Lika-Krbava, for instance, the soil is poor
and stony, but there is no other channel for investment,
and the man who has acquired a little money must and
will buy land. Competition, together with speculation,
has run prices up so that sometimes where arable land
formerly cost $60 to $80 a yoke it now costs up to $400,
and meadow land is dearer still.

In this county a very interesting official inquiry was
made as to the effects of emigration. The civil population was 208,000. In 1902, 5,619 went to America and
436 returned. It must be remembered that this represents an early phase of the movement, and that few
would be coming back so soon. In 1903 it was estimated
that 8000 were in America. In that year 2795 borrowed
money with which to go, and 4317 sent money home,
amounting, so far as known, to about $560,860, or not
quite $130 from each sender on an average. With this
money 4116 homes were bettered—by paying debts,
buying more land or making improvements. Seven
homes were reported as impoverished, and twenty-seven
as ruined (abandoned?).

Wages and land values have risen

Effects of emigration in Lika-Krbava County

It is pleasant to be able to clothe these dry bones of
statistics with the flesh and blood of Miss Gazvoda's
true story.

NOTES FROM MY VILLAGE
By a Croatian School Teacher

Today they are telling in the village that fifteen are going
tomorrow to Fiume by the early train—men, women and young
girls on their way to America. They were all blessed by the
priest after mass. The prayer for their happiness away from
home was very moving. All who knelt before the altar were
pale, struggling against the tears in eyes which may never see

this church again. On this consecrated spot they took leave of
the fatherland, our dear Croatia, who cannot feed her children
because she is not free nor the mistress of her own money. She
must let them go among strangers in order that those who remain may live, they and their children and their old people.
And the old people die in peace because they have hope; the
little ones shall fare better than ever they have done.

This morning all went early to confession. With God they
go safer on their long journey. Toward evening they can be
seen hurrying from house to house taking leave of those that
they love. Who can say that there will ever be another meeting for them? It is very late before they have finished these
visits and the family waits for them with impatience. With
impatience, how else when this evening or rather the few hours
still left are so short? This is the last supper at home. There
is no going to bed, for at three they must start for the station
as the train goes at four. It is so sad to hear them driving
through the village singing a song which expresses all the feelings
of their sore hearts.

The saddest moment of all is the departure. The train has
come, they must get on board. How many tears and sobs and
kisses in our little forest and rock-bound station. Friends go
with them to Fiume—all but the children and the old folks who
stay in the village alone.

In Fiume the girls buy what they need for the journey and a
little gold crucifix. That must be bought in the fatherland.
So must rings, too. Often the parents buy the betrothal rings
for their sons and daughters who marry in America and send
them to them. Faith and love come from the homeland.

Finally at the ship good byes must be said, the last. One
little girl whose older sister was going by train to Vienna, had
gone with her to Fiume. But when the train was about to go
the little one flung herself down upon the ground in her distress
and shrieked terribly. Everyone tried to pacify her but she
pressed her little hands over her eyes to hide the engine from
her sight, and answered, "It is easy for you to talk, but this
hateful engine is robbing me of my sweet sister." She was quite
ill with suffering and they had much ado to get her away. But
it is hardest for the mothers who let their daughters or their
sons go.

Very late, after midnight, people come home—alone. Now
come quiet tears and prayers that God may grant the travelers
a safe arrival. With what anxiety and joy do they wait for
the news from the agent that their dear ones have reached New
York in safety. There relatives are already expecting them and

the journey can be peacefully continued in their company. Our people generally go to Michigan. In one town there are so many that our people call it "New Lipa."

The money for the journey always comes from relatives or friends to whom all is honestly repaid later. The young fellows try to save the money to bring over a young girl. When she comes to America—generally she does not know her suitor—she is married. If she is unwilling, not finding him to her liking, she must pay back the money, but it very often happens that another lad pays it for her and takes her for his wife instead.

Many girls are very fortunate in America. For instance this very day a family is coming home. The wife was poor and ill-favored. Relatives sent her money for the journey to America and there she married a poor and very humble sort of man. By work and saving they have got together $6,000 in thirteen years. They have six children and with them are now returning. In those days she was poor, ridiculed, alone; now she is well-to-do, respected, the mother of a family. The women are full of curiosity about her. At noon they were all in the street in hopes of seeing her but in vain. She and her family are staying in Fiume and will come to-night, perhaps. My housekeeper is her godmother and so awaits her happy godchild with much pleasure for she is to offer her, for purchase, a large meadow which once belonged to the parents of her godchild, but which they were obliged to sell. I think that would be a very pleasant feeling, to be able to buy back again a piece of land lost in one's father's time, and to let the happy grandchildren jump and play about where once the poor grandfather worked and whence misfortune drove him away to die.

My housekeeper, who is already sixty-five, cannot tell without crying how it used to be here in the good old days. Thirty-four years ago there was no railroad. Our splendid highway, the "Lujziane," even then a century old, saw such activity as will never return. All travel was by this road and our people were happy because they always had the opportunity to work and to live in peace. In one house they kept ten servants, men and maids. Day and night the teams with their heavy loads were on the highway. Labor was very cheap, a man got about thirteen cents and a woman six cents a day. To be sure they had good food besides, bread, meat and wine as much as they wanted, and the children of the women servants were fed, too. The wages were low as I have said, yet the people were contented. Some got very rich, but the poor, too, were well provided for.

Twenty years ago two men went to America from here, the first from our place to go. Now nearly half the village is in

America.   It is hard to till the fields for there are no workers to be had.   Whoever has strength and youth is at work in America. At home are only the old men and women and the young wives with their children.   Every wife has much to do for herself. Only poor girls work in the fields.   "And they must be paid a crown (twenty cents) a day," sighs my housekeeper and thinks of the better days of old.

The women help one another and live from day to day, dragging along waiting for letters and money.   The money generally comes in autumn.   Everything is bought on credit through the year; the dealer waits, for he knows that in the autumn it will all be paid.   If not then, danger threatens the little house or at least the cow in the stall.

At Christmas and Easter, too, and at mid-summer presents of a few dollars come to the fortunate ones.   Others who have a hard lot wait months and years and never receive anything. The husband forgets his wife, the son his father and mother, the brother his sisters and brothers.   The new world with new enjoyments silences his conscience and hardens his heart.   Oh, how bitterly those at home feel this!   They not only suffer; they are ashamed that they have been forgotten.

One often sees jolly fellows at a dance and in gay company which they did not enjoy at home.   That tempts them and so one and another is lost.   If a relative is near it is not so danger-ous, for the scamp is under some control and one hopes he will become reasonable.   But when one who is quite alone gives himself up to the joys of the world then it goes hard.   Thank God such cases are very rare with us.   If one goes astray he amends even after years and is not lost.

Near me lives a woman with her husband and the wife of her younger son who came home last year.   Her elder son is still in America.   He went twelve or thirteen years ago, leaving at home his wife and two children, a boy and girl.   His tempera-ment was gay and weak.   He soon forgot father and mother, wife and children.   He did not write and sent nothing for the support of his family.   His poor young wife took it much to heart and died of a decline.   His mother had her photographed as she lay on her bier and sent the picture to her hard-hearted son.   He sent it back.   His own mother cursed him, but he did not change.

The little girl was already eight and the son nine when he sent a letter—the children were to come to him.   He sent the money, too.   The children went accompanied by the sister of his dead wife.   When they arrived he fell in love with her and married her.   Now the poor children have their aunt for their

CROATIAN SCENES

1. Fetching water; the white linen costume and the wattled fence are characteristic. 2. In a coast village; more stones than vegetation. 3, and 4. Spring ploughing.

stepmother and are very well off. The man has changed greatly
and is very watchful of his son, perhaps for fear that he might
become as he himself once was. The soul of the dead wife, I
think, is satisfied.

Another woman was also very unhappy. Her husband left
her with six children and went to America. At first he sent news
of himself, but after a while he quite forgot his dear ones. A
relative of his wife's, who was also in America, had got him in
her net and led him astray. For years the wife and children
starved. Once she tried to take her life but was saved. The
eldest daughter, a young girl as pretty as a picture, wrote con-
tinually to her father and brought it about that he sent her
money for the journey. She set forth with the firmest intention
of saving him from his danger and restoring him to her mother.
And so it was. The man quite reformed. Today his wife and
all his children are already with him. It goes well with them.
All that his poor wife suffered is forgotten. The daughter has
made a happy marriage and is living contentedly. Last year
I saw a big photograph of a wedding. The whole family are in
the picture and I was amazed to see how stout the poor wife had
grown and how happy she looked.

Once I was traveling third class on the train from Fiume
because I like to hear the talk of the common people. One
learns more in such a trip than in the best school. In the same
compartment with me was a woman, young but very sad. She
was from the village next ours, the place where the chair factory
is for which our women and girls make the cane seats by which
they earn their living. She had been in Fiume to sell something.
The empty basket stood by her. It was large and must have
been very heavy when it was full. In talking with me she gave
me a picture of her sad life.

She was very poor. Her father had long been dead. Her
mother was ailing and was very anxious about her daughter's
future. Then came a widower, no longer young, and tried to
persuade her that she ought to give him her daughter. But
the daughter could not make up her mind to it. "He did not
please me." But the mother said, "Take him, my child, and
we shall both be provided for." So she married him. Soon he
went to America. She was left alone with her little daughter,
for her mother died soon after. The child is now nine years old
and goes to school. But the father does nothing at all for his
family. More fortunate children often strike the poor little
girl when she is going home. Then she says to her mother,
"Mama, all the children have a father and nobody dares strike
them. Why haven't I a father?" Then the poor woman

weeps quietly. In America the husband leads a jolly life.
More than that, he borrows money from people and when they
want it back he says, "My wife will pay." And so people from
America keep coming to her with bills from her husband. I
tried to console her. Heaven knows whether she will ever be
happy.

What a joy the young husband in America feels when his
wife sends him a picture of their first baby. One wrote home,
"I can't write much this time for looking at my dear child as it
smiles at me from the picture." He is a locksmith and has been
in America a year. Two months ago his wife and baby safely
joined him there. She writes how hard it is for her to wear a
hat. None of the common people wear them here. But her
husband says "You may live with me for years but I shall not
go out with you unless you wear a hat." So the woman must
be fine. People require it there.

Many girls however take especial delight in the hat that they
are to wear in America. But photographs are the best proof to
what an extent dress is carried in America. One sees the most
beautiful hats and dresses on our women. "It has to be so.
It is the custom here," they write. But one must marvel at
how fine they are. And when they return they look so entirely
different. They know better how to behave and show that
they have learned something. All know English even if not
quite correctly. All Slavs, especially Croatians, have a great
talent for languages. Our peasants learn English very fast.
Years ago when the first letter came from America from the two
earliest emigrants, it was a hard matter to get it read, for as
neither of them could write someone else had written for them
but in English. The poor wife had to hunt the neighborhood
over until she found an official on a railroad who explained the
letter to her after a fashion. I have the story from my housekeeper and she tells how the poor wife who had waited months
for news moved heaven and earth to get the letter read. Now
there would be no difficulty. There are plenty in the village who
understand English. The children attend English schools while
they are in America and derive great benefit from it when they
are grown up.

The women who are left here alone almost always remain
faithful to their husbands. It is a rare case when now and then
one forgets herself. But if it does occur the men show far more
feeling and self-control than one might expect. A common
peasant in such circumstances has often more strength and
insight than an intelligent man from the better classes.

In one neighborhood a man married and went soon after to

America. His young wife remained with his parents. His un-married brother also made one of the household. Suddenly a misfortune. She bore him a child. The parents drove her from the house and wrote her husband how matters stood. She went to Fiume as a nurse and supported herself and her child. The husband not unnaturally was furious and wrote her that she need not expect him to return to her. But with time he forgave her all in the goodness of his heart and wrote for her to come to him. She answered, "I cannot leave my child." Then he wrote again, "Come and bring the child with you," and he at once sent her the tickets both for herself and for the child.

She made the journey in dread. "He will kill me"; that was her only thought. But when he met her she could not be-lieve her eyes. He first took the baby into his arms and then embraced her. They are living peacefully together. All is forgotten. He loves the child dearly, for they have none of their own. Always when he comes from the mine the poor child is waiting for him like an angel. How much magnanimity this simple peasant has. But the people here are very religious and follow the words of Christ, "Judge not."

What especially pleases them is the respect in which workers are held in America. They are better cared for, too, mentally. They have three or four Croatian papers, they have organizations and learn much that they bring home later. They have their priests and churches, but as yet only two Croatian schools. All is founded by the contributions of workingmen. They send a great deal home to the churches, too; they are supporting a poor man, and in 1903, when there were the disturbances in Croatia about the Hungarian flag and the Hungarian inscrip-tions on the railroad stations, our brothers in America sacrificed a great deal for the support of the families of those under arrest. They love Croatia dearly. Each one longs for home and wants to die here. We Slavs are so soft-natured. Homesickness is our disease. On account of it many Croatians cannot hold out and return home too soon.

The talk is all of America. Our newspapers write so much what a bad thing it is for whole families to go there as they do. But it is no use. People must eat. The stones are hard. There is too little land. The government does nothing for the good of the people. There are no factories, there is no building, no mining. So how can people live and pay taxes? And if the taxes are not paid the cow is taken from the stall, the pillows from under the head.

In Slavonia there is no need of emigration, for there the land is fertile and people can make a good living. But here in the mountain district and on the coast, in Lika, too, and in Dalmatia, people have to go to America.

Only American capital could lessen the stream of emigration. Croatia is a beautiful country. Our mountains doubtless hold great treasures, but we lack the money with which to seek them. Only American capital could bring them to light. We have the beautiful sea, the lovely Plitvica lakes and the fine district about Agram, but we cannot make use of these beauties as a rich and free people could do. We have a sufficient income, but as a public man has said, "Our pockets are in the Hungarian trousers." The Hungarians have our money and give us just enough to keep us alive. Only a free and independent nation can progress. We are like dead capital.

But we hope for our national resurrection. So many have already died in this hope. It is our ideal, our dearest one. For this Zriny and Frankopany died. The innocent blood of our best sons must at last bring us good fortune.

ON THE COAST OF THE ADRIATIC

1. Zengg, once a resort of pirates. Note the Castle of Uskoks on height to the left, and the row of warehouses built to protect shipping from the Bora, and the karst character of the country. 2. View near Ragusa.

CHAPTER X

THE ADRIATIC COAST OF AUSTRIA-HUNGARY

The very names that belong to all this region—Istria, The coast and islands Dalmatia, Montenegro, Ragusa, Cattaro and the rest— are like "magic casements opening on the foam," and it is hard to settle down to the prosaic facts of emigration. At first sight the country does not seem Slavic. Italy with her architecture and her contagious grace of life, and Turkey, with costumes and manners of the near East, overlay to the eyes the Slavic substance.

We naturally approach things on their most familiar side, and just as we are apt to know only a Germanized form of Slavic names—Agram for Zagráb, Lemberg for Lwów—so in this region it is the Italian forms of the names that are familiar. We say Fiume, not Rjeka; Ragusa, not Dubrovnik; Montenegro, not Črnagora.

But this nomenclature, the Venetian aspect of the cities, and the Italian spoken in the hotels are misleading. The Italian element is indeed prevalent in restricted parts of Goricia-Gradisca and of Istria, in Fiume, and especially in and about Trieste; but for the rest, the population of the whole Adriatic coast of Austria and Hungary is essentially Servo-Croatian. In Dalmatia, which the tourist is prone to regard as a second and more pictur-esque Italy, over 97 per cent of the people speak Croatian, or Servian, which is the same language written with a different alphabet.

This shore, from above Nabresina at the head of the Gulf of Trieste, to a point beyond the lovely Bocche di Cattaro or about as far south as Rome, stretches in an air line nearly 400 miles. Apart from the peninsula of Istria, we are dealing with a narrow strip of land, broken by fiords and bays, fringed with islands, large and small, and backed by a singularly rugged limestone range, rich in noble contours and violet shadows. It is a country very fertile where soil is to be had, but as bare as a pile of broken stone where the Bora (the north wind) sweeps it, or the salt spray driven over from the sea blights it, or where the soil has been washed away by the rain. The mountains have been robbed of their forests to make piles on which to build the palaces of Venice, to supply masts for her fleets, or for more prosaic uses since. Consequently they stand largely denuded not only of vegetation but of earth, with naked limestone flanks and peaks, and the streams are likely to be roaring torrents after a rain and dry at other times.

The whole shore is richer in charm than in means of livelihood, and of late is becoming a favorite resort for tourists and health-seekers. Abbazia, frequented the whole year round, is the best-known watering place as yet, but others are deservedly coming into prominence. Its magnificent classic ruins, notable among which are the great palace of Diocletian at Spalato and the amphi-theatre at Pola; its picturesque Italianate cities, of which Ragusa, with its brilliant political and literary history, is easily first; the wonderful fiord-like beauty of the Bocche di Cattaro, with the snows of Lovčen, rosy in the sunset, inviting to an exploration of Monte-negro; the people thronging its streets and by-ways in various and always picturesque dress in which Slavic and Oriental elements are curiously intermingled,*—all these make a whole in which each island, each town, each valley has its own special note.

The people All along the shore and the islands the peasants are at the same time fishermen and bold and skilful sailors.

---

* The costume I will not attempt to describe but will refer the reader to the many books of Dalmatian travel, or to Mr. Ernest Peixotto's charmingly illustrated "Impressions of Dalmatia" in *Scribner's Magazine* for July, 1906, or the photographs and text of an article "Where East meets West: Visit to picturesque Dalmatia, Montenegro, and Bosnia," by M. C. Coffin in the *National Geographic Magazine* for May, 1908.

In Istrea and Dalmatia

1. In Ragusa. A "Greek" woman, apparently afraid of the evil eye of the camera.
2 and 4. Dalmatian women. 3. Women of Castel Muschio on the island of Veplia, off Fiume,
carrying water in brass vessels on their heads from a spring far below the town. 5 and 6. Waiting to see the train pass. Dress of the Canale valley.

Unlike most Slavs, they are also capable traders, a fact that suggests how much environment and example have to do with what we consider national traits. Not only does their land produce articles admirably adapted for export—fish, good wine, olive oil, fruit, including figs and almonds, and of late years the well-known "Dalmatian insect powder," made from certain camomile-like flowers—but for centuries the coast was under the rule of Venice, the queen of Eastern commerce, and these Slavic coast folk proved apt pupils.

Physically the Dalmatian is a splendid type. Ethnologists note with some surprise the exceptional height of the Dalmatians, and still more that of their neighbors of Bosnia-Herzegovina. They are among the tallest men of Europe, and not only tall but sturdy and markedly fine in their carriage. They are darker than the more northern Slavs but very often the honest grey-blue eyes of the Slav look out of the swarthy or olive face of the Southerner. Greek blood, too, seems to have left its traces.

Physical traits

I wish that I could show the picture of an old man with whom I talked near Ragusa, but he refused to let me photograph him. This fear of a camera I met with more than once here, and here alone, and I wondered if it could be a trace of the eastern superstition of the evil eye. He was in full array—red Dalmatian cap, baggy Turkish trousers of blue, a series of embroidered zouave jackets, one over the other, and a wide girdle stuck full of various articles among which I distinguished only a horn knife-handle and a richly wrought silver sheath. His long pipe he held in his fingers.

He was a fine old fellow, grey-haired, erect and friendly, speaking English remarkably well—better, in fact, than he understood it. He had been in America for six years, he told me, thirty-five years ago. He went as a sailor to New York, then again by ship to San Francisco, where he worked at gold mining. He made $60 to $70 a month, working for a big company.

Characteristics of Dalmatian emigration

Such a people as the Dalmatians, so situated, would naturally be mobile, but Dalmatian emigration, which we may take as the type for this region, has a quite different character from that of any other Slavic emigration movement. It has been, as it were, a long-continued dripping of individuals, not a mass movement growing as a snowball does, like that among the Slovaks and Croatians, nor a family migration, like that of the Bohemians. The men go alone, often making the journey as sailors, and simply leaving their ship in port,—a fact which in the past has doubtless brought many into America unregistered, in so far vitiating our statistics. One local informant after another stated with great emphasis that the Dalmatian does not go "like other emigrants" at random,* but to a particular place and friend, and with a very clear idea of what he is about.

Causes of emigration general and special

There is ground enough for emigration in the general situation of a rapidly growing population with very little available soil, so that the most inaccessible spots are terraced and cultivated, and a teaspoonful of earth in a hollow is made to grow something.† But besides this general situation, special causes have been at work. First we may put the decline of the old commerce, dependent on sails, and, it must be said, on piracy. On the shores of the Bocche one sees dead towns of dream-like streets lined with deserted villas, and at Zeng the proud row of warehouses built to shield the harbor from the Bora, but now out of all proportion to the needs of trade, tells the same story of the victory of steam over sails as do the decaying merchant homes of Salem or Newburyport in New England.

A later cause of emigration was a treaty made in 1890, which for the fifteen years that it was in force depressed the price of Dalmatian wine by exposing it to Italian competi-

* For reasons for the belief that Slavic emigrants in general also emigrate not at random, but planning to join friends, see above, page 53, and Appendix IV, page 433.
† Compare for Dalmatian conditions Table 3, page 48.

tion and did much to make life impossible to the wine-grower, already hard hit by the phylloxera.   Other com-plaints are of a disease of the insect-powder plants, of failure of fisheries, and of severe winters that have done much damage.   The evil results of an extreme subdivision of land are also felt.   A yoke, or less than an acre and a half, is said to be the average holding of a small peasant. This would be insufficient if it were not that the soil is so fruitful.   I was told that a yoke of good vineyard would produce seventy hectolitres of wine, enough to support a family.   In other places one is told that a family can live from the yield of one olive tree!

It is hard to say when the Dalmatians began to go to America; it was certainly early.   One is said to have arrived in 1700 by way of India, and apparently a good many came to look for gold in California after 1849. The close in 1856 of the Crimean War, in which many Dalmatians served on shipboard, seems to have given another impulse. *Beginnings of emigration to America*

As to numbers, it is also hard to get any definite in-formation until 1899, when our immigration tables began to report as one class Dalmatians, Bosnians and Herze-govinians.   The number of these coming in 1907 was over 7,000, of whom most were probably Dalmatians. This was, however, the high tide mark up to date.   For the official American figures see the following table: *Numbers of emigrants*

TABLE 12.—IMMIGRATION, 1899–1909

Year	Dalmatians, Bosnians and Herzegovinians	Bulgarians, Servians and Montenegrins
1899	367	94
1900	675	204
1901	732	611
1902	1004	1,291
1903	1736	6,479
1904	2036	4,577
1905	2639	5,823
1906	4568	11,548
1907	7393	27,174
1908	3747	18,246
1909	1888	6,214

In 1905 a Ragusa steamship agent, then the only authorized agent for all Dalmatia, stated that three or four thousand were going yearly, three-quarters to New York and one-quarter to the Far West; of the latter, nine out of ten were going to California, the others to the Dakotas; but this is a very imperfect account of their final destinations.

Shiftings of population

As is so often the case, emigration to America is here also but one in a series of adjustments of population. The exodus to America creates a scarcity of labor which is in turn met by an influx from places that are still worse off economically. For instance I was told that the island of Lissa, where 1700 out of a population of 9914 had emigrated, drew several hundreds of workers from the mainland to carry on its agriculture, and that if the movement continued it would be felt as a great hardship. Similarly Ragusa Vecchia, and other places draw in harvest hands from Montenegro.

Remittances

As to remittances, it was impossible for me to get data of any value, though what was told me indicated that the Dalmatians dealt with larger sums than most Slavs, which agrees with their reputation for greater aptitude for commerce.

Morals and education

When the men are away, the women attend to the tillage, whatever it is, and they have the reputation of being excellent vine-dressers. They are said to have a higher standard of morality than the women further inland. In some places it is the custom that a woman shall go to no dance or festivity while her husband is on the sea; but when he is in port she knows that he is alive and probably having his share of amusement, and she goes with the rest. In general the coast population are more alert, more cultivated by contact with men and affairs than are the people of the interior.

Illiteracy

They are, however, very illiterate, especially the women. The census of 1900 showed that among the Servo-Croatians of Austria (that is, practically, the Dalmatians and Istrians), nearly 70 per cent of the men between

SOWING IN MONTENEGRO

Note the house and stall (?) in the background, the small size of the oxen, the round Dalmatian cap and Montenegrin costume of the man.

thirty and fifty years of age were illiterate, and nearly 90 per cent of the women of the same age. Even among young men between ten and twenty, over half could neither read nor write.

This excessive illiteracy is in curious contrast with the exceptionally shrewd, intelligent character of the Dalmatians. In the United States they take not only to the various kinds of work for which their lives as fishermen and sailors have especially fitted them, but to business in various lines. They have apparently especial success in managing restaurants. Illiteracy is not always as great a handicap as one would suppose, even in business. Not long ago in Cleveland I met a gentleman from one of our southwestern states who had come north to interest investors in a mining enterprise. He was a fine-looking man with the speech, bearing and address of a quiet but prosperous American. I learned that he came in 1849 from Dalmatia on his uncle's ship, which he left to look for gold during the California excitement of that time. His business acquaintances, I am told, wonder why he always leaves them to pick out the particular paper that is wanted from his pile of assay reports and other documents. The reason is that he cannot read, nor write anything but his own name. *Dalmatians good business men*

If the first generation in America overcomes its deficiencies thus, the second seems to profit to the full by American advantages. An informant in Galveston, telling me of a Dalmatian family said, "The son is an American, pure and simple; there is no evidence of a foreigner about him." Of another Dalmatian of the second generation he said, "He is a great ball player, and a thorough American in spirit. I think they are more readily digested than other people. They are strong and manly, have good morals, make money. They drink a good deal, but in ten years I have known only one drunkard. As an example of how they get on, take the family of Michael S. I doubt if he could read or write. The eldest son, Stephen, is physically one of the most mag- *Development in America*

nificent looking fellows in town.   He holds a responsible
position in a shipping agency.   The next son is a fine
stenographer, and is working in a wholesale commission
store.   The third, William, has a fruit business of his
own.   John and Michael junior are both stenographers.
One son left the parochial school for the public school
when he had made his first communion.   He went from
the sixth grade parochial to the fifth grade public, but
was then put in the seventh."

I have taken Dalmatian emigration as the type for
this region, and of this and the adjoining coast of Croatia
no more need be said here.

Istria

The Croatian-speaking part of Istria which alone concerns us is largely mountainous and extremely poor.
The emigration thence is numerically slight and quite
recent, and is apparently directly due to the opening of
the Cunard route from Fiume to New York.   It began to
be of some importance in 1903, and I was told that
Fiume agents incite it.   There are no available data.

Bosnia-Her-
zegovina

From Bosnia-Herzegovina, the province lying back of
Dalmatia, which after having been "administered" by
Austria-Hungary since the decision of the treaty of
Berlin to that effect in 1878 was so unceremoniously
"annexed" in the autumn of 1908, there is also some
emigration, though our data do not enable us to dis-
entangle it from that from Dalmatia.   In any case it
is numerically unimportant, and gives little excuse for
describing this fascinating country nearly half of whose
Servo-Croatian population are, by a curious turn of
history, Mohammedan, though monogamous by binding
custom.*

* To those interested I heartily recommend A. J. Evans'
"Through Bosnia and Herzegovina on Foot During the Insurrection, August and September, 1875."   The book includes a
delightful historical account of Ragusa, and descriptions of bits
of Croatia.
    A descriptive article by myself "A Week in Hercegovina and
Bosnia," may be found in the Bryn Mawr Alumnae Quarterly
of October, 1908, and in the Wellesley College Magazine of May,
1909.

Montenegro, Servia and Bulgaria lie outside the limits
of my study of Slavic immigration from Austria-Hungary,* but these countries have been rapidly gaining in
importance as sources of emigration, their contingent
rising to over 27,000 in 1907, and maintaining itself
at over 6000 even in the lean year 1909.† Unfortunately
our data give no hint of what proportion came from each
country.   In the case of Servia and Montenegro it is
not important to distinguish them from one another,
Montenegrins being also Servians in blood and speech,
and divided only politically from the kingdom of Servia.
Bulgarians, however, are an entirely distinct group,
Slavic in speech and affiliations, but with an unknown
element of the blood of the old Bulgars, a people of
Asiatic stock, with a speech akin to the Finnic and Magyar.‡

Montenegro I visited in 1905, but there seemed little
to learn as to emigration.   A Dalmatian emigration
agent told us indeed that as many as 2000 emigrated
yearly from this little principality of not much over
200,000 population,§ but that they go wholly to Alaska.
In Douglas, Alaska, a Servian paper is or was published,
a copy of which was shown us, containing a long
poem in which the Eagle and the Vila (the powerful
mountain goddess or fairy of Servian folk-lore) discoursed
of the destiny of the poor emigrants.   The eagle told how
they had suffered on the vessel, how a storm had arisen
and how the captain was panic-stricken till the emigrants
advised him to pray to Saint Nicholas, the patron of
voyagers, which he did, after which all was well.   I have
never observed just this relation between steerage passengers and captain, but I have seen the design for a statue to

* Other Slavic emigration districts which also lie outside this
study, as already mentioned, are Russian and German Poland
and Russia itself.   For some account of Russian immigration,
and some further data as to Bulgarian and Servian immigrants
see Chapter XIII.
† The figures are given above in Table 12, page 195.
‡ Cf. Ripley: "Races of Europe," Vol. I, page 421.
§ Population in 1900, 227, 841.

Saint Nicholas, to be erected by grateful returned emigrants in a Croatian village.

Montene-
grin emigra-
tion

We were told frequently of the then recent rejection at Ellis Island of some hundred or more Montenegrins. These men had borrowed the money for their tickets, and their forced return was a serious matter for them and theirs. For some time after this the Montenegrin government would grant no more passes; later, the central authorities issued passes, but lower officials were forbidden to do so. I judge, however, that passports are not practically a necessity, whether legally required or not. In 1904, only 54 passports were issued to America and South America, which certainly could not cover the number of those emigrating, but it was not easy to get further information. As an official in a neighboring Austrian town said to us, "Small states love secrets."

In Cetinje, the capital, we met the very usual evidence of interest in emigration to America which is shown by inquiries how to get there, this time inquiries from a tall soldier on sentinel duty; and a beautiful girl, with the rare, stately beauty of the Montenegrin women, walking home with her knitting through the early twilight to her home on the mountains, an hour away, told us that her brother was in New York.

The Montenegrin men do not seem to have a first-class reputation, in neighboring Dalmatia, as workers, but were said to find employment in Cattaro, the Dalmatian port just below Montenegro, because they would work for less money than Dalmatians, who asked two crowns (forty cents) a day. It was said that only two Montenegrin women had emigrated, one of them to Buenos Ayres. This shows, if proof were necessary, in how early a phase this emigration movement still is (or was in 1905).

Montene-
grins in
America

With their small numbers it is not surprising that I have not been able to learn much about Montenegrins in America, but I did once run across traces of a party of 35 of them in a Colorado mining camp, where they had

A Home in Montenegro

No chimney, a roof of dry grass, walls of unmortared stones without windows.

left an unenviable reputation for a low grade of living.   I
saw the rough shacks provided for them in which they
had bunked promiscuously, and I remembered the low
huts of unmortared stone, with roofs of grass and filled
with smoke and children, which I had seen on their
naked mountain sides.   I thought of the still frequent
newspaper accounts of clashes of their bands with the
Turks on the frontier, and of how close they stand to the
heroic age in which the woman alone labors, since the
man must fight and hunt.   I recalled the Homeric
figure of the blind gusla player singing epic songs in the
square at Cetinje (I suppose the only instance in Europe
of a living epic), and I did not wonder that the Montenegrins cannot meet the standards at once of the tenth
and twentieth centuries.*

   * So recently as 1875 the following episode which reads like
some mediaeval romance is said to have actually taken place.
A young man, for an aggravated crime of seduction, was given
the following sentence by the whole village acting as a tribunal.
"Milutin, in order that he may do penance before God in his
deepest soul for the sin that he has committed, and that he may
wash his honor clean before the world must, in the next fight
that may occur with the Turks, charge them unarmed, and snatch
a weapon from a Turk living or dead, and thus prove that he can
appreciate honor and courage."   In the revolt of 1875 Milutin
fulfilled his strange sentence, which reconciled what was practically a sentence of death with the Slavic horror of bloodshed;
attacked a division of Turks without any weapon and met his
death.   See Krauss: "Sitte und Brauch der Süd-Slaven," page
212.

PART II

SLAVIC IMMIGRANTS IN THE UNITED STATES

Ubi bene, ibi Patria

CHAPTER XI

THE HISTORY OF SLAVIC IMMIGRATION
PREVIOUS TO 1880

The time has not yet come when the history of Slavic immigration can be written with any thoroughness. The preliminary work must be done by local antiquarian societies, state historical associations, writers of monographs, and mainly by members of the various nationalities themselves. Meanwhile, unless the work of collecting material is vigorously and systematically carried on, much will be irrevocably lost.* I submit for criticism a rough outline for such a history so far as I have made it out.

The reader of previous chapters will find in this account a recurrence to persons and events already mentioned in connection with the various separate cradles of emigration,—persons and events which now have to be considered together in chronological sequence as they affect America. To bring together the facts bearing on the same point, wherever they are taken up, reference may be made to the index, which takes the place of some of the cross references which would otherwise be required.

Accounts of Slavic immigration needed

---

* The intelligent and foresighted effort of the Wisconsin Historical Society, under the leadership of Mr. Thwaites, to gather material on foreign settlements in the State before the memory of their early stages is lost, is one that should be generally imitated. Unfortunately, the undertaking was not completed, but some of the material has been published and some of it is accessible in the society's library at Madison.

Among the immigrants themselves it is very naturally the two older groups, the Bohemians and the Poles, who have done most toward getting their history written, and it must be said that both have made creditable beginnings. For a partial bibliography, see Appendix XIV, page 456.

FIRST PERIOD: SPORADIC ARRIVALS
BEFORE 1850.

I distinguish three periods, that before 1850, that from 1850 to 1880, and that since 1880. The first is marked by no considerable influx, but by scattered individuals rescued from oblivion by some personal distinction or some touch of the picturesque.

Individual colonists

The list is headed by a Pole, John of Kolno, previously referred to, who is said to have commanded a vessel from Danzig and to have discovered the Labrador mainland sixteen years before Columbus crossed the Atlantic.* In the seventeenth century appear a number of sturdy worthies of Manhattan, including the two Bohemians already spoken of, Augustine Heřman, Lord of Bohemia Manor, and Bedřich Filip, who reached what was then New Amsterdam about 1658.† The founder of the distinguished family of the Zabriskies was one Albert Soborowski or Albrecht Zaborowsky, who in 1662 or earlier settled on the Hackensack River in New Jersey. His signature as interpreter is found affixed to an Indian contract of purchase in 1679. One descendant was Abraham O. Zabriskie, an eminent Chancellor of New Jersey, another was the Rev. George Gray, Dean of Harvard College. The family claim descent from the Polish King, John Sobieski, but Mr. Čapek argues in favor of their Bohemian origin.‡ These men and their descendants intermarried with well-known families like that of Gouverneur

---

* I find in the *American Pioneer*, I, pages 399–400, a communication signed Polonus, which states that in "Ulisses," by George Korn, Leyden (?) 1671, it is mentioned that John Scolnus (that is, John of Kolno, a small town in Masovia in Russian Poland), a Pole in the service of Christian, King of Denmark, discovered the continent of Labrador in the year 1476. See also Kruszka: "Historya Polska w Ameryce," I, page 52.

† See pages 68–69. Additional names will be found in Čapek's "Památky Českých Emigrantů v America."

‡ See Čapek, page 9; Kruszka: "Historya Polska w Ameryce," page 53; New York Gen. Rec., XXIII, pages 26, 33, 139–47 (quoted by Čapek). See also *Who's Who in America* for modern representatives of the name. For part of my information I am indebted to a living member of the family.

MANOR HOUSE OF FREDERICK PHILLIPS
Built in 1682—Now the city hall of Yonkers, N. Y.

FIRST HOUSE IN BETHLEHEM
The place of the Moravian Settlement in Pennsylvania, 1741.

Morris, the Bayards, Jays, Morrisons, Astors and others, and, like all the immigrants of the period before 1850, were quickly merged in the general population.

Whether Zaborowsky was a Pole or not, we are informed that as early as 1659 the Dutch colonists of Manhattan Island hired a Polish schoolmaster for the education of the youth of the community.* One hears of Polish settlers in Virginia,† of Polish indented servants in southern states,‡ and Proper speaks of a small colony of Polish Protestants who, during the early years of the eighteenth century, settled in New Jersey in the valleys of the Passaic and Raritan. §

Another historical waif is the story already referred to of the unnamed Dalmatian who is said to have gone to California some time before 1700 by way of India. Less shadowy is Sodowsky, who probably settled in what is now New York City in the reign of Queen Anne. He was an Indian trader, and his sons James and Jacob were frontiersmen in the days when white men were first beginning to get a foothold in Kentucky. With Hight and Harrod, James Sodowsky helped make the first "improvement" there, when in 1774 they planted corn at Harrod's Station. This settlement was broken up by Indians. Jacob is said to have made a canoe voyage, and to have reached New Orleans by the Cumberland, Ohio and Mississippi rivers, the first white man after the Spanish and French to descend those streams. It is a disputed point whether or not the name of Sandusky in Ohio is derived from a corruption of the name Sodowsky.‖

* Conway, J.: "Catholic Education in the United States," quoted by Kruszka, I, page 53.

† Kruszka, I, page 54.

‡ Ballagh, J. C.: "White Servitude in the Colony of Virginia." Johns Hopkins Univ. Studies in Historical and Political Science, XIII, page 40.

§ Proper, E. E.: "Colonial Immigration Laws," Columbia College Studies in History, Economics, and Public Law, XII, page 81.

‖ For a fairly full though not wholly consistent account of the Sodowsky pioneers see the *American Pioneer*, I, page 119, and II, page 325. Cf. also Roosevelt's "Winning of the West," I, page 164.

There were probably other more or less distinguished colonial families, both Bohemian and Polish, but information is scarce. William Paca, one of the signers of the Declaration of Independence, was of an old and numerous family which may have a Bohemian origin.*

Moravian brethrenOf wider interest was the coming of the thrice winnowed followers of Huss, the "Moravian Brethren."† (See above, page 69.) Exiled from Bohemia as "Bohemian Brethren," they were later drawn from their refuge in Moravia to Saxony, where Count Zinsendorf gave them protection at Herrnhut. Fired with missionary zeal, a small body of this sect landed in 1736 in Georgia, where Count Zinsendorf had procured a grant of land. Here Wesley attended the dedication of their church. By 1739 they had also a missionary colony in South Carolina, but this had to be abandoned, owing to quarrels between the English and Spanish in which the Moravians would not participate and could not remain neutral. In 1740 they were accordingly transported in Whitefield's shallop to Philadelphia. Again difficulties arose, but by 1741 they were established at Bethlehem in the Lehigh Valley. From this as a centre they have founded numerous settlements, and have increased until they now number over 16,000 in the United States.

While, as has been said, this movement has an inner connection with Bohemian history, it is hard to say how far it meant an actual infusion of Slavic blood. There may be more than names would indicate, as Bohemians would have been very likely to translate their names (as Schwarz for Černy) or to conform them to German usage.

Polish patriotsOur Revolution brought from Poland the national hero, Kosciuszko, together with Pulaski, who died at Savannah, and Niemcewicz, biographer of Washington, three men who with the Frenchman, Lafayette, seem

* Čapek, page 10.
† There is a large and detailed literature of the Moravian movement, much of which can be readily consulted. Cf. Gindely: "Geschichte der Böhmischen Brüder," besides the English authorities.

to lend a touch of exotic romance to the homespun of our own embattled farmers.*

The Polish insurrection of 1831 sent us a more considerable and more abiding contingent including, among many Poles, a Bohemian volunteer in their cause, Dr. Dignovity, later of San Antonio, Texas, where his family are said still to prosper.†

A pathetic echo of the fate of some of the Polish exiles is a reminiscence of an American lady who lived as a girl in Troy, New York, some time in the early thirties. She told me that she could never forget seeing there a group of Polish gentlemen, ragged, but obvious aristocrats, working at the cobbled paving of the street with bleeding fingers. A few days later one of these men looked at his torn hands, drew out a pistol and shot himself.

The little girl in Troy was not alone in her sense of pity for the exiles, as is manifested in the current literature of the day,‡ and more practically by the grant from Congress of land amounting to thirty-six sections. Two townships were surveyed for them near Rock River, Illinois.§

* Kruszka (I, page 54 ff.) gives an account of these heroes and of many lesser early Polish immigrants.

† Čapek, pages 98–105. Čapek speaks of various other immigrants of the early nineteenth century, one of them an associate of John Jacob Astor, besides those mentioned above, page 69.

‡ In the *New England Magazine* of January, 1835, is an interesting article (unsigned) on the Polish Exiles. It refers with romantic enthusiasm to Poland's wrongs, sufferings and glories, and especially reproaches America with her ungenerous treatment of those exiles who have come thither. "There have arrived in the United States about three hundred and fifty exiles of Poland; most of them non-commissioned officers, young men—many of them boys. Of these not even fifty have found employment suitable to their education and former habits; the majority of the rest have applied themselves to hard work, such as they could find, to earn their bitter bread and pass away the dreary days of their exile until their country shall again call them to her rescue; for they will not abandon the hope of one day seeing her free, and nobly refuse to take upon themselves any engagement which will prevent them from obeying her first signal." See also Kraitser: "The Poles in the United States of America," pages 193–6.

§ Donaldson: "The Public Domain," page 212.

Refugees of
1848

The revolutionary year 1848 also sent us, as has been said before, political refugees from both Bohemia and Poland, as well as those from France and Germany of whom Carl Schurz is the best known. Of this movement a well informed Bohemian writes:

"The first emigration from Bohemia to the United States took place in the few years succeeding the Revolution of 1848 in Austria, and the cause therefor was almost entirely political dissatisfaction due to the reaction toward despotism which followed that revolution. These first settlers were of the most intelligent class of people, and in very many cases of the wealthy classes. They established themselves in St. Louis, Missouri, and in Caledonia, Wisconsin (near Racine)."*

The gold
fever

The gold fever of 1849, as also mentioned in previous chapters, brought adventurers to California, some Bohemians probably, and some Dalmatians. Dalmatians, indeed, being sailors and fishermen, either from the coast or islands of the Adriatic, have come to us now and again from very early times.

Statistics of
immigration

In the period previous to 1850 our immigration statistics published by the Treasury Department are of little value to us. They do not mention Austria-Hungary as a country of origin (this first appears in the list in 1861) but Poland and "Russia except Poland" do appear. For the whole period of thirty years, however, only 495 "alien passengers" are recorded from Poland and 907 from Russia except Poland. Immigrants are not distinguished from transient visitors. The figures are doubtless very defective in any case, apart from the fact that German Poles are indistinguishable from Germans and that Bohemians have no rubric at all.

United
States Census of 1850

The census of 1850, to which we then turn to sum up the results of this period as well as it can be done, does not specify either Poland or Bohemia as countries of

* "The Bohemian Settlements in Kewaunee County." Anonymous MSS. in possession of State Historical Society of Wisconsin.

birth.* The Polish immigrants of this period, being
mainly from German Poland and Silesia, doubtless are
merged with the mass of the German born, who already
in 1850 numbered nearly 600,000. Natives of Austria, the
bulk of whom were certainly Bohemians, then numbered,
so far as registered, only 946. The largest groups
were at the doors, so to speak, in New York City (109),
New Orleans (129) and in California (87). Inland the
beginnings of the later large Bohemian colonies in Missouri, Illinois and Wisconsin were already apparent.

SECOND PERIOD: 1850–1880.
THE OLDER SLAVIC IMMIGRATION

During this period there was a considerable immigration of Bohemians and Poles, the latter still mainly from
the German provinces. Bohemian immigration began
to be of importance earlier than the Polish, and throughout this period continued to outnumber it.

The United States figures for arrivals of alien passengers for the period are:

TABLE 13.—ARRIVALS OF ALIEN PASSENGERS AND IMMIGRANTS, 1850–1880.†

YEAR	POLAND	RUSSIA EXCEPT POLAND	HUNGARY	OTHER AUSTRIA EXCEPT HUNGARY
1851–1860	1,164	457	..	..
1861–1870	2,027	2,532	484‡	5,914‡
1871–1880	12,970	38,838§	9,960	63,009
Total for the period	16,161	41,827	10,444	68,923

* For a discussion of census data as a basis for estimating the
numbers of Slavic inhabitants see Appendix XV, page 458.

† Alien passengers through 1867–68; immigrants since that
date.

‡ 192 passengers, the country of whose origin is stated only as
Austria-Hungary, are omitted from the figures for 1868.

§ After 1871 passengers from Finland are given apart from
those of Russia and are not here included. For immigration
figures previous to 1892 see "Arrivals of Alien Passengers and
Immigrants in the United States from 1820 to 1892." Treasury
Dept. Report, 1893.

The census results for the period are shown in brief in Chart I.

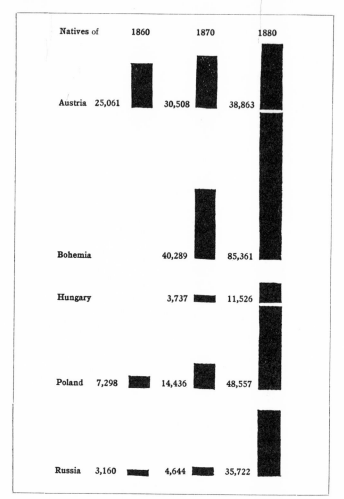

CHART I.—CENSUS DATA FOR NATIVES OF SPECIFIED COUNTRIES IN THE UNITED STATES, 1860, 1870 AND 1880.*

Since so far as our data indicate the Slavs in the United States in 1850 were a negligible quantity in

* For percentages and later figures see Table 15, page 244.

point of numbers, we may regard those registered in 1880 as added during this thirty year period. We find that in 1880 the census figures were as follows:

TABLE 14.—SLAVS IN THE UNITED STATES. CENSUS OF 1880.

Natives of Bohemia............ 85,361
   "   " Poland.............. 48,557 ⎫
   "   " Austria............. 38,663 ⎬ 122,942
   "   " Russia.............. 35,722 ⎭
   "   " Hungary............ 11,526
        Total.....................219,829

It is of course impossible to know just what these figures mean racially. The Bohemian group is evidently large, for besides the bulk of those from Bohemia a considerable number from Austria were probably Bohemians (or Moravians which amounts to the same thing). The 123,000 from Poland, Austria and Russia were probably mainly Poles and Jews, though in what proportions it is impossible to say.*

The character of the immigration of this period is essentially economic, in contrast with the earlier scattering and largely political movement. Artisans from villages and larger towns and peasants from their fields began to come in numbers, and to come as settlers, with their families and their little capital, making their way to regions that were then pioneer country. _An economic movement_

Though the bulk of those who came went West, like our own young men, to "grow up with the country," and for much the same reasons, there were of course still those (as there are today) who were influenced mainly by hopes of a freedom that they lacked at home, and various political events increased this element from time to time. The war between Austria and Prussia in 1866 sent us both Bohemians and Poles, and a further emigration of the latter was caused by the Polish insurrection of 1861 and by the course of events in Prussia _Political influence_

* It is rather interesting to note the remark in the census of 1860 (p. xxix): "Of Russians and Poles speaking the Sclavonian language, this migration has been inconsiderable in amount."

after the war with France and during the "Kultur Kampf" of the early seventies.

An instance of the spirit of the men who came for the sake of their political connections was told me by the son of a Bohemian pioneer in Texas. A friend from the old country visited the family in their new abode.

"Why, Valentine," he said, "at home your pigs are housed better than you are here."

"That is true," was the sturdy answer, "but I would rather live here in this log house than in a palace under the Austrian government."

It is not strange that the son of a man of this stamp finds himself a person of influence in his community—in this particular case, judge, editor, and member of the county school committee.

In the Chicago schools the teachers notice even today a difference among the Polish pupils between the children of men of intelligence, self-exiled for the sake of ideals, and of the Polish "man with the hoe." It must be said, however, that Polish children in general are considered good scholars.

A movement spontaneous and unorganized but grouped

In this second period appear for the first time groups of some size and cohesion. Apparently Slavs have never immigrated as organized bodies (unless we count the Moravians or some of the Russian sectaries); but though coming separately or in little bands of relatives or neighbors, they have a strong tendency to congregate in homogeneous groups, often made up of people drawn together not simply as members of the same national subdivision, but as neighbors in the same home village. This is the natural result at once of social affinities, intensified by isolation in a strange land among people with a strange tongue, and of the fact that the immigrant who finds a successful location draws over acquaintances from home to settle beside him. Yet while the bulk of our Slavic population are in larger or smaller colonies of their own, it will almost always be noticeable that representatives are to be found dispersed far and wide, the scouts, as it were, who may lead the way to new settlements.

The two chief early routes seem to have been from Bremen or Liverpool to either New York or New Orleans, though in the days of sailing vessels there was probably more variety than today in both the goal and the character of the journey. From New York the settlers went West, while from New Orleans, Galveston and the other Gulf ports they pushed inland, by the great waterway of the Mississippi, then in all the glory of its steamboating era. Many of those who entered at the Gulf ports, penetrating northward, ultimately found the same goals as their countrymen traveling overland from the east. Many, however, did not go so far but stopped as we shall see at Saint Louis or Cleveland or settled in Texas without journeying farther. *Early routes*

It seems best to consider separately the settlement first of the Bohemians, then of the Poles, and finally of other Slavic groups.

BOHEMIAN SETTLEMENT

The earliest colony of Bohemians was in St. Louis, where in 1854 they had already established a Catholic church, and this city has always remained an influential Bohemian centre. *In Saint Louis*

Texas also early drew Bohemian immigrants.* The first, it is said, was a Protestant pastor named Bergman, from Silesia, who left home in February, 1848, and came to Catspring, near Austin, where he engaged in farming. A letter from him containing most favorable accounts of Texas fell accidentally into the hands of another Bohemian named Lešikar, and through his persuasions a group of Bohemians who had been thinking of emigrating to Southern Hungary decided *Texas settlements*

---

* My account of these Texas settlers is drawn from Dr. Habernicht's "History of Bohemians in America. Part III, The State of Texas." The Study is in Bohemian and the untranslated title will be found in the Bibliography.

with Lešikar to follow Bergman's example. Their story suggests what emigration meant in those days. The voyage from Liverpool to Galveston lasted seventeen weeks. The vessel was crowded with Irish immigrants. The food, which was bad, was served out raw, and each family had to cook for themselves, an arrangement then common. *Half of the party died on the journey.**

Early
hardships

From this beginning, settlers from Bohemia and Moravia multiplied in Texas, spreading into a number of counties. Their situation was nevertheless a very difficult one. The state which had become a part of the Union only three years before, in 1845, had long been a resort for the most varied elements. The Americans generally carried on large plantations with slave labor, or else had great half wild herds. Cotton and cattle were raised for traffic with neighboring states or with Mexico. Into such a society came Bohemians, Poles and Germans, singly or in small groups, with a little capital only, buying comparatively small farms and working them themselves. The Bohemians generally held anti-slavery views which set the Americans against them and subjected them to all sorts of persecutions. When the Civil War broke out, matters naturally became worse. "They fired on people who wanted to avoid military service as if they had been rabbits, and if one were caught he had to go as a soldier." Some of the unfortunate settlers went to Mexico for awhile, others are said to have hidden in the woods and to have slept in hollow trees. Added to these troubles were the war prices. No goods came through from the Northwest, and what was brought in from Mexico was very dear.

I am tempted to cite instances of the careers of some of these early Texan settlers, for instance that of Joseph Petr, whose father emigrated from Moravia when

* Friedrich Kapp, long one of the New York State Commissioners of Immigration, in the years before the Federal authorities had assumed responsibility, gives similar accounts of the horrible conditions of the early steerage. Indeed, the literature of the subject, both history and fiction, is full of them.

the boy was eleven—one of six children who could no longer be supported in the old home.   The new farm was bought on credit, the whole family had to work early and late, and schooling was out of the question.   After five years the Civil War broke out, the eldest son died in the ranks and the sixteen-year-old Joseph was employed carting provisions for the soldiers.   After the war he learned blacksmithing, and helped with his father's farm and store.   He prospered and came to own a thousand acres of good land on which twenty Bohemian families found their living as employes or tenants. He held a number of offices, served as postmaster, and was twice elected to the state legislature.

Thus their native persistence carried the Bohemians through the dark days of their first settlement.   Since 1904 Texas seems to have again begun to attract Bohemians in considerable numbers: in the four years 1905–1908 over 4000 gave Texas as their destination.   In 1906 their number in the state was locally estimated at 60,000, a respectable and respected element of the farming districts.*

One of the earliest goals of the Bohemians as well as of Poles, Germans and Scandinavians, Belgians, and many other peoples, was Wisconsin, and the attitude of that state toward immigration probably did a good deal to bring this about.   A fact that is easily forgotten in the present state of feeling in regard to immigration is the eager and official solicitation of immigrants that was carried on for years by various states.   Mr. Gregory, in a

Wisconsin's call for immigrants

* Habernicht remarks (page 128), "The Moravians in Texas, conservative in character, have not acquired the energy and alertness, the business spirit, requisite in America; so that they do not accomplish as great a success as they might with their industry, honesty and thrift.   Of late years their main crop has suffered from the ravages of the cotton weevil."   Habernicht here speaks of Moravians.   I have used the word Bohemian as equivalent to Čech (Chekh) and have applied it to natives of Moravia and Bohemia alike.   For some further account of Texas settlement see page 228.

paper contributed to the Proceedings of the State Historical Society of Wisconsin in 1901, writes as follows:

"The men who controlled the destinies of Wisconsin . . . framed the state constitution and the early statutes in such a way as to encourage foreign settlers to feel at home here, and in this respect Wisconsin's laws have never changed. During a large part of the time since admission to the Union (in 1848), an active propaganda to encourage immigration has been carried on by the state."

Wisconsin, like various other states, appointed a Commissioner of Emigration to stimulate the inflow. In 1852 the first man to fill this office reported to the Governor that he had been in New York distributing pamphlets in English, German, Norwegian and Dutch, describing the resources of the state. These were handed to immigrants on vessels and in hotels and taverns, and sent abroad; editorials and advertisements were inserted in foreign papers, and he and his assistants talked personally with as many immigrants as possible. He himself says:

"It is hardly possible to make a true estimate of the influence exerted by the agency in New York. Information has emanated from there in every direction, and is now spread over a large and, for our object, most valuable part of Europe."

Federal encouragement

After four years this state canvass for immigrants was suspended for a time, but in 1864 the Wisconsin legislature memorialized Congress for the passage of national laws to encourage foreign immigration on the ground that labor was scarce, owing to the war, and that wages had more than doubled. Whether or not as a consequence of this request, Congress did in the same year pass an act to encourage immigration, which, however, was repealed in March, 1868.*

Again, in 1879, Wisconsin established a State

* Hall, P. F.: "Immigration and its Effects upon the United States," page 202.

Board of Immigration to increase and stimulate immigration, with authority to disseminate information. The official circulars mentioned as inducements the following points: climate, rich lands at a nominal price, free schools and a free university, equality before the law, religious liberty, no imprisonment for debt and liberal exemption from seizure by a creditor, suffrage and the right to be elected to any office but that of governor or lieutenant governor on one year's residence, whether a citizen or not (intention to become one having been declared); and full eligibility to office for all actual citizens. "There is never an election in the state," one circular continues, "that does not put some, and often very many, foreign-born citizens into office. Indeed, there is no such thing as a foreigner in Wisconsin, save in the mere accident of birthplace; for men coming here and entering into the active duties of life identify themselves with the state and her interests, and are to all intents and purposes American." We are told "The language above used is, except in rhetoric, identical" with that in an edition of 1884.

Besides this direct encouragement by the state "a similar canvass was maintained by counties and land companies, and at a later stage by railway companies, some of them sending agents to travel in Europe."* Of such solicitation at the very beginning of Bohemian immigration I found tradition still mindful in the old country. {Other forms of solicitation}

Mr. Senner, formerly Commissioner of Immigration at the Port of New York, said before the Industrial Commission (Vol. XV, 1901, page 182) that the effect of such advertisement is exaggerated.

"There is no doubt that people have been educated to take our advertisements with a large grain of allowance. They look rather more sceptically on these matters than

* For all this see Gregory, J. G.: "Foreign Immigration to Wisconsin." Proceedings of State Historical Society of Wisconsin, 1901.

they did fifteen to twenty years ago." Michigan, Wisconsin and a few other states maintained permanent colonization bureaus in Europe, "but their success is very small."

Granting that experience has led intending immigrants to discount solicitations to emigrate, it is still true that immigrants have felt themselves directly and officially invited and urged to come, and it is not surprising that one often finds them aggrieved and hurt at the tone of too many current references making foreigners synonymous with everything that is unwelcome.

Bohemians in Wisconsin
Wisconsin was, as has been explained, a favorite goal with both Bohemians and Poles. The Bohemians were at Caledonia, near Racine, on Lake Michigan, in 1844. The first Bohemian newspaper, *Slavie*, was published here, and here the Bohemian free-thought movement seems to have first taken shape. Within a few years there were settlements in Milwaukee (then a town of about 30,000), and in Manitowoc and Kewaunee counties. The latter now contains the largest colony of Bohemians in Wisconsin (excepting perhaps that in Milwaukee); in 1890 it was estimated that three-sevenths of the population of Kewaunee county were of Bohemian extraction.

It is therefore particularly fortunate that the collections of the Wisconsin Historical Society contain the unpublished account of the early days there which I have already cited, and that Miss Nan Mashek has published a spirited if brief account.* I quote from the former:

"The first Bohemian settlers in Kewaunee County came from Milwaukee. The inducement offered was the opportunity given for obtaining cheap but good farming lands for which the purchasers could pay, and support themselves at the same time from the timber found upon them. The succeeding immigrants came directly from Bohemia by the solicitation of their friends

* "Bohemian Farmers of Wisconsin." *Charities*, XIII, pages 211–214 (Dec. 3, 1904).

and relatives already settled here, and almost without
exception their reason was a desire to better their material condition.   Most of them immediately bought lands,
usually with borrowed money, and at once settled upon
them, while others worked in the large saw mills at
Kewaunee for a part of the year, and upon their lands
during the remainder.   In about 1870 the larger part of
the immigrants were already established here, and since
then but few have come.

"Though in certain parts of Bohemia peculiarities in Pioneer
dress and customs are even now prevalent, they rapidly conditions
disappeared among the settlers here, until there is now
none at all strikingly noticeable.   Very little personal
property was brought along, except the ancestral feather
bed which yet plays such a prominent part in the baggage
of the immigrants of today; each family was usually
provided with some money, though funds were not
absolutely necessary, because while clearing his newly
purchased farm the settler was sure of support from the
timber cut.   The greatest difficulties encountered were
due to the distance of the market and the lack of roads.
During the first year Manitowoc, at a distance of thirty
miles, was the nearest market, and the roads to that were
corduroys through swamp lands.   When the village of
Kewaunee was settled, the condition of affairs was improved but even then some farmers were obliged to
carry to town on their backs the split shingles they had
made, and receiving their pay in flour, return home with
the sack on their shoulders.   In the fall, supplies were
laid in for the whole winter, and if ever the flour gave
out, hand coffee mills were used to grind whatever wheat
they might have.   .   .   .   By far the greater part of the
Bohemian emigrants belonged to the agricultural and
common laboring classes in the old country."

Another Kewaunee County informant,* writing of the
old times, says:

* Letter from Louis Bruemmer.   MSS. in library of Historical
Society of Wisconsin.

"The old settlers suffered hardships; having bought lands, and their funds [being] exhausted, they were compelled to carry shingles on their shoulders, made by hand, to Kewaunee or Ahnapee in exchange for the necessaries of life, traveling on foot from twenty to thirty miles. The writer lived in an adjoining town of Mishicott in Manitowoc county, in 1854, and had his feet frozen in making cord wood at thirty-seven and one-half cents per cord, where they charged him board with $2.50 per week. He was then fourteen years old, and was expected to earn the pork and bread for the family; he made shingle vhile his feet were healing, and after being able to walk, loaded 2000 shingles on a hand sled to Mishicott, three miles distant, to trade for flour and pork; but on trying the merchants, was sorry to find that they would give 'store pay' for shingles, *except* flour and pork, which must be paid for in cash; but our cash was gone; finally the merchant relented, and furnished me with twenty pounds [of] flour at the rate of $14 per barrel, and the flour was of the same quality as middlings of the present time. Such were the conditions in this county from 1850 to 1857; there was a poor market for everything.

Success

"The soil was good, covered with heavy timber such as maple, beech, hemlock, cedar, basswood or linden, black and white ash, oak and elm. But through hard work and industry, lands were cleared, and in a couple of years they were glad that they had a log cabin, a yoke of oxen, a cow and twenty-five hens, and from five to twenty acres improved land, which partially supported the family. The money and clothing were generally earned by the heads of the families in saw mills, of which there were plenty within a radius of twenty miles, and their lot was better then—even a hundred per cent better—than in their European homes."

We will return to a consideration of this thrifty county later, in discussing farming conditions.

Another similar informant, from Crawford county

(Wis.), says that the Bohemians, who are from all parts of the old country, first came in 1857, having been in other states first. They came individually. The first six men (the original gives their names) bought land of the government, but later comers bought from resident farmers or speculators. The numbers have increased gradually. Most came from Chicago, a few direct from Bohemia on invitation of their relatives here. A few have sold and gone farther west. They are, as a class, industrious, clean, frugal, honest, patriotic, peace-loving, and intelligent. Their sons and daughters speak both English and Bohemian, but they seldom intermarry with other nationalities. They follow the American mode of farming, but are more industrious. "The effect on their neighbors is Grand, as they envy each other for the common good," says our informant.

In spite of their industry, however, not all of these early Bohemians succeeded. Many, I was told, lost their land in the panic of 1859 for a few dollars' indebtedness, and had to abandon farming and join some city colony, many going to St. Louis.

St. Louis, Texas and Wisconsin are not the only seats of early settlements. There were Bohemian colonists, says Mr. Rudis Jicinsky, in an article in the Cedar Rapids *Gazette*, at about the same time in Wisconsin, New York, Ohio, Illinois, Michigan, Minnesota, Iowa and Texas.* Yet the wooded country of Wisconsin and Minnesota, where the timber supplied a source of income from the first, was sought earlier than the more fertile prairie districts.† *Other settlements*

The Bohemian settlements on the rich levels of Iowa were generally not only later than those to the north, but were commonly made, not directly from the old country, but as a second stage by settlers moving from Wisconsin. *Bohemians in Iowa*

* Cedar Rapids *Gazette*, June 14, 1906, page 11.
† See page 324 for a comparison of timber and prairie land for settlement.

Pioneer
stories

Two stories which I gleaned from a family of these early Iowa settlers had several points of interest. The father's family, of Bohemian peasant stock, came about 1854 to Galveston, and made its way thence by steamer to Houston, Texas, then a small place. The Bohemian settlers there seemed unprogressive, the talk of yellow fever was not cheering, the water was bad, the insect plagues intolerable, and sleep out of the question. The family quickly decided to push on to St. Louis, which meant going back to Galveston to take the St. Louis steamer. On the Mississippi boat there was a set of roughs, and a row took place in which one man was killed. The mother used to tell how one of these men stood and looked at the little boy as he lay asleep.

The father was disgusted with the South after these experiences, and decided to go to Racine, Wisconsin, by way of Galena and Chicago. In Chicago the father fell sick and died, but the family finally reached Racine. They did not remain, however, but joined a party of their countrymen going to Linn county, Iowa, to settle. There were perhaps four families in the party, each with its yoke of oxen. In Iowa the son prospered, until today his fields stretch over the wide rolling slopes as far as the eye can see, and his farmhouse is given over to his superintendent, while he lives with his family in the town. In Iowa he met his wife, whose family came from Bohemia a few years earlier than his.

Loss of so-
cial status
in America

The wife's story is typical of the not uncommon case where the transition to America means a fall, not a rise, in social status. Her family were cultivated, well-to-do people. One son, being involved in the revolution of 1848, was sent to America with family money to invest. The members of the family at home understood that he was succeeding, and decided to join him, but on arrival they found themselves stranded, as the money entrusted to the son had been swallowed up in a business misadventure. Moreover, by a tragic coincidence of two accidents to letters, they lost touch with another son who had remained in Europe. He as well as the family had moved, and on both sides letters were returned as impossible to deliver. The family came first to New York, then went on to Wisconsin, and from there to Iowa, going by train as far as Milwaukee.

On their way to Iowa they stopped at a place where one of the party had a log cabin, and here they finally spent a whole season, three families sharing its inconveniences. Blocks of wood were used for chairs, and bedframes were made on the model of a saw-horse. A hole covered with boards served as a cellar in which to store potatoes.

In April, 1852, they started out again in regular immigrant fashion. The family had only one wagon for all their luggage, and the daughter, who told me the story, then seventeen, made the three weeks' journey on foot. Every few miles was a farmhouse with the sign "tavern," and at these taverns they would get their meals.

They finally reached Cedar Rapids, which now, with 25,000 people, is the sixth city of Iowa, but it was then a little place with some thirty houses, the people Americans and a few German laborers. The chief man of the settlement, a judge, asked the father if he did not have a daughter who would come and work at his house. So this delicately reared girl, who had been brought up to go to school, sew and embroider, "not even accustomed to wash the dishes," went out to service on a pioneer farm. None of the family were used to hard work, and it killed the father in a year. But the young are strong to endure, and the daughter grew up and married the prosperous Bohemian farmer whose story has already been told. Their children, girl and boys alike, have had college educations, and the son, on a recent trip to Europe, found their relatives there, one cousin a professor in the University of Vienna, another cousin teaching Greek in a seminary, and an uncle the owner of a large factory. The mother, while glad to have news of her kin, would not like to have her European relatives see her American environment. She cannot forget what she felt to be the degradation of her barefoot, hardworking girlhood.

Life in
Cedar
Rapids

Cleveland colony of Bohemians

Ohio was the seat of another early Bohemian colony, situated in and about Cleveland, where the first comers arrived about 1848. It is interesting to notice that just as Wisconsin was the first goal of Bohemians who later went to Iowa, so Wisconsin was also the intended destination of those who started the Cleveland colony. As seems to be often the case, the earliest were Jews, but true Bohemians came directly after; by 1855 there were 19 families, and in 1869 their numbers had grown to over 3000.

In spite of all the hardship of the pioneer days, doubly difficult to those who came from a very different sort of life at home, the old people often look back with regret to the "good old times" when numbers were less and intimacy more, and when the very fact of being strangers together in a strange land made internal differences of religious opinion or social class seem trivial.

One old lady who came in 1853 said: "At first it was very hard, for the Americans looked upon us with distrust or rather aversion, which I could never explain to myself. Later I learned that it was only our customs—our bare feet and handkerchiefs over our heads—that they objected to."

Occupations

Of the old settlers many were farmers, though their children, like others, have since largely come to the cities. At least a quarter, however, had trades. In 1869, when the Cleveland colony numbered 1749 males and 1503 females, there were 120 carpenters, builders, coopers, etc., 84 masons and stone cutters, 56 tailors, 50 machinists and smiths of various sorts, 44 shoemakers, 22 inn-keepers, 17 butchers and bakers, 15 storekeepers, 13 professional musicians, 11 iron moulders, while others were furriers, tanners, harness makers, upholsterers, watchmakers, dyers, cobblers, bookbinders, printers, brewers, etc. Fifty girls were at service on farms.*

* "The Bohemian Colony and Bohemian Societies in Cleveland, Ohio, in North America, published by the Bohemians of

The Bohemian settlements further west, in Nebraska, the Dakotas and Oklahoma, belong mainly in the period after 1880, although those in Nebraska began in the sixties.

The chief city colonies of Bohemians were founded early, but did not grow very rapidly. That in St. Louis, the first to be of importance, has already been spoken of. The colony in New York made its chief gains in the seventies; according to the census it rose during this decade from 1487 to 8093, multiplying itself between five and six times between 1870 and 1880, while in the twenty years from 1880 to 1900 it did not quite double. As already said, many came to New York from Kutna Hora as a result of a strike in the government tobacco factory there in 1878 (?), and this brought it about that many Bohemians went into cigar making in New York, fresh comers being drawn into a trade which already occupied many of their fellow countrymen. (See page 357.)

The Bohemian colony in Chicago, already in 1870, when the census gave it 6277, the largest in the country, closely reflects the general movement. The first settlers, coming apparently about 1851, were political exiles; later there was a more numerous and less select influx of peasants and artisans.* After the fire of 1871 came a stream of skilled laborers,† and as custom tailoring was then a good trade in Chicago, many Bohemians went into it. Unfortunately the Bohemians as well as Bohemian Jews are to be found in large numbers in sweat-shops.

City colonies; Bohemians in New York

Bohemians in Chicago

Cleveland on the occasion of the Ethnographical Exhibition in Prague in the year 1905," pages 13–27. The book is in Bohemian. The original title, untranslated, will be found in the Bibliography under Bohemians in the United States.

* The late Mrs. Humpal-Zeman in her article in "Hull House Maps and Papers" (1895) wrote: "Among these earlier emigrants were men of cultivation and energy, who loved liberty so well that they were ready to undertake all manner of menial service for her sake; and thus one would often find men of education and high social standing engaged in street sweeping, cigar making and other humble occupations; and graduates of the University of Prague working for $2.50 and $4 a week."

† Humpal-Zeman, Josefa: "Bohemian Settlements in the United States." Industrial Commission, XV, page 507.

Bohemians
and Poles in
the Civil
War

A subject which certainly should be treated in an historical account of Slavs in America, but which I can only touch upon without in any way doing justice to it, is the service of both Bohemians and Poles during the Civil War. The anti-slavery sentiment of the former has already been alluded to, and the first regiment that went from Chicago to fight for the Union is said to have been a Lincoln rifle company that some " Bohemian-Slavonian " young men had organized in 1860.* The dominating feature in the great Bohemian National Cemetery in Chicago is the soldier's monument, just such a monument as stands on every village common in New England; and perhaps nothing so much as this visible sign of blood shed in the same cause bridges the difference of national feeling.

POLISH SETTLEMENT

Polish colo-
nies in
Texas

To turn now to the other important body of Slavic immigrants of this period, the Poles, we find that they, as well as the Bohemians, came early to Texas, and at Panna Marya (the Virgin Mary) their oldest settlement in that state, the first Polish church in America was founded in 1855. I had an interesting talk with a son of one of the original colonists, who spoke gladly of the old times. Rev. Leopold Moczygemba,† a Franciscan missionary in Texas, became acquainted with an Irish Catholic who owned land and who suggested its use for a Polish colony. At first there were only fifteen or twenty families, but in all there came a hundred or more; it is not possible to get precise numbers.

The first immigrants came by sailing vessels to Galveston, up the river to Indianola, and thence by wagon, arriving in the early winter. They built huts of boughs and such other material as they could find. The con-

---

* Humpal-Zeman, Josefa: "Hull House Maps and Papers," page 125.
† For an account, with portrait, of this early settler, see Kruszka, I, Ch. III. For general conditions in Texas at this time, see above page 216.

PRIESTS AND PATRIOTS

1. Father Dombrowski, born in Poland in 1842; fought for Polish freedom in the war of '63; obliged to leave his country; entered the priesthood and came to America in 1869. In Detroit he founded a Polish seminary and introduced the order of Felician sisters for teaching, care of orphans, etc. He died in 1903, known as the "patriot priest." 2. Mr. Tomasz Siemiradzki of the Polish National Alliance. 3. Father Baraga, first bishop of Marquette, Michigan; Slovenian missionary to the Indians and author of valuable philological works on Indian languages. Born in 1797 near Laibach, Carniola. 4. Father Kruszka of Ripon, Wis., author of a history of the Poles in America.

ditions proved very hard, the climate being dry, and all the surroundings strange to them. They had no trouble with Indians, but Texas in those days was a refuge for lawless characters, and the Americans were often unfriendly and violent. "They would take a man and beat him just for the fun of it," I was told. "Several times a Pole bought a horse and in the night it was stolen from him by the men who had sold it." Those who had trades could earn money by going to town "instead of scratching in dry ground." Many left and went North. My informant was nearly eleven years old when his family came to Texas. He served on the Confederate side during the war. He had evidently prospered; his place, which lay rather apart, spoke of fairly substantial farming, the house was comfortable and solid, and the son was a good looking fellow.

The pictures that I carry away from Panna Marya are of the group of children learning their catechism in the cool stone church, the girls in pink, blue and red sunbonnets, the boys bareheaded and barefooted; of the priest's house with its veranda and flower beds; of the store, a typical country store, with a saddled horse hitched under the live oak before it; of the big, bare schoolrooms in which the children were being taught in English, not of the purest yet not of the worst either— the whole making up an impression of the quiet, rather stagnant life of men still close to the European peasant, yet by no means untouched by America; a life wholesome if not very highly evolved. *Panna Marya to-day*

The Panna Marya settlement was quickly followed by other Polish colonies in Texas, five of which founded churches the next year, and eleven others in the course of the next two decades.* In 1906 the Polish population of Texas was estimated at between 16,000 and 17,000.

* It is interesting to find that Texas attracted the only representatives of the little group of the Slavs of the Lausitz (the Wends, Lusatians or Sorbs), whom I have heard of as immigrants. Mr. Morfill writes: "In the year 1854 about 400 Sorbs, for the most part from Prussia, emigrated to Texas, under the leader-

Poles in
Wisconsin

We find that the Poles, like the Bohemians, also settled early in Wisconsin, this state now ranking fourth in its number of natives of Poland.   The earliest Polish church in Wisconsin was established in Polonia, Portage county, in 1858.   In 1906, when I visited Polonia, it counted 360 families and rejoiced in a recently completed and magnificent church towering over the country side, and built at a cost of $70,000.   Near the church is an orphanage (connected with the house of the Felician sisters at Detroit), a parish school where, besides the day scholars, are some forty boys who board during the winter, and the modest residence of the priest.   The Poles of this district came mainly from Russia, and were said to be "getting on better all the time," though in the previous year hail had destroyed most of the crops, even potatoes. The houses looked well built and homelike, and the whole impression of the place was cheerful, except for the doubt whether the expensive church did not imply a vastly disproportionate sacrifice.   It is, however, fair to note that $36,000 had been given by the present pastor and his predecessor, and that $18,000 was still unpaid.

Course of
Polish set-
tlement

The fact that practically all Poles are Roman Catholics and zealous ones, and that a Polish group is likely to found a church as soon as it is at all numerous, makes the chronology of the founding of their churches to all intents and purposes an outline of the dates and locations of their settlements.   We are fortunate in having this guide to the history of Polish settlement in the data as to the founding of Polish churches compiled by Father Kruszka.*

In the twenty-six years 1855 to 1880 inclusive, 85 Polish churches were founded; among them were 17

ship of their pastor, Kilian. Here they settled in Bastrop County and have preserved their native language till the present day by means of their schools and two churches where the service is conducted in the Wendish language."   "Slavonic Literature," page 245.

* For list of Polish churches, with dates of foundation, for the period before 1880, see Appendix XVI, page 459.

in Texas, 16 in Wisconsin, six in Michigan and six in Missouri. These were the earliest states in the list. The first, as has been said, was that at Panna Marya in Texas, the second at Parisville, Michigan, in 1857, the third that at Polonia, Wisconsin, described above. Of six founded in Illinois, three were in Chicago, the first of them in 1869; of seven in Pennsylvania, the first was in Shamokin in 1870. New York city and Buffalo appear in 1873, Minnesota in the same year with three churches, Nebraska in 1876. Detroit is dated 1872, Cleveland, 1875.

In fact, it is during the seventies that the Polish movement to this country first becomes of much numerical importance. The census shows a gain in the decade 1860 to 1870 of 7000 natives of Poland (we must remember that Polish Jews are included), in the next decade of over 34,000, figures destined to be quite overshadowed in the two decades of the next period, when the gains were 99,000 and 236,000 respectively.* Census data of Polish movement, 1860–1900

SLOVENIAN IMMIGRANTS

Although Bohemians and Poles made up the main body of Slavic immigration previous to 1880, members of other groups came also, and among these certain early Slovenians have a special interest. So far as known, the first of this little nationality to come to America was neither a political refugee nor a workingman seeking a better lot, but a Catholic missionary and saint, Bishop Baraga,† the first of a series of Slovenian priests who have Slovenians: Bishop Baraga

---

*Cf. Chart I, page 212.

† My counting Bishop Baraga as a Slovenian (rather than a German) having been questioned, I can only say that over 94 per cent of the population of Carniola today are Slovenian in speech, that Bishop Baraga is counted by Slovenians in this country as one of themselves, and that the other priests who followed him from Carniola are constantly compared and contrasted with German priests. His name, so far as I know, neither bars nor proves a Slavic origin, though Nepomuk, his father's middle name, is that of a Bohemian saint, and his mother's name, de Jencic, is obviously Slavic. That he could speak Slovenian, but perhaps as an acquired language, proves nothing either way,

devoted themselves to the spread of their religion in the Northwest.

Mission to the Indians Frederic Baraga was born in 1797 in his father's castle near the beautiful city of Laibach, the capital of Carniola. The gifted, fine natured boy was studying at the University of Vienna—law and "other useful sciences," and English, French and Italian—when he became convinced of his vocation, and entered the priesthood. After some years in a Slovenian parish he decided to fulfil his long-cherished desire for missionary work among the Indians of the American Northwest. The Leopoldine Society, established in Vienna in 1829 for this work, opened the way, and in 1831 he was with his new superior, Bishop Fenwick, in Cincinnati. Here he stayed for a few months, until the season should be sufficiently advanced for him to go into the wilderness.

Before summer opened he was in his chosen field, the pastor of a flock of Indian converts. For twenty-two years, the happiest of his life, he endured extremities of hardship and peril in the work that he loved, and his elevation to the bishopric in 1853, with its lessened opportunities for personal work, was a genuine cross to him.

His newly created see then covered not only the upper peninsula of Michigan, but a great part of lower Michigan, northern Wisconsin, eastern Minnesota, and parts of Ontario, and necessitated exhausting journeys on snowshoes and in canoes. Once, for instance, this slight, frail man walked on snowshoes twenty-four hours without resting, in bitter cold, through the deep snow, carrying a heavy pack, and with nothing to eat but a piece of dry, frozen cake. Prematurely aged by the continued strain of excessive exposures, he died in 1868, at the age of seventy. Besides his religious work, in which he was extraordinarily successful not only in converting

since if a German, this would have been necessary, going as he did to a Slovenian parish; and if a Slovenian, his family, which was apparently of high social position, would probably at the period of his boyhood have thought it bad taste to talk any language but German.

but in moulding and uplifting his Indians, Bishop Baraga distinguished himself by his philological publications, especially by an Ojibway grammar and dictionary, the first, and said to be still the standard, work on the subject.*

Bishop Baraga's career had the not unnatural result of making Catholic leaders in America desire more of his breed, while at the same time his influence, especially as exerted during his occasional visits to Austria, stimulated interest in the American field among his countrymen. This partly explains the curious fact that while the Poles in America, perhaps nearly 3,000,000 Catholics, with a goodly share of culture as well as zeal, have had no bishop of their own nationality until quite recently, the much smaller and obscurer group of the Slovenians have had five bishops, besides many priests. Of late years their own people have been immigrating in considerable numbers and need Slovenian pastors, but besides these, many Slovenian priests are in charge of non-Slovenian parishes—especially in the diocese of St. Paul, Minnesota. Speaking German as they do, practically as a second mother tongue, and being in general excellent linguists, it is not surprising that they prove a very useful class of priests.

Other Slovenian priests

Besides these ecclesiastical representatives there were other early Slovenian immigrants here and there in the country. For instance, in Calumet, Michigan, there is a flourishing department store owned by the descendants of a Slovenian who came with a fellow countryman as early as 1856 as a peddler or traveling dealer. Slovenians are said to have first appeared in Chicago and in Iowa about 1863, and in 1866 they founded their chief farming colony in Brockway, Minnesota. (See page 339.) They were in Omaha in 1868. About 1873 their present large colony in Joliet was founded. They began to

Slovenian settlements

* Those interested to know more of this fine type of a Roman Catholic missionary will do well to read his life by Father Verwyst.

come to New York about 1878, though not in large numbers till 1893. Like most of the smaller Slavic groups, however, their mass migration falls after 1880.*

Besides the three nationalities just discussed, doubtless other Slavic groups were represented in the country during the period before 1880, but none so far as my very imperfect information goes were of special importance until after the new tide of immigration set in with the eighties.

SLAVIC DISTRIBUTION IN 1880

In spite of the unsatisfactory character, for our purposes, of the information supplied by the United States census,† it does give at least certain interesting indications in regard to the distribution of Slavs in this country. We find for instance, that natives of Austria, Bohemia, Hungary and Poland, were all represented in every state and territory, with the single exception that there was no Hungarian in New Hampshire.

New York state had the largest group of natives of Austria, Bohemia, Poland and Hungary, the total being 32,000, but these of course included a very large number of Polish Jews, and other non-Slavic elements. Wisconsin probably had the largest Slavic population among the states, for her 24,000 natives of the four countries in question were comparatively free from non-Slavic intermixture. They included over 18,000 from Bohemia and Austria, and over 5000 from Poland. The Illinois total stood only 500 below Wisconsin's; in reality, considering the large Jewish contingent in Chicago, the difference in Slavic population was doubtless greater than this suggests.

Next to these three states come Minnesota, Iowa,

---

* For very interesting data, of which I have been able to make only a partial use, see the manual prepared for Slovenians in America by Rev. F. S. Šušteršič, of Joliet, Illinois, and published there by the Amerikanski Slovenec press in 1903, with the title of "Poduk Rojakom Slovencem." (See also below, page 269 ff.)

† Discussed in Appendix XV, page 456.

Nebraska and Ohio, with 11,000 to 13,000 each, mainly from Bohemia. Michigan had over 8000, of which over 5000 were from Poland, giving this state probably the largest Polish group in the country at that time.

Pennsylvania, later to be the Slavic state *par excellence*, ranked in 1880 after these eight states, with 8,333. It was, however, one of three states that then had over 1000 natives of Hungary, New York and Ohio being the others. Texas and Missouri had old and considerable Bohemian colonies. Of natives of the four countries together, Kansas had over 4000 and California over 3000, the former mainly Bohemians, the latter with a number at least of Dalmatians, though there is no way of estimating how many these were. Finally, it is to be noted that the Bohemians had already made their way to Dakota, 1300 strong.

It is at once noticeable how wide is this distribution and yet how large a part of the whole bulk is in the group of neighboring states, Illinois, Iowa, Wisconsin, Minnesota, Michigan, Nebraska, Dakota and Kansas. Of the Bohemians, the most important Slavic group at this date, over 70 per cent were in this region.

CHAPTER XII

THE NEWER SLAVIC IMMIGRATION: SINCE 1880

Changes in composition of Slavic immigration   With the coming of the eighties the original contingent of Bohemians and Poles began to be overlaid by a much larger volume of newcomers differing in various important respects from the old. In the first place, the later Slavic immigrants were largely of nationalities previously little represented in America. Since up to 1899 the American immigration data are classified only by "country of last permanent residence" and not by nationality, it is not possible to get any precise measure of this change in the make-up of the Slavic stream.

Neither can the beginning of the movement to America among the newer immigrant nationalities—Slovaks and Ruthenians, Slovenians and Croatians, Bulgarians, Servians and Russians—be dated in any hard and fast way.* Apparently, as already said, the impulse spread from the Poles in Germany eastward to their brothers in Galicia in the latter part of the seventies, and to the Poles in Russia somewhat later. The Slovaks began to come in considerable numbers in the early eighties, and the Ruthenians at about the same time.

These three nationalities converge in the eastern Carpathian district, and more or less interpenetrate one another; and emigration to America having once started, it was natural that so contagious a movement should spread through the whole Carpathian group. Moreover, among all these peoples trade is largely in the hands of the Jews, who are apt to have international

* Discussion of the origin and spread of the emigration movement among the first four of these nationalities will be found in the appropriate chapters in Part I, but for convenience it is resumed here as a whole.

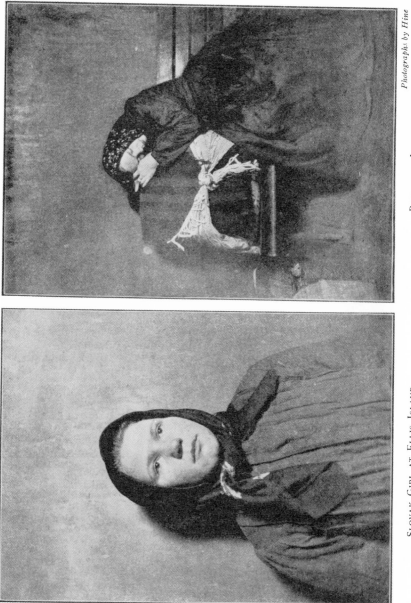

BOHEMIAN IMMIGRANT

SLOVAK GIRL AT ELLIS ISLAND

affiliations, and it seems often to have happened that some enterprising Jew first among his fellow townspeople became aware of the land of promise across the Atlantic, explored and reported on it, and thus set the stream of immigration flowing.

The South Slavs began to come to America somewhat later. Though individual Slovenians came very early, as already mentioned, it was not till about 1892 that the movement became noticeably important among them. In the Croatian group, the Dalmatians, sailors and wanderers, had sent now and then an immigrant from very early times, but it was not till toward the middle of the nineties that Croatians, and especially Croatians from the country back of the coast, began coming in numbers. Servians and Bulgarians are still more recent comers, numerous only since 1902 or so, but growing rapidly. As to Russians, of 66,000 in the last eleven years (1899 to 1909 inclusive), over nine-tenths came after 1902 and over two-thirds in the last three years.

The grounds of the earlier immigration may be said to have been, roughly, the opportunity of acquiring farming land cheaply if not gratuitously, and in a less degree the desire for the greater political and religious freedom promised by America. In the course of time both these grounds lost their importance. As the supply of desirable land to be had on easy terms diminished, this incentive to immigration grew weaker, and lessening political unrest in Western Europe allayed the other. On the other hand, the great industrial development of the United States, following after the Civil War, and especially after the hard times in the seventies, meant a great increase in the demand for labor. The Teutonic element of the older immigration, to which the Bohemian was very similar, was not looking primarily for wage jobs but for independence, especially the independence of the farm owner. The same was largely true of the British immigrants, English, Welsh and Scotch. Besides, neither belonged, in any sense, to the class of

Causes and industrial character

cheap labor.   The Irish alone were not enough to supply
the demand for "hands," and French-Canadians, while
an important element in New England, have not been
numerous elsewhere.   Italians and Slavs, proving most
available, were consequently called in to meet the want.

These newer groups of Slavic immigrants were mainly
drawn from more primitive districts than the earlier
groups; districts where the population was less in touch
with Western Europe.   They generally came, not intending to take up farms and settle, but hoping to earn money
to send back to their homes, to which they planned
to return.   To this end they sought the best paid
work that they could find in mines, foundries, factories
and elsewhere.   A large proportion of both the old and
the new comers were peasants, that is, small independent
farmers; but among the new, the proportion of men
possessing trades was less, and mere laborers were more
numerous.

Immigra-
tion induced
by em-
ployers
Historically, the American origin of the more recent
immigration, so far as such a movement can have a
specific origin, seems to have been the desire of certain
Pennsylvania anthracite mine owners to replace the
employes that they found hard to deal with, and especially the Irish, with cheaper and more docile material.
Strikes were a frequent source of friction, the Molly
Maguire affair had caused great bitterness, and it was
natural that employers should be on the lookout for new
sources of labor supply.   In a number of places these raw
recruits of industry seem to have been called in as the
result of a strike, and there probably were plenty of
instances of sending agents abroad to hire men or of
otherwise inducing labor to immigrate either under
contract or with an equivalent understanding.   These
proceedings were, of course, perfectly legal up to 1885,
when the law forbidding the importation of labor under
contract was passed.

One story is that the first comers were brought over
for a certain mine operator at Drifton, Pennsylvania,

through an "Austrian" foreman. I have never been able to verify the story nor to date it. I was interested to run across a Slovak hatter in Bartfeld, Hungary, who emigrated about 1880, and told of having gone "to Drifton, where there was an Austrian foreman," who, however, does not appear to have had anything to do with his emigrating.*

Mr. Powderly, formerly Commissioner of Immigration, testified before the Industrial Commission; "I believe in 1869, during a miners' strike which was then in progress, a man who was connected with one of the coal companies made the statement that in order to defeat the men in their demands it would be necessary to bring cheap labor from Europe, and shortly after that, miners were noticed coming to the anthracite region in large numbers from Italy, Hungary, Russia, and other far-off lands."†

It will be seen that Mr. Powderly mentions a comparatively early date at which the importation of workmen under contract was in no way forbidden. But even then such a course, while legal, would have been unpopular among workingmen, and probably always more or less *sub rosa*. This may be one reason why it is very hard to get any definite information about these matters; but indeed, on both sides of the water, the doings of less than a generation ago are surprisingly hard to ascertain.

In Pennsylvania the great early goal appears to have been, as already indicated, the anthracite coal region of the eastern part of the state. The Poles seem to have been the first to come, and right on their heels came the Slovaks. An informant from Hazleton, a district where they appeared quite early, gave me, in 1904, the following account of their first arrival:

Influx into the anthracite fields

"They began to come about twenty years ago; a few stray ones came earlier. Nowadays not so many are coming, but at one time they came in batches, shipped

---

* This man's story is told on pages 100-101.
† Industrial Commission, 1901, XV, page 32.

by the carload to the coal fields. When they arrived they seemed perfectly aimless. It was hard for them to make themselves understood, and they would be sent to a man who kept a saloon on Wyoming street. They would land at the depot, and at the beginning they would spend the first night on the platform. I have quartered many in my stable on the hay. One pulled out a prayer book and read a prayer. They were mainly Catholics, but some were Protestants, though we did not know that till later. Sometimes they would go up into the brush and build a fire and sleep, or if it was too cold, just sit there on the ground. As soon as they had earned something, or if they had a little money, they would go to the baker's or get meat of any cheap sort, regardless of its condition. Many were so poor that they came in old army suits,* their belongings all in one big bundle. At first it was only men that came."

Massachusetts farmers call in Poles

An interesting account of the coming of the first Poles to the Connecticut valley farms of Massachusetts tells how here, as in Pennsylvania, the influx was in direct response to a demand on the part of employers:†

"It was about twenty years ago that the Poles were first brought to the Connecticut valley. In the particular section under consideration, the farmers could not hire men and boys to work on their farms, or girls and women to assist in the household work. The demand was pressing. Charles Parsons of Northampton, who has since died, then a pushing, aggressive farmer, conceived the idea of going to New York and Castle Garden and there securing enough of the strong and sturdy immigrants to meet the demand for farm and domestic labor.

"The business grew rapidly. Mr. Parsons made weekly trips. Agents at New York told the incoming immigrants as pleasing stories as was necessary to make the Pole see the Connecticut Valley farms as the promised land. Being new and green to America, the Pole at first paid the highest price, and was given the small end of the bargain. The agent in New York had to have a fee for his trouble. Mr. Parsons had to advance

* Some of the peasant costumes might easily be mistaken for some sort of uniform.
† Boston *Daily Globe*, June 29, 1902.

the money to bring the Pole to the farm, and, of course, he had to have a profit also. This meant, as a rule, that the immigrant was practically mortgaged for $10 when he commenced work. It was, of course, to be taken out of the wages to be paid him for his labor. The contract was not particularly bad for either the farmer or laborer. The men came first, and were followed by women and children. How many Mr. Parsons took from New York cannot be stated. The number must have been in the thousands.

"Next Francis Clapp of South Deerfield took up the business. Mr. Clapp is one of the substantial farmers of the Mill River district in South Deerfield. He tells his story in this way:

"I began with the Poles in 1889. I continued it for six years, and then it was no longer profitable. The Poles had learned by this time to find their own places. In many cases their relatives, who had been working in this country for several years, sent for their friends. They secured places for them. During the six years I secured places for more than three thousand. I sent them to places in each of the six New England states, men and women, boys and girls. I treated them well. I found many of them suspicious, but they were 'square' as a rule. The yarns told them by some of the New York agents and by others who desired to make money out of them, at times caused trouble. One day I brought eighteen to South Deerfield. The New York agent had told them that they had friends in the vicinity. Of course I knew nothing of this. I did not have an interpreter, and we could not talk. They realized they had been deceived, and they determined to go back to New York. I succeeded in keeping only three. The other fifteen walked back to New York. They were entirely without money. They were frightened, and went in a drove.

"I had a license from the town to transact the business. I secured a girl as an interpreter who spoke seven different dialects. She could also do as much work in the house as any girl we ever had. She went back to New York after a time, married and went to work in a cigar factory. While they were waiting for places if such happened to be the case or for other reasons they were quartered at my farm.

"They seem, when they first come, to be entirely without nerves. They sleep well under all conditions. Their appetites are enormous. Of course they are given only coarse food. I have known the men to eat from ten to fifteen potatoes at a meal, together with meat and bread. They are very rarely sick.

"They make good citizens. Almost without exception they are Roman Catholics, and faithful to their obligations. They are willing to pay the price to succeed.   That price is to work hard and save.   They do not keep their money about them. They place it in the savings banks.   When I first went to New York to get them it cost the farmer nothing.   The Pole had to pay the fee for the New York agent, the money which I advanced to pay his fare and other expenses, and the profit I made.   Then, as they grew to know the custom better, the Pole paid half and the farmer half.   Now the farmer has to pay the whole when the men come from a distance.

"As a rule, the men are hired for a season of eight months, the time of outdoor work on the farms,   At first the contracts, on an average, were about $80 for the eight months.   The Poles were given little money, only as they needed it.   They had to work off the mortgage of $10 which they had contracted.   They really needed little money.   They were fed and lodged, and, as a rule, they had sufficient clothing, for they had little occasion to dress finely.   There was a chance, too, that if they had money they might leave the farmer without help, and so the settlement came at the end of the contract period.

" Roman Skibisky is a young Pole who is quite a daring specu- lator as well as farmer.   He lives in what was formerly one of the fine old mansions on the broad main street of Sunderland. For several years he has been plunging more or less in onions. Last fall he made his heaviest strike.   All told, he purchased about 6500 bushels of onions.   They cost him on an average less than forty cents a bushel.   He kept them until this spring and sold them at an average of $1.10 a bushel.

"Taking out the cost of cold storage and insurance he netted more than $4000 on an investment of about $2600.   At one time he could have sold his entire holdings at $1.25 a bushel.   His success has not given him a big head.   He works barefooted in the field this season just as though he had not made a rich strike. When Mrs. Skibisky was asked what she likes in this country she replied, 'Me happy here.'   They have three children."

"First comers"

Just as in emigration districts in Europe one hears of more than one "first man to go to America," so on this side there doubtless have been many "first comers." Sporadic and experimental trials of the land of the dol- lar, both induced and spontaneous, have opened new fields to immigrants.   As a spider throws his first thin thread across, and, his anchorage secured, gradually thickens and confirms it, so each immigrant who gets an economic foothold strengthens the bridge between the countries

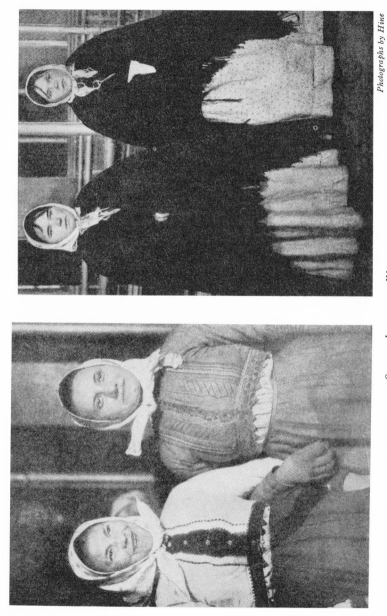

Photographs by Hine

SLOVAK IMMIGRANT WOMEN

and draws others over.   Thus among the Slavs the streams of immigration, once set flowing, have made paths for themselves, and constantly increased in volume.   As one labor market becomes supplied, new openings are sought and found.

The character of the later Slavic influx naturally produced a territorial distribution quite different from that of the older movement.   The new immigrants, guided in the main by the chances of good wages rather than of cheap land, rapidly found their way to the points where there was a demand for their undaunted though unskilled labor.   Once within the country, no contract labor law impeded the employers' agents, and men were drafted off to different places according as hands were needed in mine, coke oven, rolling mill, lumber camp or, less typically, factory.   Consequently, while the immigrants of the preceding period had mainly gone to the farming country lying north and west of Chicago, these later comers, answering primarily the call for labor in mines and related industries, found their center of gravity in Pennsylvania, and spread thence through the industrial districts, especially the industrial districts of the middle West, and above all to the various mining and metal-working centres throughout the country. *Distribution determined by demand for labor*

But though during this period agricultural settlement* has been overshadowed, it has by no means been lacking, especially among the Bohemians and the Poles.   It has taken place mainly in the group of states west of the great lakes; but in the Connecticut valley, and elsewhere in the East, the number of "Polanders" who have bought land is also considerable.   I have been surprised to see in a Bohemian paper in New York the space devoted to advertisement of Connecticut and other farms. *Farming*

This period has also seen the formation of large urban colonies of different nationalities, in various cities large *City colonies*

* Cf. Chapter XV for a discussion of this phase of settlement.

and small, colonies which often have very curious and interesting distinctive features.* Such a movement as this later Slavic immigration is, however, hard to deal with historically. It has little coherent history, and what it has is still too much in the making to be easily studied or presented.

The general facts as to the distribution of Slavic immigrants are shown on Map X, and the data as to each nationality separately are given, so far as I have been able to secure them, in the next chapter.

Numerical
increase
Census data

TABLE 15.—NATIVES OF AUSTRIA-HUNGARY, BOHEMIA, POLAND AND RUSSIA, 1880, 1890 AND 1900. UNITED STATES CENSUS.

NATIVES OF	1880	1890	1900
Austria................	38,663	123,271	275,907
Bohemia..............	85,361	118,106	156,891
Hungary..............	11,526	62,435	145,714
Poland................	48,557	147,440	383,407
Russia...............	35,722	182,644	423,726
Total..............	219,829	633,896	1,385,645
Total per cent of foreign born................	3.2	6.8	13.4

The period since 1880 has seen not only changes in the racial and economic character of the Slavs coming to the United States but a vast increase in their numbers.

* Cf., for the Bohemians of Chicago, Mrs. Humpal-Zeman's account in "Hull House Maps and Papers," and Dr. Alice Masaryk's article, "The Bohemians in Chicago," in *Charities*, XIII, pages 206–210 (Dec. 3, 1904). On Bohemians in New York see Dr. Jane E. Robbins, "The Bohemian Women in New York," *ibid.* pages 194–196.

In the same issue of *Charities* Miss Laura B. Garret has "Notes on the Poles in Baltimore," and Miss Sayles an article on "Housing and Social Conditions in a Slavic Neighborhood," which deals with Jersey City. Another study of conditions among the Slavs of Jersey City by Miss E. T. White has been published by Whittier House.

Of these various accounts those by the two Bohemian women first mentioned are much the most valuable to those who are seeking true understanding of the life of such a group as is there studied.

A rough indication of this is the large share of the foreign-born population that comes to be made up of natives of Austria-Hungary (including Bohemia), Poland and Russia. As shown in Table 15, in 1880 they were 3.2 per cent of the total foreign born; in 1890, 6.8 per cent; in 1900, 13.4 per cent. In absolute numbers they increased in the twenty years over six-fold, from something over 200,000 to nearly 1,400,000.

If we consider, not population as shown by the census, but the count of arriving immigrants, the increase is even more striking. In the last decade of our previous period, 1871–1880, Austria-Hungary and Russia* sent us 4.5 per cent of all immigrants; in the decade 1900–1909 they sent almost 43 per cent.

Up to 1899 the best material that we have consists of the figures, supplied by the immigration authorities, as to the countries from which immigration is drawn. After that year the immigration figures are also classified according to "races and peoples"† and these not only give us direct information, but throw light on the racial significance of the figures for the different geographical contingents, which are all that we have to go by for the years before 1899. We find that during the decade 1899–1908, the immigration from Austria-Hungary was six-tenths Slavic. Since there is no reason to think that this proportion would be less in earlier years, and since for the same decade 69 per cent of all Slavic immigrants came to us from Austria-Hungary (and for earlier periods this proportion would doubtless be still larger), the Austro-Hungarian contribution to our immigration may be taken as a rough index of the incoming Slavs.

A most vivid representation of the growth of the Austro-Hungarian stream is given by Chart II (page 246),

Immigration statistics

---

* Austria-Hungary presumably includes Bohemia and Austrian Poland (Galicia); Russia includes Russian Poland. That is, all Poland except German Poland is included. It must of course be remembered that these groups of immigrants are very mixed racially.

† For a criticism of this classification, see below, page 247.

drawn from the Immigration Reports, which shows how
this stream has swollen since 1867. The year 1880,
which we have taken as our landmark, shows a sudden

CHART II.

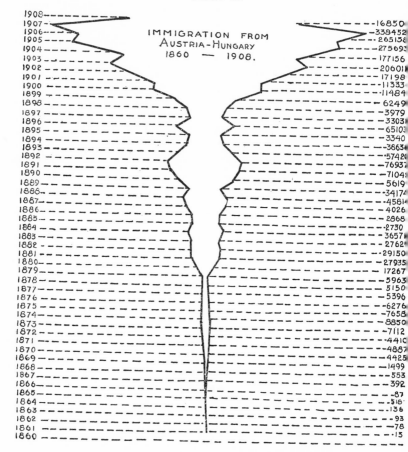

IMMIGRATION FROM
AUSTRIA-HUNGARY
1860 — 1908.

1908	16850
1907	338452
1906	265158
1905	275693
1904	177156
1903	20601
1902	17198
1901	11333
1900	11484
1899	6249
1898	3979
1897	3303
1896	65103
1895	3340
1894	3663
1893	57420
1892	76937
1891	71041
1890	5619
1889	34174
1888	4581
1887	4026
1886	2868
1885	2730
1884	3657
1883	2762
1882	29150
1881	27935
1880	17267
1879	5963
1878	5150
1877	5396
1876	6276
1875	7658
1874	8850
1873	7112
1872	4410
1871	4887
1870	4425
1869	1499
1868	553
1867	392
1866	87
1865	518
1864	136
1863	93
1862	78
1861	15
1860	

rise, the numbers of that year being almost three times
those of the preceding. From this time onward there is
an increase, which is, however, sharply checked in 1893
by the depression then beginning. It was not till 1900

that the numbers reacted from this to their level of 1892. The culminating point up to date was reached in 1907, after which the recent panic again lessened the influx, and started a new period of decline, though a brief one, since the figures for 1909 (received too late to appear on the chart), indicate a recovery from 168,509 to 170,191.*

The change spoken of above by which the immigration data are presented by racial and national groups instead of by country of last permanent residence only, is a great boon to the student of this subject. The classification was made by one of our best known ethnologists, the late Professor Otis T. Mason, but it is probably impossible to make one that shall be at once practical and quite logical. This one is open to several minor objections. Distinct nationalities like Croatians and Slovenians, Bulgarians and Servians, are lumped together, and at the same time special place is given to a group which is merely a territorial division; namely, Dalmatians, Bosnians, and Herzegovinians (who are Servo-Croatians). *Classification by "races and peoples"*

It is hard, however, to explain or excuse the practice of the immigration authorities of including Hebrews in the Slavic group, as was done, for instance, on page 21 of the 1906 report of the Commissioner General of Immigration. In the same report the Lithuanians and Roumanians are also included as Slavic, but this is less objectionable as these peoples, although they never count themselves as Slavs nor are so counted by others, and although they speak non-Slavic languages, probably have much Slavic intermixture, and considerably resemble, in culture and habits, the neighboring Slavic peoples. The same might be said of the Magyars, despite their Mongolian type of speech.

The Jew, on the contrary, even the Polish or Russian Jew, is not only remote in blood and speech from all

* The years are not calendar but fiscal years ending June 30, so that e.g. 1907 means July 1, 1906, to June 30, 1907. How differently the various Slavic groups were affected by the depression may be studied in Appendix XVII, page 460.

Slavs, but moves in another world of ideas and purposes, and plays a very different economic part both in Europe and America. To put him into one class with Slavic immigrants in a table of racial divisions can only create confusion.*

The years 1899 and 1908 are the earliest and latest for which full information as to immigrants by races is available. In these ten years the country admitted over one and a half million Slavs, many of whom, however, had been here before or have since returned. It is not uncommon for a Slovak to have made the trip to America eight times, in which case he appears in our figures as eight immigrants.

Immigration by countries and peoples

The facts for the period are shown by the tables in Appendix XVII, where we see that 69 in 100 of Slavic arrivals came, as already said, from Austria-Hungary, 25 per cent more from Russia, 2 per cent each from Germany and the territory Bulgaria-Servia-Montenegro, 1 per cent from Turkey, and only 1 per cent from all other countries combined.

The immigration from Bulgaria, Servia and Montenegro is almost wholly Slavic (96 per cent), that from Austria nearly two-thirds such (61 per cent), while the streams from Russia and Turkey are not far from one-third Slavic, and that from Germany is one-tenth Slavic.

Our previous study of conditions in Europe, combined with the American figures, indicates that we have received during the decade 1899–1908 the following groups from the countries named:

I. From Austria-Hungary:
   Bohemians (Chekhs) from Bohemia, Moravia and
      Silesia (83,698).
   Poles from Galicia (about 335,651).

* For a further consideration of this subject, see Boeckh: "The Determination of Racial Stock among American Immigrants." Quart. Pub'ns. Am. Stat. Assn., X, pages 199–221 (Dec., 1906).

Slovaks from northern Hungary (about 320,047).

Ruthenians from Galicia and northeastern Hungary (about 102,036).

Slovenians from the Austrian province of Carniola and adjacent parts (number unknown).*

Croatians from Croatia-Slavonia, Istria, Dalmatia, Bosnia and Herzegovina and southern Hungary (number unknown).*

Servians from the same territory (certainly less than 28,677).

II. From outside Austria-Hungary:

The largest of the three Polish contingents, that from Russia (369,973).

The smallest of the three Polish contingents, that from Germany (32,388).

Russians proper, from Russia (53,454), only between three and four per cent of the total of almost a million and a half immigrants that Russia has sent us in the decade.

Servians (beside those from Austria-Hungary) from Servia, Montenegro, Bulgaria (?) and Turkey (?) (number unknown).* Montenegrins are Servians from Montenegro.

And lastly, Bulgarians from Bulgaria and Turkey, which latter, I suppose, here means Macedonia (number unknown). (See page 274 ff.)

A large part of the Slavic immigrants that come from outside the five main fields ((1) Austria-Hungary, (2) Russia, (3) Germany, (4) Bulgaria, Servia, and Montenegro, and (5) Turkey in Europe) are those who give their last permanent residence as British North America or the United States.   The latter rubric was, however, provided only in the 1906 tables, in which it occupies a large space, (1059 Poles, for instance, gave the United States as their last country of permanent residence).

Turning now to the consideration of the separate national streams, we note (cf. Appendix XVII) the great Racial groups

---

* Unfortunately the immigration data are so grouped as to make it impossible to distinguish Croatians and Slovenians from one another, or Bulgarians and Servians from one another, though these are all separate nationalities with distinct languages.

numerical predominance of the Poles, who make up 44 per cent of the Slav total for the decade. The little people of the Slovaks make the second group, with almost one-fifth of the whole. Third comes the mixed group of Croatians and Slovenians, which the data do not allow us to separate, and which together make over 16 per cent. The other groups are all much smaller. The Bohemians, who were the most important group of Slavic immigrants in the earlier years, and even in 1880 were not far from twice as numerous in the country as natives of Poland, sank during this period to one-twentieth of the whole; that is, to less than the little group of the Ruthenians and to scarcely more than those newcomers, the Servians and Bulgarians.

Even within the period the emphasis has been shifting. Within the Slavic group, as in European immigration in general, the spread of the movement has trended south and east. Taking 1907, the year of the high tide of immigration, and comparing this with 1899, we see that the different groups have increased at very different rates. The Bulgarian-Servian group rose from under 100 to 27,000, or to two hundred and ninety-one times as many. The related group from Dalmatia and Bosnia increased twenty-fold; the Ruthenians, starting with 1400, rose to over 24,000, multiplying more than seven times; the Russians increased their numbers nearly ten times. The older immigration groups also increased, though at a less rate; Bohemians and Poles and the Croatian-Slovenian group all about five-fold, while the Slovaks increased less than three-fold, and reached their maximum in 1905.

"Alien departures" and net inflow

We must, however, be on guard in using any immigration totals not to overlook the fact that they represent gross, not net, arrivals. We must allow for the numbers of immigrants returning from the United States. In the appendix to the report of the Commissioner General of Immigration for 1908, an estimate is attempted of

"Alien departures," with the result that the accepted immigration figures should be reduced as follows:

1899 by 41 per cent		1904 by 37 per cent	
1900 by 31	" "	1905 by 34	" "
1901 by 28	" "	1906 by 26	" "
1902 by 21	" "	1907 by 22	" "
1903 by 21	" "	1908 by 73	" "

That is, while the total immigration for 1908 was 782,870, the real, net immigration was only 209,867, or not far above *a quarter* as much,—and for this one year the figures are not estimated but actual.* What then are we to suppose in regard to the Slavic immigration? What proportion of their total of nearly 1,700,000 during the decade 1899–1908 represents a net addition to our numbers? We get a side light on this by studying Table III of the successive immigration reports which gives the number of immigrants of each nationality who have been in the country previously. In Appendix XIX are given percentages for two years (for 1906 and, for purposes of comparison, for 1900) and I find to my own surprise that the English, Irish and Scotch have the largest proportion and thus appear to come and go the most, and that the Scandinavians and Germans also stand high. The Slovaks have nearly as high a rate of those returning as the Irish, in both years; other Slavs have smaller proportions. Jews, as one might expect, come to stay, and go back and forth less than any other class noted.

From these figures we see that while the Slavs, except the Slovaks, are (if the data are correct) less migratory than the average, there is still a large deduction to be made for those entering the country more than once, and in addition to this, for the large though hitherto unknown number who leave and do not return.

* For the first time, in 1909, we are getting actual data by nationalities of emigration from the United States. At this writing they are available for July, 1908, to May, 1909. Those for the Slavs drawn from the Immigration Bulletin for July, 1909, are given in Appendix XVIII.

Another indication of the discrepancy between immigration totals and net additions to the population is given by a comparison of the figures for immigration with the United States census. Foreign countries sent us, in the decade 1891–1900, 3,687,564 immigrants. The census of 1900, however, shows a gain of foreign born since 1890 of less than a third as many (1,091,729). Part of this difference, but not by any means all of it, is accounted for by deaths among our foreign-born population.

CHAPTER XIII

THE PRESENT DISTRIBUTION OF SLAVS IN THE UNITED STATES

As regards the distribution of our Slavic population, it is not possible to get full and satisfactory data. We should like to know, both for the Slavic body as a whole and for each of the nationalities composing it, the total numbers of the group, the size and location of its chief colonies, the states in which it has any considerable representation, and the way in which the area of settlement has extended. It would also be interesting to know how many of each group are in cities, how many in smaller industrial centers and around mines, how many in rural communities. Unfortunately much of this information is not to be had. *The data as to present distribution*

The census figures by country of parents' birth are given herewith in Table 16, but they supply no precise information as to nationalities. Where the political boundaries of one country comprise many national groups, as in Austria and Hungary, and where, on the other hand, racial groups are cut through by political boundaries, as are the Poles, Little Russians and Croatians, the country of birth tells a small part of the story. *Difficulties in using census and immigration figures*

The statistics of the immigration department as to intended destinations of immigrants, given by nationalities, for 1899 and succeeding years, are valuable as some indication of the flow of the current, though they doubtless exaggerate the degree of concentration of settlement.

In the first place, the states in which the ports of entry are situated, and notably New York state, are credited with all those who arrive with no specific address though

TABLE 16.*—NUMBER AND PERCENTAGE OF WHITE PERSONS OF FOREIGN PARENTAGE HAVING EITHER ONE OR BOTH PARENTS BORN IN SPECIFIED COUNTRIES, BY STATES AND TERRITORIES; ARRANGED GEOGRAPHICALLY: 1900

WHITE PERSONS HAVING EITHER BOTH PARENTS BORN AS SPECIFIED OR ONE PARENT BORN AS SPECIFIED AND ONE PARENT NATIVE

STATES AND TERRITORIES	Austria		Bohemia		Hungary		Poland		Russia	
	Number	Per cent	Number	Per cent	Number	Per cent	Number	Per cent	Number	Per cent
The United States†	434,617	1.7	356,830	1.4	216,391	0.8	687,671	2.7	685,176	2.6
North Atlantic division	251,618	2.3	41,123	0.4	155,542	1.5	306,335	2.9	434,938	4.1
Maine	224	0.1	34	(‡)	53	(‡)	524	0.3	1,566	0.8
New Hampshire	278	0.2	14	(‡)	104	0.1	909	0.6	1,083	0.6
Vermont	311	0.3	40	(‡)	148	0.1	247	0.4	659	0.6
Massachusetts	5,503	0.3	1,572	0.1	1,361	0.1	20,412	1.7	40,712	2.3
Rhode Island	822	0.3	58	(‡)	84	(‡)	2,533	0.9	3,783	1.4
Connecticut	7,677	1.5	907	0.2	8,283	1.6	14,315	2.7	17,505	3.4
New York	117,581	2.7	30,408	0.7	57,036	1.3	116,949	2.7	250,392	6.0
New Jersey	22,156	2.2	1,847	0.2	20,276	2.0	21,495	2.2	31,479	3.2
Pennsylvania	97,066	4.0	6,243	0.2	68,197	2.8	119,781	5.0	78,759	3.3
South Atlantic division	6,278	1.0	6,245	1.0	2,925	0.5	9,625	1.6	27,157	4.5
North Central division	123,665	1.1	279,290	2.4	51,033	0.4	353,512	3.0	187,232	1.6
Ohio	17,494	1.2	33,096	2.3	25,006	1.8	31,760	2.3	13,406	1.0
Indiana	3,457	0.7	1,152	0.2	2,131	0.4	12,689	2.5	2,099	0.4
Illinois	29,922	1.2	81,478	3.3	9,891	0.4	126,603	5.1	44,997	1.8
Michigan	9,836	0.7	5,084	0.4	1,081	0.1	61,091	4.5	6,567	0.5
Wisconsin	15,144	1.0	36,223	2.5	1,876	0.1	74,657	5.1	6,214	0.4
Minnesota	16,485	1.3	28,376	2.2	4,223	0.3	26,160	2.0	10,437	0.8
Iowa	4,671	0.5	29,203	3.0	833	0.1	1,510	0.2	3,378	0.4
Missouri	8,536	1.2	8,404	1.1	1,497	0.2	6,978	0.9	10,951	1.5
North Dakota	2,014	0.8	3,654	1.5	1,797	0.7	2,112	0.9	23,909	9.7
South Dakota	1,692	0.7	6,361	2.6	881	0.4	1,146	0.5	25,689	10.5
Nebraska	8,085	1.6	38,471	7.6	882	0.2	7,338	1.5	14,537	2.9
Kansas	6,320	1.6	7,788	1.9	935	0.2	1,478	0.4	25,048	6.2
South Central division	21,473	2.0	26,358	2.5	3,113	0.3	12,091	1.1	16,527	1.6
Western division	30,652	1.7	3,638	0.2	3,653	0.2	5,887	0.3	18,537	1.0

* U. S. Census, 1900, Population, Vol. I. Table lxxxix, page cxciv.   † Includes persons in the military territory.   ‡ Less than one-tenth of 1 per cent.

254

perhaps with no desire or likelihood of staying in the state, as well as with all those who stay there for a short time only and are later distributed thence by employment agencies and otherwise.

Secondly, too great numbers are ascribed to the states that already have the largest colonies and are best known in the home countries, and where, consequently, incoming immigrants have acquaintances or hope to get work. Many, for instance, strike first for Pennsylvania, and afterwards go from there to West Virginia, Montana, or elsewhere. The Slovak colony of a city like Pittsburgh is equivalent to a big employment and information bureau, and by no means all of those who resort to the city remain there. For example, to a mining camp in Colorado where I was, came a Slovak family just procured from Pittsburgh.

Thirdly, the totals are exaggerated by counting the same man over every time that he goes home and returns. How serious a misconception this produces has been already discussed (page 250, ff.).

Bearing these reservations in mind, however, the accompanying Map X and Table 17, summarizing the data as to the intended destinations of immigrants for the ten years ending June 30, 1908, have considerable interest. *Destinations during the last decade*

We see that much the largest total contingent of Slavs was headed for Pennsylvania, over twice as many as for New York state, over three times as many as for Illinois. The chief groups for Pennsylvania are (a) the Poles, (b) the Slovaks, (c) the Croatians and Slovenians, (d) the Ruthenians. All four of these nationalities are represented more largely in Pennsylvania than in any other state. The others are comparatively negligible, yet the largest contingent of the Bulgarians and Servians comes here, and the state has more Russians than any other except New York. The Bohemians, however, go elsewhere in larger numbers; namely, to Illinois, which takes first place, to New York, which stands second,

TABLE 17.—DESTINATIONS OF SLAVIC IMMIGRANTS DURING THE DECADE ENDED JUNE 30, 1908

STATE	BOHEMIANS AND MORAVIANS	BULGARIANS, SERVIANS AND MONTENEGRINS	CROATIANS AND SLOVENIANS	DALMATIANS, BOSNIANS AND HERZEGOVINIANS	POLES	RUSSIANS	RUTHENIANS	SLOVAKS	TOTAL
Pennsylvania	7,622	18,548	121,311	2,057	209,697	12,866	53,809	160,116	595,116
New York	15,072	7,921	22,045	7,020	159,849	17,700	21,376	41,460	292,443
Illinois	22,816	14,082	33,962	4,096	92,532	3,719	2,340	21,351	194,898
New Jersey	1,431	770	3,039	1,449	62,972	2,717	11,205	30,510	114,093
Ohio	9,914	11,743	28,822	596	25,870	695	3,478	26,001	107,119
Massachusetts	546	705	374	52	64,377	4,061	2,429	2,258	74,802
Connecticut	571	133	916	110	34,285	1,836	2,747	9,045	49,643
Michigan	1,154	1,719	7,760	91	25,733	470	522	2,646	40,104
Wisconsin	2,959	755	6,400	182	12,864	394	181	4,004	27,739
Missouri	1,934	3,765	8,304	1,122	4,604	350	798	2,565	23,532
Minnesota	1,695	1,287	8,503	464	4,175	262	445	1,496	18,307
Maryland	2,198	664	917	7	9,831	2,326	638	1,300	17,881
West Virginia	479	1,038	4,932	727	4,563	485	507	3,380	16,120
Indiana	187	3,187	2,656	103	5,069	77	167	2,249	13,695
Texas	6,307	2,126	1,029	131	1,812	923	494	221	13,043
California	211	1,020	2,863	2,884	385	2,850	100	276	10,589
Colorado	526	595	5,780	692	535	504	109	701	9,442
Rhode Island	49	62	39	10	5,672	202	617	129	6,780
Washington	185	617	2,608	810	1,061	518	135	364	6,208
Nebraska	3,999	44	332	11	1,205	183	14	79	5,867
New Hampshire	6	145	8	3	3,795	421	278	46	4,702
Vermont	28	33	42	5	3,817	232	314	400	4,404
Delaware	26	1	32	2	644	71	303	70	4,322
Kansas	707	108	2,100	7	193	301	93	233	4,193
Montana	74	675	2,207	400	381	14	23	278	3,864
Iowa	1,589	108	1,662	13	794	69	22	216	3,460
North Dakota	746	14	72	11	138	1,172	380	94	3,247
Louisiana	61	936	1,108	454	341	337	78	73	3,185
Virginia	158	371	536	75	1,994	380	75	439	2,375
Maine	1	88	35	14	141	91	30	461	1,814
South Dakota	408	168	269	283	257	240	46	57	1,612
Wyoming	131	170	714	63	20	18	19	178	1,550
Arizona	40	626	377	281	21	150	..	21	1,515
Utah	10	1,066	..	38	21	..	..	35	1,210
Oregon	31	39	499	294	93	94	13	104	1,203
Alabama	25	75	219	14	54	13	15	290	1,185
Tennessee	12	56	806	5	103	24	..	35	1,041

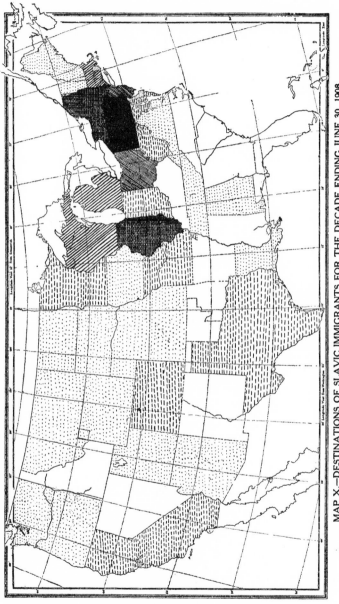

MAP X.—DESTINATIONS OF SLAVIC IMMIGRANTS FOR THE DECADE ENDING JUNE 30, 1908

Data from Annual Reports of Commissioner General of Immigration. Numbers indicate total of Slavic immigrants reporting a specified destination.

Black: over 500,000.   Pennsylvania, 595,116.
Cross-barred: 190,000–300,000.   N. Y., 292,443, Ill. 194,898.
Close diagonal: 100,000–120,000.   N. J. 114,093, O. 107,119.
Coarse diagonal: 25,000–75,000.   Mass. 74,802,   Conn. 49,643, Mich. 40,104, Wis. 27,739.
Broken cross lines: 9000–25,000.   Mo. 23,532, Minn. 18 307, Md. 17,881,
W. Va. 16,120, Ind. 13,695, Texas. 13,043, Cal. 10,589, Col. 9442.
Dotted: 1000–7000.   R. I. 6780, Wash. 6208, Neb. 5867, N. H. 4702, Vt. 4404, Del. 4322, Kan. 4193, Mont. 3864, Iowa, 3466, N. D. 3347, La. 3185, Va. 2375, Me. 1814, S. D. 1612, Wyo. 1550, Ariz. 1515 Utah, 1210, Oregon, 1203, Ala. 1185, Tenn. 1041.
White: Less than 1000.   All other.

17   257

and third, to Ohio; Pennsylvania ranking as fourth choice and just above Texas.   The Dalmatian group also made Pennsylvania its fourth choice, after New York, Illinois and California (the latter sought by about 2900).*

Settlement   If in addition to these data as to the trend of the current, we wish to know the actual numbers and locations of the colonies of the different nationalities, we have to rely mainly on estimates and on indirect indications.   From printed and manuscript matter in various languages, and from personal inquiry, I have gathered what I could, with the following results.†

BOHEMIANS IN THE UNITED STATES

Bohemian immigration grown less important   Of late the relative numerical importance of Bohemian immigrants has decreased; they have ceased to stand to Americans as the type of the Slav.   In 1909 they were only about four in a hundred of the Slavic arrivals, and in the period 1880 to 1900, while the census showed an increase of nearly eight-fold for natives of Poland (Jews included), of nearly seven-fold for natives of Austria, and for natives of Hungary an increase of nearly thirteen-fold, the number of natives of Bohemia did not double.   The census figures are: natives of Bohemia, in 1880, 85,361; in 1900, 156,891.

More urban in character   To some extent the character of the Bohemian immigration has also altered, and not apparently for the

---

* Outside of the thirty-seven states given in the table, no state has a total of 1000.   Arkansas, Indian Territory, New Mexico and Oklahoma taken together show 3426, including over 700 Croatians and Slovenians in Arkansas and New Mexico, and over 300 Bohemians in Oklahoma.   Nevada and Idaho together have nearly 500, mainly in Nevada, and most of them South Slavs.   South Carolina attracted over one hundred each of Poles and Bohemians.   Mississippi and Kentucky each attracted over 100 Croatians and Slovenians.   A few South Slavs (over 150 in all) have sought Georgia.   Florida and North Carolina have trivial numbers only (100 and 55); Hawaii still fewer (51), including 35 Russians; Porto Rico 30; the Philippines none.   Alaska on the other hand was the goal of 342, including 78 Russians and 243 South Slavs, of whom Montenegrins probably made a considerable part.   (Compare page 199.)

† For numbers of the various Slav groups engaged in farming, see Chapter XV.

better. For one thing, it seeks the cities somewhat more than it did. In 1880 the fifty largest cities of the country held somewhat under 40 per cent of the natives of Bohemia, in 1900, 50 per cent. This change is due largely to the great growth of the colony, or rather colonies, in Chicago, which added nearly 25,000 natives of Bohemia in this period. Cleveland gained something over 8000, New York not quite 7000, and Baltimore over 1000. St. Louis lost in relative importance as a Bohemian centre, having attracted practically no newcomers, and the other Bohemian city colonies did not receive many. Omaha (with South Omaha) had in 1900 a colony of 3283; I have no figures for this city for 1880.*

More interesting are the gains, as shown by the census, for the districts outside of these few large city colonies. Nebraska added over 7000 natives of Bohemia, making it the third Bohemian state, and barely less than New York (16,347 and 16,138). In no other state do the Bohemians make so large a proportion (9 per cent) of the foreign-born population. Oklahoma, with 7 per cent, comes next, and Texas, if Moravians were not counted as Austrians, might show nearly the same proportion. Texas, in spite of being such an old colony, received nearly 6000 (besides Moravians), Minnesota received 3400, the Dakotas together 2400, Oklahoma nearly 1200. These are the chief growing points, and they certainly suggest a wholesome distribution. Pennsylvania, such a lodestone to the Slovaks, Croatians, Poles and other Slavs, to say nothing of Italians, attracted to its heavy tasks less Bohemians than went to the prairies of the Dakotas alone. *Gains outside the cities*

It is interesting to note that these figures give a somewhat different impression from the table of destinations.† This is doubtless because many Bohemians who have been in the country for some time move farther west, *The westward movement of old settlers*

* See United States Census, 1900, Population, Part I, Table 35, for statistics of foreign born in cities.
† See Table 17, page 256.

their places being filled by newcomers from the old country whose influx they neutralize in our census totals. Thus, the data in regard to destinations by no means fully reflect the push westward. Note for instance that the old Bohemian strongholds of Wisconsin and Iowa, though still to a considerable extent the goal for immigrants, made only slight net gains.*

The southern states gained but few Bohemians, or else lost some of the few that they had. New Jersey, Massachusetts and Connecticut gained merely some hundreds each (New Jersey the most with 631). If we add Kansas, with a gain of 571, we exhaust the list of any important changes of distribution, so far as registered by the census figures for natives of Bohemia.

Bohemians in feeling Of more interest than this information as to the number of those born in Bohemia is information as to those who count themselves Bohemians, and who constitute the real strength of the group. In a tenacious race like the Slavic, which has had its national feeling intensified by the fight it has been obliged to make to preserve its national existence and above all its own tongue, the third or even the fourth generation may still count themselves as belonging to their ancestors' stock, and be none the worse Americans either. Have the English sympathies of a descendant of a Winthrop or a Lee disappeared in half a score of generations?

Estimates of "Bohemian" group I estimate from a number of data that in a community perhaps fifty years old, the census figure for those born in Bohemia must be multiplied three or four times to give the number of those who count as "Bohemians." Fortunately, however, we are not reduced to deductions of this sort, for we are dealing with a very intelligent and self conscious group who know their own numbers pretty well. The Reverend Valentine Kohlbeck, writing in 1906 in the *Champlain Educator*, gives a series of esti-

* Bohemians destined to Wisconsin in ten years ending June 30, 1908, 2959. Increase in Bohemian-born in Wisconsin, 1880–1900, 297. The corresponding figures for Iowa are 1589 and 255.

mates which are not likely to be without error, but which doubtless indicate, at least in a rough way, the distribution of the group, and which are shown in Table 18 along with the census figures for purposes of comparison.

TABLE 18.—BOHEMIANS IN THE UNITED STATES.

STATE	Rev. Mr. Kohlbeck's Estimate of "Bohemians," 1906*		Census of 1900. Persons with both Parents Natives of Bohemia†	
	Rank	Number	Rank	Number
Illinois	1	110,000	1	77,329
Nebraska	2	57,000	2	35,115
Texas	3	48,000	8	20,253§
Iowa	4	45,000	7	24,944
New York	5	40,000	5	29,135
Wisconsin	6	38,000	4	31,074
Ohio . . . . }	7	30,000‡	3	31,416
Minnesota . . . . }		30,000	6	24,960
Kansas	8	20,000	10	6,802
South Dakota	9	18,000	12	5,660
Missouri	10	15,000	9	7,222
Maryland . . . . }	11	12,000	13	5,292
Michigan . . . . }		12,000	14	4,443
North Dakota	12	10,000	15	3,285
Pennsylvania	13	8,000	11	5,923
New Jersey	14	6,000	17	1,752
Oklahoma	15	5,000	16	2,467
Indiana . . . . }		2,000	19	1,003
Arkansas . . . . }	16	2,000	23	566
California . . . . }		2,000	21	756
Colorado	17	1,500	22	606
Massachusetts . . . . }		1,000‡	18	1,533
Virginia . . . . }	18	1,000	24	478
Washington . . . . . . }		1,000	21	756
Oregon	19	800	25	430
Connecticut	. .	No estimate	20	852
Montana	. .	" "	26	319
Scattered	. .	2,000		1,029
Total for U. S	. .	517,300	. .	325,400

* Kohlbeck, Rev. Valentine: "The Catholic Bohemians of the United States." The *Champlain Educator*, XXV, pages 36–54. (Jan-Mar., 1906.)

† Census, 1900, Population, Part I, Table 38.

‡ Doubtless too low.

§ Here and elsewhere the presence of Chekhs from Moravia, who make one group with the Bohemians but do not appear in the census figures for natives of Bohemia, help to cause a discrepancy. Cf. page 217.

POLES IN THE UNITED STATES

Father
Kruszka's
figures

Since the census figures for "Natives of Poland" include Polish Jews and others, they are of little use for our purpose, so that it is particularly fortunate that we have so devoted a student of Polish conditions as the Rev. W. X. Kruszka of Ripon, Wisconsin, to fall back upon. The latest estimate of his that I have seen printed was in the *Polish Press* (*Prasa Polska*), a little bi-lingual sheet published in Milwaukee, under date of March 2, 1907. This table shows a total of only a little over 2,000,000 (2,199,411), but Father Kruszka has since written me, under date of January, 1907, that he then put the number at about 3,000,000.

A later estimate appeared, unsigned, in the *Polish Press* of December 15, 1908, with the remark, "Polish immigration, especially from Russian Poland, has been increasing so fast during the last eight years that it is hard to keep track of it. According to Polish immigration and colonization agents, the Polish population in the United States numbers 4,000,000, distributed in the following states."* Both estimates are given in Table 19.

These figures refer, of course, to all those who, whether themselves born of Polish parents or not, count in the community as Poles. By divisions of the country Father Kruszka's table shows 1,082,000 in the North Atlantic states, 1,033,000 in the North Central, or over 96 per cent of the whole in the North and North Atlantic region.

City colo-
nies of Poles

As regards the urban population, it is impossible to tell what proportion of the Poles are city dwellers, but

---

* Mr. Siemiradski of the Polish National Alliance writes me, August 25, 1909: "The data of Father Kruszka were about as correct as possible for 1907. The last two years did not bring much increase, as during the financial panic many Poles left for the old country, and the influx of new immigrants was not considerable. But of course many Polish children were born in this time, and it would be safer to put the whole number of Poles in the United States as over 3,000,000, and together with Canada about 4,000,000."

TABLE 19.—POLES IN THE UNITED STATES. ESTI-
MATES OF REV. W. X. KRUSZKA AND OF THE
"POLISH PRESS"

ESTIMATE OF REV. W. X. KRUSZKA *Polish Press*, MARCH 2, 1907		ANONYMOUS ESTIMATE IN *Polish Press*, DECEMBER 15, 1908	
State	Number	State	Number
Pennsylvania	422,790	Pennsylvania........	525,000
Illinois..........	388,745	New York..........	500,000
New York.......	355,725	Illinois.............	450,000
Wisconsin........	197,945	Massachusetts......	300,000
Michigan.........	160,830	Wisconsin..........	250,000
Massachusetts....	128,515	Michigan...........	250,000
Ohio............	96,110	New Jersey........	200,000
New Jersey......	92,785	Minnesota..........	140,000
Minnesota........	88,805	Connecticut........	125,000
Connecticut......	61,490	Ohio..............	125,000
Indiana..........	41,335	Indiana............	70,000
Missouri.........	21,400	Missouri...........	60,000
Maryland........	19,415	Maryland..........	50,000
Nebraska........	18,770	Nebraska..........	50,000
Texas...........	18,740	Rhode Island.......	40,000
Rhode Island.....	10,310	Maine.............	35,000
Delaware........	8,630	Texas.............	25,000
California........	6,600	West Virginia......	25,000
North Dakota....	6,270	Delaware..........	20,000
Kansas..........	5,455	North Dakota......	15,000
New Hampshire..	5,320	Kansas............	8,000
Washington......	4,480	California..........	8,000
Colorado........	4,100	Washington........	7,000
Iowa............	3,755	Colorado..........	6,000
South Dakota....	3,360	Iowa..............	6,000
Kentucky........	3,340	Oklahoma..........	6,000
Maine...........	3,215	Oregon............	6,000
Oklahoma	2,780	Vermont..........	6,000
Oregon..........	2,656	South Dakota......	5,000
Tennessee........	2,610	Kentucky..........	5,000
Arkansas........	2,575	Montana..........	5,000
Montana.........	2,065	Tennessee..........	5,000
Indian Territory..	1,995	Other states	Less than
Vermont.........	1,795		5,000
Georgia..........	945		
Alabama.........	865	Total including Can-	
Louisiana........	840	ada.............	c. 4,000,000
South Carolina ...	815		
Mississippi.......	650		
North Carolina...	375		
Florida..........	210		
Total..........	2,199,411		

of Polish city colonies certain estimates are given in Table 20, below. Father Kruszka also in the first volume of his "Historya Polska w Ameryce"* gives a set of estimates of city colonies for 1903, which are attested in each case by the mayor as, to the best of his information, the number of inhabitants "of Polish nativity and origin." These are as follows: Chicago, 250,000; Buffalo, and immediate suburbs, about 70,000; Milwaukee, 65,000; Detroit and immediate suburbs, 50,000; Pittsburgh and immediate suburbs, upwards of 50,000; Cleveland and immediate suburbs, 30,000; Toledo, 14,000.

TABLE 20.—POLES IN CITIES. ANONYMOUS ESTIMATE IN "POLISH PRESS," DECEMBER 15, 1908.

Chicago and suburbs................	350,000
Greater New York	250,000
Buffalo and suburbs................	80,000
Milwaukee and suburbs.............	75,000
Detroit and suburbs................	75,000
Jersey City, Toledo, Cleveland, Bay City, Manistee, South Bend, St. Louis, Kansas City, St. Paul, Winona, Omaha and various other cities....	Considerable, but unknown number.

Course of settlement

As to the dates of settlement, Father Kruszka's figures for the founding of Polish churches give some information.† In the decade 1880–1889, the North Central district continued to be the most important. Wisconsin shows twenty churches founded during this time, Minnesota seventeen, Michigan sixteen, Nebraska seven, Dakota two. Some of these were in the cities (as Milwaukee, St. Paul, Detroit, and Omaha), some in little places with picturesque Polish names (as Pulaski, Sobieski, Krakow, Gniezno, Opole, Wilno, Tarnow, Chojnice).

About the middle of the eighties Pennsylvania began to gain rapidly, with twenty-seven churches in the decade 1884–1893. Previous to this there had been eight Polish churches in the state, beginning at Shamokin in 1870 and Shenandoah 1873. Massachusetts had

* Vol. I, page 90 ff.　　　　　† See above, page 230.

a Polish church in Boston in 1880, in Chicopee in 1887, in Fall River in 1890; Connecticut had one in Meriden in 1891. In the four years 1888–1891 New York gained twelve Polish churches, four of them in Buffalo. All of this represents the growth of mining and factory centres among the Poles, in contrast to the homestead settlements farther west.

In the next period, during the eleven years 1890–1900, this growth in industrial districts continued. Pennsylvania added twenty-eight churches, Illinois twenty-six, including the fourteenth Polish church in Chicago. In New England, Worcester and Holyoke in Massachusetts, New Britain, Ansonia, Bridgeport and Norwich in Connecticut, and Providence, Rhode Island, gained Polish churches. The more agricultural districts were not, however, at a standstill. Wisconsin added twenty-one parishes, and Texas took a fresh start and added eight. On the Pacific, Tacoma was added to the list in 1890 and several other places in Washington soon after.

The immigration reports also throw some light on the distribution of Poles. During the ten years ended June 30, 1908, Poles to the number of 743,151 entered the country, being, as already shown, 44 per cent of the total Slavic arrivals for the period. Of these Poles, nearly 210,000 sought Pennsylvania, and nearly 160,000 New York state, together almost a half of the Polish immigration of the decade. Illinois, Massachusetts and New Jersey, Ohio, Michigan and Wisconsin, were next in order of popularity. No other state ran to six figures, but thirteen states were the goal of 1000 Poles or more. *Immigration data as to destinations*

SLOVAKS IN THE UNITED STATES

It is particularly hard to estimate the numbers of this nationality. From the immigration reports we can learn how many have come in since 1899 but not how many came earlier, how many have gone away nor how many have been born or have died here. The census lumps them indistinguishably with all the other natives *Number of Slovaks hard to estimate* of Hungary. But though the word Hungarian is often used in this country to mean Slovak, and though the Slovaks are probably the largest group of immigrants who have come to us from Hungary, they probably make less than a third of the Hungarian contingent—to judge from the immigration figures of 1905, the only ones which give the data for Hungary separate from those for Austria.*

The fact that the Slovaks are divided religiously makes it harder to get trustworthy estimates for them than for a nationality which, like the Poles, is practically all included in one religious body. The larger number of them are Roman Catholics, but some are Lutherans, some Calvinists, and some members of the Greek Catholic church in which they are hopelessly confused with the Ruthenians. (See Table 28, page 386.)

Accordingly estimates of their numbers in this country vary widely. One informant says 750,000, another 500,000. Mr. Čapek, in his very interesting book "The Slovaks of Hungary," published in 1906, to which I have several times referred, puts them at "well-nigh 400,000." The immigration figures show over 300,000 landed in the last decade alone, but this doubtless includes many double counts, as the Slovak immigrant is prone to go back and forth. In 1905 nearly a quarter of those arriving had been in the country before.

Destinations of Slovaks

As to their distribution in this country, the data for intended destinations of immigrants during the last ten years show that every state and territory † (and Alaska and Porto Rico besides), was given as a destination by

* In 1905 Hungary sent us 163,703 immigrants, of whom 51,000 were Slovaks, 22,000 Croatians and Slovenians, 3000 Ruthenians, and 3000 other Slavs (Slavs of all sorts making in that year 48 per cent of the immigrants from Hungary). Of non-Slavic nationalities she sent Magyars (or Hungarians proper) 45,000, Germans 26,000, Hebrews 6000, Roumanians 7000. These proportions doubtless vary from time to time.

† When the "states and territories" are here mentioned, Alaska, Porto Rico, Hawaii and the Philippines are not intended to be included unless specially named.

at least two or three representatives of this pathetic people, so dispersed, yet so devoted to the home that poverty and oppression combine to shut to them.

Along with this wide dispersal, however, goes a very marked concentration of their forces in Pennsylvania, to which were destined over half (or 169,116).* New York's share was about 13 per cent (41,460), New Jersey's about 9 per cent, and so on down through Ohio, Illinois, Connecticut and Wisconsin, to West Virginia with something over 1 per cent. A thousand or two went to each of the following states: Michigan, Missouri, Massachusetts, Indiana, Minnesota and Maryland (1300). Colorado was given by 701 as their destination.

RUTHENIANS IN THE UNITED STATES

This is another group for which it is as yet impossible to get anything like satisfactory data, and for which estimates vary widely. An elaborate study of Ruthenian conditions in America was undertaken by Mr. Baczynski, of Lemberg, in 1906, and when this is published (and translated) we may hope to know more. In 1904 Mr. Ardan wrote in *Charities*,† "Even the most conservative cannot today place the number of Ruthenians in the United States much below 350,000. In addition there are 60,000 in Canada and about the same number in Brazil and other South American republics." Other estimates are, "300,000 or more," "250,000," and finally, "200,000 besides a like number in Canada." *Ruthenian numbers*

The first Ruthenian church, built in 1885 in Shenandoah, Pennsylvania, as already stated, roughly locates the Ruthenians' starting point geographically as well as chronologically. Yet if the greatest number went at first, and still go, to Pennsylvania, they also early found their way west. For instance, in Minneapolis I found that they dated back to 1884. *Beginnings*

* But note the warning as to deductions from such figures, page 253 ff.
† Vol. XIII, page 246 (Dec. 3, 1904).

Destina-
tions

For distribution I have again to depend on the declared destinations of immigrants during the last decade. Of something over 100,000 arrivals, almost 52 per cent (53,899) gave Pennsylvania as their goal, and nearly 20 per cent (or 21,376) New York, but this probably exaggerates the numbers settling in the latter state. New Jersey is according to figures the third favorite goal of the Ruthenians, with over 11,000 intending to go there, but I suspect that many who appear as destined to New York really go to New Jersey. It is significant that while it was not until 1905 that the Ruthenians founded a Greek Catholic or Uniate church in New York City, Jersey City had one fifteen years earlier, and long served the religious needs of the Ruthenians of New York as well as of those of Newark, Hackensack, Bloomfield, Elizabeth and Elizabethport.

The only other states named by as many as 1000 Ruthenians were Ohio, Connecticut, Massachusetts and Illinois, in this order, but only four of the states and territories had none (namely, Georgia, Tennessee, Arizona and Nevada).

Seeking
farms

Ruthenians who wish for farms commonly go to Canada, either directly from the old country or after saving money here. The movement from the United States to Canada, or more specifically to Manitoba, is said to have begun in 1896, and has probably drafted off some of the pick of the Ruthenians coming to this country.* There are, however, Ruthenian farming settlements in the United States, though I have no clue to their numbers. Instances that have been cited to me are Clayton and Royalton, in Wisconsin, and some places in North Dakota.

* For an anecdote bearing on this point see page 352. See also pages 139 and 338.

SLOVENIANS IN THE UNITED STATES

The Slovenian missionaries and other early comers have already been spoken of, but how much connection there was between these and the mass movement that set in during the early nineties I do not know.* | Only estimates available

As to the numbers of the Slovenians we have only estimates, since census figures merge them with all others of Austrian birth or parentage, and the records of the immigration authorities treat them and the Croatians as one group. But as the Slovenians are a compact nationality, homogeneous in religion (practically all are Roman Catholics), and apparently with no special factions, the estimates can be considered fairly trustworthy.

The figures given me in 1907 by Mr. Valjavec, editor of the *Glas Naroda* (combined here and there with data from other sources), are as follows.

In the United States and Alaska there are a little over 100,000 Slovenians. Of these, only a few thousand are in the South, most being in the North Atlantic and North Central region. In Pennsylvania there are 25,000 in twenty-three or more places;† in Ohio 15,000, largely in and about Cleveland (which has 8000 or 9000 by itself);‡ in Illinois over 10,000, besides big colonies in Joliet (with 3000, or, according to a local estimate, 9,000), and Chicago and South Chicago (with 2000);§ in Michigan 7000 (the largest group being 3000 or 4000 in | Locations and occupations

* See, however, page 339.
† Of these Mr. Valjavec writes that they are "generally coal miners, laborers in steel works, business men (saloonkeepers, of course ! ! !), proprietors of real estate, and local politicians (especially in Forest City, where, during the last few years, Slovenic aldermen were elected)."
‡ This colony has five Slovenian churches in and about the city, and is made up mostly of factory laborers, with "a few business men, doing business, of course, with their countrymen only."
§ Two churches; colony made up of "factory laborers, business men, real estate."

Calumet and the adjacent copper mining settlements);*
in Minnesota 12,000, many of them farmers, in twenty
places;† in Colorado 10,000 in ten places or more, including Pueblo,‡ Leadville, and smaller mining centres;
in Montana 5000 about the mines and smelters of Anaconda, Butte, East Helena and so on; in California 5000;
in Kansas 3000 (farmers and miners); in Washington
15,000 (farmers); and 1000 or so in Utah, Wyoming,
Idaho and the mines of West Virginia. Some are farming
in Indiana, Nebraska and Iowa, some are in the Southwest and South (in Texas, Arkansas, Tennessee, Alabama,
Louisiana and Mississippi), often as stave makers and
lumbermen—in fact, there are said to be Slovenians in
almost every state and territory except Georgia.

The guidebook for Slovenians in America by the Rev.
F. S. Šušteršič of Joliet, already mentioned, gives not
only a list of places where there are Slovenian colonies,
but often the date of settlement and other information
of much interest.

Few in the
North
Atlantic
states

The small number of Slovenians in the North Atlantic
division, outside of Pennsylvania, is striking. In New
York city and Brooklyn the guidebook just referred to
finds only 1000, and no church; and in all New York
state there is mention of only one other colony—150
persons in Little Falls. New Jersey does not appear in
the list at all.§

* "In Calumet is the second generation of Slovenians, very
prosperous and Americanized. There have they large stores
(Vertin Brothers' department store, one square block, is the
largest department store north of Chicago in the United States)."
† "The first Slovenians coming to America went to Minnesota (homesteaders). They founded a town, by name Krain-
town, about forty years ago; there lives now the second generation, all farmers, very prosperous and good Americans." Slovenians in Minnesota are largely farmers and miners. Bishop
Trubec of Minnesota is a Slovene.
‡ They are said to have 3000 business men, "real estate, etc.,"
in and about Pueblo, and 1000 "stockholders of mining property, real estate, etc.," in Leadville.
§ See above, page 231 ff., for accounts of earlier Slovenian immigration. The immigration data as to destinations are discussed in connection with the Croatians in the next section.

CROATIANS IN THE UNITED STATES

I here take the term Croatian to include all immigrants, Estimates of numbers from whatever province, speaking the Croatian language. One estimate puts them at 400,000 in the United States; another at from 250,000 to 300,000 divided as follows: from Croatia 150,000, from Dalmatia 80,000 to 100,000, from Istria 25,000, from Bosnia 20,000, from Herzegovina 15,000 and from Servia 5000, besides of late some from the Banat in Hungary.

The inhabitants of the Adriatic shore and islands Sources and destinations whom we roughly designate as Dalmatians, were, as already stated, early comers, and the colonies of natives of Austria in New Orleans and San Francisco, mentioned in the census of 1850, 1860 or 1870, were doubtless theirs.* Croatians from Croatia came later, and their location has been determined, not like the Dalmatians', by opportunities for waterside industries and fishing, for business and for farming, but by opportunities to labor in mines, furnaces, rolling mills and factories. Nevertheless, they are said to be in every state and territory, including Alaska. "They are said to be," since for them as for the Slovenians, neither census nor immigration reports give any distinct data, so that estimates alone are available.

The largest group of them, however, is undoubtedly in Pennsylvania, where they are put at from 80,000 to 100,000, or according to one estimate, 130,000. A large proportion of these are in and about Pittsburgh and Allegheny. Illinois is credited with 40,000, perhaps half in Chicago, but the estimates of the Chicago colony vary too much to be of any value. Ohio, including the large Cleveland colony, is given 35,000. Other considerable groups are in New York, New Orleans, San Francisco, St. Louis and Kansas City; in Montana at Great Falls, Anaconda and Butte; in Colorado at Pueblo, Cripple

* Natives of Austria: New Orleans, 1850, 129; 1870, 253; San Francisco, 1870, 476.

Creek, Crested Butte and Denver; and in Michigan at Calumet. The oldest colonies are said to be those in San Francisco, New Orleans, Mobile and Chicago.

Occupations One informant writes that not many are engaged in farming, but that most are engaged in mining different ores, many in railroad work, steel mills, stockyards and stone quarries. Workingmen with trades are chiefly from the larger cities of Croatia and Istria; stone-cutters especially are from Istria. "Dalmatians are mostly business men, especially in California, New York, New Orleans, Mobile," and I might add Galveston. "The coast has many Dalmatians who have large oyster plants." "It gives me pleasure to state that a large percentage are now starting to settle in the United States for good; many have recently purchased little homes of their own, many are prepared to receive their families from abroad to settle here."

Destination figures of immigration department The immigration data as to destinations are in this case not distinctive, Croatians being put in one group with Slovenians; but even so, the mixed figures have a certain interest, especially since for the Croatians we have so little American material. We see that the combined group reached a total of 275,800 for the last ten years; of these, 121,311, or 44 per cent, were headed for Pennsylvania. The next largest groups were Illinois (33,962), Ohio (28,822), and New York (22,045); then, at a long interval, Minnesota, Missouri, Michigan, Wisconsin, Colorado. No other state had as many as 5000, but every state and territory, even Alaska, Porto Rico and Hawaii, was the goal of a few of this hardy group of wanderers.

SERVIANS IN THE UNITED STATES

Countries of origin Servians come not only from Servia and Montenegro, where they compose practically the whole population, but from many neighboring countries, where they form a scattered minority more or less substantial, or where they have colonies. The chief sources are Dalmatia, where the Greek Orthodox population, which is the same thing as saying the Servian population, makes 4 per cent of the whole; Bosnia and Herzegovina, where they are over 40 per cent; Croatia, where they are a quarter; and the Banat and elsewhere in Hungary, where they number between 400,000 and 500,000, or $5\frac{1}{2}$ per cent.

The United States census does not include Servia or Montenegro in the list of countries of birth with which it deals, and the unfortunate classification of the immigration reports, which, as has been explained, combines Servians with the totally distinct nationality of the Bulgarians, prevents our having any precise data as to numbers or country of origin. The 22,677 "Bulgarians, Servians and Montenegrins" who arrived during the last decade from Austria-Hungary, were probably mainly Servians from Bosnia and Herzegovina, Croatia and the Dalmatian coast and the Banat in Hungary. — No separate official data

Of the "Bulgarians, Servians and Montenegrins" who in the same period came from "Bulgaria, Servia, and Montenegro" there is no way of guessing how many were Servians from Servia and Montenegro, how many were Bulgarians from Bulgaria.

Taken together, they are an immigration group which rapidly increased in importance till checked by the late depression. The figures for the last eleven years were as follows:

TABLE 21.—BULGARIAN, SERVIAN AND MONTENE-GRIN ALIEN ARRIVALS, 1899–1909.

1899........	94	1904........	4577
1900........	204	1905........	5823
1901........	611	1906	11,548
1902	1291	1907........	27,174
1903........	6479	1908........	18,246
		1909	6214

Of the Servians in the United States, the Very Reverend Sebastian Dabovich, Administrator of the Holy Servian Orthodox Catholic Church in North America, estimates* that there are about 200,000, "or 150,000 — Numbers estimated

* Under date of April 8, 1907.

certainly." He places them as follows: New England, 50,000; Southeastern states, 5000; North Middle states, 20,000; South Middle states, 15,000; Northwestern states, 25,000; Southwestern states and territories, 15,000; Alaska, Canada and British Columbia, 5000; Mexico and Central American countries, 5000, besides 10,000 "more or less unidentified roaming, unsettled (gipsies), professionals, etc." A Croatian correspondent estimates Servians from Servia and Montenegro alone as about 10,000 in the United States.*

BULGARIANS IN THE UNITED STATES

No official data available

As already said, Bulgarians and Servians are combined in the immigration tables, and the census does not mention Bulgaria, so that for Bulgarian numbers in the United States we have to rely on estimates.

Mr. Albert Sonnichsen, the best authority on the subject known to me,† wrote as follows in the summer of 1909:

Estimates of Bulgarians in the United States

"The general estimate is that between forty and fifty thousand Bulgars (from Bulgaria and Macedonia) have come to this country, including those in Canada. Their principal centre was here in Granite City, an outlying suburb of St. Louis, but during the last year the majority of the 10,000 who were here have migrated westward. At present there are less than a thousand here. About 10,000 are now working on the railroad lines in Montana, the two Dakotas, Iowa and Minnesota. The belief is they will return here in autumn, but my own impression is, there will never again be 10,000 of them in Granite City.

"Other important centres are Seattle, Butte, Montana, Chicago, Indianapolis, and Steelton, Pennsylvania; but they are too shifting a people to make estimates of their numbers in those centres of any value.

* For discussion of immigration data as to destinations see the next section, on Bulgarians.
† Author of "Confessions of a Macedonian Bandit," and àgent on Bulgarians for the Immigration Commission.

"I hope you are not making any racial distinctions Bulgarians are Bulgarians whencesoever they come between Bulgars and Macedonians. I believe the Bulgars who have come from Macedonia are registered on Ellis Island as Macedonians, which is bound to be confusing and inaccurate, for Macedonians may include Greeks, Vlachs, and even Turks. The distinction between the Bulgars from Bulgaria and those from Macedonia is purely political. Many of those who are registered as Greeks are so in church affiliation only, being Slavic by race and tongue.

"The majority (I should say about 80 per cent) of the Bulgars in this country are from Macedonia, and nearly all are from one small district in Monastir vilayet; Kostur, or Castoria. Their reasons for coming are fundamentally economic, but the immediate causes are the revolution of 1904, when half the people in Monastir were rendered homeless by the burning of their villages, and the continued persecution of the Greek Church since then, which closed Greece to them as a market for their labor. Not five per cent of the Bulgars in this country came before four years ago.

"There seems to be a conspiracy among students of immigration to have all Bulgars from Bulgaria. They remind me of a railroad roadmaster I met some weeks ago. I asked him about one of his gangs, about eighty men, and he told me they were mixed Bulgars and Macedonians. I asked him how he knew the difference. He said he had a keen eye for race characteristics. He had looked the gang over, and one by one picked out the Bulgars; they were darker, bigger, stronger, and the foreman had declared them to be rightly classified. When I visited this gang, I found every one to be a Macedonian, most of whom I had met in the old country.

"Within the last month I have visited about ten large gangs of Bulgars working on the railroads. In some I found not a single native of Bulgaria, and in some from two to seven, the gangs averaging fifty men. To one who knows the language, there is no mistake in distinguishing. There is as much difference in speech and intonation as between Missouri and County Clare, though the Bulgarian of Bulgarian schools and Macedonian schools is the same. . . .

"I have been quite surprised at the similarity between the speech of the Bulgars and Croatians (Horvats). I found I could converse quite freely with them, and that they took me for a Horvat coming from a different province from their own. . . .

"I am especially interested in the Slavs. I have great faith in their virility as a race, in proportion as they are unmixed with Turkish or Greek blood."

Bulgarian-Servian distribution

The immigration data give at least some indication of the flow of the Bulgarians and Servians, considered as one group.* Of the total of 76,047 arrivals, 42 per cent came from Bulgaria, Servia, and Montenegro, 25 per cent from Turkey, and 29 per cent from Austria-Hungary. This immigration movement is still in so early a phase that it is doubtful, as Mr. Sonnichsen intimates, if the statement of destinations has much bearing on any permanent location. We see however, that, as with most Slavs, the greatest number (almost a quarter) are first attracted to Pennsylvania. Illinois and Ohio are next in importance, then New York, Missouri and Indiana. But in scattering numbers they have sought every state and territory, including Alaska and Hawaii; Porto Rico and the Philippines alone do not appear on the list. Such a dissemination of the peoples of the earth sometimes fills one with amazement. How did 110 Servians and Bulgarians happen to intend to go to Alaska, or 116 to Oklahoma, or 137 to New Mexico, one wonders.

RUSSIANS IN THE UNITED STATES

Census figures useless for Russians

The census figures for natives of Russia are valueless as an indication of the numbers or whereabouts of Russians who, as we have seen, make a very small per

---

* For some discussion of these data see the preceding section on the Servians.

cent of the immigrants from their country, the greater part being Jews, Poles, Finns, Lithuanians and Germans.

Russians form the smallest of the Slavic groups of immigrants,* only 66,282 having arrived during the eleven years ended June 30, 1909, but during the years 1902–1908 inclusive their numbers increased with marked rapidity. The figures are as follows for the eleven years:

Immigration data

TABLE 22.—RUSSIANS; ALIEN ARRIVALS, 1899–1909.

1899........1774	1904........ 3961
1900........1200	1905........ 3746
1901........ 672	1906........ 5814
1902........1551	1907........16,807
1903........3608	1908........17,111
	1909 10,038

It is noticeable that the figures did not decline in 1908, when immigration generally fell off on account of the hard times, and that even in 1909 they declined comparatively little. It is interesting to see how differently the Russian and the Servo-Bulgarian flow was affected: in 1907, the former was 16,807, the latter 27,174; in 1908, the numbers were 17,111 and 18,246 respectively; in 1909, 10,038 and 6214, so that where the Russians were, in 1907, the less by over 11,000, in 1909 they were the greater by almost 4000. This may indicate that the Russian emigration is due to political exigencies rather than to economic considerations.

As regards the number of Russians in the country, I have never found any one bold enough to attempt an estimate. But as a considerable portion of the immigrants are women, and children under fourteen (indicating a family element), and as those who have been in the United States before are a small fraction of those entering (indicating a small proportion of the bird of passage

Numbers here unknown

* That is, of groups arranged on racial lines; the classification of the immigration report isolates one portion of the Servo-Croatians on a geographical basis as "Dalmatians, Bosnians and Herzegovinians," and this is the smallest Slavic group of the reports.

element),* it seems not unreasonable to conclude that births in Russian families in this country must have at least counterbalanced both deaths and the outgo of returning emigrants and emigrants' children.† If then we neglect all Russians who entered the country before 1899 (both them and their descendants), we should still have at least sixty or seventy thousand among us, the total number who have entered the country since 1898 being, as said above, 66,282.

Destinations

The table of destinations of these Russian immigrants shows New York as the goal of 17,700, and Pennsylvania of 12,866. Then follow Massachusetts with 4061; Illinois with 3719; California with 2850; New Jersey with 2717; Maryland with 2326; Connecticut with 1836; and North Dakota with 1172. The only places under our flag to which none were going were Utah and the Philippine Islands. Thirty-five were bound for Hawaii and eleven for Porto Rico.

Colonies

There have long been Russian religious colonists in the country. The census of 1880‡ speaks of "35,722 Russians (predominantly Mennonites) of whom a large majority were those in Kansas (with 8032), New York (with 5438), and Dakota (6493)." Catherinenstadt, in Kansas, has, I am told, a Russian settlement, and there are Russian "Stundists," in this case Baptists, who have settled within six years or so at various points in North Dakota. These are, however, "Little Russians" like the Ruthenians, not "Great Russians" or Russians proper, and came from about Kiew or Kherson. The most famous instance of this sort, however, is the body

---

* It is interesting to compare the Russians with the Bulgarian-Servian group in these respects. During the last three years among the former, women made 13.2 per cent of the immigrants, among the latter 3.6; for children under fourteen the figures stand 6.2 per cent and 1.5 per cent respectively, and for immigrants previously in the United States, 2.3 per cent and 2.6 per cent. The Russian movement thus appears to be of a more permanent sort than the other.

† It would not be surprising to learn, however, that considerable numbers leave the United States for Canada.

‡ Vol. I, page 468.

of Doukhobors* who were settled in Canada some years ago, to the number of 7000 or so, under the auspices of the Society of Friends.

But for emigrants who are leaving home not for America or reasons of religion, nor politics, but for economic motives, Siberia America has to compete with the vast back country of Siberia. The director of the emigration department in St. Petersburg was quoted by the newspapers under date of April 20, 1907, as saying, "This year, owing to the political and economic crisis, 300,000 Russian subjects will emigrate to America. Hitherto the yearly exodus has been about 250,000, of whom two-thirds were Jews and only 3 per cent orthodox Russians, 1 per cent being farm hands. Now the percentage of Russians and farm hands has increased. Most of the emigrants will go west to Illinois, Minnesota, Nebraska and the Dakotas. They come from the Volga, Dnieper and Don districts, and are hardy and industrious. Though illiterate, they are intelligent and unbigoted. The Government is endeavoring to direct the stream of emigrants to Siberia, but only the poorest go there, the wealthier preferring America. Steamship lines from Libau, Odessa and Helsingfors make the passage across the Atlantic cheaper, easier and surer than that to Siberia, while clever steamship agents canvass the villages and hamlets, securing desirable emigrants."

Something more than a year later, the following paragraph appeared:

"St. Petersburg, Aug. 31,1908. A great new nation is forming in Siberia. One of the greatest migrations in history has been proceeding so quietly that the world generally has not noticed the movement. During the past twelve months over 500,000 Russians have gone to Siberia, or equal to half the number of immigrants the United States received during that period from the whole world. Prince Vassiltchikoff, minister of agriculture,

* See Elkinton: "The Doukhobors," *Charities*, XIII, pages 252–256 (Dec. 3, 1904).

has furnished the Duoma with the following figures of the migration across the Ural Mountains. For several years before 1906 it was 60,000 annually. In 1906 it was 180,000. In 1907 it was 400,000. In the first three months of this year it was 420,000, comprising 70,000 families. The accounts of Siberia brought home by the soldiers returning from the Russo-Japanese war, impressed the poverty stricken Moujiks with glowing ideas of Siberia's wealth. They also have little faith in the measures the Grand Council of the Empire is taking to settle the burning agrarian question. The emigrants seldom go singly, or even in families, but gather in colonies for the exodus.''

ESTIMATES OF TOTAL SLAVIC POPULATION

Wide distribution

Is it not noteworthy as one studies these figures how widely the country is being tried; how, with all the massing of numbers at the great occupation centres, there are scouts as it were of almost every race in almost every quarter? Even to Porto Rico, Alaska, and Hawaii Slavs of the most varied nationalities were found to be making their way. And wherever one emigrant finds an opening others follow.

TABLE 23.—ESTIMATES OF TOTAL SLAVIC POPULATION IN THE UNITED STATES—BY NATIONALITY

NATIONALITY	LOWER ESTIMATE	UPPER ESTIMATE
Bohemians..............	500,000	500,000
Slovaks................	400,000	750,000
Poles..................	2,000,000	4,000,000
Ruthenians............	200,000	350,000
Slovenians.............	100,000	100,000
Croatians, including Dalmatians..............	250,000	400,000
Servians...............	150,000	200,000
Bulgarians.............	40,000	50,000
Russians...............	60,000 (?)	70,000(?)
Total................	3,700,000	6,420,000

It is obvious from all that has been said, that there is no way of knowing anything like the precise numbers, either of the foreign born of this group of nationalities, or of those who count as belonging to them. For the latter, those who count as Slavs in the community, I have offered such estimates as I have been able to get. These doubtless contain much guess-work, some exaggeration, and perhaps, in cases like that of the Croatians and Servians, some overlapping. Yet they unquestionably have a certain value especially where a group is homogeneous as regards religious faith.

The following table brings together these estimates, and it seems to me reasonable to conclude that we probably have not much less than 4,000,000 Slavs in this country at present, and very possibly well over that number.

CHAPTER XIV

THE ECONOMIC SITUATION OF THE SLAV IN AMERICA

Chief occupations

The Pennsylvania coal operator imported the Slav laborer, and to this day it is with the Pennsylvania products—coal and coke, iron and steel—that he is mainly busied. He does not take to the various lines of petty street traffic, such as peddling of small wares and fruit selling, which so often make the first industrial step of the Greek, Syrian, Italian and Jew. When the Slav goes into trade it is generally a round higher up, and marks on his part a great rise in the world. Neither are the Slavs characteristically day laborers like the Italians. Of course they are to be found doing rough, undifferentiated work, especially on railroads, but this is not typical. Many are on farms also. But their most characteristic occupation is the often highly paid employment about mines and foundries. No work is too onerous, too exhausting, or too dangerous for them.

Minor callings

But though the Slavic group is absorbed chiefly in these four occupations—mining, metal work, common labor and agriculture—it also includes many skilled mechanics in building and other trades. Bohemians especially are very frequently to be found in the upper ranks of labor, whether in small independent establishments of their own or as skilled workmen in large factories; they are found, too, in large numbers in the more modest ranks of the business and professional classes. Unfortunately they are also working to a considerable extent in the sweated tailoring shops of Chicago and cigar-making shops of New York. Poles and other Slavs also work in large numbers in factories in Massachusetts and Connecticut, in New York, New Jersey, Ohio, Illinois and elsewhere. They are employed, for instance, in textile factories, sugar refineries, wire factories, oil works, stockyards and packing houses.* Worthy of special note is a pearl button factory, imported, work people and all, I am told, as a consequence of the McKinley tariff which ruined the pearl button makers of Austria at a blow, reducing to poverty those who did not emigrate to Ameica.†

Among special aptitudes may be mentioned that of the Croatians, who are skilled axemen, for work in lumber camps, stave cutting, and so on. Also that of the Dalmatians for all sorts of waterside industries; one hears of them as longshoremen, fishermen and sailors, and as oystermen about New Orleans. They seem also to have a special gift for the catering business, and manage restaurants in places as far apart as Galveston and Boston.

Each local and racial group of any size soon comes to Professions support its own saloons, priests, stores, doctors, lawyers, bankers and editors—evolving them, perhaps, roughly in this order. Thus there develops within the group a business and professional class from which most of the national and party leaders are drawn. But the number who come to have a clientage or reputation outside their own group is, naturally, relatively small, though very interesting. Several are professors in universities, of whom Professor Pupin, of Columbia, is probably the best known.

While there are many music lovers among Slavs in Music and America, and while an amazingly large proportion of the art distinguished names on our concert programs are Slavic, I believe that these are almost without exception of Euro-

* The charts appended to this chapter, and the remarks under the different national heads in Chapter XIII, give some further information as to occupations. Mr. Koukol's remarks as to the Slovaks are worth quoting: "The Slovaks when they come here are poor, illiterate, have no training, are inured to oppression; yet they have pluck, perseverance, enterprise and courage. From their ranks are recruited many of the foremen in the mills, and an ever-increasing number of merchants." Koukol: "A Slav's a Man for a' that." *Charities and the Commons*, XXI, page 594 (Jan. 2, 1909).

† For the Bohemian end of this story see pages 78–79.

pean birth and training, artists of whom the Polish Pader-
ewski, the Bohemian Dvořak and the Croatian Ternina
may stand as types.* Slavs, like Germans, seem not to
produce in our country their finest intellectual and artistic fruits. This is doubtless partly our fault, partly
theirs, and partly simply the result of recent transplanta-
tion. A Croatian sculptor in Chicago explained to me
with the conscious tolerance of a cosmopolitan that in
America he found himself obliged to do merely commercial work on buildings and so forth. Said he: "Of course
America has not yet reached the point of development
where she can care for sculpture. It will come in due
time. Croatia is an old country and naturally it is different there." As I had seen something of the vigorous
and beautiful work of Frangeš and other native artists
at an exhibition in Agram (Agram in population not the
equal of Peoria), this point of view struck me as less
grotesque than it might have done otherwise.

Wage rates

To discuss the wages of Slavic workers would be simply to discuss general wages in all the lines in which
they are employed. For apart from a certain discount
if he cannot speak English or is very "green," the Slavic
immigrant receives the usual wages of the place, the
industry and the season.

In Pitts-
burgh mills
and mines

Nevertheless, the Pittsburgh district is of such preponderant importance for Slavic immigrants that it may
be worth while to cite some of the prevailing wage rates
there as given by Professor Commons in his study for
The Pittsburgh Survey.†

* I note, however, that the Rev. Alois Kolisek in an essay on
"Slovak Popular Melodies" (page 384) says, "The American
Slovaks have recently produced a promising young composer,
Vladimir Šaško, a teacher of music at the Music School in Chi-
cago. His 'Slovak Rhapsodies' are worthy of note." The
essay is contained in Seton-Watson's "Racial Problems in
Hungary."
† "Wage Earners of Pittsburgh." *Charities and the Commons*,
XXI, pages 1051–1066 (March 6, 1909).
Though printed in 1909 the article appears to refer to condi-
tions before the depression of 1907.
Further figures for wages of Slavic immigrants based on data

SLAVIC WORKINGMEN, PITTSBURGH

The two great classes of employment that interest us are work in and about the steel mills and in and about the mines. The latter, as we shall see, is the better paid. The unskilled laborers in the mills and yards who have little or no knowledge of English and who, as the case stands, have no labor union to help them, get wages varying from fifteen cents to sixteen and a half cents per hour. They earn, that is, in prosperous times, $1.35 to $1.65 for a ten-hour day. Section hands on the railroads, who are however mostly Italians, get less than this, perhaps thirteen and a half cents an hour. In general a knowledge of English raises the pay two cents an hour. *The value of English*

"Eight to ten dollars for a week of sixty hours is thus the level toward which the wages of the unskilled gravitate when competition is free and English unessential."

In the mines of the Pittsburgh district the common laborer underground gets $2.36 for an eight-hour day. The same class of men in the mills would be getting only $1.80 to $1.98 for a twelve-hour day. Other men in the mines paid by the ton but practically also common laborers earn $2.40 to $3.00 in eight hours, while corresponding work in the mills brings only $2.28 to $2.41 for twelve hours. *Wages of skilled and unskilled*

When we consider more skilled work, it is hard to generalize. We find men in the mines who are earning $3.25 to $5.00 in eight hours, who for somewhat similar work in the mills would be paid an average of $6.25 for twelve hours. There are, however, in the mills certain positions requiring peculiar skill which command exceptional pay; for instance, the work of rollers in the rolling mills which yields from $7.00 or $8.00 up to $10 or

from New York employment agencies will be found in the article by Frank J. Sheridan, "Italian, Slavic and Hungarian Immigrant Laborers in the United States," Bulletin of the United States Department of Labor, No. 72, pages 403–486 (September, 1907). A table of wages taken from this article will be found in Appendix XX, page 464.

$16 for a twelve-hour day. The men who hold these positions are immigrants as well as native born, but they are more properly to be ranked as a sort of foreman than as workmen. The mines offer nothing comparable to these most highly paid jobs in the steel work.

Effect of immigration on wages

One of the most important questions in regard to our immigration is the question how this vast addition to our labor supply has affected the price of labor.

Since the pause due to the Civil War over 21,500,000 have entered our ports,* the majority of them laborers. Vast numbers have indeed returned (in the decade 1899–1908 alone, 3,275,589,† more than one-seventh of the whole number) and thousands more have died here. Yet in 1900 there were at work nearly 9,000,000 white men and boys of foreign parentage,—not very far from half (43 per cent) of all male white workers. One would suppose that America could not have absorbed these myriads without bringing wages down with a run.

The course of wages

Notoriously this has not been the case. Chart III, drawn from the carefully computed tables in Dr. Edith Abbott's study of the wages of unskilled labor ‡ seems to show a general upward trend of wages, other than those of farm laborers, from 1840 to 1890, interrupted by the abnormal rise and fall, between 1860 and 1880, caused by the Civil War and the depreciation of the currency. From 1890 to 1900 this gain seems not to have been maintained. Yet I suppose that few would hold that the workingman in America has on the whole lost ground economically.

Retrogressions

Granting this, there has been loss and retrogression for certain classes and at certain points. Some trades,

---

* June 30, 1862–June 30, 1909; 21,663,203.

† Ann. Report Comm. Gen. of Immig. for 1908, page 228. See also pages 250–252, 294–296 and appendix XVIII, page 463.

‡ "The Wages of Unskilled Labor in the United States, 1850–1900." For criticism and explanation of the tables the student is referred to the original. See also, for tables and chart showing relative money wages, real wages and hours of labor, 1840–1899, Bull. of the U. S. Dept. of Labor, No. 38 (Jan., 1902), page 123 ff.

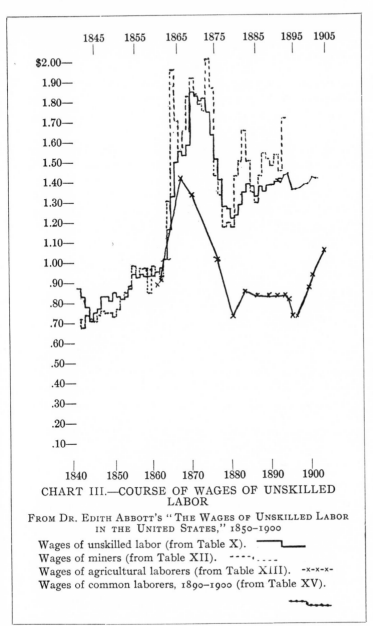

CHART III.—COURSE OF WAGES OF UNSKILLED
LABOR

FROM DR. EDITH ABBOTT'S "THE WAGES OF UNSKILLED LABOR
IN THE UNITED STATES," 1850–1900

Wages of unskilled labor (from Table X). ▬▬▬
Wages of miners (from Table XII). ‑‑‑‑·‑‑‑‑
Wages of agricultural laborers (from Table XIII). ‑x‑x‑x‑
Wages of common laborers, 1890–1900 (from Table XV).

chiefly those subjected to sweating (and of these notably the needle trades), have suffered from the influx
from Europe. Furthermore, specialization of industry
and exaggeration of the seasonal character of production
have tended to degrade whole classes of workers, including the tramp labor of the farm; and the abundant
supply of immigrant labor has facilitated both specialization and seasonal concentration.

Wages in the steel industry of Pittsburgh have just
been considered. But if we look a little further back
for comparison we find that this industry seems to have
offered less and less favorable conditions for the past
fifteen years or so. Hours have increased and wages
have declined. "It is estimated by many who are in a
position to know, that the actual earnings of skilled
workmen in the steel mills have declined 20 to 50 per
cent since 1897,"*—of the *skilled* workmen, we must
notice. The unskilled laborers, on the other hand, men
paid by time, not by the ton, "have had their wages
advanced in recent years, while the earnings of tonnage
men were declining." The explanation offered by Mr.
Fitch, in his admirable Pittsburgh Survey study of the
steel industry just quoted, is that the company cuts the
wages of those men on whose speed the output depends,
in order to increase their exertions. In any case, the
class which has been flooded by immigrant labor is not
the class which has lost ground, but the reverse is the
case.

Clogging
effect of
immigration
on the labor
market

I think we may conclude that the earnings of the rough,
manly labor of the country have not in general been
pushed backward by the inrush of these hosts of workers
with low standards of wages and comfort. On the other
hand, it seems impossible to doubt that if there had been
no such influx wages would have risen in some degree
which it is not possible to calculate. Had our legislation

* Fitch, John Andrews: "The Steel Industry and the Labor
Problem." *Charities and the Commons*, XXI, pages 1079–1092
(March 6, 1909).

shielded labor by anything corresponding to the protection accorded to employers, it would have greatly retarded and curtailed, both for evil and for good, the exploitation of our resources and the growth of our production. Capitalists would have been bidding against one another for "hands" just as their wives have been actually bidding against one another for servants, with results upon which this is not the place to speculate.

That the depressing effect of the immigrant on the labor market has been chiefly of this merely negative character—clogging the rise of wages instead of causing a sharp decline—is due to three main causes.

Reasons why no worse

First, the vast expansion of industry has supplied new work for the new workers (or for old workers whose empty places the newcomers have then filled), thus minimizing the competition of immigrants with those already in the country.

Secondly, labor organizations have done a substantial service, not merely to their own members nor to the working class in general, but to the whole country, in standardizing wage rates within their own fields, and to some considerable extent outside them also.

Thirdly, we have to thank the particular character of the immigrants themselves, especially those of the newer type represented by Slavs and Italians, for the fact that they have not done more damage to our wage standards.

The first point, the expansion of industry, needs little elaboration. The total value of our manufacturing products has been given by the census as for 1870, four billion dollars; 1880, five billion; 1890 (the close of the first decade of the new immigration), nine billion; 1900, thirteen billion dollars.

(1) Expansion of industry

As a single illustration of the relation of this expansion to Slavic labor I may take the great Punxsutawny coke district, north of Pittsburgh. Practically all the labor about the coke ovens is done by Slavs, and to the question, "Who did this work before these men came?" the answer was, "It was not done."

This aspect of the situation was especially prominent in the flush times of 1906, when I was visiting various Slavic centres in this country; at that time the effects of the general expanding trend of our production were intensified by the special effect of the prosperity of the moment. At Galveston I found employers competing with one another on the wharf for the services of arriving immigrants; in Tercio, Colorado, a few months later, mines could not be worked to the full for lack of men, and from the harvest fields of the Northwest a great cry was going up that there were not enough laborers to gather the crops. When the demand for labor is so great as this we may absorb a million immigrants a year with comparatively little injury to the laborers who are here.

(2) Organization of labor

As to the second point, the steadying of wage standards through organization; though the Slavs come mainly from districts in which labor and capital have not undergone their modern development, they have proved surprisingly available union material, as was shown in the great strike of anthracite miners in 1902, and in the strike in the Chicago slaughter houses in 1904.

Even when the Slav does not join the union he often seems to have an instinctive class consciousness, quite without theoretical basis, which keeps him from being a "strike breaker." A Croatian physician said to me, "Our people are not in the union, but they respect its rules. It is not that they are afraid and not that they sympathize, but a class feeling." And this among men as innocent of socialism as a Maine farmer could be!

In spite of the terrible simplicity which at home too often makes the Slavs the prey of usurers, they can be made to understand the advantage of paying out their hardly won dollars and wasting their costly American time in idleness for the sake of future benefit. An observer of the slaughter-house strike wrote:

"Even the young women, the pleasant-looking Slav girls, told very simply and very distinctly what the strike was for—no family could live when wages were fifteen or sixteen cents an hour and the number of hours of work amounted to but $5.50 to $7.40 a week. The Slavs live on very little, and the strike meant that they were becoming Americanized to the extent of attempting to raise their standard of living; for there are many people who are living on a margin in the stockyards district all the time. When the girls give a ball they give it for the death fund.''

The Slav is apt to have a certain mild, immovable Discipline stubbornness which is a valuable quality to take into an industrial struggle. Moreover, in spite of his individualistic temperament, he has shown in the unions capacity for cohesion and discipline. To quote again from the account of the slaughter-house strike:

''Another strike order was that they were to stay at home, to stay away from the saloon and the street corner, and not to 'rush the can,' and though the Germans and Irish did not observe this literally, you could see the Slavs actually within their own gates, filling the front porches and spending the morning sitting on the high steps obeying the order implicitly. . . . . The police said afterwards there were fewer arrests this last summer in the stockyards district than in any previous summer. . . . . At the outset Michael Donnelly had cards printed in four languages, in which it was ordered that all the laws must be obeyed; that any violence would not be tolerated. It was no uncommon thing to see the foreign men beneath the electric lights, puzzling out, with their fingers on words which came difficultly, the meaning of the order.''

This adaptability to union life means a political sense (in the best meaning of the word political) with which the Slav has not commonly been credited.* It means

* Interesting in this connection is the McKees Rocks strike of the summer of 1909 (on which see various articles in *The Survey*, *e. g.*, Mr. Paul Kellogg's article in the issue of August 7, 1909, pages 656–665, and articles by Rufus D. Smith and M. T. C. Wing in the issue of October 2, 1909).

among other things that men inheriting all sorts of racial feuds and animosities, which have been systematically fostered by government for centuries, can and do sink those hatreds in cosmopolitan unions. At one meeting, for instance, interpreters will address their people in Slovak, Polish, Bohemian and Lithuanian. Of whatever unwisdom, and worse, unions may stand accused, they teach at least a nobler, more intelligible and more practical lesson in democratic self-government than most ward politics.

Unorganized steel workers *vs.* organized miners

In the two great industries of the Pittsburgh district, mining and steel work, Professor Commons shows a most striking contrast in both conditions and earnings between the steel trade, in which unionism has collapsed completely, and mining, where it has thriven to the advantage of both employers and men.* He reckons that while "in 1897 the conditions in the mines were similar to those in the mills," since that date, the conditions of the poorest paid laborers in the mines have improved 100 per cent and that of their fellow workers in steel perhaps 20 per cent, so that today, "measured by the hour, to the Slavs employed by the same company are paid 90 per cent to 100 per cent more as mine workers than as steel workers." Not only are the miners' hours less and their wages per hour more, but the miners have better housing at lower rentals. "Taking everything into account—wages, hours, leisure, cost of

---

* "With a national union able and willing to discipline its local unions, the leading coal operators assert that they can carry on their business to better advantage with the union than without. If there were no union they would be menaced by petty strikes whenever a few hot-heads stirred up trouble, and at times when the operator might be tied up with contracts to deliver coal. But under the annual agreements with the union the operators are safer in making long contracts, and they can conduct their business on even a closer calculation for labor than for materials whose prices and supplies fluctuate." Commons, John R.: "The Wage Earners of Pittsburgh." *Charities and the Commons*, XXI, pages 1051–1064 (Mar. 6, 1909).

Further references on the subject of immigrants and trade unions will be found in the Bibliography under Labor Organization.

living, conditions of work—I should say that common laborers employed by the steel companies in their mines are 50 to 90 per cent better off than the same grade of laborers employed at their mills and furnaces; that semi-skilled laborers employed at piece rates are 40 to 50 per cent better off in the mines; and that the highest paid laborers, the steel roller and the mine worker, are about on a footing." (Pages 1063, 1064.)

The trouble in the steel work, then, has apparently not been the presence of immigrant labor. In both cases a large part of the workers are Slavs, and a large part of the Slavs are unskilled, but while the miners' union has been dominated by the interests of the unskilled, and has prospered, the steel workers' disastrous experience was, as Professor Commons shows, under the guidance of the highly skilled and in their interests. What the absence of unionism has meant in the steel industry not only as to wages but as to morale and loss of personal and political liberty is strikingly shown in Mr. Fitch's study of the Pittsburgh steel industry.*

These two things, the expansion of production and the organization of labor, have meant that both the temptation and the opportunity for the immigrant to undercut wages have been less than they would have been otherwise. The Slav especially has gone largely into employments in which wages have been stiffened by both expansion and unionism. But a third element in the situation has been, as already said, the character of the recent immigrants themselves. (3) Character of Slavic immigrants

In the first place, they have come here to get money; their hearts are set on saving money, either to send home or to use here, and their main object, therefore, is to find the best possible wages. Nothing else matters much, and to this end each nationality forms a sort of spontaneous system of industrial intelligence. Consequently the underbidding of the Slavic immigrant (a) Their aim, high earnings

* Fitch, J. A.: "The Steel Industry and the Labor Problem." *Charities and the Commons*, XXI, pages 1079–1092 (Mar. 6, 1909).

comes less in the shape of taking smaller pay, which he is loath to do, than of "putting up" with more than the English-speaking workingman will tolerate—with poorer accommodations, harder work, longer hours, and especially with greater danger. This is a serious matter, but I am now discussing money wages.

(b) Their mobility

Besides being thus set on good wages, they are in the second place extraordinarily unhampered in moving to seek them. Adam Smith's dictum that men are of all luggage the most difficult to be transported does not apply to them. They are largely single men unencumbered by families, and many of those who are married are here without their families, supporting them "on the other side." Both are entirely mobile through being alone and without any sort of local ties. The Slavs at least have no special bias toward great cities, nor anything more potent than social affinity to bind them to the colonies of their own kind. Whereas Jews, so far as they are not deHebraized, are tied down by their need of "kosher" food and the synagogue to places which support a considerable Jewish colony, the Roman Catholic Slavs, on the contrary, find their church practically everywhere and, Catholic and non-Catholic alike, are ready to try any locality. They do not "congest" except as conditions of employment require it.

(c) Return to Europe an alternative

In the third place, the little farm in the old country, which so many Slavic and Italian immigrants still own, does for them, to a certain extent, what free land in the West did through so many generations for American workingmen and for the earlier immigrants. It gives them, namely, an alternative to wage offers. In other words the employer has not got them in a corner. They came here for high pay, the highest obtainable; if they do not get what they want in one place, they will go to another, or, if it seems best, they will go home. They thus serve as a sort of shifting ballast. Our periods of industrial shrinkage would be far worse than they are were it not that the usual supply of incoming immigrants is then cut down, while large numbers leave the country for the time at least. Thus within two months of the breaking out of the anthracite coal strike of 1902 many Slav miners had sailed for Europe, and in the lean years 1894 and 1895 besides the fact that immigration greatly fell off, those emigrating were nearly three-quarters of those immigrating.

Even more interesting was the contraction in the hard times that began in 1907, when not only did immigration fall off by over half a million, or to less than two-thirds of what it had been for the three years before, but the outgoing tide rose from some 400,000 to over 700,000, or to over 77 per cent of the incoming.* The estimated

TABLE 24.—ALIEN ARRIVALS AND DEPARTURES, 1904–1908.

Year	Total alien arrivals	Total alien departures
1904	840,714	332,019[1]
1905	1,059,755	385,111[1]
1906	1,166,353	356,257[1]
1907	1,438,469	431,306[1]
1908	924,695	714,828

[1] Estimated.

Annual Report of the Commissioner General of Immigration for 1908, page 228.

net alien inflow fell from over 1,000,000 in 1907 to about 200,000 (or to little more than one-fifth as many) in 1908; and of four nationalities, Croatians, Slovaks, Italians and Magyars, more went than came, actually lessening their numbers in the country to a marked degree.*

TABLE 25.—IMMIGRATION AND EMIGRATION OF CERTAIN RACES DURING THE YEAR ENDED JUNE 30, 1909.

Nationality	Immigrant Aliens admitted	Immigrant Aliens departed	Net Loss
Croatian and Slovenian...	20,472	28,589	8,117
Italian (South)	110,547	147,828	37,281
Magyar	24,378	29,276	4,898
Slovak	16,170	23,573	7,403

Immigration Bulletin, June, 1909.

* For further facts on this subject see above, pages 250–252, and Appendix XVIII, page 463.

A contrac-
tile labor
supply

We have thus an elastic labor supply on a large scale, and this is an inestimable advantage. The bird of passage has been so much, and often so stupidly, inveighed against that it is worth while to emphasize this point. While England appoints commissions on the unemployed, starts relief funds and subsidizes emigration of her own flesh and blood, our Slovaks or Sicilians return to their farms, when work is not to be had here, and employ themselves at home—vastly to their own advantage and to ours. Conversely when new works are to be opened up, there is a reservoir of indefinite capacity to draw from.

The unem-
ployed im-
migrant

On the other hand, when newcomers do find themselves stranded in this country without the means to return, they are of course extraordinarily helpless. Take Miss Grace Abbott's account of the Bulgarians in Chicago in the spring of 1908.* Here we have an immigration movement in its earliest phase, men coming through the inducements of transportation agents and without relatives established in America who might help in case of need. Unwittingly they came at a bad season of the year and, far more serious, in a year of depression. Had they been acting on the advice of relatives and friends, this would not have happened. The men studied by Miss Abbott had been, on the average, about five months in this country when on April 8 the Chicago newspapers "told the story of 600 unemployed and starving Bulgarians who had marched on the City Hall and demanded work," a "demonstration as harmless as it was ineffective." Sixteen had had no work at all in this country, and only sixteen had been employed for as much as three months. They had been swindled by agents and contractors. They possessed neither money nor credit; most of them (78 per cent) had mortgaged their farms in Bulgaria to get here, and they had no means of returning. "News began to come from home that the mortgage was

* "The Bulgarians of Chicago." *Charities and the Commons*, XXI, pages 653–660 (Jan. 9, 1909).

due, the wife sick or the children needing food." No wonder that they were in despair.

Even worse than the situation in large cities was that of unemployed foreigners in some of the many places where the population practically consists solely of the employes of one or more great industries. When these closed, hordes of men with no natural affiliations found themselves out of work in a community which had no means of meeting their needs whether through taxes or philanthropy, except in so far as the employer assumed responsibility.

Three reasons have been given why the American labor market has not suffered more than it has done by the influx of immigrants. Allowing for all these favorable circumstances, it is still true that the presence of a limitless supply of unexacting, unskilled foreign laborers, anxious to get standing room in American employment on any terms, is an infinitely serious fact for the workingman and for every person who cares for America's future. It means for one thing, even granting all that has here been advanced, that Slavic workmen have largely displaced English-speaking workmen, with higher standards, in whole branches and districts. A notable example of this displacement is in the Schuylkill hard coal field.*

Displacement through immigrants

The peculiar arrangement in coal mining by which the miner is himself a sub-employer of labor, made it at first appear to the advantage of the English-speaking miner not to oppose the coming of the "foreigners." As Dr. Warne says: "It was not only by the operators and railroad mining companies that the Slav was at first welcomed. Under the contract system in vogue in many collieries, the skilled miner was also able to draw advantage from this cheaper labor. This self-interest of the

Anthracite coal mining

* For full accounts compare Dr. Peter Roberts' two admirable studies, "The Anthracite Coal Industry" and "Anthracite Coal Communities" and Dr. Warne's briefer but important account, in "The Slav Invasion and the Mine Workers." Further data, from an article by Frank J. Sheridan, will be found in Appendix XXI, page 467.

English-speaking miner removed the only obstacle then strong enough to have prevented the Slav's entrance into the industry, and the latter then rapidly spread throughout the region, especially in the southern field."

The result of this to the laborer employed by the miner was that he "was forced either to work more cheaply or to withdraw from the competition; and in a market usually over-supplied with mine labor, owing among other things to the lack of regular employment the year round, there could be but one result. In a short while the English-speaking laborer was being forced out of that position."

But the pressure exerted by the new element was not long confined to the laborers. With poetic justice the newcomers whom the miners had been glad to exploit, ousted the miners themselves as well as their laborers in the end. To quote Dr. Warne again:

"In course of time the Slav became not a mere pair of hands but a skilled worker,—to use the terms common in the mines, not a *laborer*, but a *miner*. As he had been a cheaper laborer, so he was a cheaper miner."

In spite of having moved up a step in his employment he was still un-American in his ways, "had his fewer wants, his lower cost of living, and his lower price for his labor. Moreover, he brought to his new work as a skilled miner that characteristic indifference to difficult conditions which had made him a useful laborer. He would work in poorer seams than the English-speaking miner, and in more dangerous places, and so, as he had driven out the laborer of the older industrial group, he now began as surely to drive out the English-speaking miner.

"Yet the pinch of the new conditions for the English-speaking miner lay not so much in a reduction of the wage rate paid him—for that remained practically unchanged from 1880 to 1900—as in those elements which determined his net earnings. The tendency was for these to decrease. The miners' tools grew greater in number and their cost rose; the poorer seams, which must now be worked, yielded less coal for a given amount of powder and energy; certain allowances for what was once called extra work were withdrawn; insurance became at once more necessary and more expensive as the ignorant, daring Slav made mine working more hazardous; the number of pounds required for a ton and the size of the mine-car gradually increased; the dockage system, under which the miner was charged for impurities in the coal he sent out of the mine, also worked more and more to his disadvantage."

Down to the strike of 1900 "it was in general true that the real *net* wages of those of the older industrial group who remained miners were constantly being lessened. Not only did many voluntarily leave the industry; not only were workers being forced out of the mines, but many were compelled to lower their standard of living; others were prevented from raising their standard, while to many the struggle to exist became a most severe battle for the necessaries of life. The pressure on some mine workers was so great as to force their boys of tender years into the breaker and their girl children into the silk mill, in order that their pittance might add to the family income."

Thus, although as has already been said the underbidding of the Slav has been felt less in lower wage rates than in worse conditions, these harder terms may easily mean lower actual earnings even with an unaltered wage rate. Even if earnings are not decreased, the man of American standards may object even more to accepting poorer social conditions for himself and his children than to adapting himself to a smaller income.

It is of course not only in the mining world, nor only in these precise ways, that the pressure of immigrant competition makes itself felt. The employer, whether or not he himself directly or indirectly evokes the ever-flowing stream of fresh labor, is not slow to use the advantage that it gives him. He profits unreservedly by

The reserve army

this self-renewing supply for which, too often, neither he nor the community feel any responsibility. The old phrase, "the reserve army," recurs to one at a sight like that to be seen at the doors of the great Chicago packing houses in the early morning, when the process that is usually more hidden stands nakedly out. Although I was there in a season when the labor market was in general understocked, and at an hour when most of those who were to be taken on for the day had been already selected, there was still a crowd of eager men and boys waiting in the yard on the chance that more hands would be needed later. Now and then a foreman came out and ran them over with his eye and picked out those that he wanted. "He looks for the round-toed shoes," some one said to me; "he wants those fresh from the old country, not Americanized enough to wear factory-made footwear. When they are squeezed dry he can get other fresh comers."

Over-exertion, accident and injury

Here we touch on the most terrible indictment of American employment—the rate at which it uses up men. I have already told how in Hungary and Croatia and Carniola and Bohemia it was constantly said that emigrants returned from the United States exhausted if not maimed. Men, we were assured, could not stand American labor more than a few years, after which they came home with their earnings, not worth much for hard labor thereafter. This fact, that he does not expect to have a long earning time in America, makes the Slav miner or steel worker the more eager to earn "big pay day" so long as he is in the country, and also more indifferent as to how he is housed and what his working conditions are while here.

Thus, the American workingman has to meet the competition of men who not only are used to living more cheaply than he, but who are working on a spurt, spending energy which has not been tapped before, at a rate which will exhaust their strength in a few years' over-exertion.

I have spoken before of the Slav's apparent indiffer- Indifference to danger
ence to danger, and I certainly do not pretend to explain
it. A certain degree of instinctive fatalism is probably one
component; the familiarity that breeds a most dangerous
contempt is another; another may be physical endurance.
In a mining company's hospital a nurse told me that if
an injured Italian screamed and "took on," they thought
little of it, but if a Slav complained they knew that he
was very badly, if not fatally, hurt. This indifference
to danger may be one of the many elements that go to
swell the terrible and excessive death roll of American
industry, notably in mines and in metal work.

One of the great services of the Pittsburgh Survey Accidents in
has been the study of industrial accidents. The black Allegheny
record for Allegheny county, in which Pittsburgh is situ- County
ated, shows for the year ending June 30, 1907, 526 men
killed and probably over 2000 injured in their work; this
is likely to mean 150 hopeless cripples, 97 men with only
one hand to use, 75 with only one eye, 470 children left
fatherless, and so on. Of the 526 men killed, 189 were
born in Austria-Hungary; of these, 117 were killed in
steel manufacture, 15 in railroading, 34 in mining and
23 in other work.*

Mr. Koukol, Secretary of the Slavonic Immigrant Society, states that the report for 1905–6 of the National
Croatian Society shows that out of a membership of
about 17,000, 95 were killed by accident (almost a third
of all deaths) and 85 were permanently disabled.†

A study of the causes of nearly 400 accidents led Miss Causes and
Eastman to attribute nearly equal numbers of cases compensa-
(respectively 27.85 and 29.97 per cent) to the victims or tion
their fellow workers, and to employers or their repre-

* Eastman, Crystal: "One Year's Work Accidents and their
Cost." *Charities and the Commons*, XXI, pages 1143–1175
(Mar. 6, 1909).
See also, "The Temper of the Workers under Trial," by the
same author. *Charities and the Commons*, XXI, pages 561–570
(Jan. 2, 1909).
† Koukol, Alois B.: "The Slav's a Man for a' That." *Chari-
ties and the Commons*, XXI, pages 589–599 (Jan. 2, 1909).

sentatives. Both are concerned in about 16 per cent and in about 27 per cent neither.* The compensation was miserably inadequate measured by the loss of earning power. Six men whose aggregate loss of income she estimates at $123,000, received together $520. This may be an extreme case, but in over half of the cases not a dollar to take the place of lost income was received from the employer; i. e., nothing at all in cases of injury, nothing over the equivalent of funeral expenses in fatal cases. At best it is bad enough, but the foreigner is almost sure to be at a special disadvantage. In Pennsylvania the law exempts the employer from paying anything to the family of an alien on his death, if the family lives in a foreign country,† and in other ways it is more difficult for the stranger to get those meagre rights of compensation which the law allows.

Relief funds The Carnegie Relief Fund and the various relief associations in which the employers interest themselves to some degree, mitigate the situation somewhat, and so do mutual benefit societies, of which the Slavs have a surprisingly good provision. (See page 380, ff.) Miss Eastman states that the National Croatian Society provides a sick or accident benefit of $5.00 a week for nine months, and a death benefit of $800 for a payment of fifty-six cents a month.

Prevention I do not know how far it is fair to the employers to suppose that there would be less waste of life, health and vigor if the labor supply were less abundant, if the men who work for them were nearer to their sympathies in race, religion and tradition, or if, finally, the burden of the injured and the worn-out fell more surely and heavily on the taxpayers, if not on the particular employers.‡

* Eastman: "One Year's Work Accidents." Table VI, page 1157.

† Of the 526 men killed in Allegheny county in a year, 149 left dependents in Europe.

‡ Mrs. Florence Kelley, speaking out of her own experience as factory inspector in Illinois, says in her Pittsburgh Survey article on "Factory Inspection" (*Charities and the Commons*, XXI, page 1113), "In the United States and particularly in

As it is, some corporations do feel a genuine sense of responsibility, shown, among other things, by the maintenance of hospitals, of which that of the Colorado Fuel and Iron Company at Pueblo, under Dr. Corwin's enthusiastic care, is a fine example. And even more important, there are signs that we are on the eve of effective policies for conserving human life as well as other national resources. The federal experiments looking toward lessening the loss through mine explosions is one such sign; another is the recently established inspection service of the United States Steel Corporation, and perhaps the most important is the gathering demand for adequate compensation, the burden of which shall be so placed as to lead to the utmost practicable measure of prevention.

In spite of the grisly deduction that must be made for injuries, if we cast up the debit and credit of the immigrant's situation from his point of view we find, I feel confident, a generally favorable balance. He comes, not only to earn his living, but to save, and he usually succeeds in doing so. At first the results of his thrift are remitted to Europe, or carried home on his

Savings

Pennsylvania, there is greater need than in other industrial communities for effective factory inspection, because the courts have deprived employers of the usual business incentives to caution and effort for the highest efficiency in life-saving. Under the fellow-servant laws, even as amended, and the assumption-of-risk laws, with the custom of carrying casualty insurance, employers are so largely absolved from paying damages that an unparalleled indifference to the safety of employes has developed within the past quarter century. The waste of life, limb, health and nervous energy of workingmen in the prime of life is so conspicuous in factory work in Pittsburgh that for one with technical, professional acquaintance with the processes of industry in other communities, the abiding impression following visits to Pittsburgh is one of horror and depression. Relatively little of this is inevitable." Note also Miss Crowell's comment (in the same study, page 909), on the neglect of certain Company tenements. "Its mills, with their equipment, were repaired and improved in order to increase the quality and quantity of their output. But common laborers were too easily replaced for an effort to be made to conserve their health or well-being by repairing or improving these houses in which they lived. If ten men fell out, ten more were ready to step in and fill their places."

return, but these remittances grow less with the years. "When they first came they used to send home 80 per cent of their wages in savings; the Italians still do so, but the Slavs now send less, perhaps 20 per cent,"—so said a Dalmatian banker in a New Jersey city, a man who is the trusted adviser of a whole group of Slavic nationalities and of those Americans who are trying to get into touch with them. Whether these precise figures are generally true or not, they represent a widespread effect of two causes—of the degree to which families and family interests have been permanently transplanted to this country, and of the rising standard of living.

Savings are likely at the beginning to take the shape of hoarding, and the first purchase of the newly arrived immigrant is apt to be a trunk, so that he may have some place under lock and key. But he quickly acquires enough confidence and intelligence to prefer a bank. Sometimes it is an employer whose timely advice brings this about. I remember a Jersey City manufacturer telling me how he learned that one of his men was keeping $800 in his room, and induced him to deposit it. Sometimes representatives of a man's own nationality on the board of directors help to win his confidence, though in one case it was said that the Lithuanians objected to depositing money in a bank where their priest was a director, for fear that he would know how much money they had.

Deposits and remittances

Whether as places of deposit for savings or as channels of remittance, private banks are generally not as secure as they should be, and the shame of this is ours so far as we do not provide proper legal safeguards. The report made in 1909 by the New York Commission on Immigration shows that in that state the known liabilities of insolvent banks with merely nominal assets amounted in one year to nearly $1,500,000. Ten states, including Illinois, Ohio and Wisconsin, report no legislation as to this species of bank. The Commission states that "the losses among Jews and Slavs, though very heavy, could not be determined with any exactness."*

Besides their too frequent insecurity, banks where savings may be deposited are in many places not within reach, and where they are so they are generally less available than they might be because of the custom, only slowly being broken in upon, which keeps them closed evenings and Saturday afternoons, the very times when they are most needed.

In spite of all obstacles and discouragements to thrift, both the deposits and remittances of immigrants reach imposing figures.† In Hazelton, the centre of an important anthracite district, I was told in one of the banks that two-thirds of the $5,000,000 of deposits in the three banks of the town were those of the "foreigners." Few of them, I was told, would deposit less than $20 a month, many as much as $50; a man depositing the larger sum would be getting perhaps $75 a month. Incomes are greatly helped out by boarders, and some "boarding bosses" save $100 a month.

Another very important and early developed form of thrift is membership in one of the many National Societies which, along with their various other functions, serve as mutual benefit societies. Some account of these is given in Chapter XVII. *Mutual benefit societies*

As the centre of gravity of the immigrant swings to this country, his savings, instead of being laid by for use in Europe, are accumulated for the sake of some sort of investment in America. Many buy farms with their savings, but many more buy a house and lot for a home. In some mining places the companies own all available *Purchase of homes*

* Report of the Commission on Immigration of New York State, appointed pursuant to the provisions of chapter 210 of the laws of 1909, transmitted to the legislature April 5, 1909; pages xiv, 252. See especially pages 24–38 and 190–194.

† In Appendix XXIII will be found a discussion of this subject, with tables, drawn from the article by F. J. Sheridan previously referred to, showing the number and amounts of money orders sent to Italy, Austria-Hungary, and Russia for each calendar year, 1900–1906.

20

land, and pursue the policy of refusing to sell any, but in spite of this difficulty large numbers of the men do acquire homes. For instance, in the mining town of Shenandoah, Dr. Roberts estimates that "Slavs" make up about 60 per cent of the population, and own as individuals 25 per cent of the real estate, besides $120,000 worth of property in churches, parsonages, parochial schools and so forth, the whole amounting to $1,320,000 acquired in fifteen or twenty years. If we add three other towns, the total rises to $2,500,000, an average of about $100 apiece.*

Building and loan associations

Building and loan associations for the co-operative purchase of homes have been of great assistance. Dr. Roberts reports sixty-five such associations in the anthracite district. These are made up mainly of mine employes, and in 1900 had helped to put up 583 houses. The report for 1904 of J. S. McCullough, the Illinois auditor of building, loan and homestead associations, contains the following remarks as to Bohemian and Polish societies of this sort in that state:

"I deem it appropriate to call special attention to the organizations which are designated in this office as the Bohemian and Polish Associations of Chicago. Their simple and economical business methods (occasionally quite crude), their steady growth and general success, the fact that the great majority operate in the territory bounded by Twelfth street on the north and Halsted street on the east, embracing the great stockyards district, and the further fact that the membership is composed almost exclusively of persons of Bohemian and Polish nationality or extraction, renders a separate classification justifiable. Some of the significant features of their methods are that books, in many cases, are kept

* Roberts, Peter: "Anthracite Coal Communities," page 41. It should be said that Dr. Roberts uses Slav in this connection to include Italians—a sense which may perhaps be justified by local usage and convenience, in spite of its ethnological inaccuracy.

For some data as to Poles in a Massachusetts farming village, see below, pages 328-9.

Croatian Saloon in Chicago

Croatian Saloon in Hibbing, Minnesota

in the foreign language, all payments of dues and interest are weekly, moneys are received only on meeting nights, no regular office quarters are maintained, officers' salaries are nominal, economy seems to be the watchword, and among the members a fraternal feeling is cultivated. This particular list comprises eighty-one associations with $6,200,000 in assets, 220,000 shares in force, and an approximate membership of 28,000. Of the above number all but seven show an increase of assets during the year—a remarkable exhibit. The industry, thrift and ambition to own a home, prevalent to such a marked degree among these classes, is responsible for the standing and splendid record of these institutions. The people, believing and trusting in them, deposit therein their savings, and hundreds of homes have been and will continue to be acquired through this popular agency."*

Occasionally savings may be invested in shares of stock; for instance, in the town of Calumet, Michigan, one hears of workingmen buying copper mining shares. But far more commonly a man who has margin enough for saving, accumulates with the idea of going into business for himself. As Dr. Warne says:† *Business investments: (1) Stores*

"At first the Slav was found only in the 'patch'— the small group of buildings usually located near a colliery. But today he is filling up and overflowing the small town, and is appearing in the principal thoroughfares of the mining cities with his saloon and his butcher shop. He is even reaching higher in the business world. Only recently a banking house has been opened in Shenandoah, conducted exclusively by Slavs. In Mahanoy City Slavs are also largely interested in one of the banks, and its business is growing rapidly."

A few hundred dollars will start a little store, perhaps dark and unattractive to American eyes, but stocked with an assortment of simple goods such as the countrymen

* Thirteenth Annual Report of the Auditor of Public Accounts of Building, Loan and Homestead Associations of the State of Illinois, pages viii and ix.

† "The Slav Invasion," page 105.

of the shopkeeper desire, including, very likely, highly ornamented prayer books in Slovak or little Russian, gay printed head kerchiefs, sheep's milk cheese from Liptó, dried wood-mushrooms from Bohemia, the little tin lamps that the miners wear in their cap fronts underground, and whatever may happen to be wanted of cheap American drygoods or groceries. With this may be combined the sale of steamship and railroad tickets and perhaps an informal employment agency.

It seems remarkable that the Slavs, who have been so often accused of lack of individual initiative, and who many of them are commercially very primitive, lacking in all business experience and too often accustomed to being patiently exploited by middlemen in countries where Jews practically monopolize all business, have here succeeded as well as they have done in commercial undertakings. Their honesty, and a strongly marked vein of shrewdness, are probably their best assets. One constantly hears praise of Slavs in business dealings, especially for being prompt and sure in payment.* In Massachusetts, in Connecticut, everywhere, I hear it said that the local merchants prefer them as customers.

(2) Saloons What is more lucrative and far more desired than keeping a store is keeping a saloon. It takes more capital,—the estimate for a Polish saloon of the poorer sort in Chicago is $500 for furnishings and an equal amount to pay for the license,—but it gives much more social importance. All the Slavic groups drink a great deal, and at home in Europe the inn or dram shop or public-house, or whatever one chooses to name it, is an important institution. The Irish-American development of the saloon, with all the threads of influence that radiate from it, is an alluring model. The saloon keeper of a Slavic group may be the best man in it; he is at least very likely to be the most influential. It is very probably he who acts first in the matter of building a

* One dealer, however, is said to have remarked, "They pay cash because they could not get credit."

church, and perhaps piety and business combine when he secures its location on a corner opposite to his place of business.

Still higher in the social scale than the saloon keepers are the bankers, whose business ranges from small local concerns in mining and farming towns to big city banking houses. The bankers carry on the bulk of the business in steamship and railroad tickets as well as in the transmission of money. Many of them are well known and very influential men, often with a large political or semi-political following, like Mr. Rovnianek of Pittsburgh among the Slovaks. One does not often hear, I think, stories of defaulting bankers, such as are so pitifully frequent among Italians.

(3) Banks

Neither do the Slavs appear to have been afflicted with any serious development of the padrone system, such as has flourished among Italians, Greeks and Syrians,—a fact the more surprising when one considers the circumstances and the way in which many groups of Slavs have been accustomed to have all their business transacted for them by Jewish middlemen.

Absence of padrones

Very interesting developments, significant, one may hope, though not yet on a large scale, are various co-operative undertakings among Slavic groups; for instance in Yonkers, where under the lead of a public spirited Ruthenian priest a model tenement was built on a co-operative plan, and other co-operative enterprises were started; at Calumet, where Croatians have started a promising co-operative store with a capital of $30,000 and about one hundred members, mostly "trammers" in the mines, besides masons and other outside workmen; and in Lorain, Ohio, where the Slovaks are just now incorporating a co-operative store said to be capitalized at $10,000 and to propose to deal in groceries and provisions, dry goods and hardware.

Co-operation

The total amount of Slavic capital would naturally be impossible to compute, but it must be enormous. Father Kruszka estimates that in 1900 Poles owned $600,000,000 worth of city property alone. As early as 1887 the Chicago *Tribune* calculated that Poles in that one city owned real estate worth $10,000,000.

It must not be supposed, of course, that every family has a margin from which even Slavic thrift and abnegation can save, or even that they all have an income sufficient to maintain strength and independence. The Slavs, like other working people, have to meet the problems of inadequate pay, rising prices, and above all, of growing needs. As the Ruthenian priest already spoken of said to me, "The laborer cannot afford to be an American. It costs too much. A man must earn at least $2.00 a day to be an American." Again he said, "My people are perishing for lack of vision." The two lacks—lack of vision and lack of what is materially necessary to satisfactory human living under modern conditions—are in some degree two aspects of the same thing, and neither is confined to any one nationality.

NOTES ON CHARTS SHOWING OCCUPATIONS OF SLAVIC IMMI-
GRANTS BY NATIVITY OF PARENTS: MALES 10 YEARS
OLD AND OVER

The best that we can do toward getting information
from the census as to the Slavic group is to study the
statistics for those born of natives of Austria, Bohemia,
Hungary, Poland, and Russia. In the following notes
and charts I use the word "Slavs" to designate this
group. These figures unfortunately include not only
Slavs but vast numbers of Jews, besides many Germans,
Magyars, Lithuanians, a few Tyrolese Italians, and
other non-Slavs.

Where we are dealing with hard manual labor, which
does not attract the Hebrew element, it is probably fair
to assume that these statistics represent a group substantially Slavic, with some intermixture of Germans,
Magyars and Lithuanians. This would not be true of
the professions, mercantile pursuits, nor of work like
tailoring or cigar making. Although it is certain that
the number of Slavs in these occupations is large, it is
impossible to isolate and count them.

It is also impossible to get from the census any data
as to the total number of Slavs in this country, so that
no estimate can be made of what proportion of all Slavs
(or of any single Slavic nationality) is engaged in a
given occupation.

The figures on which the charts are based are drawn
from Table 23 in the volume on Occupations (Census of
1900).

Chart IV shows the number of Slavs in those groups of Chart IV
occupations in which they are most numerous, namely
miners and metal workers (including census classes
86, 95–100, 112–116); laborers not specified (census
class 35); in agricultural pursuits (census class 2, which
includes not only farmers and farm laborers but those
in lumbering, dairying and stock raising); and finally
those that I have collected in one group as "mechanics."

This last group is intended to include those that in Germany would be called *Handwerker*, men with trades, and includes workers in the building trades, leather trades, cabinet makers, coopers, bakers and butchers (census classes, 71–8, 87, 88, 101–4, 108, 109). Blacksmiths and machinists are not included here but with the metal workers.

 Chart V   While this first chart shows the facts for the Slavic group as a whole, it is interesting to see how much the various

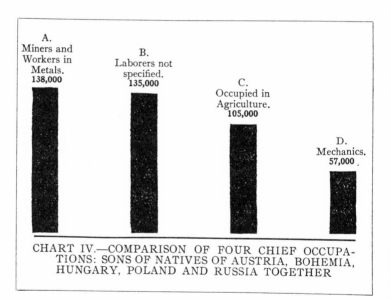

CHART IV.—COMPARISON OF FOUR CHIEF OCCUPA-TIONS: SONS OF NATIVES OF AUSTRIA, BOHEMIA, HUNGARY, POLAND AND RUSSIA TOGETHER

Slavic nationalities differ among themselves as shown in Chart V. Taking the laborers as 100, we see that the Bohemians have in agriculture (laborers and farmers together) 296, or nearly three times as many, that mechanics are more than three-quarters as many as laborers, and that miners are few. At the other end of the scale, Hungary has more miners by a third than she has laborers, while agriculture and the work of mechanics take relatively very few. It is interesting

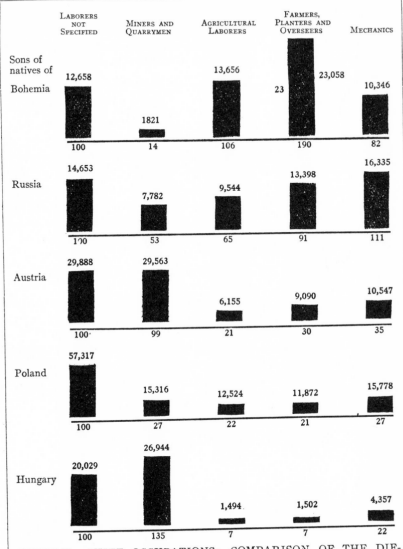

CHART V.—CHIEF OCCUPATIONS: COMPARISON OF THE DIF-
FERENT NATIONAL GROUPS

For each national group the number of laborers is taken as 100 and the
other occupations are represented by columns adjusted to this.

The numbers above the columns are the actual numbers recorded for the
specified groups, the numbers below the columns are percentages in terms of
the number of laborers.

to note the excess of farmers over farm laborers among those of Bohemian and Russian extraction.

Chart VI shows the proportion of Slavs engaged in certain occupations to the total number of persons so engaged. Here the actual size of the totals in the different occupational groups modifies the showing. Thus the agricultural group among the Slavs, though large absolutely, proves to contribute only eleven in a thousand to the enormous aggregate of nearly 9,500,000 persons engaged in agriculture (of whom over 7,000,000 are of native parentage). On the other hand, in certain minor trades like coke-burning and tanning Slavs make a substantial fraction of the whole, and it is notable how large a proportion they make—143 in a thousand—in the important group of miners and quarrymen. If the census data permitted us to exclude the quarrymen from this group, the results would be even more striking, since quarrying is a trade which attracts Italians, Finns and others, but apparently not many Slavs.

Chart VII compares the Slavs in six occupations with the three other groups of foreign parentage which are most largely represented in that occupation. It should be noted that in this chart the actual size of the different occupational groups is not shown, and that the numbers of the various nationalities in each occupation are represented only in terms of their proportion to the Slavs taken as 100. Italians appear in the table among the laborers and the coke burners. The Scandinavians, on the other hand, appear only in the agricultural group. For the rest, the Slavs are brought into comparison with Irishmen, Germans, English and Welsh, and are greatly outnumbered by them in agriculture, as mechanics (in the sense here given to the word), and less markedly as iron and steel workers and as simple laborers, while in work in mines, coke ovens and allied occupations they lead.

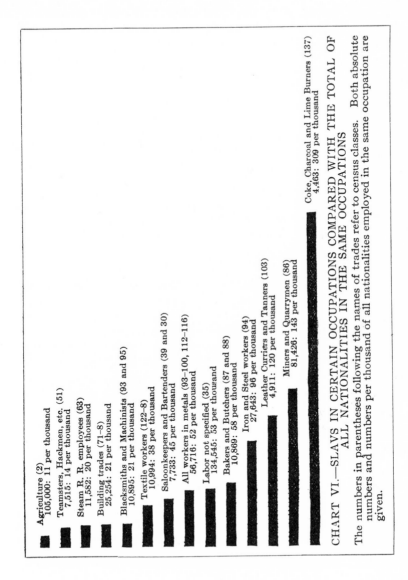

Agriculture (2)
105,000: 11 per thousand

Teamsters, Hackmen, etc. (51)
7,515: 14 per thousand

Steam R. R. employees (63)
11,582: 20 per thousand

Building trades (71–8)
25,254: 21 per thousand

Blacksmiths and Machinists (93 and 95)
10,895: 21 per thousand

Textile workers (122–8)
10,994: 38 per thousand

Saloonkeepers and Bartenders (39 and 30)
7,733: 45 per thousand

All workers in metals (93–100, 112–116)
56,716: 52 per thousand

Labor not specified (35)
134,545: 53 per thousand

Bakers and Butchers (87 and 88)
10,869: 58 per thousand

Iron and Steel workers (94)
27,643: 96 per thousand

Leather Curriers and Tanners (103)
4,911: 120 per thousand

Miners and Quarrymen (86)
81,426: 143 per thousand

Coke, Charcoal and Lime Burners (137)
4,463: 309 per thousand

CHART VI.—SLAVS IN CERTAIN OCCUPATIONS COMPARED WITH THE TOTAL OF ALL NATIONALITIES IN THE SAME OCCUPATIONS

The numbers in parentheses following the names of trades refer to census classes. Both absolute numbers and numbers per thousand of all nationalities employed in the same occupation are given.

COKE, CHARCOAL AND LIME BURNERS (137)

Slavs......4,463.   100%

Germans... 795.   18% of the Slavs in this occupation.

Italians.... 681.   15%

Irish 565.   13%

MINERS AND QUARRYMEN (86)

Slavs 81,426.   100%

English and Welsh...70,031.   86%

Irish..............51,320.   63%

Germans 35,931.   44%

IRON AND STEEL WORKERS (94)

Slavs 27,643.   100%

Germans. 49,580.   179%

Irish..............47,365.   171%

English and Welsh...19,775.   72%

LABOR (NOT SPECIFIED) (35)

Slavs 134,545.   100%

Irish..............270,027.   199%

Germans..........241,553.   178%

Italians........... 93,901.   69%

MECHANICS (71–8, 87, 88, 101–4, 108, 109)

Slavs 57,363. 100%

Germans 329,577. 575%

Irish 168,324. 293%

English and Welsh 78,591. 137%

AGRICULTURAL PURSUITS (2)

Slavs..........105,492.   100%   Germans 775,452. 735%

Scandinavians...304,502.   288%

Irish............277,155.   263%

Percentages of total Slavs in the specified occupation.

CHART VII.—COMPARISON, FOR CERTAIN OCCUPATIONS, BE-
TWEEN SLAVS AND THE THREE OTHER FOREIGN GROUPS
THAT HAVE THE LARGEST NUMBER IN THE GIVEN OCCU-
PATION.

The Slavs in each occupation are taken as 100 and the columns representing other nationalities in the same occupation are proportioned to this.
Both their absolute numbers and the percentage of Slavs in the same
occupation are given.   Figures in parentheses following names of trades
refer to census classes.

CHAPTER XV

SLAVS AS FARMERS

Why do peasants from Bohemian beet fields or Croatian vineyards betake themselves to mines and foundries, making no use of the experience of a lifetime and of a skill which if often primitive is sometimes of a high order? It is not, as is often assumed, because they are eager to taste city life or because the hard tasks and narrow round of country life are irksome, but, with most of them at least, because of the hard necessity of the case, especially in the beginning.

Why immigrants do not take up farming

The explanation of a Polish writer quoted by Father Kruszka* fully bears out this conclusion. At home, he says, the Polish immigrants either had no property at all or owned at most only a tiny piece of land. In either case the money that they are able to raise when they leave home is hardly more than enough to bring them to America. They cannot think of buying a farm. The position of a farm laborer is not attractive to them because not only does it mean lower pay than other employments that are open to them, but it lasts only a part of the year; so necessarily they settle in the city. By the time that a family has saved the considerable sum needed to buy land and begin farming, its members are so accustomed to city life that it would be hard for them to change.

There are other difficulties besides those named by this Polish writer. First, we must remember that the obstacle of language is far more serious on the farm than in the factory. A man once taught his special task in

---

* "Historya Polska w Ameryce," III, page 111. This whole chapter on the agricultural situation and the general economic condition of Poles in America has much interesting matter in it, hardly to be found in English.

any highly organized work is, once for all, initiated; after the first it is mere repetition. Moreover, in a large industrial group there is likely to be a fellow countryman at hand to interpret. On the farm, in contrast to this, there is a constant change of tasks and an endless opportunity for costly and annoying mistakes from inability to understand orders.

Further, it is an infinitely less trying change to go from home to a group of countrymen in a foreign country than it is to leave that group to go alone among Americans. Farm life is made forbidding to the foreigner by the strange food, the lack of his own church and, above all, by his separation from those of his own speech and ways. In Europe country life is for the most part village life. There are cases where peasants live scattered, each on his own land, but the typical settlement is a village, clustered close, with a church and an open place where perhaps the boys and girls dance on Sunday afternoons and fields about it stretching out on every side. A man may have a long tramp morning and evening, but that is all in the day's work as he conceives it. The isolation of the American farmhouse is a drawback both to life as a farm hand and to life as an independent farmer.*

---

* Mrs. Humpal-Zeman lays much stress on this contrast between the lonely farm in America and the traditional holidays, feasts, processions, national music and games which make life gay in the old country. (Industrial Commission, Vol. XV, page 508.) An interesting discussion of conditions on western farms is Mr. E. V. Smalley's "The Isolation of Life on the Prairie Farm," *Atlantic Monthly*, Vol. 72, p. 378 (1893). See, too, the admirable discussion of this point by Miss Jane Addams. She says: "Regret is many times expressed that, notwithstanding the fact that nine out of every ten immigrants are of rural birth and are fitted to undertake that painstaking method of cultivating the soil which American farmers despise, they nevertheless all tend to congregate in cities where their inherited and elaborate knowledge of agricultural processes is unutilized. But it is characteristic of American complacency when any assisted removal to agricultural regions is contemplated, that we utterly ignore the past experiences of the immigrant and always assume that each family will be content to live in the middle of its own piece of ground, although there are few peoples on the face of the earth who have ever tried isolating a family on one

Another point that we overlook when we accuse the Reasons for "clannish-ness" immigrant of being clannish is that he sometimes really fears the hostility or the over-reaching greed of American neighbors, with their too common contempt for "foreigners." I find a Bohemian guidebook advising settlers that in certain localities they will find no fellow countrymen "so that the immigrant must settle among perfect strangers, in great part cunning and capable of anything, and might easily, in consequence of his ignorance of the language, be deprived of the land that he has taken up and in some cases partly cultivated." On the other hand, among a group of settlers, neighbors at home and now strangers together in a strange land, there is an especial degree of mutual helpfulness and comfort. This has great economic as well as moral value. For instance, in a Nebraska county which lost nearly 2000 of its scanty population in the three bad years that followed the panic of 1873, the Bohemian and German homesteaders held

hundred and sixty acres, or on eighty, or even on forty. But this is the American way—a survival of our pioneer days—and we refuse to modify it, even in regard to South Italians, although from the day of mediaeval incursions they have lived in compact villages with an intense and elaborated social life, so much of it out of doors and interdependent that it has affected almost every domestic habit. Italian women knead their own bread, but depend on the village oven for its baking, and the men would rather walk for miles to their fields each day than to face an evening of companionship limited to the family. Nothing could afford a better check to the constant removal to the cities of the farming population all over the United States than the possibility of combining community life with agricultural occupation. This combination would afford that development of civilization which, curiously enough, density alone brings and for which even a free system of rural delivery is not an adequate substitute. Much of the significance and charm of rural life in South Italy lies in its village companionship, quite as the dreariness of the American farm life inheres in its unnecessary solitude. But we totally disregard the solution which the old agricultural community offers, and our utter lack of adaptability has something to do with the fact that the South Italian remains in the city, where he soon forgets his cunning in regard to silk worms and olive trees, but continues his old social habits to the extent of filling an entire tenement house with the people from one village."—"Newer Ideals of Peace," pages 65–67.

Much of what Miss Addams here says applies to Slavs as truly as to Italians.

out, as the Americans could not, against the grasshopper plague, the drought and the hard times. And the reason for this, my American informant assured me, was that Bohemians were more ready to help one another than were the Americans.*

Number on farms

In spite of all the difficulties, we do find considerable numbers of our Slavic population on farms. The census indicates that they are about 100,000, the majority being independent farmers. They are fairly widely scattered, for twenty-six states each have at least 200 of them. Wisconsin has the largest number, with over 13,000, and South Dakota has the largest proportion, with about 11 per cent of its whole farming population belonging to the Slavic group.†

Bohemians and Poles doubtless make the great majority of the Slavic farmers in the United States. The Bohemians certainly have a larger proportion of their total number on farms than has any other Slavic group and it may be that they have a larger absolute number though an exact knowledge of the facts is impossible. It is common to estimate that one-half of the Bohemians in the United States are living in country places and occupied either with farming or with some one of the various employments incident to rural life, from shoemaking to keeping store or acting as notary public. If the comparison be extended to all groups of foreign parentage, Bohemia‡ shows a larger proportion engaged in agriculture than any foreign countries except Switzerland, Denmark and Norway, surpassing even Germany and Sweden. It is interesting to note that Italy has a very low rank in this regard; even Poland and Russia surpass her, lowered as their place is by the large non-agricultural Jewish element, and only Hungary is below her.

Of the Poles, Father Kruszka thinks that barely

<hr />

* An instance of this occurs in " The True Story of a Bohemian Pioneer " which follows this chapter.
† See Appendix XXII, page 469.
‡ The statements refer to persons of specified parentage.

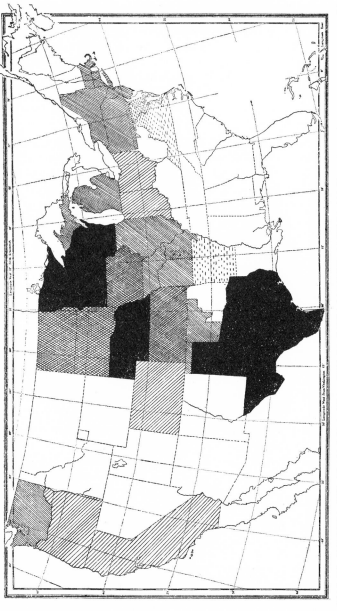

MAP XI.—FARMERS AND FARM LABORERS: ONE OR BOTH PARENTS BORN IN AUSTRIA-HUNGARY, POLAND OR RUSSIA. NUMBERS BY STATES.*

Black: over 10,000. Wisconsin 13,327; Minnesota 11,394; Nebraska 11,361; Texas 10,915.
Cross-hatched: 5,000 to 10,000. S. Dakota 8,466; Kansas 8,134; N. Dakota 6,800; Iowa 5,951.
Fine diagonal: 1000 to 5000. New York 3,750; Michigan 3,645; Oklahoma 2,229; Illinois 2,117; Connecticut 2,036; Massachusetts 1,845; New Jersey 1,594; Missouri 1,594; Pennsylvania 1,232; Washington 965.

Coarse diagonal: 500 to 1000. Ohio 949; Indiana 875; California 780; Oregon 604; Colorado 580.
Broken line: 200 to 500. Arkansas 468; Maryland 345; Virginia 226.
White: under 200. All others.

* Census of 1900, Vol. on Occupations, Table 41. Males ten years of age and over engaged as "agricultural laborers" or as "farmers, planters and overseers."

one-third are on farms, yet for 1901 he estimates that 700 out of 900 Polish settlements were agricultural. The total number of Poles on farms, including hired laborers, women and children, he puts at 500,000. Among these are 70,000 farm owners, possessing, as he calculates, an average of about 80 acres apiece. This would give to Polish landowners a total area equal to over two-thirds of Rhode Island.

Besides Bohemians and Poles there are larger or smaller numbers of farmers among most of the other Slavic groups and probably among all; certainly Slovaks, Ruthenians, Slovenians, Croatians, Dalmatians and Russians furnish farmers. Among Servians, Montenegrins and Bulgarians I do not happen to have learned of any, which does not, however, prove a negative.

Varieties of farming districts

Map XI shows where the Slavs have chiefly taken up land. They are in roughly five groups of states representing five kinds of farming.

1. *The Wooded States*—Wisconsin, Michigan and Minnesota—where the settler had to clear his land and where he today raises wheat, potatoes, dairy products, fruit and vegetables for canning, and so forth.

2. *The Prairie States*—Iowa, Nebraska, Kansas and the Dakotas—where the settler found the virgin prairie and where he now raises corn and wheat.

3. *The Southwestern States*—Texas, Oklahoma, Missouri and Arkansas—where, in parts at least, cotton is king.

4. *The Pacific Slope*—Washington, California and Oregon—where fruit and especially grapes are grown, and where Bohemians, Dalmatians and Slovenians have settled.

5. *The Eastern States*—New York, Connecticut, Massachusetts, New Jersey and Pennsylvania—with diversified and "truck" farming. Settlements in Illinois, Ohio, and Indiana, Maryland and Virginia share many characteristics with this group.

Polish Market Scene, Stevens Point, Wisconsin

When the Poles and more especially the Bohemians Western settlers; pioneers and land-owners began to come, scatteringly in the forties and in considerable numbers in the fifties and later, they passed almost without stopping through the Atlantic states and through Ohio, Indiana and Illinois, and went on to the states where they could then get land free as homesteaders or at cheap rates.   Consequently they settled first in Wisconsin, Michigan and Minnesota, where it was necessary to cut timber to clear the land, and somewhat later in the prairie states farther west, in Iowa, Nebraska and the Dakotas.   Those that came up from the Gulf ports settled, too, in Texas.

The Bohemian settlements in Kewaunee county, Wisconsin, the early hardships of which have been described in Chapter XI, are a good example of farming in the timber belt.*   Today the hard old times seem far behind, and it is pleasant to see signs of prosperity on every hand; the roomy farmhouses of wood or of yellow brick, with rows of poplars about the yard, the big, well-built barns, the thrifty fields, and the cheese factories.   "Ten years ago every other farm was mortgaged; today not one in seven," I was told.   Land is worth five times its old value.   Where twelve years before Bohemian farmers were borrowing at 8 or 9 per cent, in 1906 they paid 4 per cent.   They have a good bank of their own, and altogether are a very substantial class.

The Poles were generally poorer than the Bohemians when they began, so that they commonly secured inferior land, harder to clear and less fertile when cleared. Yet they have done well, too.   Portage County, Wisconsin, is a great Polish district, and about Stevens Point and Polonia† in that county I found very good looking Polish farms with great stacks of yellow wheat straw behind the barns.   At Stevens Point it was quaint to see a typical Galician market scene, minus the element of

* See also Miss Mashek's admirable article already referred to, "Bohemian Farmers of Wisconsin." *Charities*, XIII, pages 211–214 (Dec. 3, 1904).

† For further data as to this settlement, see above, page 258.

costume,—the big square littered with straw and full of farm wagons and hobnobbing country folk.*

Farming on wooded land

Not only were the wooded states easier to reach at first, but it was and is possible to begin with less capital in timber than in prairie country. Today the advantages are probably even more than they were earlier. A land agent in Nebraska connected with a Bohemian farming paper says, "Breaking prairie costs two or three dollars an acre, while land that has been cut over and partly cleared can be planted at once among the stumps without preliminary expense and yields besides wood enough for buildings and fences. To remove the stumps immediately costs too much, and if they are of soft wood it takes them twenty-five years to rot away. The whole plan of farming is different on the two kinds of lands, even different ploughs are needed, but no one ever fails who settles in the timber."

"Two hundred and fifty dollars," I was told, "is enough to begin farming under such conditions. A man works for two or three or four years in a city, and then makes a start. Many begin with only $50 or $100. Nowadays they buy perhaps 40 acres at $5.00 or $10 an acre, clear as much of it as they can, and build a little shanty. Somehow or other they manage to get an old horse. All the family work, and in winter the man very likely goes off to the woods where he can earn good wages, $35 or $40 a month, with board."†

Prairie states

On a prairie farm conditions differ considerably. No one wants less than 160 acres, and besides land the

* An interesting early Polish settlement dating back to 1876 or before was that at Radom, Illinois. The settlers there had worked in Chicago factories till they had saved enough to buy land. They are said to have very comfortable houses, a church, school and hotel, to use the best agricultural machinery, and to enjoy the services of an exceptionally good teacher. The latter was a priest and a patriot, who had lost one arm in the Polish Revolution, He held a position in a Canadian university when he heard of this colony and went there to teach the Polish children.

† See for a similar account Kruszka: "Historya Polska w Ameryce," III, page 118, where detailed data are given.

farmer must have buildings, machinery and stock. For this at least $1500 is needed. "I always say I will pay no attention to any one with under $1000," the agent said. "They are afraid of mortgages, and pay cash, at $5.00 an acre; therefore they need $800 for the land alone. The rest goes for stock, machinery, breaking the land, and the support of the family till returns begin to come in."

Iowa, which formerly attracted many Bohemians, and eastern Kansas are now what Ohio was in the early days; that is, too fully settled and too expensive for the newly arrived immigrant, since land costs perhaps $125 an acre. Yet I was told that a family might even now begin with only $500 by hiring a farm at $3.50 to $4.00 an acre, or by farming on shares (the terms being one-half of the corn crop, two-fifths of the oats).

In a town which I visited in Iowa the settlement of Bohemians was an old one, dating back to the fifties and sixties. They are now well established. The old log houses have been replaced by good frame cottages, the old isolation is largely done away with by rural free delivery, and the telephone is in general use. They have a bank and good stores, but I imagine that the great mail order houses in Chicago, which publish special Bohemian catalogues, do a good business among them. We visited the house of one such Bohemian farmer, who came to this country when a child. The house was not large, but a comfortable clapboarded cottage, nicely furnished, and very neat. Behind it stood what remained of the original little loghouse, now used for some farm purpose. One little daughter played the parlor organ, self-taught; all eight children went to the public school, and talked English among themselves, but Bohemian with their mother.

All through this western region, covering our first three groups of states, the independent farmer is the type. Here the immigrant did not start as a hired laborer and work his way up, but began at once on his arrival

Independent farmers the type

to farm on his own account. To do this he had to come with his capital in hand ready to invest. We do not realize how much this sort of thing still goes on. For instance, I was told of a group of seven Bohemians going to Nebraska in June, 1906. Most of them had $3000; the poorest had $1900. They had come without their families, whom they were to return to fetch when they had selected their land. In a little town in Texas I met a Bohemian couple who had just arrived with a considerable sum with which they proposed to buy land. A Bohemian pastor was helping them to select a location, and as he had a fine place of his own with a charming vineyard, they had the benefit of skilled advice. And how good those endless stretches of dark soil on which the cotton was just beginning to sprout must have looked to them.

The Pacific slope

Of the Pacific Slope I know nothing at first hand. I am told of fruit raising, and especially of vineyards and the production of wine carried on with great success by Bohemians and by various of the South Slav groups, notably Dalmatians. One informant tells me of a Dalmatian farm in California through which it takes three-quarters of an hour to drive with a good horse, past corn on the one hand and wheat on the other. This estate is said to be worth from one to two million dollars. Another large enterprise is that of the Bohemian firm, F. Korbel Brothers, founded in 1862 and incorporated in 1903.

The census figures give insignificant numbers of Slavs in agriculture in California and Oregon, and even fewer in Washington.* It must be remembered, however, that in California both Bohemian and Dalmatian settlement dates back to the early days and on this account the figures may not fully represent the presence of Slavic stock.

On farms in the East

Slavic farming in the eastern states (meaning here the group of states included under 5 in the classification given above) has a different history and is of a different

* Cf. Appendix XXII, page 469.

type. It began later, and occupies more Poles and fewer Bohemians. Whereas in the three western groups of states the majority are independent farmers who came from the old country with money to buy land in America, in this group the hired farm laborer predominates.* Arriving with no means, he earns perhaps $25 a month besides his board.† Before long it may be he marries a Polish girl (who has meanwhile been saving a good part of her weekly wage of $3.50 as a servant) and goes to farming for himself.

Interesting examples of Polish farming may be found at many places in the Connecticut valley,‡ for instance in Massachusetts in the stretch between Northampton and Greenfield,—in Hadley, Hatfield, Sunderland and South Deerfield. The numbers in these places are small compared with those in the neighboring manufacturing centres like Chicopee and Webster, (credited with 5000 Poles each), or Holyoke, Worcester, Palmer, Ludlow, Westfield, Ware, Greenfield, Turners Falls, Clinton and Fitchburg, with their smaller but still considerable

---

* While in the states that I have included in my two western groups the Slavs showed in 1900, nearly seventeen farmers to every ten farm laborers, in the eastern group there were forty-four farm laborers to every ten farmers. By Slavs is here meant persons whose parents were born in Austria, Bohemia, Hungary, Poland or Russia. For an explanation of this usage see page 311.

† A local informant supplies the following account of monthly wages of farm laborers for the neighborhood of Deerfield, Mass.

1875–80 (before coming of Poles) $30–$35.
1880, for Poles, $8–$10 at first.
$16–$18 after 3 to 5 years.
for Americans, $16–$25.
1907 for Poles, $20–$28.
for Americans, $25–$32.
1909 for Poles, $18–$22.
for Americans, $23–$28.

‡ This invasion of the Connecticut valley by Poles has attracted considerable attention. See an article by E. K. Titus in the *New England Magazine*, Oct., 1903, and a more recent study by Miss Elizabeth S. Tyler in the *Smith College Monthly* for June, 1909; also articles in the *Boston Daily Globe*, June 29, 1902, the *Springfield Sunday Union* of January 7, 1906, the *New York Herald* of January 14, 1906, and the *Boston Evening Transcript*, May 8 and August 4, 1909. For an account of the bringing of Poles to this district see above, page 240, ff.

Polish industrial colonies.   But the significance of the country settlements lies not in numbers but in the proportion of the Poles to the native-born, and in the permanence of their position as land-owners.

Poles in Old Hadley   The most striking settlement is at Old Hadley, in Massachusetts.   Here, where Goffe, the regicide, is said to have once helped beat off an Indian raid, two-thirds of the births in 1906 were Polish.*   All up and down the beautiful elm-shaded street the old colonial mansions are occupied by Poles.   Probably one cause of the attractiveness of these New England farms is the compact village life, so different from western settlements, with each man on his isolated quarter section.

The way up   As already said, the typical case here is the immigrant who begins as a hired man at a monthly wage.   In this position he learns to raise tobacco and onions, the staples of the district, and after a time may either buy or hire land, or take it on shares.   In the latter case the landlord furnishes one-half the seed and all the fertilizer, and receives in return one-half the crop.   This plan makes it possible to begin with almost no capital, but many buy outright when they have only $200 or $300, borrowing the rest (perhaps $1000) either from relatives or on a mortgage.   Relatives generally take no interest on loans to one another.   Tobacco land is valued at perhaps $180 an acre, onion land at perhaps $150.

Amount of property held by Poles   Advancing in this way, many have bought farms, or at least a house and lot of land.   In 1906, out of 13,000 acres of assessed land in Hadley over 700 acres, or more than a twentieth of the whole, was in Polish hands.   Of persons paying taxes on property, they made one in ten. Their holdings were below the average in value, as is natural, but forty-four persons among them owned,

---

* In 1905 natives of Austria and Russia (who are here practically synonymous with Poles), made 372 out of 570 foreign born in a total population of 1,895; that is, they were approximately two-thirds of the foreign population and one-fifth of the whole.   The other foreign born were Irish 110, French Canadian 33, Italian 23, scattering 32.

IN OLD HADLEY

1. The home of four or five Polish families.   2. A home of a poorer class, the front used for a small store.   3. O of three farmsteads owned by successful Polish farmer and onion dealer.   4. A colonial home of Old Hadley that n houses four or five Polish families.   5 and 6. Polish door yards.

together, real estate assessed at nearly $57,000, or almost $1300 each, besides an average of about $150 worth each of stock and other personal property owned by thirty-seven persons. That is, Poles making not quite 20 per cent of the population of the town owned 5.3 per cent of the taxable area, 5.7 per cent of the taxable value in real estate, and 3.1 per cent of the personal property.

These averages and aggregates naturally cover a considerable diversity of individual circumstances. Among the owners of real estate, for instance, they range from one man with over one hundred acres of land, a house, a barn, tobacco sheds, farm stock, etc., to a man with three-quarters of an acre of land and a house and barn worth $300. In a neighboring town we found a man who is said to have made a fortune by "cornering" onions, who owns three farms, and lives with his family in a good, old-fashioned New England farmhouse.

When the Poles hire the old American houses, they may use them as tenements, four or five families to a house. Moreover, they may take boarders, and this practice is said to be on the increase except among the well-to-do in towns. One hears stories in Hadley of overcrowding and of payments of fifteen cents a night for a place to lie on the floor. Generally a boarder pays perhaps $4.00 a month, which covers cooking, but he buys his own food. The farming of the Poles is regarded as inferior by the Americans; their great economic advantage lies in the fact that not only do they themselves work instead of hiring labor, but that all the members of the family, women and children as well as men, work in the fields.*

Housing and labor

* A friend in Greenfield writes: "The women and girls, as is necessary in onion weeding, dress like the men in overalls and without shoes and stockings. It is a familiar but picturesque sight, and one typically representative of their great patience, dogged perseverance and thrift, to see them, in blue jeans and huge straw hats, slowly crawling on their hands and knees up and down the long rows, astraddle the slender green onion tops, pulling out the tiny weeds which no machine can reach. They

Citizenship   It seems surprising that with so many property owners there are only ten Poles in Hadley who are naturalized. One American, at least, who talked with us about it, was much opposed to their gaining the vote, and if this feeling is common it may be the reason why so few have become citizens.

Polish increase   The figures as to property are striking enough, but much less so than the Hadley vital statistics, which show that in the year 1906 the Poles account for 48 per cent of the deaths, 52 per cent of the marriages, and 66 per cent of the births; that is, that they are increasing out of proportion to the native element. In school the children are 136 out of 573 (24 per cent), an increase over the year before of 19.3 per cent for the Polish children, while the whole number of children increased only 10.5 per cent. In estimating the importance of this situation we must bear in mind the small scale of it all, and that the figures are for a single year only. We must not suppose, either, that there are many Hadleys; but all these qualifications do not rob the situation of significance.

Girls often come over alone as servants, and readily get places. Of thirteen Polish marriages in Hadley in 1906, the bride was entered as servant or domestic in all except one, where she was called a "housekeeper." The bridegrooms were ten "laborers" and three "farmers." They do not seem to marry excessively early, as the youngest Hadley bride was eighteen, the youngest groom twenty years old.

However well one may think of the Pole, the New Englander may be pardoned a pang of regret as he sees the old American stock shrink away, partly through withdrawal to the money-making centres, partly by a sort of racial dry rot which shows itself in the miserably

do not stop to rest even on the hottest days, and at noon the women go back to the house, prepare the meal, and bring it out to the men." A very similar account of Polish onion raising in Orange County, New York, is given in an article "The Black Dirt People" by Henry H. Moore in *The Outlook* for Dec. 25, 1909, pages 949–957.

deficient birth rate. It is with a rather rueful smile that he observes the swarms of funny little tots, with their tow heads bundled in kerchiefs, that cluster about the doors of the old white farmhouses. But if any one is to be blamed, it is certainly not the hardworking newcomer who has left home and all for his chance here.

Another difference between East and West is that in the East there is of course no pioneer element. The farms bought or hired by Poles, Bohemians and other Slavs anywhere east of Wisconsin and Iowa are farms that Americans have let go. This contrast between the pioneer who brings wild land under the plough and the settler in old communities deserves emphasis because some writers on immigration, as for instance Professor Mayo-Smith, make much of the difference between "colonists" prior to the Revolution and "immigrants" since, on the ground, in part at least, that the latter have done none of the hard work of settling the country. As a matter of fact, a large part of the colonists came to dwell in settled and orderly communities, while from the Revolution to the present moment, and from Kentucky to Alaska, the immigrant has been among the frontiersmen and has worked in the van in the conquest of the continent.

The immigrant as pioneer

I shall always recall with pleasure an evening spent on a cool, wide piazza in a little Nebraska town, listening to the story of my Bohemian hostess, which I have tried to reproduce as "The True Story of a Bohemian Pioneer." It was hard to realize that the quiet-voiced, middle-aged lady beside me had lived as a girl in a dug-out, had herself "broken prairie"—heart-breaking labor for a man—had endured storms and famine, rattlesnake bites and plagues of grasshoppers, droughts and floods. It seemed strange that she could have lived to see the treeless and uninhabited prairie covered with stacked wheat and shaded farmhouses, and the scattered sod houses replaced by a pleasant, well-built town with a friendly, honest Bohemian air; with good houses, gardens and shade trees;

with a court house, churches, a Bohemian cemetery, and an "opera house" for Bohemian theatricals.

Agricultural settlement spontaneous One of the most interesting aspects of the facts here presented is the considerable degree to which Slavic peasants are taking root in the land without any artificial stimulus. So far as I know there has not been any concerted effort to promote their distribution,—nothing, at least, comparable to what has been done to open opportunities for agricultural life to Jews and Italians. The Slavs present no such problem of congestion as do the Jews, to render Americans uneasy, nor have they, like the Jews, a body of wealthy men to aid the poorer among them. Neither does any home government concern itself to forward their interests, as Italy concerns herself for her expatriated citizens.

One might suppose that the race of the Mir and the Zadruga, the communal village and the "house communion," would have developed co-operative farming colonies here, but aside from the Doukhobor settlement in Canada, this does not seem to be the case. From time to time co-operative colonies of one sort and another have been proposed and actually undertaken, but they appear to fail regularly. "It never does among Slavs," agreed three informants in chorus, a Slovenian, a Slovak and a Bohemian.*

The rôle of the land agent The initiative toward settlement on the land doubtless comes largely from the energy of those who have lands to sell and who use every art to induce settlers to come to them. The so-called immigration departments of the southern and western railroads are vast enterprises,

* An instance cited was an agitation started by a Slovenian priest about 1896 for a co-operative farming colony in California with a capital of $40,000. But "they expected too much" and failed. Mrs. Humpal-Zeman, too, writing of the Bohemians, says that attempts at "colonies" fail, and tells of one started on a co-operative basis on a plantation in Virginia by an association formed for the purpose. The plan was started in 1897 in Chicago as a result of the depression of that time, but the families who actually went to the spot did not stay long, and the whole thing broke up. See Report of the Industrial Commission, XV, page 508.

spending freely on advertising, traveling agents, excursions for "colonists" and "home-seekers", on "Northern settlers' conventions" and on every possible method of attraction. For instance, the Santa Fé road has strips of model gardening along its tracks in various places to demonstrate the qualities of soil and climate. These efforts are aimed mainly at drawing settlers from other states, but the suction affects the immigrant from Europe as well as the native American. Moreover, various southern states, through official boards and otherwise, have done much active canvassing for immigrants from abroad. Though they seem not yet to have made the discovery, they are likely in the course of time to learn that in the Southern Slav, as well as in the Bohemian and Pole, they have a thrifty, hard working people, many of whom are used to fruit culture and to a hot sun.*

Besides the railroads and the state commissions, there are, of course, numerous private land agents and promoters. One hears that there have been occasional abominable land promotion schemes, decoying settlers on to wretched land, and one such, real or fictitious, has found a place in literature in Sienkiewicz's heart-rending story, "After Bread,"† which reminds one of nothing so much as of the similar picture in Martin Chuzzlewit.

In Chicago I had an interesting talk with a real estate agent who was colonizing Bohemians and Poles in places

* For an account of Southern efforts to attract immigrants, see Fleming, W. L.: "Immigration to the Southern States." *Pol. Sci. Quar.*, XX, page 276 (1905).

† It is only fair to say that the story is said to have been written in the interests of the Polish landlords with the intention of deterring from emigration. The following frank admission which occurs in this story is interesting, coming from so good a German hater as Sienkiewicz.

The land company having failed to survey and allot the land among the settlers, "a body of Germans," says Sienkiewicz, "would have combined together to clear the woods, build houses, and then would have measured off to each man his portion," but the Poles, "at the beginning, wanted each to settle on his own land, to build his own house and to cut down trees on his own lot. . . . Thereupon arose contentions."

in Lake County, Michigan. He claimed that a family could "make a nice start" with $500. "They would buy, say, eighty acres at $3.50 to $5.00 an acre, making a first payment of a dollar an acre. They could pay up in five years, and after the first two years it would be easy. Building material for the house would cost $100, and they could put it up themselves with the help of the neighbors. Outfit and team would cost $200, and they would have $100 left to live on. A cow and twenty-five chickens would almost make a living." The school authorities had agreed to put up a school house for any three families. He arranged settlements of each nationality by itself. The Bohemians liked sandy soil, the Poles wanted clay and preferred Wisconsin to Michigan. It would have been interesting to hear the other side and learn how the settlers' actual experience compared with this prospectus.

An example of similar efforts on a larger scale is the work of the business agent (himself an American) of a Bohemian farming magazine published in Omaha. He selects a location belonging to some land company, visits the place and judges its characteristics, and proceeds to procure settlers by writing it up, article after article.

Guides for immigrants Another aid to settlement are handbooks for immigrants, giving information as to the relative advantages of different localities, as to fields of employment, range of wages, price of land, crops, and so forth. Of these I have seen two admirable specimens, one for Bohemians,* one, already spoken of, for Slovenians,† both written by men of the nationality in question, in their own language. Here again, in contrast to Professor Ellis's "Guida per gl'Immigranti Italiani," or Mrs. Severance's guide published in many languages, the undertaking represents no outside influence, but comes from within the group itself.

* Rosický, Jan: "Jak je v Americe." *Národní Tiskárny* Press, Omaha, Neb., 1906.
† Šušteršič, Rev. F. J.: "Poduk Rojakom Slovencem." *Amerikanski Slovenec* Press, Joliet, Ill., 1903.

The most important question with regard to this whole matter is not how many peasant immigrants have taken up farming on their arrival here, but rather how many of the much greater numbers who have gone into industry and mining leave those pursuits later for the farm. The younger generation, brought up in the city, are not likely to go "back to the land" as they grow up. Their associations, ambitions and habits will all be of the town, and there is no immediate outlook for such a change of direction in our school education, or such a shifting of comparative wages and profits in the economic world, as to induce a return current from the city. The first generation, the immigrants themselves, must make the change if it is to be made. "When they arrive is the time to talk land to them but then they have not the money," said one informant, and if they have not saved the needed money before losing their land hunger, then that chance is gone. There are those, however, who save and go to farming with their savings. While most of those who have bought farms have hitherto belonged to the comparatively small number who come with money in hand for this purpose, there are also those who have earned the money here. Sometimes, as seems to be commonly the case among the Poles in the Connecticut valley, the necessary money for independent farming is earned by work as hired farm laborers. In Hadley, for instance, the Polish landowners have been recruited, not from the neighboring industrial centres where Poles and other Slavs are numerous, but direct from Poland, the newcomers arriving with no money in hand, and working first for hire and perhaps later on shares.

Sometimes the money to begin farming with is earned in industrial pursuits. How often this is done, it is impossible to estimate. Even in Hadley I was told that men did sometimes come from Pennsylvania mines with their savings. In Pennsylvania itself there are very interesting instances of this current back to the land. In an anthracite county town, in 1904, I had an instructive talk with a real estate dealer whose signboard (except the name) I copy.

"George Smith spredava loti (lots), hauzi (houses), farmi (farms) za hotove penezi. Ofic (office) jeto pod no. 17½ na West Broad strice (street)."

The words in parentheses I have inserted to mark the English words which have been adopted in a more or less Slavonized form. My informant said: "Today the Americans are leaving the farms for the cities and factories; the farms are ruined by the factories making it impossible to get servants. The Slavs are the people who take to farming. The movement has been going on only for the last five or six years, but if it continues at the present rate, they will be in the majority in the farming districts in this neighborhood. A Slav miner will save $1000 to $2500, seldom more. This would give him a farm of perhaps 50 to 75 acres with a house. If he had only $1000 he could still buy 10 or 12 acres with a little house. They make good farmers. They raise more hay and less 'truck' and stock than the Italians. They are much cleaner. The nationalities represented are chiefly Slovaks, Magyars and Poles, with some Russian Jews."

Not only in Pennsylvania but scattered here and there in other states, one comes across larger or smaller numbers thus graduating from industry to the farm.*

Among the Slovaks Several of the minor nationalities, though they have far fewer representatives in agriculture than have the Poles and Bohemians, have farming settlements that are very interesting and many of these were made as a result of American savings. Of the Slovaks, one of their leaders, Mr. Rovnianek, wrote in 1904:

"At first there was a disposition among them to return to their native country, but in a little while some decided to stay. Then it was that they began to look around them for opportunities to settle on farms and return to the manner of life which they had led at home. There

---

* Cf. the Radom settlement mentioned in note, page 324.

Photograph by Hine

SLOVAK WOMEN AT ELLIS ISLAND

Photograph by Hine

A SLOVAK FAMILY BOUND FOR THE WEST

are now hundreds of Slovak farmers in Pennsylvania, Connecticut and Ohio; and in Minnesota, Arkansas, Virginia and Wisconsin there are colonies of them where for miles on every side the land is entirely in their possession. It would scarcely be possible to name a state in the Union where a few Slovaks have not settled and obtained farms which they own, having bought them with money earned previously during the time of their employment in the industrial centres."*

Father Stephen Furdek of Cleveland, who perhaps knows the Slovak situation as well as any one, is of the opinion that when they get a little money and a little more independent spirit they will turn to farming quite generally.

One of the interesting Slovak farm settlements is a place called Slovaktown, near Stuttgart, Arkansas, of which the Rev. J. A. McQuaid writes me,† "There are 250 Slovaks, 50 families, most of them Roman Catholic and a few Lutheran. All own farms, some have 40 acres, some 80, some more. A few young men work for wages away from home; otherwise they are employed on their own land. They were born in the old country, but came to Slovaktown mostly from Pennsylvania and Illinois, where they had worked in mines and factories and on railroads. When they had saved enough money to pay for 40 acres, they would buy from the Slovak Colonization Company of Pittsburgh, but the land being wild and unimproved they would stay on at their old jobs till they had saved enough more money to afford to fence the land and build temporary homes. Some had only $20 or $25 to start with, after the land was paid for, and yet they have succeeded well. They own the land clear, with no mortgages. The chief crops are corn, oats, hay, fruits and vegetables, besides milk for the creamery. They are better farmers than any other

A Slovak colony in Arkansas

* Rovnianek, P. V.: "The Slovaks in America." *Charities*, XIII, pages 239–244 (Dec. 3, 1904).

† This is not given *verbatim*, but condensed from Father McQuaid's letter.

22

nationality. They have comfortable, tidy houses, surrounded by fruit trees and rich gardens; they have barns, and live stock such as cows, horses, mules and hogs. They live and dress well, and instead of having to buy meat, potatoes, sauerkraut, corn and the other things that should abound on a farm, but not always do, they generally have some to sell. The children go to the American public schools, of which there are two in their neighborhood. They learn to read and write both English and Slovak, the former at school, the latter at home from their parents. They are on excellent terms with their American neighbors, who respect as well as like them. They are industrious, honest, of steady habits, intelligent and able-bodied. They love peace and home. Five are school directors and one is a road overseer."

This is certainly a cheering account.

Croatians buying farms

Among the Croatians there are also instances of settling in the country after saving money at other work in America. For instance, in the copper mining town of Calumet, Michigan, I was told of a movement beginning among the Croatians there to buy farms in the South and elsewhere. Ten or fifteen families, with savings of $1000 or $2000 each, had gone to Georgia. One man went to Minnesota, where he paid $1500 for his land. Three or four families went to Canada. "They have spent $35,000 on their church in Calumet, but in ten years they will all be gone and will be farming," said my informant.

I was also told (what I have not verified), that their colony in Chicago had been 5000 or 6000 strong a few years before, but had in 1906 dwindled to 1000 or 1500, as a result of the numbers that had distributed themselves thence—many to mines and factories, but many also to farms.

Ruthenians go to Canada

As we had already learned in Europe, Ruthenians who come meaning to farm generally go directly to Canada. But many also save money from their earnings in the

United States and then go to Canada with it, as was done by the Ruthenian whose story is told on page 352 below. In Canada, settlers can get a "quarter section" on homestead terms and keep what money they have as free capital. Galicians (Ruthenians) are said to succeed better than any other immigrants in Canada, to be "all over the country," and as numerous in Canada as in the United States.* In the United States also they have some farming settlements, but apparently not any considerable number. I was told of a settlement in Royalton, Minnesota, made up of men nearly all of whom had worked for five or six years in Minneapolis, and saved perhaps $500 to $1500. Some have log houses, some ordinary frame houses,—"the only thing that costs money is the glass." Another Minnesota settlement was made by men from McKees Rocks near Pittsburgh.

The Slovenians' chief farming colony seems to be that at Brockway, Minnesota, near Saint Cloud, but this apparently does not belong in the class of agricultural settlement succeeding an industrial phase. This colony dates back fifty years. I understand that one of their Roman Catholic missionaries to the Indians brought over

Slovenian farmers

* Some interesting articles on Galicians in the Canadian Northwest appeared in the Boston *Transcript* in 1905. The following passage from the first of these, under date of October 17th, seems worth quoting:

"Here they have quite overcome the prejudice at first aroused among Canadian-American people, by their sheepskin costume, strange tongue and devotion to the various Greek churches. They have 'made good.' It is hard to see how the Alberta townspeople of other races could get along without them. Their daughters wait on the public tables alertly and mannerly. They are the hotel chambermaids. Housewives depend on them and are well rewarded for teaching them how. At country stopping-places Galician men are hostlers and bartenders at once. They labor on the railways and roads. Not even Yankees are of more adventurous and individualistic spirit. They have initiative, as if by blood. A Galician will join any gang of any nation, he alone, if he sees good money to be earned so. It is because these people, as seen in the towns, are singularly interesting, that one goes for a long drive to their farming settlements, wishing to see them at home, confer with their teachers and clergy, get a correct idea of their cabins, methods and whole manner of life. As yet, at Fort Saskatchewan, we are scarcely on the verge of their main settlement."

from upper Carniola a group of 'his countrymen, who cleared the forest and took up homesteads. Even to-day they are said, young people and all, to preserve their own language, to its minute local peculiarities.*

Advantages of return current to the land

Of the return current to the land from the larger centres it is impossible to get any adequate measure, but it certainly exists, and whatever its amount, it seems desirable on several accounts. As contrasted with immediate settlement on a farm it brings the Slavic peasant into the more isolated life of the country after he has had a chance to acquire a tinge of American ideas and American standards. He has not lost his thrift and his splendid courage for work, or he would not be there; and he has had a chance to learn something of the new country. Although the fact that some of the more successful and energetic leave the city colonies may deprive those colonies of possible leaders, still their going away tends to draw others after them from the tenement districts to the land.

Mr. Commons is convinced that the foreign family is "assimilated" faster on the farm than in the city. Of this I am not sure. I remember that our only population of long standing in the country which still speaks a foreign language, the "Pennsylvania Dutch," is eminently rural; and recalling my own observations, the city life, in spite of its foreign quarters, seems to me the stronger solvent.

Skill of Slavic farmers

As to the quality of Slavic farming, one naturally hears different reports. I suspect that the American often thinks the Pole or Bohemian a poor farmer because he works on a different plan, while the foreigner, used to small, intensive farming, thinks Yankees slovenly and wasteful. Especially when he takes up old, worn-out farm lands in Virginia or Kentucky, he has small respect

* In Rev. F. S. Šuteršič's guide for Slovenians in America, I find Slovenian farm settlements mentioned in Iowa, South Dakota, Idaho, and Washington, besides Minnesota. See also above, pages 233, 269–270.

POLISH BERRY PICKERS IN MARYLAND

for the methods of his predecessor, who, he says, "robbed the soil."*

The American business agent of a Bohemian farming paper, already quoted, could not say enough in praise of the Bohemian farmers. They farmed better than the Americans. They invested freely in farm machinery. Nothing was too good or too big for them. In the eastern half of Butler county, Nebraska, there were seventeen big steam threshing outfits among Bohemians—something to which you could find nothing parallel in the same area anywhere in the United States. The Bohemian paper of which he was agent had seven times more advertising of farm implements than any other paper in the United States.

While the above statements are those of an interested party, all the available evidence points the same way. It would seem, moreover, as though in certain lines, new to us and familiar in Europe, the immigrant should be able to supply very valuable skill. This seems to be especially the case in the sugar-beet industry, in which the labor of Bohemians, who understand beet culture well, is much sought.

Of the financial success of Slavic farmers I see no reason to doubt. My inquiry was undertaken in a time of great general prosperity, and allowance must be made for that fact. Certainly I ran across no "hard luck

Standard of living

* The following Massachusetts testimony is interesting: "The Polish farmer uses as up to date methods and implements as the American does. The crops of the Poles compare very favorably with those raised by Americans. In one particular the Pole has taught the American a lesson. Before the coming of the Poles to Sunderland all the farmers crowded down on to the meadow land near the river. The upper terraces were deserted because the soil did not contain the rich river loam. The Poles came and began working these upper lands with which the Yankees refused to have anything to do. They have now demonstrated clearly that the lighter soil is exactly as good for tobacco as any other and as a result the terrace lands have risen tremendously in value. The Pole's faith in the light soil is well justified by the fact that tobacco raised on it was judged the best produced in Sunderland last year."—Tyler, E. T.: "The Poles in the Connecticut Valley." *Smith College Monthly*, June, 1909, page 581.

stories." The only complaints that I heard were from Americans, and they feared not the failure of the foreigners but the low standard of living which made for their economic success.

Where, as in parts of the Connecticut valley, there is a large drifting body of farm laborers of the poorest class hired for a few months at a time, one hears of drunkenness, cutting affrays with the police and with one another, of a low moral standard and brutish overcrowding, of dirt, and of low standards generally. Again, even in this same region, one hears the other side*—they are clean, they Americanize sooner than any other nationality, business men would rather deal with them than with any class, the elders drink less than they did, and the young people much less than their elders, and they are saving and gaining ground all the time. Probably the most widespread contrast with American ways is the custom of women as well as men working in the field. The children work too, and the foreigner's great advantage is that he hires no labor and that a big family is an advantage, not an expense. While this has its bad side, on the other hand it facilitates early marriages and consequently rural morality, and the getting the farmer's wife out of doors has its hygienic advantages.

That the standard of living of foreigners is not higher than it is, is certainly to be regretted. But it is rising, and meanwhile a lower standard of living in the country and among independent farmers does not threaten the standard of living of competitors in nearly as dangerous a fashion as among industrial wage laborers.

Cases of financial success

The large money successes of which one occasionally hears are apt to be made on the speculative side of farming. But the strictly legitimate acquisition of wealth in rich sections is considerable. A farm like the Dalmatian one in California, spoken of above, is naturally

* See extracts from an article entitled "Absorbing the Alien," Boston Evening *Transcript*, August 4, 1909. Appendix XXIV, page 473.

a rarity. On the other hand, a Nebraska farmer who is worth $50,000 or $75,000 is by no means a wonder, and while the majority farm on a smaller scale, they tend to become a substantial class of property owners.

The success of those who do succeed advertises farming and stimulates ambition. It also tends to originate new and higher standards of living within the foreign group, where new refinements or comforts among their own people are far more powerfully suggestive than the same things among Americans. When the farmer's son, and sometimes his daughter, goes to the state university or the normal school, or otherwise secures a higher education, the group acquires leaders of its own with a broader outlook.

But more important than the exceptional successes are the large number of thrifty farmers' families, poor but "getting on," which offer to the next generation a fair chance of education and advance.

THE TRUE STORY OF A BOHEMIAN PIONEER*

"I was a little girl when we came to America. My father had been a poor man in Bohemia, and one day a neighbor, a well-to-do farmer, came to him and said that he wanted to go to America but that he knew no German (which he regarded as indispensable for the journey), and that if my father, who could speak German, would come with him and help him he would pay his expenses. So it was arranged that way. We got as far as Manitowoc, on the Wisconsin shore of Lake Michigan, where there was a large Bohemian settlement, and there our farmer decided that he could shift for himself and left us. We sat there on the dock by the lakeside, my father, my mother, my little brother and myself without one cent among us. *The journey to Wisconsin*

" Well, we got along somehow. I went to school and learned to read, progressing as far as the Fourth Reader, and father saved a little money. At that time Nebraska, which was not admitted as a state till later, in 1867, was attracting settlers and my father decided to migrate from Wisconsin to Nebraska territory.

" We started in the autumn of 1866 with a little party of Bohemian families. I was eight years old then and my brother *Removal to Nebraska*

* Reprinted by kind permission from the *Chautauquan*, February, 1908.

several years younger. My father had eight hundred dollars to make a start with, and it seemed a great deal to us, but no other of the families had so little.

"We got as far as Saint Joseph on the Missouri River, just south of the Nebraska line, and there my father was persuaded by a blacksmith with whom he had made friends to stay over the winter. This was very good advice, and if any of the party had been more experienced they would not have started till spring in the first place.

"So we stayed at Saint Joe, where the traces of the war were still to be seen—remnants of the fortifications, and chain and other débris on the bank where they had been shot from across the river. But the other families went on into Nebraska that fall and got themselves established in a provisional way. But that was all they could do; it was too late to start any farming and the men, all except one cripple, came back and wintered at Saint Joe, where they could get employment, leaving their families on the prairies in the sod houses with the one crippled man.

"Also, by the blacksmith's advice, my father bought a pair of oxen, good ones, which proved to be an excellent investment and far more serviceable than the old army horses that the others bought. The horses were cheap, but they turned out to be quite useless; they always balked and finally, when we got to our destination, they ran away. Father also bought my brother a good little Indian pony.

"When spring came we started out again and traveled some weeks. The women and children slept in the wagon and the men under it. Going up hill, father would fasten the pony on ahead of the oxen to help them up.

"When we got to the Blue River father said: 'According to the map my land should be across there, as I figure it out,' and he was right. We looked about for our neighbors but we could see nothing. Then we heard a cock crow, but still we could see no house, for we were not used to sod houses. At last we found a bridge of felled tree trunks leading across the river to our neighbor's home.

Dug-outs   "In those days men either built their houses of sods piled up on the flat prairie or else made dug-outs in the bank of the river. At first we lived in an old dug-out already made, later we made quite a nice one for ourselves. It was tall enough to stand up straight in and the earth sides were whitewashed, but for some time we had no door, having nothing to make one of. Once, that first summer, my father had gone to break some land for a neighbor twelve miles away and had taken my brother with

him so that my mother and I were left alone and there came up a
fearful storm. That was while we still had no door. In those
days when you were driving across the prairie in the dark, you
had to be careful not to break through into people's dug-outs.
Heavy rains made trouble. Water would leak in and sometimes
rats and snakes would come through. As soon as they could
the settlers would get into houses made of logs plastered with
mud.

"Our oxen proved of the greatest advantage to us when it
came to 'breaking prairie.' Horses were not strong enough for
that work. Father not only used the oxen himself, but loaned
them for nothing to the neighbors. In those days all were the
best of friends. It was all for one and one for all. Father also
made money with his oxen, 'breaking prairie' for American farmers. When new emigrants came out, father would go to Nebraska
City, sixty-four miles away, to fetch them with his oxen. It
took him four days. He had trained them to run and they went
fast. So in more ways than one our oxen helped us to get a
start. Later father also broke steers for use and this was
very profitable. *Oxen of great use*

"At first there were many kinds of hardship. The climate
was much worse then than it is now. In winter big blizzards
would come and last a week; now we never have them more than
a day and night at a time. In summer there were hot winds,
such as we have not had now for years, and terrible droughts.
In those days there were no trees except along the banks of the
rivers. As the country has got settled up and trees planted all
about, and especially as the prairie has been ploughed up and
cultivated and fields of alfalfa sown, it has made a great difference.
The hot winds are said to start in the prairie country; it just
breeds them. *Climate*

"One winter, I think that it was the first year, father went to
Beatrice, about twenty miles away, with the yoke of oxen and
the wagon and nine bushels of wheat. We had had one big fall
of snow before he started but soon after another big storm came
and he was kept away a week. He had been afraid of what was
coming but the neighbors laughed at him. Mother was almost
wild when he did not come back. The snow was so deep that
where the creek ordinarily was there was now a hill of snow. She
went to a neighbor and wanted him to go and look for father,
but he had no boots that he could go in. Mother had barely
come back to the house to get him a pair when father got home
with just the oxen and what he called a 'smick.' He brought
nothing with him, but he was glad enough to get back at all.
The oxen had refused to face the storm (they never will) and had
turned around and broken everything. So he had come home *Snow storms*

as he was, leaving the things in care of a man that he knew who lived near the place where it happened, which was twelve miles off. Mother decided to go back with him to fetch what he had left, leaving me at home alone. Another storm came up and they could not get back for four days. I was only nine years old. After a time I had eaten up all the bread and burned all the wood. I had sense enough to make my way to the river and follow up on the ice to a neighbor's. A woman came back with me and chopped wood for me. Then father and mother got home. They had been only twelve miles off and had expected to return right away, but it had been impossible.

A flood

"In the spring when all that snow came off at once and rain came besides it made a flood. The land was under water for miles. Everybody had to move out, up on to a hill. The mills could not grind and there was not enough to eat. We used flour mixed with shorts. We gave away almost everything. Mr. H., a well-to-do neighbor, came and borrowed a little corn meal.

Famine

"That summer we had nothing. The pony ran away and was gone seven weeks. The oxen were used to his leading and would not plough without him. Father went to hunt for him and when he returned he was so worn and changed that we did not know him. We got the pony back, but he was ruined and we sold him for twenty-five dollars. We had no money and nothing to eat. We did have plenty of clothes; we had brought those with us. Many, who had not, used sacking. One time we had nothing but corn meal, not even salt, and we could not swallow it. Mr. V. came once and spent a week with us. He had brought all sorts of things with him and he laughed at us. He had raisins and prunes and so forth. Next year he was in the same straits that we were. He had spent all his money and no more came in.

"Now-a-days settlers have a very different experience. It is not at all so hard. They can earn money and buy things and there are railroad facilities. In those days work was often paid for with an order on the store. In 1868 the Northwestern Railroad came to Omaha and other lines soon came to nearby points, but at first there was nothing of the sort. Once father carried a bushel of corn for his chickens ten miles on his back.

Locusts

"Even worse than the blizzards and floods were the plagues of locusts which came later. We had had them in '69 or '70, but at that time they were not so bad here and did not do so much damage as when they came again. In '74 they were much worse and in '75 they hatched here. They have never been so bad since. We heard a sound and it grew dark and we thought that a storm was coming. The sun was hidden. We thought that it was the end of the world. Then they began to come down. In one hour they had eaten everything, even the tobacco. They bent down little trees with their weight. They were so thick on the ground that when we took a step they were over our ankles and our feet made holes, like footprints in the snow. The river was covered with them so that in some places we could not see the water. They would eat the paint off a house and chew up lace curtains. Sometimes they were so thick on the rails that they stopped the trains. The masses of them in the river made a terrible smell afterwards, but it did not seem to cause any sickness.

"In those days Indians used often to come through. They were Omahas and Pawnees and they used to visit one another annually, by turns. Sometimes there would be five hundred in a party. They went in single file, five or ten paces apart, at a sort of little trot. It was the government's orders that, to avoid trouble, they were not to go in a bunch. They would gather, however, to camp. They would be two or three days going through. Some traveled on foot but the squaws were mostly on ponies with crossed sticks trailing behind, with the children and goods loaded on the middle. The sticks were young trees and they were fastened with the brush of their tops dragging, which made them springy and elastic. The Indians then were superior to those that we see now-a-days. They looked livelier and were better dressed. Indians

"Often, when you least expected it, you would suddenly find a big Indian standing beside you. Shivers went right through a person. They had a regular snaky walk. They would come up and ask for a little flour or want to swap something, but they never bothered. They were all right if they were treated right. Some people treated them mean and would not give them anything so of course they suffered. If an Indian got mad or excited he did not care what he did. If we gave one a chicken we just pointed it out in the bunch and he shot it with an arrow. Once my brother wanted a pretty whip that one of them had and gave him a dog and a pair of shoes for it. (A dog the Indians would kill at once and eat.) The Indian said my brother could have the whip, but that first he wanted to carry it with him on his visit and that he would leave it on his return. My brother did not feel that he could make any objection, but he did not expect to see the whip again. On the return however, the Indian brought it.

"I grew up a very strong girl. I did all sorts of work, even to breaking prairie, which is hard work for a man. Once I was ploughing with the girl that my brother married. I was managing the oxen while she held the plough. After a time she said that it was too hard work, she could not hold the plough into the Breaking prairie soil. So we changed work, but she was not used to the oxen and said *gee* when she should have said *haw* and they broke and ran. After that she held the plough. Another time she wanted to ride the mare. I told her that she did not know how, but she insisted and was thrown and a good deal hurt.

"Two separate times I was bitten by a rattlesnake. There was no doctor and we did what we could. It was a week before I could put my foot to the ground.

Reading Bohemian

"I do not know why my father never taught me to read Bohemian. In the evenings he used to read aloud to us in Bohemian and I knew my English reader almost by heart. But it was not till after my marriage that I taught myself to read Bohemian. It was not difficult, as I could speak it and the spelling is perfectly regular when once you understand the system. After my marriage I was delicate for a time. I suffered from my early overwork and exposure. I had leisure and read much in English and Bohemian."

Today

This, as nearly as I can repeat it, is the story told me in the soft twilight of a recent Fourth of July by my Bohemian hostess in a Nebraska county town. Out on the lawn her son was setting off fireworks to amuse an adopted grandchild. Indoors her husband, also a Bohemian, the well-to-do owner of grist mills on the near-by river which had figured in her story, was reading his paper. Everything spoke of peace and plenty and I wondered what it must feel like to have seen such changes and to have been oneself so active an instrument in bringing about the development from prairie wilderness to tamed and civilized settlement.

CHAPTER XVI

HOUSEHOLD LIFE*

Women are for the most part so scarce among our Slavic colonies that they do not present a special industrial problem. As yet more men than women immigrate. Among the Slavic immigrants of 1906, for instance, the women were only about one-third of the men, and among those nationalities which have most recently begun to come to us, the Bulgarians, Servians and Montenegrins, there was not one woman to twenty-five men. Of course many of these immigrants are leaving wives in Europe, yet there is a great excess of unmarried men,† and since they seldom marry outside of their own national group, wives are much in demand. Consequently the girls very generally marry upon their arrival in America, or as soon as they are old enough, though some work a few years before they marry. Women scarce and valuable

Women have indeed not only a scarcity value as wives, but considerable economic importance. The man who is so fortunate as to be married can take boarders and lodgers from among his own countrymen, and thus perhaps double the family income, besides gaining in social importance as a "boarding boss." It is, however, not only the desire to make money which leads the Slav, who loves privacy in his family life, thus to open his house. He feels that the young relative or the neighbor's son has a personal claim, and it is often more as a matter Taking boarders

* The best and fullest treatment of the various subjects discussed in this chapter will be found in Dr. Roberts' "Anthracite Coal Communities."

† The Carniolan figures seem to show nearly twice as many single as married men. Appendix XII, page 451

Miss Byington reports 300 Bulgarians in West Homestead among whom were only three women. *Charities and the Commons,* XXI, page 916 (Feb. 6, 1909).

of kindness than of business that he makes room for him. Where else should the poor lad go? he thinks. He has neither money nor work nor serviceable speech. Very likely the price of his ticket has been already advanced, and it is the part of prudence as well as of kindness not to let him run up bills to strangers. He must be sheltered, fitted out with clothes less eloquent of the green newcomer, and above all he must be helped to a job. Under these varied inducements married couples are apt to have their houses full, and too often more than full.

Not wholly an evil This situation has both its good and its bad sides. Americans see the overcrowding and the occasional rows, and are perhaps scandalized at the presence of one woman in a house full of men. They do not realize that for a young fellow to camp with a number of others in one room in the house of some relative or acquaintance may be not demoralizing but a safeguard. It is indeed fair to construe much of the poorest, most crowded living as a temporary "roughing it" on the part of men who have gone out to seek their fortunes; as something intended only as a transition arrangement, just as our own eastern college boys are content for a time with rough living in the far West. It does not represent their standard of living in the sense of what would content them permanently.

Cooking arrangements Sometimes the men pay only for a sleeping place; sometimes they are regular boarders. In a Colorado mining camp $10 a month is a usual price in the latter case. Another arrangement that is very common is for the men to pay a certain sum (perhaps $2.00 a month, perhaps $4.00), for lodging, washing and cooking, and to buy their own food. A singular custom that one hears of over and over again, and which seems to be peculiar to the Slavs, is for the men to buy, or get the woman to buy for them, each his own separate daily supply of food.* If a woman has fifteen boarders she may have

---

* Miss Byington, writing of a Bulgarian boarding house in Homestead, Pa., says: "The financial arrangements of such an

the butcher cut off and weigh fifteen pieces of meat, and the men may sit down to supper together, each with his own separately cooked piece before him. A still stranger arrangement which sometimes occurs in the coal mining camps is for the contract to include the services of the woman, not only in having ready, against the return from work, a tub of hot water for the absolutely necessary daily bath (which makes the dirty looking coal miner one of the cleanest of workingmen) but in lending her motherly help in the bathing operation itself. She comes in and scrubs the grime off the miner's shoulders where he cannot get at it!

In spite of the fact that the necessities of the situation often seem so well met by families taking boarders, there are grave objections to the custom, as tending to result in overcrowding and in a lowering of the tone of family life, which make it one of the main objects of American criticism. The people chiefly concerned are quite conscious of all this, and as the family prospers and the children begin to grow up, they show happily a very strong tendency to abandon this source of income. A Slovak priest in New York gave me an interesting account of his observations: *Objections to boarders in the family*

"In the far West the women often make $80 a month, with ten or fifteen boarders. That is as much as the man makes. Yet when the children get to be five or six years old, the parents leave the mining or factory settlement where there are no chances for education, and come to the city where there are schools and kindergartens. There the man earns only $1.50 a day in a factory, and the wife stays at home and earns nothing. *Evidences of rising standards*

establishment are simple. The boarding boss runs the house, and the men pay him three dollars a month for a place to sleep, for having their clothes washed and their food cooked. In addition, an account is kept of the food purchased, and the total is divided among the men at each pay-day. The housewife purchases and cooks what special food each man chooses to order: beef, pork, lamb, each with a tag of some sort, labeling the order, and all frying together. A separate statement is kept of these expenses for each boarder."—Byington, Margaret F.: "The Mill Town Courts and their Lodgers." *Charities and the Commons*, XXI, page 919 (Feb. 6, 1909).

In New York city she seldom takes boarders—at most a relative or two. Most women have a child almost every year, and by the time the eldest child is six there are enough little ones to keep the mother busy. The Slovaks do not want to farm, for the American agricultural system is not suitable. They are used to living in farm villages, not on scattered farms;* they have large families, and on a farm the children cannot go to school. Many did go into farming, but returned to the city on account of the education of the children."

The taking of boarders seems indeed to be a transition phase, both for individual families and in general, decreasing as the balance of the sexes in this country becomes more normal.

A mission-
ary's story
Interesting in this connection was the story told me by a Protestant missionary in one of the most neglected factory slums that it has ever been my lot to see. A Ruthenian who had been coming to his services told him one evening that there had been a christening at his home the day before, that "the evil had conquered him" and there had been drinking; but it was the last time that liquor should come into his house. He notified the eighteen boarders, who, in day and night shifts, occupied the two upstairs rooms of his little house, of his ultimatum; they might of course go to the saloon, but if they stayed on with him, they must bring no drink home. Some left, most remained. The man himself soon after joined the church, and later, through his influence, sixteen of the eighteen boarders did likewise. A little later he came one day to the minister and asked him if he thought it would do to take fewer boarders; his wife had no time to go to church. The minister naturally encouraged him to do so, and he cut the number down by successive reductions to four men, trying to give his wife more time so that he could teach her to read. Finally he said that he wanted to live like the Americans, with no boarders and a parlor "where no

*On this point see above, page 318.

one slept." This, too, was accomplished, and the man and his wife and little children occupied a three-room house, with no outsiders. But at this point in his career he had saved money enough to go to farming (if I remember rightly, $3000), and like most Ruthenians who go into farming he moved to Canada.

In spite of the state of the marriage market, the number of Slavic women who work for wages is absolutely, if not relatively, a large one. The census showed among women whose parents were natives of Austria, Bohemia, Hungary, Poland and Russia, 145,292 gainfully occupied, of whom 36,000 were servants and waitresses alone. {Women wage-earners}

I give the following census data for what they are worth. The presence of Hebrew and other non-Slavic elements lessens their significance for our purposes.

TABLE 26.—FEMALES OF SPECIFIED PARENTAGE ENGAGED IN GAINFUL OCCUPATIONS

COUNTRY OF BIRTH OF PARENTS	ABSOLUTE NUMBERS	PERCENTAGE OF ALL FEMALES OF SAME PARENTAGE	PERCENTAGE OF ALL OCCUPIED MALES OF SAME PARENTAGE
Hungary	14,631	15.7	16.0
Bohemia	25,719	14.6	25.0
Austria	25,590	13.9	15.0
Russia	40,816	12.7	20.0
Poland	38,536	12.3	18.0

Compare with these data the following :

COUNTRY OF BIRTH OF PARENTS	ABSOLUTE NUMBERS	PERCENTAGE OF ALL FEMALES OF SAME PARENTAGE	PERCENTAGE OF ALL OCCUPIED MALES OF SAME PARENTAGE
Ireland	634,201	24.8	35.0
Canada, French	78,979	20.1	30.0
Germany	538,192	14.1	20.0
Italy	26,093	8.9	9.0
Total of native parentage	3,247,907	13.2	22.0
Total of foreign parentage	2,071,490	16.5	23.0

Based on Table lxxii, Volume on Occupations, United States Census, 1900.

23

TABLE 27.—LEADING OCCUPATIONS FOR FEMALES OF EACH SPECIFIED PARENTAGE. ABSOLUTE NUMBERS AND PERCENTAGES OF ALL FEMALE WORKERS OF THE GIVEN PARENTAGE

	Number	Per Cent
Hungary:		
Servants and waitresses	6087	41.6
Textile mill operatives	1350	9.2
Bohemia:		
Servants and waitresses	6316	24.6
Tailoresses	3468	13.5
Tobacco and cigar factory operatives	3367	13.1
Austria:		
Servants and waitresses	8909	34.8
Tailoresses	1613	6.3
Seamstresses	1579	6.2
Dressmakers	1534	6.0
Poland:		
Servants and waitresses	8815	22.9
Textile mill operatives	5793	14.9
Tailoresses	3291	8.5
Tobacco and cigar factory operatives	2224	5.8
Russia:		
Tailoresses	6256	15.3
Servants and waitresses	5853	14.3
Seamstresses	5419	13.3
Dressmakers	3014	7.4

Volume on Occupations, U. S. Census, 1900, pages ccxi–ccxii, and ccvii.

In households

The wages of such girls engaged in housework vary, of course, from place to place. In Hadley, Massachusetts, $3.00 a week seemed to be a medium rate, "perhaps $2.00 to $2.50 for a quite green girl; at any rate, not over $3.50 for general housework." In Jersey City a Ruthenian agency was placing wholly green girls at $8.00 a month, and those with some experience at $15 and $16. I have generally found that housekeepers who have had Slavic girls give them enthusiastic praise as very clean, very hard-working, and devotedly loyal to the family. Of course one also hears complaints, but it is fair to consider that language is in this case much more of a barrier than with German or even Scandinavian girls.*

In factories

The number of Slavic women working in shops and

* An amusing and sympathetic little story of a Polish girl in housework is "A Bright Green Pole," by Alice Ward Bailey. *The Outlook*, Feb. 6, 1904.

"Griner" Girls (Slovenians) in a Cleveland Hardware Factory

factories is also large. These are mainly, I think, unmarried girls, but the Bohemian families in New York city and elsewhere have, as is shown later, the reputation of sending their wives and mothers into tailoring and cigar-making shops to an excessive degree. The kinds of work at which Slavic women are engaged of course vary greatly, from that in a Cleveland hardware factory, where Slovenian girls are engaged in handling iron parts of considerable weight,* to the other extreme of the finest of lace work and embroidery for fashionable New York dressmakers, in which Bohemian and Slovak girls find their old-world handicraft in modified shape standing them in stead here. From a purely aesthetic point of view, no one need wish to see a prettier sight than a Passaic handkerchief factory full of Polish girls in kerchiefs of pale yellow and other soft colors, the afternoon sun slanting across the fine stuff on which they were working. Others work in Yonkers factories, where the preparation of rabbit skins is as offensive to every sense as it is destructive to the lungs; others again pack fuses in Connecticut works, in imminent risk of explosions. Large numbers, especially of Poles, are in the textile mills of Massachusetts, and so on through an endless variety of occupations, down to the women in a mining settlement who take in washing as their family cares allow.

For a more detailed study of Slavic working women I refer the reader to Miss Butler's "Women and the Trades," a study of working conditions in Pittsburgh. She finds the American and German girls turning over the inferior and unpleasant work to newcomers from Poland and Russia, and "these same newcomers, sometimes by sheer physical strength, sometimes by personal indifference and a low standard, are found *competing on the basis of lower wages with men. Work that would other-*

* Miss Butler found, in and about Pittsburgh, 1954 women in metal work, two-thirds of them Polish and Croatian, some of whom were doing extremely heavy work. Butler, Elizabeth Beardsley: "Women and the Trades," page 228.

wise never have been given to girls to do, has come into the hands of Polish women."* "A determination to work and earn is uppermost. Marriage is not suffered to act as a hindrance." "These women have the same reputation as have their men-folk for willingness to work hard and put up with poor conditions." . . . "They are in the factory," says Miss Butler significantly, "*too much on sufferance for grievances to be worth their while.*" This I am convinced is the real meaning of much of their supposed indifference to "unpleasant" conditions. Another part of the explanation of such conditions is elsewhere noted by Miss Butler, who says that workrooms that would not long be tolerated by Americans—employers or the general public—have been regarded with indifference when occupied by immigrant workers "*perhaps because of inability to share the sensations of a foreigner.*"

"The Polish women have not the conservatism which keeps the Italian girl at home; they have not the same standard of close knit family relationship," is an observation of Miss Butler's which I am inclined to question. I think it is not that the family is less closely knit, but that custom does not impose on Polish girls the seclusion that Italians regard as incumbent on their girls and which makes it improper for Italian girls to attend, for instance, any evening classes at a settlement, (as all other nationalities freely do), or in general to move about unchaperoned on pain of loss to the family reputation.

"The Polish women," according to Miss Butler, "have pushed their way into a wider circle of industries than have the Jewish girls," which seems surprising, but in these various industries they "are limited by lack of training and by trade indifference, as well as by the stolid physical poise that cannot be speeded at the high pressure to which an American girl will respond. They have not an industrial standard that would tend to

---

* Miss Butler seems to use the term Polish to roughly designate the Slavic group. The italics in these quotations are mine.

react progressively upon the character of their work and the arrangement of the workrooms. They accept positions that girls of other races regard as socially inferior. They consent to do . . . the work that leads and can lead to nothing except coarsening of fibre and a final break in strength." Here we meet again the constantly recurring note of the destruction of Slavic workpeople by the conditions of their American employment.

The Polish working women are, however, not all of this stolid make and in this lowest grade of employment. In canneries and cracker factories Miss Butler found "Polish girls who are lighter handed, fairer, more delicately built. . . . These girls have rapid work to do. They have the nervous energy to pack or to fill cans at high speed, . . . the quickness that can be spurred higher and higher to the breaking point; who can in two years or three be worked out and thrown aside."

Of special historical interest is the part played in the New York cigar making industry by Bohemian women. Dr. Abbott* says that they began to emigrate in 1869. I have often been told of an exodus to this country of women cigar makers, following a strike in tobacco factories of the Bohemian government in Kutna Hora (Kuttenberg) in the seventies.† It is said that "five or six wives would come over together, work at cigar making as they did in Bohemia, and send money back for their husbands' passage." "In Bohemia the men had worked only in the fields, and their wives taught

Cigar makers

* See the excellent historical study of women in cigar making which makes Chapter IX of Dr. Edith Abbott's "Women in Industry." The quotations are taken from this source. See also Miss Butler's study, in Chapter V of the book referred to above, on this industry in Pittsburgh.

† In a visit to the government tobacco factory at Budweis, in 1905, we found all but fifty of the employes women, two-thirds of whom, we were told, were married. They are given a preliminary physical examination, and if accepted as sound, receive instruction for three months, and are then put on piece rates. There are both sickness and death benefits and disability pensions after ten years' service. The work-people are not organized, and are said to be "very Catholic."

them," after they came over, the relatively unskilled work of bunch making, while the women still did the more skilled and better paid rolling. "The entire united family would take up the manufacture of cigars, emulating the industry of the mother," says an article in the New York *Tribune* of Nov. 6, 1877, quoted by Miss Abbott. The women were considered by Americans to be more intelligent than the men.

The effect of the Bohemian influx was demoralizing to the trade. It was complained that the women displaced men, and worked for prices that an American would not work for. Probably most serious was the fact that they worked in their tenement homes and helped to make cigar making in New York for a time a sweated industry, till the factory again reasserted itself over the home workroom.

Married women in the factories.

Another count against the Bohemian cigar makers is that among them there is "less prejudice against the work of married women than among most other nationalities."* "Many of them say it 'pays' to go on with their work and 'hire a cheaper woman' to do part of their housework and look after their children." The effects on family life are discussed by Dr. Jane Robbins† as follows:

"Home life among the Bohemians exists under peculiar difficulties. The mothers work in cigar factories, and besides the factory work they have the bearing and rearing of children, and sewing, cooking, washing and cleaning to do in their homes.

"The first result noticed is that every one keeps early hours. At nine o'clock on a winter evening, a block occupied by Bohemian families is wrapped in slumber,

---

* "The percentage of married women employed in the manufacture of cigars and tobacco is larger than in any other industry in the list given under the manufacturing group, with the single exception of seamstresses; 11.18 per cent of the women in the whole group and 16.4 per cent of those in 'cigars and tobacco' were married." Abbott, page 211.

† Robbins, Jane E.: "The Bohemian Women in New York." *Charities,* XIII, pages 194–6 (Dec. 3, 1904).

the windows of the houses are dark, and there is almost no one on the street. The working day begins at half past five, and the tired mothers must have their children at home and in bed at an early hour.

"The most noticeable effect of having the mothers go to factory is that the ordinary masculine aversion to doing woman's work is greatly moderated. The boys run home from their play after school hours, to start the kitchen fire, so that the water may be boiling when their mothers come home. They make beds and sweep and clean house. I have known a boy of eleven to acquire sufficient knowledge of housework so that, at his mother's death, he was able to do all the work for a family of four. Several times I have come into a home and found the strong young husband washing, and not at all embarrassed to be caught at the washtub.

"The older children, both boys and girls, take care of the younger ones. They are trained to responsibility from their earliest youth, and make great gains in both strength and charm of character. A girl of thirteen often has the care of several younger children, besides doing much of the housework for the family. A grandfather or a grandmother, even if very feeble, is a great addition to the family life in furnishing the adult point of view in the absence of both parents. A neighbor, too, in case of sudden emergency, often acts *in loco parentis*, and a very motherly person will sometimes mother a whole neighborhood.

"One woman that I knew had ten fine, healthy children—she had never lost a child—and she had been in factory the greater part of the time through the twenty-five years of her married life.

"To those theorists who look for great progress when women shall obtain a position of economic independence, the Bohemian women cigar makers ought to be an interesting study. The wife, with her quicker fingers, often makes better wages than her husband. I asked a thoughtful Bohemian of the educated class why the women did not demand more power, since they contribute so largely to the family finances, and he answered, 'Because they would not consider such a demand fitting.' Husband and wife seem to go on much as they have always done since 'male and female created he them'.

"The Bohemians are cut off from the life of the city, partly by their inability to speak English, and partly by their being so overworked that they have no time even to see what other people are doing."

Home conditions of working girls

One occasionally hears of Slavic working girls hiring a room or rooms together and living in a co-operative group, boarding themselves. I have been told that Ruthenian girls do this in New York city. Very commonly, too, they board in families. In Jersey City, for instance, I was told that the girls in the tobacco factory lived in this way paying very reasonable amounts for their accommodations.

The standard of living

Though the Slavic woman has her importance as working woman, as servant girl and as "boarding boss," she is infinitely more important as homemaker, helping to set the family standard of living. Standard of living—convenient phrase to indicate so much! What can one say of the standard of living of a group of several millions of people, of nine distinct nationalities, representing various degrees of comfort at home and most diverse fortunes here, from the millionaire at one extreme to the "charity organization case" at the other.

Americanization

One thing can be said,—the standard in general is rising, thanks to American wages, and is constantly and powerfully influenced by American ways. To one who does not believe that wisdom begins and ends with the "Yankees," this one-sided imitation does not seem all gain. For instance, the flaunting hat, especial badge of Americanization, is not so pretty nor so rational in any way as the discarded kerchief, and American housewives might learn many an appetizing and nutritious dish from foreign neighbors. But in spite of involving some loss, the process of amalgamation through imitation

In a Pennsylvania Mining Patch

The "company" houses, without clapboards or shingles, have little to recommend them. The fences and summer kitchens, built by the tenants from refuse wood, improve the comfort but not the appearance of the homes. The gutters are really open sewers. The bird houses which add a picturesque touch to these dreary villages are common among the Slavs.

is inevitable. The prestige of American customs as compared with imported ones is overwhelming, and gives one model to the diverse newcomers. Imitation prepares the way for mutual understanding and co-operation among neighbors of different origins. For instance, to an American, bare feet (certainly for grown women) would mean the extreme either of slatternliness or of poverty. To a Slav it means neither, any more than it did to sturdy Scotch women not so long ago. But what does not detract from the woman's health or self-respect does prevent her from being respected by her neighbors, so that shoes and stockings are a necessary preliminary to desirable relations with them, and are soon adopted.*

Another thing which gives a false impression of poverty and degradation is the absence of the kind of underclothes to which we are accustomed. A child may be the darling of prosperous working people, well fed and well cared for, yet fill an American visitor with a dismayed sense at once of destitution and indecency. Yet the visitor needs to know only a little social history to realize how recent are our own more prim fashions of underclothing. Here again imitation of American ways is the first step toward equal intercourse.

The question of housing for the Slavic laborer is the Housing question of working-class housing in its entirety. Only here the evils are intensified by the ignorance and helplessness of the tenant, and by a feeling, more or less unconscious perhaps, on the part of employers and public, that what is not good enough for Americans is good enough for foreigners. Life in a tenement has at best a temporary and unhomelike feeling which deadens the desire to get rid of evils that may not be for long; and with the Slavs the desire to own a home, which is widespread and intense among those who have made a permanent settlement here and who have their families

* Cf. the remark of the Cleveland Bohemian quoted on page 226.

with them, often makes the hired home appear only an interim arrangement.*

Overcrowd-
ing

Overcrowding† is likely to be the most serious side of a low standard of living—serious from its relation to both disease and immorality. To sleep huddled in feather beds in a stuffy peasant hovel is bad enough, but there what air does come in is drawn from all out-of-doors, not from an airshaft, and in summer, at least, women as well as men are in the fields by day letting the fresh air wash their lungs. It is a different matter when the same overcrowding takes place in a city tenement, where the mother stays all day long, and whence the children go to an ill ventilated school room, and the father to a dust laden factory.

Above all, overcrowding is objectionable when it brings strangers into the close quarters of the little home. This is the chief evil of the custom of taking boarders into the family, but overcrowding is not always due to an unwise thrift. Too often it is a necessary corollary of prevailing wages and prevailing rents.

And I am tempted to quote further Miss Byington's realistic picture of such an overcrowded boarding house, where twenty-four souls were housed in two rooms.

"One of these homes consisted of two rooms, one above the other, each perhaps twelve by twenty feet. In the kitchen I saw the wife of the boarding boss getting dinner, some sort of hot apple cake and a stew of the cheapest cuts of meat. Along one side of the room was

---

* I note that Miss Byington says, "This instance I introduce because it is well to recognize that low standards are not necessarily permanent. When Slavs do buy their homes, the size and attractiveness of them indicates that the unsanitary surroundings and crowded quarters of early days were simply tolerated until the ambition could be attained. With a house on the outskirts of the town, a garden about it, and a glimpse of the larger out-of-doors, they begin to feel that the dreams of their emigration have come true."—"The Mill Town Courts and Their Lodgers."

† A very valuable study of overcrowding in Homestead will be found in Miss Byington's article, "Households Builded upon Steel." *Charities and the Commons*, XXI, pages 1093–1104 (Mar. 6, 1909).

an oil-cloth-covered table, with a plank bench on each side, and above, a long row of handleless white cups in a rack, and a shelf with tin knives and forks on it. Near the up-to-date range, the only real piece of furniture in the room, hung the 'buckets' in which all mill men carry their noon or midnight meal. A crowd of men were lounging cheerfully about, talking, smoking, and enjoying life, making the most of the leisure enforced by the shut-down in the mill. In the room above, double iron bedsteads were set close together, and on them comfortables were neatly laid. Here, besides the 'boarding boss' and his wife and two babies, lived twenty men. The boss himself was a stalwart Bulgarian who had come to this country several years ago, and by running this house, besides working in the mill, had accumulated a good deal of money."

Slavs more than Italians seem inclined to use enlarging income to procure hearty food, and especially their two great luxuries, meat and beer. At first they buy mainly soup meat, and it is hard for the butchers to get bones enough to supply their demand, but soon, though they continue to save, they Americanize their marketing and get the best cuts. **Diet**

Miss Byington's tables of expenditure* show an exceptionally large percentage for food and an exceptionally small percentage for rent, and this result, though based on too few families to be conclusive, tallies with my impressions. **Household budgets**

The nearest to a family budget that I have been able to secure is the following list, given me by a Croatian co-operative store in Calumet, Michigan, as a typical monthly expenditure for groceries by a miner's family:

June 16, rice, $0.25; kidney beans, .25; navy beans, .25; macaroni, .25; vermicelli, .25; noodles, .25; salad oil, .50; onions, .10; cabbage, .25; catsup, .25; chicory, .10.

June 20, flour, $2.75; corn meal, .65; rye flour, $1.25; matches, .10.

* See "Households Builded upon Steel," page 1095.

June 21, eggs, $0.22; smoked ham, 1.83; bacon, .90.
June 26, rice, $0.25.
June 27, s. oil, $0.50; vinegar, .10; eggs, .22.
June 28, salt, 0.10.
July 5, onions, $0.10; eggs, .22.
July 9, Peerless, $0.18.
July 10, kerosene oil, $0.15; salt, .10; yeast, .25; onions, .10.
July 13, sugar, $0.25; garlic, .20; eggs, .22.
July 16, rice, $0.25; cabbage, .35; s. oil, .50; manna, .15; chow-chow, .65; stock fish, .30; soda, .93; coffee, $1.00; tea, .60; caraway seed, .10; chicory, .10.
Total, $18.42.

The members of this co-operative store are mostly "trammers," men who earn less than the miners proper. With incomes of $58 or $60 a month, when working every day, a co-operative store bill like this of $15 or $18 would be common. Besides this, money must be found for the butcher's bill, the drink bill, the dry goods bill and the rent. At a Calumet meat market where Croatians trade I was told that they eat more meat than Germans or Americans, a working man eating two or three pounds a day. A family would commonly have a butcher's bill of $25 a month, this amount covering eggs and cheese as well as meat, but not milk, as many kept their own cow. They eat much veal and pork, also fowl.

In a Colorado mining settlement I was told at the "company store" that the "Austrians" (*sc*. Slovenians) buy just about what Americans do—good flour, tea, coffee, sugar, "the necessary staples" such as crackers, canned goods, vegetables, fruit and meat; in all amounting to from $30 to $60 a month or more for a family of five or so. For rent these men pay the company $2.00 a month per room; as they ordinarily occupy a four-room cottage, this makes a monthly rental of $8.00. They also pay $1.00 a month to the company for medical and hospital service. The furniture, which they themselves own, is simple and scanty, for they move often; as for clothes, they often have no church which they attend, and there is small demand for "dressing up." For a suit a man

A Croatian Butcher's Shop in Globeville, Colorado

Croatian Copper Miners, Calumet, Michigan

pays perhaps $10. Fuel is cheap, coal costing only $1.15 a ton, besides which the women and children can often pick up enough to keep the family supplied. Of course such instances are merely illustrative. Anything exhaustive or of the nature of an authoritative average is out of the question.*

The expenditure for drink is undoubtedly apt to be large among Slavic laborers. The southern Slavs, like the Italians, are accustomed to use light wines; the northern nationalities are accustomed to liquors, and all seem to take to beer like ducks to water. Indeed, in Croatia a common answer to questions as to what returning immigrants said of America was, "They say that in America beer is cheap, but that a man is arrested there for getting drunk, and just the same even if he is rich." Besides the immense number of saloons which American Slavs support, they also drink a great deal at home, especially in the boarding houses. Miss Byington's table previously mentioned shows a great excess of expenditure for liquor by Slavs. *[margin: Drink]*

Mr. Fitch in his study of the Pittsburgh steel industry† speaks of the special temptation to drink caused by the heat and dust of the mills. Besides this "the great majority are possessed of sincere belief that they must either drink or fail. A daily stimulant they consider essential to an endurance for long of the daily twelve-hour battle with heat and exhaustion. As a result, the saloons are taking more of the steel workers' money than any of the legitimate business establishments of the mill towns. I was told by a man who was in a position to know accurately the facts of the saloon business of McKeesport in 1906, that there were eighty saloons in this city of about 30,000 population. On the Thursdays preceding the semi-monthly pay days, *[margin: Heat and thirst]*

---

*Some further data may be found in F. J. Sheridan's article on "Italian, Slavic, and Hungarian Unskilled Immigrant Laborers in the United States," already quoted.

† "The Steel Industry and the Labor Problem." *Charities and the Commons*, XXI, pages 1079–1092 (Mar. 6, 1909).

which fall on Fridays and Saturdays, the three leading saloon keepers of the city drew from their bank accounts from $1200 to $1500 each in dollar bills and small denominations to be used as change. Other saloon keepers drew varying amounts, and the total thus drawn each fortnight was over $60,000. On the Mondays after pay days the saloon keepers usually deposited double the amount drawn. The periodic leaps in deposits never failed to coincide with pay days, and the inevitable conclusion is that about $60,000 of steel workers' wages were regularly expended in the saloons within the two days."

Celebrations

The breweries often send around wagons full of kegs on Saturday night, and where the company controls a mining settlement, as in some places in Colorado, and allows no liquor on the premises, they can do nothing to prevent sales from the "wet bread wagon" on the highway. On Saturdays liberal provision is apt to be made for the next day; often several men club together to buy a keg of beer which they join in drinking at the home of one of them.

One hears stories of such a party putting whiskey in a wash tub and sitting about it, dipping it out as wanted, replenishing the tub with beer or cheaper liquor as the original supply grows low and appetite less particular if not less insistent. In many of the small, unkempt places about Pittsburgh, places like McKees Rocks, for instance, a Monday morning sees a portentous accumulation of empty kegs lying in the mud at the doors of the Slav boarding places.

The heaviest drinking, however, is on ceremonial occasions, especially at weddings and christenings (not at funerals). Friends are invited, or in small places perhaps all comers are welcomed, and prolonged merrymakings take place. These festivals lasting for days are old customs, and take place in the old country among entirely self-respecting people. But here such occasions too often turn into debauches, and too often they end, not unnaturally, in brawls. This does more to injure the reputation of Slavs in this country than everything else put together, and some priests, to prevent the evil, perform weddings on Monday instead of on Saturday. When sober, Slavs are generally exceptionally peaceable and gentle, but when drunk they are quite the reverse.* One does not hear of murders from motives of revenge or rivalry, as among Italians, but among the roughest class and in the most neglected Slavic neighborhoods brutal and sometimes bloody rows are too common. Often they are due to old racial or religious feuds. Perhaps the Ruthenians are having a feast, and it strikes some Polish lads that this would be an auspicious moment to look in on them. The result is likely to be about what might be expected to follow an encounter of two Bowery "gangs."

It is only fair to add that in Pennsylvania where an Unjust antiquated court system of payment by fees still persists, justice one constantly hears the complaint that such fights are frequently started by officers who come in and make trouble in order to pocket the goodly amount of money that wholesale arrests bring them in.† The Slavs do

* "One officer, who had been on the force for nine years, said that while in general these men were a good-natured, easygoing crowd, and *in all his experience he had never arrested a sober 'Hunkie,'* when they were drunk there was trouble." (The italics are the author's.) Byington: "The Mill Town Courts and their Lodgers."

† The following quotation from Mr. Koukol throws light on what is liable to happen.

"One deplorable trait that I frequently met with among the Slavs was contempt for American law. The existence of this trait is largely due to the teaching of experience—and experience of one particular sort. The story of Vilchinsky, a Ruthenian boarding-boss, is such a common one, it illustrates so well a wide-spread condition in the administration of law by the petty aldermen's courts of the Pennsylvania industrial districts, that it is worth repeating for the sake of its general significance.

"October 14, 1907, one of the boarders was celebrating his patron saint's day. This meant a lot of drinking by all, and during the festivities they got more or less under the influence of liquor, but they were in their own home, there was no public disturbance, and toward midnight they all went to bed. About two o'clock in the morning, however, when they were all asleep, policemen came to the house, wakened everybody and loaded

not seem to have any characteristic national weapon of offence like the Englishman's fists, the Irishman's shillalah, the Italian's stiletto, the Negro's razor or, most deadly of all, the American's revolver.   Men who are very gentle when sober, when maddened by drink will strike with anything that comes to hand—chairs, lamps, knives.

Confirmed drunkards few

It is interesting to run across the following testimony from Massachusetts.   Miss Tyler says, "Aside from these festivals there is but little harmful intemperance.   The village doctor of Sunderland says that there is very little confirmed drinking among the Poles.   This is the worst phase of intemperance among the Irish and really does more lasting harm than the spasmodic hard drinking of the Pole.   Because the Poles' intemperance is so very apparent at certain times it makes a worse impression than is really deserved."*

them into patrol wagons and buggies and took them to a police station.   The boarding-boss, four girls and three men were all taken before the magistrate, charged with disorderly conduct. Without any regular hearing—none of them could speak English and there was no interpreter—the squire asked for twenty dollars apiece for the boarders, and fifty dollars for the boarding-boss. All but two girls paid the fine immediately, and these two were then sentenced to the county jail.   During the following day, their friends succeeded in collecting enough money to pay their fines and the $1.50 extra for board in the jail.

"Abuses such as this are generated by the fact that aldermen and constables obtain fees out of the fines, which makes it to the financial interest of these officials to get as many cases into court as possible.   Many men I have talked with have stated that the constables often provoke disorder when none exists, for the sake of the profits in the arrests.   The Slavs know that they are victimized, and at the same time they realize their help-lessness; the natural result is a bitter contempt for law.

"Huh!" sneered Vilchinsky, "the police are busy enough all night stopping disorder when the men have got money.   But when there's hard times, like there is now, a man can make all the noise he pleases and the police won't arrest him.   They know he hasn't money to pay a heavy fine and costs.   It ain't law they think about; it's money."

Koukol, A.: "A Slav's a Man for a' That." *Charities and the Commons*, XXI, page 596 (Jan. 2, 1909).   See also H. V. Blaxter, "The Aldermen and their Courts." *Charities and the Commons*, XXI, pages 851–858 (Feb. 6, 1909).

* "The Poles in the Connecticut Valley." *Smith College Monthly*, June, 1909, page 583.

This confirms my own conclusion that the strange and encouraging fact is that with all this drinking there are few drunkards. For instance, one will be told in a Pennsylvania mining town that there is not a Slav in the place who loses workingtime through intemperance, not one whose wife supports him by taking in washing while he loafs and drinks. Typical is the statement of a Jersey City doctor whose practice lies largely among Ruthenians: "They drink, but few are drunkards, or hurt their health with alcohol. If a man does get drunk he is likely to be violent. If he strikes his wife she defends herself if she can, but she does not complain, for 'she knows that he has a right to hit her' and that makes a great difference." Dr. Morritt, of the Sociological Department of the Colorado Fuel and Iron Company, says of the Colorado miners, "All Slavs drink, . . yet the Slav loses less time from work by intoxication than his British or American brother." In other places, indeed, one will hear of broken work days following Sunday debauches, but the man with whom drunkenness is a disease, as it is with so many Americans, English and Irish, is certainly not typical of the Slavs in this country.*

There is among the Slavs, however, often little or no condemnation of a man's being drunk on occasion. The objections felt against intemperance are economic, not ethical. The saloon in particular has no moral stigma upon it. It still carries with it, I think, associations of the old-world inn, and in some cases is openly frequented by women as well as by men. The saloon keeper is apt to be an influential figure and a leader in group undertakings. As already said, it is often he who stirs up the men of his colony to call a priest and build a church. Under

Public opinion and drinking

---

* An eminent Bohemian who knows the conditions both in Bohemia and in the United States, said to me that many a young man drinks to excess at home in the dull village because it offers him no excitement or healthful interest, that it is the brightest and most energetic fellows who are most likely to do so and that when such men get to America and have an outlet for their energies, they stop drinking.

such circumstances it is hard for the priest to energetically and honestly fight intemperance. Some priests indeed are not in a position to preach against overindulgence with a good grace and many are not much more advanced than their flocks in their feeling about it. That some priests do combat intemperance effectively is all the more to their credit in view of all this. "He speaks to them right from the altar," said an admiring Irish policeman of a certain Polish priest. It is perhaps worth noting that this priest was partly if not wholly educated in America.

Another influence making for temperance is that of the women. Where they are scarce they can afford to pick and choose their husbands—in biological terms, they become an effective selective agency—and women usually have a prejudice against drinking husbands.

Growing Americanization is also often a powerful force against the old drinking ways; one frequently hears it said that the young people drink less than their elders, and though this is not always true of the second generation, I am confident that it will generally hold of the third.

Dress   Clothes are the most conspicuous index of the standard of expenditure, and are of course largely valued as such, by the Slav as much as by any one. The intending immigrant often buys and puts on for the first time "European clothes" as a preparation for his journey. Few of those who wear a peasant costume at home arrive in it at Ellis Island. They leave their beautiful embroidered garments behind, carefully instructed to do so by the friends in America. They know that such things would excite derision here, and indeed they themselves are prone to despise them in comparison with the cheap, ready-made goods which they buy at the port where they embark, if not before leaving home. Often, however, they purposely buy few and cheap things in Europe, waiting to fit themselves out to better advantage in America. "Then the Americans think that we never owned any good clothes before," they have complained to me.

Once established here, the process of expansion of wants is a rapid one. An American minister in a mining city said to me, "They become Americanized sooner than any element. In a few months they lose all marks except physical ones. They begin as day laborers. First a man gets himself a tailor-made suit of good style; then he gets a trunk to lock up this and his money in. Then he buys a watch. As soon as he gets confidence he begins to deposit money."

Nothing is too good for them, especially for their children and the young women. As some one has said, "A striking hat, corsets and clothes of modern cut do not look well on the mother, but they do on the daughter." "When they have come under the rules," an Irish shopkeeper in a little mining city in Pennsylvania said to me, "they want the best goods and they want them up to date. If they do not know themselves what is the style, or if they do not speak English, they bring a friend with them who does."

From the point of view of beauty they suffer immeasurably by this change to our sweatshop and factory-made clothes. Perhaps they will not lose all their old sense for color, even so; I was pleased to be told by an artist that he had been struck with most agreeable surprise at the choice of colors, brilliant but harmonious, in the dress of the Polish girls gathered in a Catholic church. The hat has to these women a symbolic value which is not generally appreciated by us, perhaps not even by Miss Johnson, though she makes her charming story, "The Wife from Vienna," turn upon it.* It means to

The hat

* This story, which appeared in the *Atlantic* of January, 1906, is one of several delightful sketches which Miss Johnson, of Pittston, has given us. Though they generally deal with Lithuanians they reflect quite closely the atmosphere of Slavic life in a mining town. "A Ticket for Ona," "Landless Men" and "Wocel's Daughter," appeared in the *Atlantic* of January, 1908, March, 1907, and June, 1906, respectively. "The Younger Generation" appeared in the *American Magazine* for September, 1906. On the significance of the American hat see pages 106–7 and 188 above.

them stepping out of the serving class, and out of the ranks of the peasants, for at home no woman below the middle class would wear a hat, however well off.

The trousseau

In the Pennsylvania mining towns it is the custom among the Slavs and Lithuanians for a young man who is engaged to be married to take his future wife to buy her outfit. He stands by, awkward and pleased, while she makes her purchases, for which he pays. You see them coming down the street together—conscious, happy, and laden with parcels.

The home

The home of a Slav miner is often a quaint mixture of old and new-world features. Over the door are crosses and the initials of the Three Kings, drawn there in chalk last Twelfth Night by the priest when he came to bless the house; round the walls of the living room a row of gaudy colored prints of sacred subjects in cheap frames, hang just under the ceiling. There are much-washed lace curtains at the windows, and covers of home-made crocheted lace lie on the cheap shellacked sideboard and table. Everything is spotless, and if the invading Americanism shows itself in hideous bric-a-brac and crayon portraits of members of the family, it at least speaks of hope, movement and purpose.*

Music

A Slavic family are likely to spend what margin they can afford above food, clothing and shelter, in different ways from the average American family; for one thing, the dust-breeding carpet comes later and the piano

* One observer hits off a prevalent type so well that I quote her description: "This home has neither the air of poverty, nor of prosperity, but somehow nicely preserves the balance between the two. . . . The native tastes of these people are plainly shown in their homes, where the most striking feature is the excess of decoration; for the household gods of the Slavic home are orderliness and decoration. A superabundance of paper flowers and crocheted lace in the form of tidies, draperies and curtains shows the native industries of the Slavic women. The elaborate altar-cloths and priestly garments seen in their churches are the handiwork of the Polish women. They complain of no time for lace-making in America, but their little girls are taught it, nevertheless, in the public schools, just as they themselves were taught it in the schools at home."—White, Elizabeth T.: "Investigation of Slavic Conditions in Jersey City," page 8.

BETTER TYPES OF "COMPANY" HOUSES FOR SLAVIC MINERS

In a settlement where the owners are interested to improve conditions. The fences are trim, trees have been set out and gardens flourish.

earlier, since music is the gift and the joy of the Slav. This is one of the comparatively few generalizations which it is safe to make as to the whole group of Slavic nationalities. (And I say this, who have been guilty of so many such generalizations!) It is not uncommon to find a large upright piano wedged between two immense beds in a little bedroom. I shall not soon forget a call on a family of Slovak coke burners on a blizzard-lashed hillside above Punxsutawny. They occupied one half of a bare company house built of upright planks painted the usual cheap, dull red. Indoors one son, just returned from work, was playing (as appeared to my unmusical comprehension) with great beauty on a really good piano. As it happened that I knew their priest at home in Hungary, a scholar and rarely gifted linguist, there was comparatively little difficulty in breaking the ice of shyness which usually makes the approach to acquaintance with Slavs so slow and difficult, and I learned that one other son was a priest, another a seminary student preparing probably for a secular profession, and one daughter a nursing sister.

Where a piano is out of the question there are less expensive instruments, fiddles, harmonicas, and the various guitar-like instruments used by the Croatians.

Though few things compare in forlornness with a Pennsylvania "mining patch," this is due mainly to the industry as it is there carried on; to the shocking desolation of the stripped hillsides; the "cave-ins," the mountain-like piles of culm·and refuse, the buildings (especially the company tenements), erected without a thought of anything but economy; and worst of all, the streams choked and overflowed with drifted coal refuse. The homes of the Slav miners have not that grassless, hen-ridden lock which so often marks the yards of even fairly well-to-do Irish people. The Slavs generally love a garden, and during the coal strike some of the Slav and Lithuanian miners used their enforced leisure to grade and grass their little yards and to make gardens which they have ever since found time to cultivate.

Surroundings: the "mining patch" settlements

Unfortunately their very fondness for a garden contributes to the miserable aspect of things in a mining patch, as in order to protect the vegetables and flowers they make a fence of such wood as they can find, of old mine props, broken and blackened, of railroad ties and odd sticks of all sorts. Of similar material they also build a more or less ramshackle shed for a summer kitchen, adding greatly to the family comfort in the heat. Appearances, however, suffer by these attempts that really mean thrift, ingenuity and love of beauty and comfort. The little bird-house with which the Slav loves to top his home adds an oddly attractive and picturesque touch to the clustering shanties.

Cleanliness and progress As to cleanliness, in spite of serious drawbacks the Slavs deserve in general a high rank. Those who have seen dirty households or individuals will dissent vigorously, but more of those who know will, I am sure, agree. Many of these people are exceedingly primitive, but they are the reverse of a slatternly people. In all this matter, and especially if we undertake the gratuitous folly of invidious comparisons, we must remember that we are viewing a process. "The Irish lived far worse when they first came to Wilkes-Barre than the Slavs ever have done," I was told. "The Irish used to make dug-outs in the hillsides, and live in them with their animals." The living conditions of some of our German immigrants, too, were on a very low level when they first came. But opportunity has meant rise, and there is no doubt that the same rise is occurring rapidly among our Slavic fellow citizens.*

As a bit of evidence, I will repeat what was said to me on this point by a Ruthenian informant in western Pennsylvania:

* Miss Garret writes of the Poles in Baltimore: "The houses are cleaner than those occupied by any other group of foreigners among us. The halls are whitewashed once or twice a year, the floors are scrubbed (the tenants in turn doing the general work) and the rooms are kept wonderfully neat. . . . Neighbors, business men, doctors, teachers all lay stress on the extreme neatness and cleanliness of the Polish people." *Charities*, XI, page 273 (Dec. 3, 1904).

"Formerly our people could save and send money home; now if a man has a family he cannot. Prices have risen faster than wages have done, that is one reason; but the chief reason is that they demand more and live better. For instance, formerly the men never wore an overcoat, no matter how cold it was. They wore blue overalls, no collar and no tie. They had no churches, no societies and no papers. All these things mean expense. They still live pretty crowded, but less so than before. From fifty to one hundred of them used to live in one house, not a big one. There were no women among them, and other people would not take them to board. If there was a man who had a wife, all flocked to him. There would be twenty-five boarders in a family, where now there would be eight or ten. Ten years ago they used to have plank shelves for bedding round the wall in some mining patches. Now-a-days all have regular beds."

The whole impression left on one's mind is that of an ambitious set of people, eager to get on, of enduring fibre, not at all afraid of hard work.

No effort has been made to describe household conditions among Slavic-Americans other than those of the laboring class. Among business men and men of the professions the standard of living is regulated as is that of similar American families. The only distinctive characteristic that I note is a greater simplicity, a warmth and quiet intensity of family life, a marked love of music and often of intellectual pursuits, and what seems to an American eye a rather uncritical aesthetic sense. According to circumstances the European or the American note prevails in the blended tastes of the household,— in the table, the dress, the furniture, the reading. *Upper and middle classes*

Physically they seem for the most part a rugged people, especially the picked contingent of young ambitious men and women who emigrate. As a general thing they appear not to suffer from our climate, though it is sometimes complained of. As one sees them at home in Europe, they often seem to be almost insensible to either *Physique* heat or cold. They come largely from districts subject to severe changes of temperature, often very sudden changes. Emil Franzos describes snowstorms blowing across the Galician plains which outdo a Dakota blizzard, and the limestone country, the Karst of the South Slavs, is also a country of violent extremes.

On the other hand, the change to city life is very taxing.*

Tuberculosis claims its own in unsanitary tenements and workshops. There is a great deal of anaemia, and when the roses fade in the cheeks of a flaxen-haired Polish girl, she is shockingly pale. The Bohemians of New York seem to supply an inordinately large share of cases of hysteria and of suicide.

The peasant women of the first generation amaze our women by their endurance. One of their own mid-wives told me that they have as hard confinements as Americans, but that they recover more quickly. In Allegheny a settlement friend went to see a neighbor and found her at nine o'clock barefoot in the yard hanging out clothes. She had borne a child at midnight, after which she had arisen and got breakfast for the men of her family and then done the washing.

Even if a woman is physically able to do this sort of thing, she is aged by it—by that and the continuous child-bearing. Yet this is their ideal. "What do your

---

* Miss White in her "Investigation of Slavic Conditions in Jersey City" notes: "The majority of the men and women, all of whom spent their youth in their native land, were found to be strong and hearty. But the children, born and reared in this country, are pale and sickly looking. It is a disheartening fact that they are not profiting by the strength that is theirs by right of inheritance." "Undoubtedly the confinement of these out-of-door children in unsanitary houses and worse than unsanitary backyards, is the cause of their physical degeneration." (Page 4.) Compare also Miss Byington: "The Slavs themselves, moreover, are people used to the limitations of country life, and are ignorant of the evil effects of transferring the small rooms, the overcrowding, the insufficient sanitary provisions which are possible with all outdoors about them, to these crowded courts under the shadow of the mill. And, as we said, their ambition to save and buy property, here or in the old country, is a further incentive to overcrowding." ".The Mill Town Courts and their Lodgers," page 922.

people think of Americans?" I asked a Slovenian priest. "Our women despise American women because they have small families," was the prompt reply, and this is a sentiment frequently met with.

A very interesting question, and one that is hard to answer, is that of the personal position of the women. My own impression is that the real, not nominal, balance of power in the household adjusts itself in any country to the relative personal force of the individuals in each case; that common sense, business acumen, temper and quiet force of will, all have their effect, regardless of sex, regardless of theory; and I should confidently look for henpecked husbands in harems and for enfranchised women tyrannized over by men with not one tittle of legal advantage. *Position of women*

This is not to say, however, that law, and still more, custom, do not affect the position of the sexes profoundly, and it is suggestive to be told that in Croatia wives warn their husbands that in America things will be different, for women have more power there. Indeed, we found in Croatia especially a widespread and wonderful legend of the position of women in America. "Is it true," an anxious man asked, "that when there is a lawsuit the woman goes to court and attends to it, and the husband stays at home?" I think that it is true that in this country the men learn more respect for the women, and acquire gentler manners toward them; and doubtless, as already said, the relative scarcity of women gives them more weight.* One hears of the husband putting all his earnings into the wife's hands to manage, as is so generally the custom among the better class of American workmen—a custom that is likely to make for thrift and wise expenditure. In a higher range of society, among the Bohemians especially, the women are quite active and well organized. They have their own associations and their own papers.

* The improved status of immigrant wives in America is a subject frequently and entertainingly illustrated by anecdotes in Mr. Steiner's "The Immigrant Tide."

CHAPTER XVII

THE ORGANIZED LIFE OF SLAVS IN AMERICA*

Slavic organizations

One of the most surprising facts in the life of Slavs in America is the degree to which they are organized into societies. There seems to be nothing in their previous history or experience to lead one to expect this, and it has been an historical commonplace to reproach the Slav with a congenital inability to combine. Yet in their new environment they are notable for the contrary tendency.

Many of their associations are small local affairs of the most various sorts. In a New York Bohemian paper I found a list of 95 local societies among this group of perhaps 35,000 people. Many were mere "pleasure clubs," to use the current East Side phrase, while many were lodges of various of their great "national" societies.

The national societies

Each of the main Slavic nationalities in the United States has one or more of these national societies, all apparently organized on much the same plan, with a central co-ordinating committee and numerous branches, founded primarily for the object of mutual insurance but also serving many other purposes, and with a membership defined by national or national-religious lines.

When one considers the scattered groups of poor and ignorant immigrants, totally unused to organization and foreign to all ideas of parliamentary procedure, from which these societies must draw a large part of their membership it is remarkable how rapidly they have grown, how highly developed and successful they are.

* The facts in this chapter were gathered mainly in 1907, and reference is in general to data of that year, except when otherwise stated.

378

A SLOVAK MASS MEETING IN CLEVELAND

A protest against Hungarian outrages

A POLISH HALL IN CHICAGO

When men are scattered in a strange country, the Grounds of cohesion "consciousness of kind" with fellow countrymen has a very special significance. As has been said in a previous chapter, to many an immigrant the idea of nationality first becomes real after he has left his native country; at home the contrast was between village and village, and between peasants as a class and landlords as a class. In America he finds a vast world of people, all speaking unintelligible tongues, and for the first time he has a vivid sense of oneness with those who speak his own language, whether here or at home.

The idea of national or racial patriotism is not so new to those from localities in Europe where different nationalities or different churches are intermingled and struggling for power, and where the fires of party zeal are always kept alight. From such districts men often emigrate, already full of national or party consciousness. This is especially marked in the case of leaders, some of whom come to America to enlist recruits for their side in European issues, and to make use of the awakening intelligence of their emigrated fellow countrymen to prepare them to play a more manly part under oppression, and to secure for themselves and their brethren fair and reasonable treatment at home.

But it is not only common speech and ways, and in Common needs and mutual aid some cases common political aims, that draw the different groups of immigrants together, but also the sense of economic weakness. The especially dangerous character of the work in the mines and foundries which employ so many Slavs is calculated to enhance their appreciation of the advantages of mutual aid.

The result is this great number of Slavic societies, the total membership of which it is impossible to calculate, especially as one man may belong to several societies. Taking the figures as they stand, however, we find for the Bohemians alone about 66,000 members in a dozen or so chief societies. The Slovaks, who are probably about as numerous in this country as the Bo-

hemians, appear to have over 120,000 society members.*
For other nationalities I have no estimates of totals,
only figures for certain individual societies.

The
Č. S. P. S.

The oldest existing Slavic society was founded by the
Bohemians at St. Louis in 1854, under the name of the
Chekho-Slavonic Benevolent Society, or as it is commonly
called by the initials of this name in Bohemian, the
Č. S. P. S. In the religious controversies which soon
divided American Bohemians into two camps, this came
to represent the free thinking, anti-Catholic side. It
numbers about 23,000 members in 216 branches.

Polish National Alliance

The largest single society appears to be the Polish
National Alliance, with a membership of 53,000 in 780
branches. This, like the preceding, is much more than a
mutual benefit society, though it is that also. In its
fine building in Chicago it has not only central offices
and committee rooms, but a museum and library and

* Rev. Stephen Furdek of Cleveland, in a pamphlet on mutual
benefit associations, dated 1908, gives the following figures for
Slovak associations:
   I. Katolicka Slovenská Jednota (First Catholic Slovak
Union); members, 33,000.
   Národný Slovenský Spolok, (National Slovak Society);
28,000.
   Grécko Kat. Sojedinenie (Greek Catholic Association);
20,879.
   Pennsylvánska Gréc. Kat. Slovenská Jednota (Penn. Greek
Catholic Slovak Union); 6,000.
   Evanjelícka Slovenská Jednota (Evangelical [sc. Lutheran]
Slovak Union); 8,000.
   Telovična Jednota Sokol (A gymnastic Society); 3741.
   Clevelandská Slov. Jednota; 1000.
   Passaická Slovenská Jednota; 1000.
   Neodvislý Nár. Slov. Spolok (Independent National Slovak
Society); 2000.
   Slovenský Venec (literally, Slovak Garland); 1061.
   Kalvinská Slov. Jednota (Calvinistic [sc. Presbyterian]
Slovak Union); 1000.
   I Kat. Slov. Ženska Jednota (First Catholic Slovak Women's
Union); 8000.
   Živena, 6000.
   Pennsylvanská Slovenská Ženska Jednota; 3000.
   Evanjelícka Slovenská Ženská Jednota; 1000.
   (The last four are women's societies.)
   I find this reference, which may also be useful. Furdek,
Stefan: "Život Slovakov v Amerike," (Life of Slovaks in Amer-
ica) in Tovaryšstvo, III, Ruzomberok, Hungary, 1890.

the printing establishment of its organ, *Zgoda* (Unity). It has special sections or committees for Education, Agriculture and Industry, Young People, Music, Gymnastics, Charity and the Kosciuszko monument which the Poles are erecting in Washington. It maintains about thirty scholarships, and ninety-two libraries, besides distributing books and pamphlets. Each member contributes twenty-one cents a month, besides assessments to cover death benefits and one cent a month for charity.

One of the most remarkable of these organizations is the National Slavonic (*sc.* Slovak) Society, which, between 1906 and the time of its foundation in 1890 had paid over $3,500,000 in death benefits, and in the three years ending April 30th, 1906, $350,000 in sick benefits. This society has a markedly patriotic character; it assists Slovak students, ("some 124" in the last year of which I have information), it encourages and disseminates Slovak literature, raises funds for Slovak political prisoners in Hungary (where the Slovaks are so bitterly oppressed), organizes patriotic meetings, and generally acts as representative of the nationality. It is interesting to note that it requires members to become American citizens within six years of joining the society. National Slovak Society

Comparable with these societies are the National Croatian Society, with 22,000 members, the little Russian National Union with 10,000, and the Slovenian National Benevolent Society. The Croatian National Society is undertaking to found a National University in this country and is appropriating money to this end. Other national societies.

Besides these organizations, which are all on a more or less anti-clerical basis, there are societies often much larger organized on a church basis, Roman Catholic, Greek Catholic (Uniate) and Orthodox, and among the Slovaks an Evangelical Union numbering 8000 members. Societies on religious lines

The main life of these societies is naturally in the local organizations or lodges, about which the social life of the group tends to centre, especially among the freethinkers, to whom their society largely stands in lieu The life of the lodges of a church. Many have handsome buildings of their own. Here there are usually a restaurant (full of the smell of beer and smoke, but entirely respectable, and frequented by family parties), a large, well-equipped gymnasium, perhaps a library, committee rooms of course, and, more important than all the rest, a large hall for meetings, lectures, dances, concerts and last but not least, theatricals. Singing and choral societies, often with picturesque, reminiscent names, are many. The Polish Singers' Alliance counts about 1,000 members.

Gymnastic
societies

The Sokols, which correspond to the German "Turnerbunds" or gymnastic societies, are as popular and widespread as they are desirable. They give opportunity for exercise dignified by a sense of the relation between good physical condition and readiness for service to one's country. Women and children, as well as the men, have their own divisions, classes and uniforms, and the Sokol exhibitions are important and very pretty social events. In Prague, in the summer of 1906, the Bohemian Sokols had an anniversary international meet, at which the American societies were also represented, and performed evolutions, literally in their thousands, in the open air.

Drama

Theatricals, whether given in some local hall or in a regular theatre hired for the occasion, are, as in Europe, a favorite employment for Sunday afternoons or evenings. Classic pieces, both literary and operatic, are much enjoyed; for instance, among the Bohemians, Smetana's opera, *The Bartered Bride*, is often given. On the other hand, one will see a very simple spontaneous little exhibition given with the greatest abandon and delight by a club of hard-worked, elderly women, whose triumphs are hugely enjoyed by their families and neighbors. It is an especial pleasure to them to reproduce the pretty costumes of their old-world youth. Worthy of especial mention are the club, called Snaha (Endeavor), of Bohemian professional women in Chicago,

TITLES OF SOME OF THE SLAVIC NEWSPAPERS PUBLISHED IN THE UNITED STATES

and the clubs organized for reading and study among the Socialists of different nationalities.

Closely connected with the societies are the news-papers, which also have attained a surprising develop-ment here. Among the Slovaks, and perhaps among some other nationalities, the circulation of papers in their own language is greater in America than it is at home where the press of a discontented nationality has to meet every sort of political hindrance.* Of daily papers the Bohemians support nine, the Poles seven, the Slovaks, Croatians and Slovenians one each. The number of weeklies is much larger, the Poles heading the list with fifty-four. In Poland (German, Russian and Austrian) the Polish press issues the large number of 657 papers, some appearing two and three times a day.

The Slavic-American press represents, of course, very divergent points of view. Many of the papers are conducted by priests for purposes of edification, some are political, of which a part are labor and socialist sheets, and a substantial number find their *raison d'être* and support as organs of certain of the societies. Of this type are *Zgoda*, organ of the Polish National Alliance, with a circulation of about 55,000, or the *Organ Bratstva*, organ of the Č. S. P. S., which is published by the Supreme Lodge of the society at the rate of forty cents a month to each member, and which prints at the beginning of each month the list of deaths and the consequent assessment.

Another feature which gives these papers their hold is the news which they bring to homesick exiles of happen-ings, big and little, in the old country. One often finds in them more and better European political intelligence than in our first class papers, and on the other hand, no village occurrence is too small to be reported. Especially in Slovak papers I have noticed the columns of quaint individual happenings, arranged county by county.

* The figures furnished me by the kindness of Mr. Rovnianek of Pittsburgh, show twelve Slovak papers published in America with a combined circulation of 112,500, and twenty published in Hungary, with a combined circulation of 48,300.

Some of these publications, especially the monthlies, are literary reviews, others are comic sheets, while others again serve special interests, as for instance the Sokol papers, the Polish *Harmonia*, the *Polsky Farmer* and the Bohemian *Hospodar* (Farmer).

One paper, the *Ženske Listy* of Chicago, is the organ of a woman's society, and is printed as well as edited by women. It is not devoted to "beauty lessons" and "household hints," but to efforts toward woman's suffrage and the "uplifting of the mental attitude of working women." Its 6000 subscribers include distinguished Bohemians all over the country, men as well as women.

Church organization If the spontaneous and luxuriant growth of private organizations among the Slavs in America is a surprising fact, it can of course be no surprise that they organize, or are organized, for religious purposes in this country as in the old.

The Roman Catholics are of course the largest group, and they find their own church, the same here as at home, already established and prepared to welcome them to its familiar services. The Protestants, who are perhaps a fourth among the Slovaks, a small percentage among the Bohemians, and negligible among the other Slavs, have got into touch, more or less, with the corresponding churches here, which are willing and eager to help them to establish and extend their organizations.

The Orthodox church under the Holy Synod of Russia has some fifty churches in the country outside of Alaska, where there are as many more, not counting the Servian mission, the Syro-Arabian mission, and sixteen churches in Canada. Not only—nor indeed mainly—Russians make up these congregations, though they are subsidized from St. Petersburg. The priests, often very able men, are carrying on an active propaganda among the borderland peoples, and especially among the Uniates or United Greek Catholics, who occupy a curious intermediate position, as has been already explained. This propaganda seems to have had considerable success among Little Russians (Ruthenians) and Slovaks. In Minneapolis I was interested to find among the Little Russians a Uniate church which had gone over bodily from Rome to Russian Orthodoxy. The Bulgarians are Greek Orthodox, but independently organized under the Bulgarian Church. In Table 28 an attempt is made to bring together the facts as to the different national groups by denominations.

A condition in America which doubtless strikes as strange all these newcomers equally, and which it takes them some time to understand, is the disassociation here of church and state. To some this comes with a grateful sense of relief, as for instance, to the Bohemian free-thinker. On the other hand, the impression that the country makes seems to be the reverse of irreligious. "The American nation is a believing nation," says Father Šušteršič in his Slovenian guide, "Poduk Rojakom Slovencem," and he cites the fact that Congress is opened with prayer, and the motto *In God we trust* on our coins. Of course, the independence of church and state means to the newcomers the unaccustomed burden of building their own churches and meeting all the cost of maintaining their services. In general, these new demands seem to make for more devotion rather than for less, and it is astonishing to see the number and magnificence of the churches with which these migrant laborers have sown the land in so few years. A little mining city, like Hazleton, Pennsylvania, will often have five or six Slavic churches, representing different nationalities and sects. In cities like Chicago, Milwaukee, Cleveland and Detroit, and even in quite small places also, one finds Gothic and Renaissance edifices of great size, elaborateness and evident expense, and sometimes of much beauty.*

Separation of church and state

---

* While this is in press I hear of the dedication of a Polish church in Ware, Massachusetts, to build which $60,000 is said to have been raised in less than three years. See also page 230.

28

TABLE 35.—CHURCH AFFILIATIONS OF SLAVS IN THE UNITED STATES

	ROMAN CATHOLIC	UNITED GREEK CATHOLIC	GREEK ORTHODOX	PROTESTANT	FREE-THINKING
POLISH........	Apart from a recent schism practically all R. C.* 500 churches and missions (1905).				
BOHEMIAN.....	50 to 70 per cent R. C.† About 125 parishes with resident priests, 166 in all.			Perhaps 2 per cent Protestant. 70 churches, viz.: 24 Presbyterian, 11 Congregational, 9 Methodist, 14 "Brethren", (all in Texas) 6 Baptist, 6 Reformed.	Perhaps 15 to 20 per cent free-thinking.‡ The Č. S. P. S. has 216 local societies.
SLOVAK........	Perhaps 50 per cent R. C. 110 churches.	A considerable number of churches.	10 churches.	Perhaps 20 per cent Protestant. Lutherans, 87 congregations, 51 churches and 55,000 people. Calvinists, about 15,000.	
RUTHENIAN....		80 churches.	26 churches.	2 churches. Some Stundists (Baptists) in Dakota.	

SLOVENIAN.....	Practically all R. C. 42 priests and 2 bishops. Perhaps 20 parishes.	
CROATIAN.......	10 churches.	2 or 3 churches.
RUSSIAN.........		About 50 churches in the U. S., (including the above?). In Alaska, 16 churches and 36 chapels.
SERVIAN........		6 churches, 12 priests, 59,000 regular communicants.
BULGARIAN.....		

* For this schism see page 389. For Protestantism among Poles see Bibliography under Polish Religious History.

† Dr. Roberts puts the proportion at 30 to 40 per cent.

‡ Dr. Roberts estimates free-thinkers as fully half of the Bohemians. For accounts of the religious status of immigrants see Grose, Howard B.: "Aliens or Americans." Other references are given in the bibliography under Churches.

The Roman
Catholics
    Among the Slavic Roman Catholics the Poles easily stand first, both in numbers and in zeal. As has already been explained (page 125) they, like the Irish, have been so situated historically, that their political and religious antagonisms coincide, intensifying both. The schismatic Russian tyrant, the heretic Swedish invader, and the Protestant Prussian oppressor with his hated schools—all have tended to make devotion to church and country one indistinguishable sentiment. To people so minded, the situation in America was a strangely confusing one. They found the Catholic church in this country, at least as they came into contact with it, practically an institution of the Irish, and the Irish have too generally shown themselves contemptuous of "foreigners," and have not always earned for themselves the love of other classes of immigrants. But apart from any such influence, the natural desire to have a priest of their own tongue and traditions would have made itself felt. Not only the Poles, but other national groups of Roman Catholics, form churches of their own just as soon as they can. They may go for a time to the "Irish Catholic" church, but it is hard to hold them there or in any other church not of their own people. In a certain Colorado mining settlement full of Roman Catholics (Slovenians, Mexicans, Italians, Slovaks), the only Catholic church was a little adobe building, where mass was served at intervals by a Spanish-speaking priest. I found it full of kneeling Mexicans, their heads bare or covered with black mantillas; but of all the other Catholics in the place, I saw only one person, a devout old German woman known to every one in the camp as "Grandma." The religious appeal could not make itself felt through the racial barriers.

    [Besides this instinctive segregation there has been a good deal of friction and discontent as to ecclesiastical administration and office. Until a short time ago the Poles, in spite of their numbers and zeal, had not been able to secure the appointment of a single Polish bishop,

SLAVIC CHURCHES OF ONE MINING TOWN

1. Slovak Roman Catholic.   2. Lithuanian Roman Catholic.   3. Slovak Lutheran.   4. Polish Roman Catholic.   5. Greek Catholic.   6. Greek Orthodox

while the much smaller group of the Slovenians, for instance, had had five bishops.*

A curious and unexpected phenomenon, probably not unrelated to all this, has been the occurrence of a Polish schism and the formation here of a so-called "Polish National Church," or Independent Polish Church, which in 1906 was said to number thirteen churches, but which Dr. Peter Roberts reports, in September, 1909, as having 90 churches. Quite apart from this movement, there is another very interesting ferment at work in the Polish churches. Every newspaper reader in districts where there are many Poles, must have frequently run across paragraphs like the following:

Divisions in the churches

"WESTFIELD PRIEST SUES PARISHIONERS.

"Westfield, Sept. 20.—As a result of dissensions that have arisen in the Holy Trinity Parish here, twenty suits in action of tort alleging slander and conspiracy to slander have been brought by Rev. X. Y. against leading Poles of this town. In addition to these suits there are four others entered in the Superior Court by Father X. Y., the whole number aggregating $40,000. So serious have been the disagreements that during the services last Sunday the entire police force was obliged to be present at all services to prevent a riot when the dissenting faction made an attempt to collect the funds of the church, independent of the regular collectors appointed by Father X. Y."

Apparently these oft-recurring clashes have no doctrinal significance. Rather, they are an effort toward liberty and self-government, embodying itself, like the historic struggles of the English, in the shape of a contention as to who shall control the purse strings, and doubtless due to the new financial responsibility of the laity in an unestablished church. A priest may have been used to take with his people a tone of absolute authority which they are led by all the influences of American life, and perhaps not least by the sight of the freer relation of American priests with their flocks, to resent. Then they hear, it may be, of a priest, originally a poor man,

* For facts which help to explain this anomaly see page 233.

dying and leaving a private fortune to relatives. They themselves, spurred on by the priest, arrange a church entertainment to help pay off the church debt. They spare no pains and are apparently successful, but the priest refuses to let the church trustees know how the balance stands, or to give any account of receipts and expenditures in general. They insist, and it leads to an open break. The priest comes to morning mass and finds himself locked out of his "own church" by his church officers. He then calls in the police to force an entrance, and the American newspaper gives the affair a paragraph that makes it appear mere rowdyism or irreligion, which it is very far from being.

The free-thought movement Among the Bohemians the religious situation is peculiar and deeply interesting. Its roots lie deep in Bohemian religious history. The reformation movement of Huss and his followers having been stamped out in blood after 1620, the Catholicism which Bohemia was forced to accept was apt to be lukewarm when it was not merely nominal.

In the nineteenth century the liberal movement of the forties had a religious as well as a political side, and an intense reaction against clericalism and dogma set in. In the free air of America, and under the influence of Robert Ingersoll and the works of Thomas Paine and Herbert Spencer, this resulted not merely in a widespread ferment of ideas, but in organized and aggressive propaganda. Under the onslaught, Bohemian Catholicism acquired a new vigor, there was bitterness on both sides, and Bohemians in this country were split into two antagonistic parties. As has been said already, the society known as the Č. S. P. S. came to be a free-thinking organization, and its lodges in some degree represent congregations. They frequently carry on free-thought schools, where on Sunday mornings, Saturday afternoons, and other leisure times, the children can be trained in Bohemian grammar and history, and in the views of the free-thinkers. For this purpose a catechism has been written. There is also a profoundly pathetic little hand-book of addresses,—they can hardly be called services,—for use at their funerals.* The funerals are often conducted by the president or other member of the lodge of the deceased; in the women's lodges by the women for women.

As far as an outsider can judge, this movement is rapidly losing momentum. It is difficult to keep the interest and enthusiasm of the young people. They find little to feed on in teachings so largely merely negative; nothing in their experience answers to their parents' rancor against the corrupt side of priestcraft as they had seen it in Austria, and the ties of race and speech, which are so powerful a bond among the first generation, influence the later born much less. The free-thought movement was essentially religious, in spite of the crudity of its materialist philosophy and of its propaganda in favor of atheism; it was the work of men, for the most part not of the most highly privileged class in respect of opportunities for culture, but to whom questions of religious belief were the supremely important and the supremely interesting thing in life, and to whom intellectual sincerity and courage were the breath of their nostrils. As a Bohemian doctor in New York once said to me, "Two Bohemians cannot meet without beginning to talk of religion." The tone of their thought at its best may be illustrated by the following quotation from a lecture on "Free-Thought in America," by Anton Jurka: "Let us be strong. Let us firmly believe that we are maintaining the position which answers most loyally to the nobility of Nature. Let us, according to our strength, draw from deeds both past and present, faith in a better future, and let us help to build this better future by faith, hope and love; by faith in the noble final goal of mankind, by hope that humanity will reach its goal and will be thoroughly imbued with a culture and enlightenment not yet dreamed of by us; with a love pure,

* See Bibliography under Free-thought.

self-sacrificing, to Nature, to man, to humanity as a whole."

Now that the critical and destructive work is done, there seems to be a great deal of mere indifference to all religious matters, and, as one hears, a good deal of self-indulgent, rather gross living on the part of some who are "free-thinkers as much as they are anything." On the other hand, one also hears of the children of the old fighters for free-thought joining one or another of the Protestant churches, partly perhaps from social reasons, partly, doubtless, from a hunger which negations could not satisfy. In one instance I hear that the free-thinkers, as such, have affiliated themselves with Unitarianism.

Socialism An element of life which, if not universal like religion, is common to all civilized countries, is the modern industrial system—the system under which capital, labor and science produce an amount of wealth unknown to history, but at the cost of enormous waste of life, health and happiness. The man who is conscious of this as a problem calls himself for the most part a socialist, and such a man, when he comes to America from Europe, finds himself in a very different position from the nationalistic patriot; he does not leave his problem, his ideal aim in life, behind him. The essential features of the new situation, so far as they are industrial, not political, are already familiar. He does not feel himself an outsider with nothing to do but to criticize; on the contrary, he is consciously one, not with his own little group alone, but with working people everywhere, and he finds his old task here.

Of the Slavs who come to us, a comparatively small part are from industrial centres where these ideas are in the air. There is, however, a socialistic contingent among them, especially among the Poles and Bohemians, though by no means comparable to that supplied by Germans and Jews. In this country I judge that their numbers do not grow as fast as one might expect. Acquisition of property makes for conservatism, and the sense of opportunity and at least nominal political equality makes for individualism. Sometimes this individualism has a more theoretical basis, and is a legacy of old struggles against oppressive governments. A Pole or a Bohemian has at least more excuse than an Englishman for transferring his jealousy of government as an alien and selfish power to a country where all authority is, or should be, his own representative and agent. I was talking with a Texas Bohemian, son of a man self-exiled for the sake of liberty, an editor, judge and school committeeman, and I said something of the need of compulsory education laws. Instantly his eyes flashed, and his voice rang: "That would be tyranny."

As to the existence or extent of that state of acute Anarchism social exasperation which is what is popularly meant by anarchism and which, at the time of the assassination of President McKinley, appeared to exist among a section of the Poles, I can unfortunately give no information, as I have never come across any traces of it or references to it.

Where the next generation will stand on all these The next matters it is hard to forecast, but I suspect that it will generation adopt the same standpoints as Americans under the same conditions. A very radical American friend values our immigrants as good future revolutionary material; the younger generation, he says, grow up quite emancipated from the old, narrow ideas of their parents and equally free from the political and social traditions that hypnotize Americans. My impression is that this view was suggested to him by experience among the Jews of the East Side, and that it would be more nearly true among that race of thinkers than elsewhere. Nevertheless, the Slav seems to share with the Frenchman and the Jew the power to think out a logical theory and to carry that theory into action.

American politics for the most part have not been Politics such as to command great interest apart from purely local considerations. Since the days of the anti-slavery movement, which enlisted the generous sympathies of the old generation of liberal immigrants, our politics have involved few questions of wide significance with the exception of some of our social-economic issues. The educated European remains on the outside of American life quite as much because it is provincial as because he is. Consequently, unless he is made over into a complete American, the foreigner is likely to take part in our politics only as a matter of business, which is to say corruptly. Among the simple-minded yet shrewd fellows at the bottom this is often quite naïvely and innocently the case. A librarian who is a good friend of the various nationalities who work in her town, asked the Poles who were coming in and out of the library on one election day what they were voting for. They replied cheerfully, pleased that she took an interest in their affairs and that they had so good a market to report, "For two dollars." The whole situation is one which naturally lends itself to log-rolling and political trading. When there are groups of men with their full numerical share of political power, with no use to which they want to put it, and full of clannish feeling, it is very easy for a leader of their own kind to "vote" them as a unit. If he is bid for by the offer of some petty office, it gratifies not only him but his whole group, who feel themselves vicariously honored in the person of the candidate.

While the conviction that American politics are corrupt draws in some men, it keeps out others; as a Slovak minister said to me, "My people are not interested in politics; they say, 'Das ist mehr Geldsache'" (that is mostly a matter of money, anyway).

Party affiliations As to political affiliations, both parties count Slavs as members. In the ante-bellum days the slavery issue tended to draw Bohemians and Poles, both of whom supplied gallant soldiers to the Union, into the Republican ranks. It is interesting to find that the Poles voted for Grant in 1872, the first election in which they were notably interested, not only because of his war record, but because he recognized the French Republic during the Prussian war, while his opponent Greeley was supposed to have favored Austria in Italy and Germany in Alsace-Lorraine. Another reason for Republicanism has been the simple and intelligible one that the Irish were Democrats. On the other hand, in Chicago both Bohemians and Poles are said to be "normally Democrats," and the explanation given by Miss Masaryk in the case of the Bohemians is that Republicanism meant the Administration, and that Bohemians were readily led by their past experience to join the opposition.

How far Slavs in this country are naturalized it is Citizenship impossible to say, the census figures on the subject being unusable in this case. In Hadley, Massachusetts, as I have already stated, while 47 Poles own property and 123 more pay a poll tax, only two are naturalized, and I judged that the Americans were far from desiring to have more become voters. The policy of the more enlightened Slavic leaders, on the contrary, is to urge citizenship and, as has been said, one at least of the national societies requires it.

In many places the Slavic vote is an important con- Slavs in office sideration. In the Illinois state campaign of 1906, both Republicans and Democrats nominated a Pole for the office of state treasurer. One of these nominees had already served in Chicago as alderman and as city attorney. A number of Poles have sat in state legislatures, both in the lower chamber and, in one instance at least, in the State senate, and there is a pretty story of a Wisconsin Bohemian whose desk in the House was reserved for him on his election as a sort of family perquisite, or rather as a courteous recognition of the services (if I remember the circumstances rightly) of his father and brother, who had preceded him in office. Mr. Sabath, a congressman from Illinois, is said to be a Bohemian.

CHAPTER XVIII

THE QUESTION OF ASSIMILATION

Forced as-
similation

Assimilation is much talked of in the United States. Its desirability is so taken for granted that any and every method of hastening it may seem acceptable, until something brings to our attention what bad company this very assimilation keeps. Wherever in the world there are people crying, "We are oppressed," there you are likely to find another set of people protesting, "This is no oppression; it is assimilation—benevolent assimilation." The shout of "Islam or the sword," wrought probably the most rapid assimilation on record.

Modern de-
velopment
of national
feeling

It is a commonplace of history that while the constitution of centralized states on a territorial basis, putting an end to feudal disorganization, was the characteristic accomplishment of the sixteenth, seventeenth and eighteenth centuries, the active ferment of the nineteenth century has been the principle of nationalities. Each group with a racial or cultural unity, and above all with the type and sign of this, a common speech, has been eagerly struggling toward autonomy, or at least toward the right to develop along its own lines and to use its own language.

Everywhere this nationalistic movement has revealed fresh human treasures and called forth some of the rarest and finest blossoms of the spirit of mankind. In literature it has given us highly differentiated types of new and poignant beauty, doubly welcome in a leveling and cosmopolitan age. Folk lore, art and philology have also felt its vivifying touch. It has evoked the most intense devotion and been the cause of the most heroic sacrifices.

On the other hand, it has divided peoples who before

were hardly conscious of differences, and has narrowed men's sympathies to their own little group,—in striking contrast to the cosmopolitan humanitarianism of the eighteenth century. It has lighted indescribable fires of bitterness. Perhaps no moral agony is greater than to see the language and tradition of one's fathers, one's spiritual birthright, strangled to death by a contemptuous rival. The Pole in Germany, the Slovak in Hungary, the little Russian in Russia—and how many more—all feel the hand at their throats. It is cruel enough in a case like that of the Germans of the Baltic provinces of Russia; though they see their children forcibly Russified, yet they know that across the border Germany is continuing her progress without thought of check. To the Slovak, who knows that if his idiom becomes obsolete in Hungary it nevermore can take its place among the living tongues of men, what must it be to see his school funds confiscated, his press harried and his children systematically taught to despise the language and nationality which he loves with a Slav's obstinate intensity?

With these things in mind one turns to the United States and finds there a process of Americanization going on which must be seen to be comprehended, and which becomes the more impressive the more it is studied. Here are over 75,000,000 people, representatives of an indefinite variety of human stocks, yet presenting in general an almost painful degree of uniformity. For local color, the short story writer must generally have recourse to sheltered and backward communities, to frontier outposts or to colonies of recent newcomers— all now rapidly losing their peculiarities. It reminds one of the old fable of the traveler's cloak; the wind which boasted that he could easily remove it only made him hug it the closer to him; in the warmth of the sun he felt it a burden, and voluntarily cast it aside. *The American situation*

Yet even in the United States assimilation is not quite without signs of difficulty and apprehension and conflicting purposes—signs of dread and jealousy, on the part of Americans, of the alien influences brought in by the streams of newcomers, and, on the part of the immigrants, of jealousy of American influence and dread of Americanizing pressure.

A Polish view

One comes sometimes with a sense of shock to a realization of points of view strange to one's own. Take, for instance, a conversation that I once had with a Polish-American priest. I had said something about "Americans," that they were not apt to be interested in Polish history, or something of the sort. Instantly he was on fire.

"You mean English-Americans," he said. "You English constantly speak as if you were the only Americans, or more Americans than others. The History of the United States, published by Scribners, is written wholly from the English point of view, and that is very common. Even such a great paper as the Chicago *Tribune* is written by men who are just over from England, and who yet speak of foreigners when they mean any Americans but English. For instance, in a recent bank failure they said that many 'foreigners' would lose, referring to German-Americans and others who had been in the country for generations. A priest born in Baltimore of Italian parents, speaking English and Italian equally naturally, will see priests, new come from Ireland, promoted over him because he is a 'foreigner.'"

I remarked that if I went to Poland he would not consider me a Pole.

"No, that is different," was his reply. "America was empty, open to all comers alike. There is no reason for the English to usurp the name of American. They should be called Yankees if anything. That is the name of English-Americans. There is no such thing as an American nation. Poles form a nation, but the United States is a country, under one government, inhabited by representatives of different nations. As to the future, I have, for my part, no idea what it will bring. I do not think that there will be amalgamation, one race composed of many. The Poles, Bohemians and so forth, remain such, generation after generation. Switzerland has been a republic for centuries, but never has brought her people to use one language. For myself, I do favor one language for the United States, *either English or some other*, to be used by every one, but there is no reason why people should not also have another language; that is an advantage, for it opens more avenues to Europe and elsewhere."

He was indignant at the requirement of the naturalization law of 1906, making a knowledge of English a condition of citizenship. I advanced as an argument for it the fact that the proceedings of Congress are carried on in English, and that to vote intelligently a man must be able to follow them. "In our Polish papers," he said, "the Congressional debates are as fully reported as in the English-American papers, and politics can be as intelligently followed." I did not feel that I could urge that many English-speaking voters seek familiarity with the debates in full in the *Congressional Record*.

The views that I have tried to reproduce here are, I think, not typical, but they certainly suggest a reconsideration of various questions, among others, "What are Americans?"

In a composite people like the American, it is inevitable that the color of the whole should appear different to those who view it from different points. The Englishman is apt to think of the United States as literally a new England, a country inhabited in the main by two classes; on the one hand descendants of seventeenth century English colonists, and on the other newly arrived foreigners.

America as seen from Europe

The continental European, on the contrary, is apt to suffer from the complementary illusion, and to believe that practically all Americans are recent European emigrants, mainly, or at least largely, from his own country. Frenchmen have insisted to me that a large proportion of the United States is French, and Germans often believe that it is mainly German, and that one could travel comfortably throughout the United States with a knowledge of German alone. This is very natural. A man sees his own country-people flocking to America, perhaps partly depopulating great tracts of the fatherland; he receives copies of newspapers in his own language printed in America; if he travels in America he is fêted and entertained everywhere by his own countrymen, and is shown America through their eyes. "I visited for two weeks in Cedar Rapids and never spoke anything but Bohemian," said a Prague friend to me. An Italian lady in Boston said, speaking in Italian, "You know in Boston one naturally gets so little chance to hear any English," much as Americans make the corresponding complaint in Paris and Berlin. On each side such exaggerated impressions are very hard to shake off. What are the facts?

The composition of the American population
The figures were given and the subject discussed in another connection (see pages 4 and 5), but it seems desirable to recapitulate here. In 1900, Negroes, Indians and Mongolians made 12 per cent of the population of the United States; foreign born white persons made 13 per cent more, native born white persons of wholly or partly foreign parentage 21 more, leaving a little over one-half (53 per cent) native whites of native parentage.

Of the foreign born and their children, however, over a tenth are English in origin, and something over a third, including the Irish, are English by inherited speech. On the other hand, of the 53 per cent of persons of native white parentage, many have non-English blood, some of them little and remote, some through all four grandparents.

During the period in which statistics of immigration have been recorded (i. e., 1820–1909), nearly 27,000,000 immigrants have been counted at our ports, of whom the major part have been neither English nor English-speaking. But the diversity goes back, not to 1820, but, as every one knows, to the colonization of the country. Some of the settlements which occupy a place in history, like that of the Swedes in Delaware, did not contribute much blood to the country, but others did so; and what with original non-English settlements, and with the immigration of Germans, Huguenots and, above all, of Scotch-Irish (movements which relatively to the times were very important), it has been estimated that at the time of the Revolution fully one-fifth of the population spoke some other language than English, and that not over one-half were of Anglo-Saxon blood.

Such an estimate is uncertain, and it is to be hoped that the publication of the returns for the census of 1790, now under way, may give us some new light; but at least the statement helps to emphasize the fact that pre-Revolutionary America was by no means wholly English.

After the constitution of the Republic, whole populations were annexed *in situ*, adding considerable non-English populations—the Spanish of Florida, the Spanish-Mexicans of the southwest and California, and the French of Louisiana, St. Louis and the old Northwest. "But in spite of all temptations to belong to other nations," the background and basis of the population is and always has been essentially English.

Background and basis of population English

It was a group of English colonies that united to form the Republic. The strain that has predominated, the men that have shaped and led the nation, have been mainly English or English-speaking, from the men of Virginia and Massachusetts in the Revolution, to the Southerners, New Englanders and "Yankees" who supplied the native element in the westward movement. The America of John Smith and Cotton Mather, of George Washington and Samuel Adams, of Emerson, Poe and Whitman, of Lincoln and Lee, of Sam Houston and Zebulon Pike and the "forty-niners" of California, of Cyrus Field and Edison, of Jay Gould and Morgan, of Joseph Smith and Mrs. Eddy, of President Eliot and President Jordan, of Aldrich and Howells and James, of

Whistler and Sargent—this is what the world understands by America, and it is essentially English in blood, and more so in literary and political tradition.

Language wields an influence beyond all calculation, and language has tended to keep the country open to English thought, and comparatively inaccessible to other outside currents.* Not only is English generally spoken throughout the country, but it is spoken with surprising uniformity, having much less dialectical variation than the languages of old countries like England and Germany, France and Italy.

A new
nation

Yet granting all that has been said as to the English in the United States, it remains true that the other elements which have made a component part of the country since the beginning have not been either thrust out by the English or simply absorbed or altered over by them into their own likeness. There has been thus far an amalgamation, a fusion, creating a new stock which is no longer English, but something distinctive and

---

* According to the census of 1890 persons unable to speak English did not amount to four in a hundred of the total population over ten years old, and of this non-English speaking group nearly four-fifths were foreign born. Among native whites of foreign parentage the numbers sink to nine in a thousand, among native whites of native parentage to under seven in a thousand, or 168,149. This native non-English group included the Spanish speaking population of the Southwest and California, the French speaking population of Louisiana (white and colored), some French Canadians of the second generation in New England (certainly under three thousand) and the Pennsylvania Dutch.

It is interesting to find that these last decreased by more than fifty per cent between 1890 and 1900, and this sudden decrease of the non-English speaking class among a population settled in the country before the Revolution is a surprising testimony to the accelerating force of the tendency toward English speech.

In general the 1900 census gives no information as to inability to speak English among white persons of native parentage, (always speaking of those over ten years old,) but among foreign born whites their proportion has fallen from 15.6 per cent in 1890 to 12.2 per cent in 1900 and among native whites of foreign parentage from 9 in a thousand to 6, showing, at every point when we can institute a comparison, a gain in knowledge of English in spite of the very heavy immigration of the preceding period.

For these data see census of 1890, Population, Part II, pages lx–lxv and 253–277; and census of 1900, Population. Vol. II, pages cxxiii–cxxvii and 489–501.

different,—American. Even our English speech is not the English of England. Our physique, our bearing, still more our tone of mind and spiritual characteristics not only are distinguishable from the English, but mark a national type as distinct perhaps as any.

In spite of my Polish interlocutor's belief that America is not a nation, it has in truth the deepest right to consider itself such. It is an organic whole, inter-sensitive through all its parts, colored by one tradition and bound together not only by love of one material motherland but by one conception of the country's mission and of the means—liberty, enlightenment and prosperity—by which that mission is to be accomplished.

Many Americans feel bitterly that this unity is now seriously threatened by the increasing variety and number of the new contingents of immigrants. In the five-year period following 1900, the immigration other than English and English-speaking amounted to one in twenty of the population in 1900.* Moreover, the foreign population is known to multiply faster than the native element, at least in parts of the country where data have been collected, and perhaps generally. It is therefore clear that as long as conditions remain unchanged, the relative amount of old American stock must progressively lessen. *Is immigration swamping America?*

We say, as long as conditions remain the same, but any of these conditions may change. For instance, on the one hand the volume of immigration may fall off from economic causes, or it may be checked by American action. On the other, the foreign element may reduce its rate of multiplication to the American rate or less as it becomes Americanized. As regards the volume of immigration, it is obvious that we need not stand passive, as before an uncontrollable natural phenomenon. It stands open to us to permit or refuse admission to the country. *Immigration policy*

* This is gross reckoning without allowance for emigrants returning to Europe. Cf. pages 250, 294 and Appendix XVIII, page 463.

Results to
the race

Doubtless the most important issue involved is the racial one. But here we are paralyzed by our comprehensive ignorance of the actual results of race crossings. Those who should be expert give the most contrary opinions. "Only pure races are strong." "Only mixed races are strong." "Mixture within certain degrees of unlikeness is desirable; beyond that line, disastrous."

The investigations of the Immigration Commission under Professor Boas, as just now reported in a preliminary way, appear to point to an unexpected and very rapid assimilation of physical type among the children of immigrants, quite apart from racial intermixture.

Economic
interests
govern

Whatever the truth as to national eugenics, in practice all other considerations are dwarfed by the economic interests involved. The question is and should be discussed in its physical, ethical, humanitarian, social and political aspects, but it is decided, in our present stage of moral development, by bread and butter considerations, from the point of view of American interests. But economic interests themselves diverge and conflict. So far as the nation desires to increase national production, commercial prosperity, dividends and rentals, so far it favors the inflow of labor to increase the product of our national "plant,"—of our land capital, and directing energies. On the other hand, so far as the nation desires to raise the standard of living of the mass of the citizens, to extend democracy within the country on economic and social as well as on political lines,—in a word, to raise wages and increase the influence of the workingman,—so far it is opposed to the admission of new and cheaper competitors in the labor market.

Hitherto the first set of interests has prevailed, with one main exception. Where, as in the case of the Chinese, race prejudice has reinforced the economic interests of the employe, those interests have prevailed and the aliens have been excluded. Otherwise the employer's policy has prevailed, subject to certain modifications,— to provisos as to personal character, health, etc., which are qualitatively valuable but negligible in a quantitative consideration. The same is true of the law against importing labor under contract, which modifies in the interests of the employes the terms under which immigrants may enter the country, but which is easily substantially evaded, does not necessarily cut down the number of arrivals, and is in several respects a two-edged weapon.

In this counterpoise of conflicting class interests it is conceivable that the views of those who try to consider the interests of no one class, of no one nation, might turn the balance, or at least make themselves felt to some effect. But the idealists differ among themselves.

Some see in the American republic the trustee for humanity of an experiment in democracy, the greatest in scale, the most favored in conditions, of which there is any hope. They believe the Anglo-Saxon to have peculiar ability and tact in self-government, and they see in the dilution of this stock by others, and in every new complication of the problem by extraneous difficulties, a threat of a world-tragedy—the shipwreck of the American enterprise in democracy. *Conflicting fears and hopes*

On the other hand, with still wider horizon and still more daring faith stand those who see in this enormous migration a new advance in the slow process of the growth of humanity. They see the newcomers drawn from layers of population where pressure is greatest and progress least possible, into situations where for the first time they meet opportunity; where they not only "have their chance," but where they, and still more their children, do actually gain, not in comfort only, but in freedom, thoughtfulness and self-respect; where with all that they lose, they on the whole profit as men. They see this new freedom, these new demands on life, together with the skill and enterprise to make their realization possible, this new spirit of hope and progress, reacting in turn on the old countries, helping them to reach higher levels. At the same time they hope that the newcomers in America will bring fresh, vigorous blood to a rather sterile and inbred stock, and that they will add valuable varieties of inheritance to a rather puritanical, one-sided culture rich in middle class commonplace, but poor in the power of creating beauty except in the one great field of literature.*

Before such a vast world movement as the modern wage migrations it is impossible not to feel awestruck, not to realize how little it is possible for contemporaries to gauge the results and to compute advantages. In the face of this doubt, the burden of proof seems to be on those who would interfere, who would turn back to their crowded homelands the hordes who are moving in the direction of promised advantage to themselves, drawn by the demand of those who desire their services.

The cost of exclusion
It is easy to talk lightly of more or less arbitrary exclusion rules, of illiteracy tests, and so forth, until one realizes the sort of social surgery that they involve. It is not possible to lower the portcullis without cutting into living flesh. A large proportion of those excluded will necessarily be people bound by the tenderest ties to those already in this country. The individual cases as they occur make this only too real to the spectator in an immigration inquiry court room. The most reasonable rules of exclusion work personal havoc. I have seen a mother fainting before the judges who excluded (as they were bound by law to do) her little feeble-minded boy. The father and elder children were irrevocably planted in America. A return to pogrom-smitten Russia with one child out of her brood would have been bad enough, but she was, as a matter of fact, too far advanced in pregnancy to be able to make the journey. The helpless, weak-minded child had to return without her, to heaven knows what fate, one of the older children being sent back with it. Such cases are inevitable under any hard and fast rule, and one must face them as one

* Mr. Joseph Lee contributed an interesting discussion of this chapter in its original form to *Charities and the Commons*, XIX, pages 1453–5, Jan. 25, 1908, under the title, "Assimilation and Nationality."

A Christmas Manger in a Croatian Church in Pennsylvania

A Croatian Wedding Party in Allegheny, Pennsylvania

faces the cruel by-results of any well-meant legislation; but it should at least be realized that every exclusion provision multiplies such cases. There is no point at which the stream of immigration can be severed without the most tragic results to individual families. Certain measures can, however, be urged with a united front by persons of the most diverse opinions. Among these measures are, first, the abolition of the steerage and the requirement of the equivalent of the present second-cabin accommodations for all passengers; and secondly, the presence of a United States official and above all of a matron on every vessel bringing any considerable number of immigrants. These requirements, in making immigration more expensive, would restrict it in a natural way and without increasing the number of debarments and deportations.

But whatever the future dimensions of the stream of immigration, it has already irrevocably planted here a great collection of representatives of different peoples. Obviously, if the old unity is to be maintained or regained it must be in one of two ways. Either there must be actual fusion through mingling of blood in intermarriage and the creation of one new common stock, with the unity that this implies, or short of this it must be a spiritual fusion alone—assimilation—the growth into similarity in speech, ways and thoughts. *Fusion*

As to the question of racial fusion, we are, as already said, as yet hopelessly ignorant. The biologists are not even ready to go beyond the very vague rule that too wide differences and too little variety are both probably bad.

As regards the Slav in particular, there is not very much to be said in regard to racial amalgamation. It might be hoped that the elaborate census tables, excerpts from which may be found in Appendix XXV, page 475, as to intermarriage would give information, but little of interest can be derived from them, and one is forced back upon generalities and personal impressions. *Slavic amalgamation*

In the first place, then, there is no physical barrier

to intermarriage between Slavs and Americans, nor even so much physical unlikeness as in the case of Italians and Jews, with their more southern characteristics. A Slav of the second or third generation in America would be likely to look, for better for worse, much like "anybody else." I should judge that on the basis of bodily appearance the much mixed Slavic peoples were at least as similar to the much mixed American stock as, say, the French or the Scandinavians.

The barrier is social and psychical, not physical. This barrier is probably overcome most easily in the highest and lowest social classes; on the one hand, in the circles of society where people belong to a more or less cosmopolitan *monde*, on the other, at the bottom, where attractions of sex and personal convenience are not complicated by much regard for estranging abstract ideas.

The social barrier
Elsewhere intermarriage is likely to be deferred till the sense of national difference in the individual case has almost reached the vanishing point. The newcomer is likely to overcome his stand-offishness sooner than the old resident. Partly on this account, but more because of the scarcity of foreign women, cases of mixed marriages in which the man, the active party in bringing about a marriage, is foreign while the wife is native born, are, as the census figures indicate, over twice as many as cases of a foreign wife with a native husband. It is also interesting to notice that it is nearly five times as common for a foreigner and a native to marry, as for foreigners from two different countries to intermarry. Native, however, may mean of the same nationality as the other partner, only of the first generation in America.*

* The figures that we have to go by are those of the last census in regard to the parentage of white persons born in this country, and their meaning is subject to many qualifications. It must not be forgotten, for instance, that what appear to be mixed foreign marriages may involve no more mingling than a marriage between Russian and Polish Jews, or Austrian and Bavarian Germans. On the other hand, the 9,000,000 persons born of unmixed foreign marriages doubtless represent largely marriages contracted before coming to America. See Appendix XXV.

I am led to believe that native does mean this in many cases of intermarriage between the native and the foreign born by seeing how persistent and powerful the sense of difference remains, even after all contrasts in speech and way of life have passed away. For example, I recall how a Bohemian-American acquaintance, an enthusiastic lover of his own people, told me with not unnatural indignation of the offensive attitude of the family of an American girl who was marrying a young Bohemian lawyer, her superior in means, social standing and cultivation.

This deep-seated antipathy or contempt for the unlike—less than kin being regarded as naturally "less than kind"—is especially to be regretted in a country like ours. The incoming groups bring it with them, and they find it here—and not only among the ignorant. The story comes to me of the wife of a Harvard professor who was relating what a pleasant call she had had from a visiting professor from Paris. "He was very agreeable, but then, after all, he was only a Frenchy," she concluded. *Race preju-dice*

Especially is there always a tendency to undervalue any nationality which is known in real life only by representatives of its lower social strata. A rather imposing New York lady whom I met returning from Europe told me that she had been much surprised to find Italy such a civilized country. I must have shown my wonder, for she excused herself by saying that of course she knew better, but she always thought of it as a country of fruit peddlers and dirty, ignorant laborers. To many a New England child the appreciation of the fact that there are Irish people of social prestige comes rather late and with some sense of surprise. So the Germans, the Greeks, the Jews, the Swedes, the Chinese, suffer in the estimation of the half-educated and snobbish wherever they are represented by the poor immigrant class.

It is a shock when we meet, not with humiliated acquiescence in our supercilious judgments, but with a corresponding contempt for ourselves; when we learn, for instance, that we are physically unpleasant to the Japanese owing to a personal odor which they associate with our meat eating.   It is indeed hard for the idea that others do not admire us to penetrate our American minds, but when it does enter it lets in light.

Segregation

The reciprocal feeling of repulsion shows itself especially in the tendency of different nationalities to draw apart.   The phenomenon is familiar enough in the tenement districts, but the same thing occurs, for instance, in a Texas country town where I found that the Germans and Bohemians, who were the main inhabitants, seemed to mix as little as oil and water.   Each of these two nationalities had its own separate public school; in the one, named Germania, both English and German were taught; in the Bohemian school English only, Bohemian not being permitted by the authorities (county or state, I do not know which).   The Americans who used to live in the place had, most of them, moved away.   There seemed to be no friction, only a desire not to mingle. One constantly runs across this fact, that the old settlers tend to withdraw as soon as they begin to be irked by a foreign atmosphere.

Assimilation inevitable

Fusion, then, we can expect only as we outgrow these antipathies and invidious comparisons.   Aside from these there is nothing to keep white peoples apart, and it is hard to resist the conclusion that after a lapse of time which no one can forecast, a fused and welded people will be the outcome, and that we are beholding the gradual creation of a new race of mankind.

To turn to the previous question, assimilation as distinct from fusion, it is clear that the difficulty often lies in the fact that the process is regarded as a one-sided one, as mere absorption or, indeed, as a form of conquest and extirpation.   "We two shall be one and I will be the one."   As a matter of fact, men grow alike in intercourse as inevitably as two communicating bodies of water reach the same level.   But the level reached is a new one, not that of either before the interchange began.

Men mentally copy one another, and Tarde has made *The laws of imitation* the laws of imitation the subject of brilliant sociological generalizations.*   He shows how the choice between the customs in which men differ is sometimes selective—a conscious or unconscious acceptance of the better adapted of the different copies.   More often, perhaps, the choice is determined, not by intrinsic superiority, but by some general rule of preference.   In a state of society where custom reigns, the preference is for the old and established, as such; where fashion and progress are the ruling ideas, what is novel is preferred for that reason.   Again, that which has prestige of any sort is regularly preferred; the rural mode copies the urban; the boy, the man; the socially inferior, the socially superior; backward nations, the leading nation of the day; the minority, the majority, and so on.

In America each immigrant group exerts a certain *American influence preponderant* influence on the community into which it comes, and some newly imported customs take root, either because they are attractive or useful in themselves, or because the newcomers are so represented as to have local prestige; but the laws of imitation work out on the whole to effect a much greater change in the immigrants than in the old settled American community.

In the first place, the convenience of unity makes for Americanization.   The different immigrant groups neutralize one another's influence.   In the steerage of an eastward bound liner one finds perhaps Roumanians, Croatians, Jews, Germans, Italians, using English as their *lingua franca,*—men, some of them from the same village at home, yet unable to speak with one another until now.   It is *E pluribus unum* in a new sense.

Again, in America the way to success on a large scale, (whether political or financial or social or literary success), the only way to a national influence or position, is the way out of the Ghetto, Little Italy or "Bohemian

* Cf. his "Laws of Imitation," translated from the French by Mrs. Parsons.   Holt, 1903.

Town." Thus American ways have practical value, whether good or bad in themselves.

Further, the prestige of numbers is on the side of the American example, and the more so the more scattered the newcomers are. In a close colony the influence is the other way for those inside, yet even so, the attraction of the American mass makes itself felt. As in a teacup one sees the little bubbles drawn to the larger ones and merging instantly when once in contact, so the larger life tends to absorb the smaller group. Indeed, the prestige of America, and the almost hypnotic influence of this prestige on the poorer class of immigrants, is often both pathetic and absurd. They cannot throw away fast enough good things and ways that they have brought with them, to replace them by sometimes inferior American substitutes.

Altering
family
names

Especially deplorable is the way in which men alter or discard their family names. The mine boss or petty official hastens or inaugurates the process by refusing to be bothered with what he calls "outlandish" names which he cannot spell. One Lithuanian family explain carefully their real name and add, "We are called Bruno just because father was put down in the boss's book under the name of an Italian who had gone away." In the Pennsylvania mining towns one finds Slavs who call themselves by such names as John Smith or Tim O'Sullivan or Pat Murphy, in the effort to make Americans of themselves. It is a great pity. The descendants of these men have a right to their paternity, and to the clue to family history given by a family name.

Thus under the joint influence of convenience, ambition and the natural human desire to be like other people, and especially to be like those who occupy the high seats in the synagogue, the unifying change goes on. The early Polish immigrants, patriots and men of education, melted into the common life so completely that later comers could find no point of attachment with them. The recent Slavic immigrants, Poles and others, have

POLISH CITIZENS OF MASSACHUSETTS

1 and 3. Church goers in Northampton, drawn from Polish settlements in Hadley and elsewhere.   2. In Old Hadley.   4. A Polish home in Sunderland

come in much larger numbers; they have formed considerable colonies, and their hearts are set, with a strength of desire which we can hardly conceive, on having their children speak their own language as their proper tongue. The consequence is some degree of success in this aim, but it means, I am convinced, only a retardation of the process.

In Cleveland a Bohemian-American teacher who took the school census found one or two young people in their early "teens," born in this country, yet unable to understand English. This was considered, however, very unusual. I was told of a Hungarian who went to live in Prague, but there in the capital of Bohemia he never learned the language, as he found he could get on with German which he knew. Later he moved to Chicago and lived in the Bohemian quarter, where he found it indispensable to learn Bohemian, and did so, with toil and pains. I have heard of graduates of Polish schools in Chicago and Baltimore who do not understand English. I have been in a Polish "sisters'" school where the children were singing Polish songs. *The unassimilated*

> "We are little exiles;
>   Far from our dear home
>   We weep night and day,"

or something like that, the little round-cheeked boys just in from play on a Chicago sidewalk were chanting.

A thousand more items to show the separateness of the foreign life in our midst might be piled together, and in the end they would all be as nothing against the irresistible influence through which it comes about that the immigrants find themselves the parents of American children. They are surprised, they are proud, they are scandalized, they are stricken to the heart with regret,—whatever their emotions they are powerless. The change occurs in different ways among the educated and the uneducated, but it occurs in either case. *The second generation American*

The prestige of America and the hatred of children for

being different from their playmates is something the parents cannot stand against. The result is often grotesque. A graduate at one of our women's colleges, the daughter of cultivated Germans, told a friend: "My father made me learn German and always was wanting me to read it. I hated to have anything to do with it. It seemed to me something inferior. People in the West call a thing 'Dutch' as a term of scorn. It was not till I was in college that I realized what German literature and philosophy have meant in the world, and that to be a German is not a thing to be ashamed of." Less educated parents, or those using a language less important than German, have a still more difficult task to hold the next generation. "I ain't no Hun, I'm an American," expresses their reaction on the situation.

In a Nebraska county town, in a district largely settled by Bohemians, one father of a family told me his experience. The older children, he said, spoke Bohemian excellently, they used to take part in private theatricals in the Bohemian opera house in the town and did well; but the younger children he simply could not induce to take to it. They knew so little that if he sent them with a message in Bohemian they were likely to make mistakes.

This, I think, is typical. In remote country settlements, or in city colonies of a marked national character, there are plenty of exceptions, but I am confident that the rule is as stated by the Nebraska Bohemian. I have found instances of individual Americans learning Polish, Bohemian or other languages as a matter of convenience, business or pleasure, or as children among playmates, but I have never heard of a community where the process worked in general away from English, not toward it.

Should they learn English only? With the acquisition of English the children are apt to lose their parents' language. Against this the parents strive. It is very common, for instance, for the parents to endeavor to have the children speak only the old language until they go to school, knowing that this is their one opportunity to acquire it, and foreseeing that after the children have entered school, they will speak English not only outside of the home but within it, too, so that it will be impossible to keep English from becoming also the family language. Henceforth the parents must talk with their own children in a foreign medium in which they are consciously at a disadvantage. Is it strange if the parents desire to avoid these difficulties?

What should be the American's attitude toward this question? I personally have no doubt that the right thing to do is to wish the parents Godspeed in their endeavor to have their children learn their language. One of the great evils among the children of foreigners, as every one who knows them realizes, is the disastrous gulf between the older and the younger generation. Discipline, in this new freedom which both parents and children misunderstand, is almost impossible; besides which, the children, who have to act as interpreters for their parents and do business for them, are thrown into a position of unnatural importance, and feel only contempt for old-world ways, a feeling enhanced by the too common American attitude. One hears stories of Italian children refusing to reply to their mother if spoken to in Italian.*

In addition to these considerations, and to the sufficiently obvious fact that to possess two languages instead of one is in itself an intellectual advantage, it is to be remembered that the leaders and teachers of the newcomers must be men who can speak both languages, and that it would be a national misfortune if these were solely men of foreign birth, including none of the second, or later, generations in this country. A final and less important consideration is that to know any immigrant language is money in a man's pocket.

An unfortunate element of difficulty is a common

* Cf. the wise and brief article on "The Struggle in the Family Life," by Miss McDowell of the University of Chicago Settlement. *Charities*, XIII, pages 196–7 (Dec. 3, 1904).

American jealousy of any speech but English. I was amused at the tact with which this feeling was disarmed when some Bohemians once wanted to get permission to use a public schoolroom out of hours for a Bohemian class. "If there should ever be a war," their spokesman said, "our boys would be among the first to volunteer. The Bohemian lad at the front would have to write in English to his mother, and though she could not read his letter she could readily find some one to translate it to her. But the Bohemian letters which he received from her, and which, amid the demoralizing life of the camp have such precious possibilities of influence, would be entirely useless, for he would not be able to read a word of them." The use of the schoolroom was granted.

Parochial schools

We cannot be surprised, however much we may regret it, that the duty of maintaining separate schools is urged on their people by clerical and other leaders, on both patriotic and religious grounds. Among the Slavs the Poles have done the most in this field. Both good priests who fear change on account of its threat to all that they hold most sacred, and greedy priests who desire to keep their hold for lower reasons, naturally strain every nerve to encourage parochial schools. Father Kruszka estimates that at the beginning of 1901 there were in the United States about 70,000 pupils in Polish Catholic schools alone. These schools undertake to train the children in religion and in the Polish language and Polish history, as well as in the regular public school branches. English is taught as a subject throughout the classes, and generally some of the other subjects are taught in English, as, for instance, geography, United States history, and bookkeeping and algebra for those who get so far. It is claimed by those interested, that children leaving these schools for the public schools enter classes above or on a level with those they have left.* I have seen

* There are, however, on the other hand critics of the parochial schools, not only among Americans, but among Poles. In Appendix XXVI, page 477, will be found a clipping on the subject from a Polish paper in Milwaukee.

parochial schools that were subject to criticism from the point of view of modern arrangements for the health and comfort of the pupils, and which were primitive in various ways (the same might be said, alas, of some public schools), but one must admire the devotion of these often very ignorant and poor people, who out of their slender means build and support all these schools, when free schools are already provided out of the taxes.

Outside of the Roman Catholic groups—for instance among the Greek Catholic Ruthenians and the free-thinking Bohemians—it is very usual to find part-time supplementary schools for religious or patriotic instruction, or both. This would seem highly desirable on one condition—that the strain on the children is not too great. Sunday schools and any reasonable amount of vacation schooling seem quite safe, but it is easy to imagine that such extra work is not always relished by the children, and this is one more element of friction which makes it difficult to modify or delay the Americanizing process.

While it can be only an advantage to children to learn their parents' language, there can be no question-that they should in any case learn English, and learn it well. A child has a right to be furnished with this key to success on precisely the same grounds that he has a right to be given a knowledge of those indispensable arts, reading and writing. And in some cases the state, as guardian of the rights of children, may have to require this, just as it has to require universal primary education. *The claim of English*

Beyond fulfilling this duty to the children growing up in our midst, there should be no compulsion in this whole matter, no suspicion of coercion or interference, but a confident faith in freedom, a candid recognition of the right of all to be as different as they please, with no reserves and no jealousies. Public libraries should follow the good example of Passaic and other places, and provide books in the languages in which they will be read. The complaints of Poles in a certain district that they lose their mail because postal employes can speak only English, should be met with a businesslike and cheerful response to their wants.

Apart from the prime reason that this is the just and friendly course, any other breeds ill will and discord out of all proportion to the points at issue. We are dealing often with men sore and irritable from European experiences. A panicky desire to denationalize our immigrants would result in unspeakable disaster, and would have no shadow of excuse. The process of change goes on too fast and too superficially as it is; it needs not forcing, but rather guidance toward what is best in America.

Bad example

Language is not the only, not even the main channel of influence. The example of personal conduct is even more effective. Biologists show us by what natural laws animals take the color of their environment; for different reasons, but as surely, people do the same. Unfortunately, from the nature of the case the immigrant generally begins at the bottom. His helplessness makes him sought for as prey by sharpers and grafters; it is all that the immigration officials can do to keep them off as he lands. As soon as he leaves the paternal care of Ellis Island they attack in force. Boarding-house runners, shady employment agents, sellers of shoddy wares, extortionate hack drivers and expressmen beset his way. One hears all sorts of stories of abuses from both Americans and Slavs—of bosses who take bribes to give employment or to assign good chambers in the mine, of ill usage at the hands of those who should be officers of justice, of arrests for the sake of fees,* of

* For an illustrative anecdote see page 367. Some account of abuses from which immigrants have suffered in judicial proceedings, at the hands of "shyster" lawyers, interpreters and others will be found in the Report of the Commission on Immigration of the State of New York, 1909, especially pages 54–61. See also Blaxter, H. V.: "The Aldermen and Their Courts." *Charities and the Commons*, XXI, pages 851–858 (Feb. 6, 1909), and Koukol: "The Slav's a Man for A' That," ibid., pages 589–598.

unjust fines, of excessive costs paid rather than incur a greater expense. The litigiousness of the Slavs is exploited by "shyster" lawyers till the immigrants learn wisdom by experience.

The suffering and loss are less serious—bad as they are—than the evil lesson. In school the boy who has been cruelly hazed is apt to be cruel to the next crop of victims, and in the same way fraud and harshness tend to reproduce themselves in the larger world.

But it is not only direct ill-treatment that is a peril; the economic pressure and low standards of our lowest industrial strata are in themselves disastrous.

"My people do not live in America, they live underneath America. America goes on over their heads. America does not begin till a man is a workingman, till he is earning two dollars a day. A laborer cannot afford to be an American."

These words, which were said to me by one of the wisest Slav leaders that I have ever met, have rung in my mind during all the five years since he spoke them.* Beginning at the bottom, "living not in America but underneath America," means living among the worst surroundings that the country has to show, worse, often, than the public would tolerate, except that "only foreigners" are affected. Yet to foreigners they are doubly injurious because, coming as they often do, with low home standards but susceptible, eager, and apt to take what they find as the American idea of what ought to be, they are likely to accept and adopt as "all right" whatever they tumble into.

I have been in places in Pennsylvania where all one can say is that civilization had broken down.† Being

* Father Paul Tymkevich, a Ruthenian Greek-Catholic priest of Yonkers. Had he been spared, he could have helped his countrymen and us. See "A Shepherd of Immigrants," for some account of his work. *Charities*, XIII, pages 193-4 (Dec., 1909).

† Some of these conditions have since been studied and made public in the Pittsburgh Survey. The worst conditions seemed to be in Allegheny and in outside boroughs.

in a city, people could not help themselves individually, as they might have done in the country, and the family with the most decent ideas was dragged down by the general degradation of the environment. From the dance hall at one end of the street, to the white door-bells, all up and down its length, which openly denoted kitchen bar-rooms, everything smelled of lawlessness. The water was known to be infected with typhoid, and had to be boiled to be safe—a considerable expense and trouble, and an excellent reason for drinking other things. In the spring the refuse of the winter stood in heaps before the doors. The deep clay mud made some streets absolutely impracticable in wet weather. The neighbors mended them by pouring on ashes and miscellaneous dumpage. Assaults, in some cases ending in death, took place night after night, and although the identity of the offender was supposed to be known, or rather because of that fact, no one dared move in the matter. The mayor stood for "running the town wide open," and was said to have investments not only in saloons but in immoral resorts.

This is a composite picture. I saw or heard of each thing on the spot, but not all were in the same place. Now consider that it is into surroundings like these that we put our new employes; that this is the example that we set before our new fellow citizens. Under such circumstances the Americanization over which we are so complacent is by no means all gain. The change is often, also, a change for the worse among those who do not have to begin at the bottom.

The intoxi-
cation of
making
money

The intoxication of the change from homes where there is no money to be made and no chance for any sort of advancement, to the boundless financial opportunities (or what appear such) of America, often results in a moral degeneration. Too often the educated immigrant has been imbued by what he has read before coming here with the idea that America is "the land of the almighty dollar," and arrives neither expecting nor desiring any-

A CROATIAN PICNIC ON LAKE SUPERIOR

thing else of the country than the opportunity to get as rich as possible. It is a tragi-comedy to see at once the native American upbraiding the newcomer with having come here solely to make money (while he himself, very likely, is living in a town which he has chosen purely for the same reason, and which he makes no effort to serve), and the newcomer, making no move to get into touch with American strivings towards ideals, proclaiming to every one that America is a country where no one cares for anything but material success.

Is it strange that a Croatian physician wrote to me from Pittsburgh as follows?   *Two views of America's meaning*

"The great question appears to be how soon immigrants can be assimilated, to what degree, and if they are going to be good citizens. It has been found that everybody who gets Americanized becomes a good citizen, i. e., a shrewd business man who knows his value at the polls, who knows how to outwit the intricacies of the law, and how to be ashamed of his origin, his name and his religion. . . . So far, good citizenship is associated with the ideal of a policeman, alderman, political boss, financier, and so forth, all of whom we can reach and see as good American citizens with rather dubious moral qualities, while educated and fine feeling people are out of reach; the immigrant knows nothing of their existence. There is no need to fear that, so long as the flesh pots are full in America, assimilation and the making of 'good citizens' will meet any obstacle; individuals, families, nations will readily submit to everything American if it only means their material advantage, while they don't expect in this country any moral profit, as there is none to get—for them. I think that it would be a good thing if some one would show to the Americans their real moral standing in the world. Unquestionably, with their freedom and their natural resources there should be much more feeling for righteousness, for tolerance and for art in this country. Had the Americans not the right men in Washington, they would develop in a few years into the most zealous worshippers of the Golden Calf and of nothing else. All this is, of course, merely my opinion, but it is based upon actual observation of the people during seven years. I believe in American, that is in human, ideas, and will hope that the minority will be able to win over the majority and make the people what they ought to be: first of all, honest."

This letter is the more impressive because the writer is in the habit of pointing out to his countrymen at home the advantages which emigration, which is very unpopular in Croatia, may bring to the country, and what America has to teach. Like Professor Muensterberg, he is heroic enough to tell unpalatable truths to both sides. May they be like Mrs. Browning's anti-slavery message—"very salt and bitter and good."

After these disillusioned words from one Slav who has known America in person, it is with a sense almost of heartbreak that one reads the Ode to Columbia which the Slovak poet Hurban Vajansky wrote in prison in Segedin.* He begins by describing the situation in Hungary of those struggling to preserve their nationality:

> The old men die beholding only ruin,
>> Their eyes behold no hope, no truth in life,
> The young men fall away, at once or slowly,
>> Even the strong give up the ceaseless strife;
> Only a handful still keep up the fight,
> Only a few lights burn amid the night.
>
> Suddenly rises proudly from the ocean
>> A giant woman with majestic face;
> Shining the drapery of her snowy garments,
>> Her eyes like flames upon the altar place;
> Her god-like breast like marble fair to see.
> "You poor forsaken children, come to me."

* For his personal history, political position and literary standing, see Čapek's "The Slovaks of Hungary" and Seton-Watson's "Racial Problems in Austria-Hungary."

"O come; I know you bring but humble packets
    That from your fatherland no gems you bring,
That murderous wrath has chased you from your dwellings,
    From the ancestral soil to which you cling;
No gifts I offer, but this one reward—
Time for free work, for human rights regard."

And they, disgraced here in their native country,
    Lift up proud heads since o'er the seas they came,
And there he speaks aloud who here was silent,
    And glories there in what he here thought shame.
Columbia to him self-knowledge gives,
Surprised he finds that only now he lives.

Hail to our brothers whom their stepdame cruel
    Drove from their simple huts, their native sod.
Columbia, thou hast smitten off their fetters,
    Lifting them up to manhood, heaven and God.
O land of Christopher, may Christ repay
What for my brothers poor thou dost today.

O sons of mine, O sisters, O my people,
    I from my distant prison speak to you.
O holy, holy heights of Tatra's mountains,
    Our fathers' fields, naught is on earth like you.
This sinful, wretched world does not command
Aught lovelier, brothers, than the Slovak land.

So in the rigid torment of my prison,
    Weeping, I call to you my countrymen.
Oh, be you faithful to our speech, our music,
    And if it may be, come, come home again.
If not, yet still in heart with us remain.
I cease, the jailer shakes the clanking chain.*

Another view of what America is to the Slav is that
of Father Tymkevich, whom I have already quoted.

* A version of the whole poem, by Miss Alice Stone Blackwell,
appeared in the Springfield *Republican*, Jan. 14, 1908; from this
I have borrowed freely, while not adopting it as it stands, as I
wished to preserve the metre of the original. Both versions are
based on an English prose translation kindly made for me by
Miss Ethel J. Cablk of New York.
    It is interesting to compare with this the Ruthenian ode to
Canada, quoted in part in Appendix XI, pages 449–450.

Economically he thought they gain by coming here, "physically and morally, no. In the city they need more morality." Then again, with deep wisdom, "They have no habits. The first step in civilization is to acquire habits, and where can they acquire them? On the streets? In the saloon?

"What my people need most is leaders,—leaders to form themselves upon, to give them a standard of ambition. Other people have leaders of their own, strong and influential men among the immigrant body, and Americans who know something about them and are ready to take an interest in them."

And again, almost like a cry, the phrase I have previously quoted, "My people are perishing for lack of vision."

The isolation of the immigrant "The Slavs are orphans in this country," he said. And it is in a sense true. It is not chiefly that they have no government of their own, concerned for them as Italy is concerned for the Italians; it is far more that coming to America they are cut off from the life of their old country, without getting into contact with the true life of their new home, from which they are shut off by language, by mutual prejudice, by divergent ideas. To them, both parents are dead, the fatherland that begot them and the foster-mother that supports without cherishing them.

In some ways this isolation is harder for the educated than for the laborer. A man like Father Tymkevich himself is in a position of almost intolerable loneliness. Intelligent, sensitive, separated from his own people by all that separates a scholar from peasants, he was a complete stranger in a community unused to look for friends and associates among foreigners.

America's duty What then ought we to be doing for these strangers in our midst? If we ought not to try to "Americanize" them, have we no obligations toward them at all?

It is obviously our plain duty to give the immigrant (and every one else) fair treatment and honest government, and to maintain conditions making wholesome, decent living possible. This is the minimum required at our hands, not by the Golden Rule—that asks much more—but by the most elementary ethic of civilization. Yet as a matter of fact, this simple, fundamental thing we cannot do. It is not in our power.

We can and must do what in the end will be a better thing. We must get our new neighbors to work with us for these things. If their isolation is not to continue, America must come to mean to them, not a rival nationality eager to make them forget their past, and offering them material bribes to induce them to abandon their ideals. We must learn to connect our ideals and theirs, we must learn, as Miss Addams has demonstrated, to work together with them for justice, for humane conditions of living, for beauty and for true, not merely formal, liberty.

Clubs and classes, libraries and evening schools, settlements and, above all, movements in which different classes of citizens join to bring about specific improvements in government or in living conditions, are of infinite value as they conduce to this higher unity, in which we may preserve every difference to which men cling with affection, without feeling ourselves any the less fellow citizens and comrades.

APPENDIX

APPENDIX

STATISTICAL, BIBLIOGRAPHICAL AND OTHER NOTES

I

POPULATION OF AUSTRIA-HUNGARY BY LANGUAGE

I. Population of Austria by Language. 1900.

The facts are expressed in percentages. Where a language is spoken by less than one per cent it is omitted.

a. Non-Slavic Languages

Province	German	Italian-Ladinish	Roumanian	Magyar
Lower Austria.........	95.0	..	..	..
Upper Austria.........	99.4	..	..	..
Salzburg..............	99.5	..	..	..
Styria	68.7	..	..	..
Carinthia.............	74.8	..	..	..
Carniola.............	5.6	..	..	..
Trieste and district	5.9	77.4	..	..
Goricia-Gradisca	1.6	36.0	..	..
Istria.................	2.1	40.5	..	..
Tyrol.................	55.5	44.3	..	..
Vorarlberg...........	94.7	5.0	..	..
Bohemia..............	37.3	..	..	..
Moravia..............	27.9	..	..	..
Silesia...............	44.7	..	..	..
Galicia...............	2.9	..	..	..
Bukowina	22.0	..	31.7	1.3
Dalmatia	..	2.6	..	..
All Austria...........	35.8	2.8	.9	.03

429

b. Slavic Languages

Province	Bohemian, Moravian, Slovak	Polish	Ruthenian	Slovenian	Servo-Croatian
Lower Austria......	4.7	..	..	..	..
Upper Austria......	..	..	..	..	..
Salzburg...........	..	..	..	..	..
Styria.............	..	..	..	31.1	..
Carinthia..........	..	..	..	25.1	..
Carniola...........	..	..	..	94.2	..
Trieste and district..	..	..	..	16.3	..
Goricia-Gradisca....	..	..	..	62.4	..
Istria.............	..	..	..	14.2	42.6
Tyrol..............	..	..	..	..	..
Vorarlberg.........	..	..	..	..	..
Bohemia...........	62.7	..	..	..	..
Moravia	71.4	..	..	..	..
Silesia	22.0	33.2	..	..	..
Galicia	..	54.8	42.2	..	..
Bukowina..........	..	3.7	41.1	..	..
Dalmatia	..	..	..	..	96.7
All Austria........	23.2	16.6	13.2	4.7	2.8

For all Austria: German 35.8, Slavic 60.4, Italian 2.8, Other 9.

Austrian Census of 1900.
Die Summarischen Ergebnisse der Volkszählung, page xxxix.

II. Civil Population of Hungary by Language. 1900.

Language	Kingdom of Hungary, Inclusive of Croatia-Slavonia		Hungary Proper, Exclusive of Croatia-Slavonia	
	Number	Per Cent	Number	Per Cent
Magyar.............	8,679,014	45.4	8,588,834	51.4
Roumanian.........	2,785,265	14.6	2,784,726	16.7
German.............	2,114,423	11.0	1,980,423	11.8
Slovak.............	2,008,744	10.5	1,991,402	11.9
Croatian...........	1,670,905	8.7	188,552	1.1
Servian.............	1,042,022	5.5	434,641	2.6
Ruthenian..........	427,825	2.2	423,159	2.5
Other..............	394,142	2.1	329,837	2.0
	19,122,340	100.0	16,721,574	100.0

Hungarian statistical year book, Vol. XIV, page 20.

The racial complexity is greater than is indicated by the statistics of language, since we must add Jews and Gipsies. Of the former there were 826,222 registered as "Israelites" in Hungary proper in 1900 besides an unknown number of Christianized Jews. Gipsies according to a special count in 1903 numbered 274,940 of whom 104,000 counted themselves as Magyars. If these and the Jews be deducted from the Magyar population, this would lose over a million of its eight or nine million total.

It must be remembered, too, that Hungarian statistics are the subject of much criticism by the minor races of Hungary as understating their numbers. Cf. Čapek: "The Slovaks of Hungary," page 145.

For further comment on the validity of these statistics see above, p. 12.

II

A PEASANT MILLIONAIRE

The following picturesque account of a Hungarian peasant appeared in the New York *Tribune:*

Johann Bagi, the peasant millionaire of Hungary, never dropped the old patriarchal custom of presiding at table, around which the men and women and boys of his great farm sat, ranged according to the rank held by each: the overseers nearest the youngest members of the master's own family, the head servants, male and female, next, opposite to one another. Then came the keepers of the linen, the fodder, the granaries, followed by the chief coachman and the rest—ploughmen, horsemen, cattle keepers, cheese and butter women, milkers, men of all work, and maids and boys.

Though Johann Bagi and his family and visitors ate off silver as heavy as that used in the Hofburg, he never wore a coat indoors, nor outside, weather permitting. Once, in the good old absolutistic days, he was found some three hours from home, tramping his fields, when a gendarme rode up and asked for his passport.

"Need none, as I am on my own ground."

"Where do you live?"

"If you ride sharply, you may reach the house in two hours and a half."

"And you insist that this is your property?"

"Yes, all around is mine, as far as your eyes travel."

Of course the gendarme thought Johann an impostor, and conducted him to the town lock-up. He was put in a dirty cell, and immediately asked for a bucket of water to clean up. While thus engaged, the governor of the province came to inspect the jail, and discovered the man, with whom only recently he had dined at the emperor's table.

Soon after the revolution had abolished feudal landlordism in Hungary, Johann's forn er master, Count George Karolyi, got into trouble, and the family sent for a Vienna lawyer of high repute to straighten out matters.

"I came to see if I could not be of some service to the highborn gentleman," said Johann, introducing himself to the new administrator.

"My good man," replied the lawyer, regarding the millionaire peasant's unpretentious dress, "no use troubling thee. We want a capitalist with about 200,000 florins in cash."

"Sorry," said Bagi, "that I did not know the exact figure. I brought what I had in the local bank—180,000 florins—but the rest can be had from Budapest in about three days. Will that do, your honor?"

III

AUSTRIAN TAXES*

The average taxation in Austria in 1899 was 38 crowns per capita. The chief taxes and their sources in 1903 were as follows:

DIRECT TAXES	IN MILLION CROWNS
Land	53.6
House tax	89.9
Tax on industries	87.7
Personal income tax	55.1
Dividend tax	8.6
Salary tax	2.2

INDIRECT TAXES	IN MILLION CROWNS
From alcohol	86.0
beer	76.0
sugar	100.9
mineral oil (kerosene, etc.)	18.8
meat	16.3
salt monopoly	46.3
tobacco monopoly	225.2
stamps and fees	154.7
railway tickets	16.8

* Twardowski, Dr. J.: "Statistische Daten über Oesterreich." Vienna, 1902.

"Finances and General Economic Conditions of Austria-Hungary for the years 1900–1904." (British) Foreign Office, April, 1905.

IV

SLAVIC IMMIGRANTS NOT COMING TO JOIN RELATIVES OR FRIENDS

Based on data in Annual Report of Commissioner of Immigration for year ended June 30, 1908, page 15.

NATIONALITY	TOTAL ADMITTED	NOT COMING TO JOIN RELATIVE OR FRIEND	
	Number	Number	Per Cent
Bohemians and Moravians...............	10,164	202	1.9
Croatians and Slovenians...............	20,472	1006	4.9
Dalmatians, Bosnians and Herzegovinians ..	3,747	352	9.3
Poles..................	68,105	1010	1.4
Ruthenians............	12,361	389	3.1
Slovaks..............	16,170	256	1.5
Together..............	131,019	3215	2.4
Bulgarians, Servians and Montenegrins	18,246	2410	13.2
Russians..............	17,111	1169	6.8
Together..............	35,357	3579	10.1

V

STATISTICAL SOURCES OF INFORMATION AS TO EMIGRATION FROM AUSTRIA-HUNGARY

There are several sources for data of a statistical sort in regard to Slavic emigration from Austria-Hungary, but even taken all together they are far from giving complete information.

The American immigration and census figures are considered elsewhere; the European sources seem to be as follows:

I. "EMIGRATIONS-TABELLEN"

Under the old régime the right to emigrate at will was not admitted. By legislation of 1820 and 1823 the political authorities were required to keep so-called *Emigrations Tabellen*, or registers of all persons who "betook themselves to a foreign state with the intention not to return" whether they went with or without official permission. It was not, however, till 1850 that these tables were regularly published (and then apparently only those for Austria). These figures may be found partly in *Mittheilungen aus dem Gebiete der Statistik*, partly in the successive numbers of the *Statistische Monatschrift*. They are also quoted at some length in Professor Buzek's "Das Auswanderungs-problem" and a few data are given above, page 72.

In 1867 freedom of emigration was granted and from this time these official figures became increasingly unreliable, until in 1884 they were given up as too remote from the truth to be useful. The figures show province of origin, sex and age, but not destination. For the period 1850 to 1868 inclusive, i. e., the time during which the data are comparatively valid, they are as follows:

EMIGRATIONS TABELLEN, 1850–1868

PROVINCE	MALE	FEMALE	TOTAL
Lower Austria	757	583	1,340
Upper Austria	1,214	1,027	2,241
Salzburg	218	222	440
Styria	148	100	248
Carinthia	57	33	90
Carniola	135	87	222
Istria, Gradisca-Goricia, Trieste and District	660	469	1,129
Tyrol and Vorarlberg	1,865	962	2,827
Bohemia	22,351	21,294	43,645
Moravia	1,365	1,243	2,608
Silesia	745	609	1,354
Galicia and Bukowina	943	513	1,456
Dalmatia	92	34	126
Total	30,550	27,176	57,726

BY AGE—ALL AUSTRIA

AGE	NUMBER
0–7 years	11,723
7–17 "	12,683
17–40 "	23,798
40–50 "	6,859
50+ "	2,663
Total	57,726

Although the law requiring the registration of emigrants referred to the monarchy, and therefore included Hungary, the Hungarian data are not available so far as known to me.

II. FIGURES FROM THE AUTHORITIES AT THE PORTS OF EMBARKATION

As a second source of information we have the figures of the authorities at the various ports which serve as gateways for the floods of emigrants. Until comparatively recently this meant for Austro-Hungarian emigration mainly Hamburg and Bremen. Many, however, who started from these German ports went to England and made the journey to America thence. In later years Amsterdam, Rotterdam and Antwerp, Havre and Marseilles, and quite recently Genoa, Naples, Fiume and Trieste, have all become important points of departure.

Since the Austrian government felt the need of the information which the old Emigrations Tabellen had at least essayed to provide, the Ministry of the Interior in 1889 requested the various ports to furnish more complete data and itself collated these figures for its own use. They appear in the *Oesterreichische Statistische Handbuch*. The International Statistical Institute in 1891 also passed a resolution looking toward completer and more uniform reports. Different countries, however, still differ in the fullness of the records which they keep of emigrants leaving their ports. In Germany the embarkation figures are published in the yearly *Berichten des Deutschen Reichscommissärs für das Auswanderungswesen* and similarly in various other countries. England only distinguishes emigrants as English and foreign (which is of the less importance here as Austrian emigrants going *via* England have already been registered at a continental port), but generally emigrants are distinguished by countries, Austria and Hungary being given separately. For a study on racial lines, however, like the present one, such data afford little information, as an "Austrian" or a "Hungarian" may be of any one of many nationalities.

The following figures for the years 1902–1907, are taken from the *Oesterreichisches Statistisches Handbuch* for 1907 (page 46), and are based on the figures furnished by the authorities of the different ports. They give a good idea of the relative importance of different routes, which however differs for emigrants from different provinces, the Fiume route being convenient for Istria, Dalmatia and Croatia, German routes for Bohemia, and so on.

The corresponding figures for Hungary are published in the Hungarian statistical yearbooks of which I have used the official French version, the *Annuaire Statistique Hongrois*.

I. FIGURES FROM PORTS OF EMBARKATION FOR EMIGRANTS FROM AUSTRIA.

PORT OF EMBARKATION	1902	1903	1904	1905	1906	1907	TOTAL
Trieste	...	19	1,981	8,750	8,265	8,893	27,908
Fiume (by Cunard Line)	...	...	1,145	1,632	2,643	1,975	7,395
Hamburg	24,331	37,231	28,172	28,621	36,647	51,890	206,892
Bremen	51,321	44,793	30,698	49,466	52,549	61,389	290,216
Amsterdam		1					1
Rotterdam	8,408	8,592	5,403	5,074	4,797	8,083	40,357
Antwerp	8,053	9,849	9,551	20,336	22,005	36,721	106,516
Havre	?	?	?	7,167	5,595	5,752	18,514
Other French Ports	?	?	33	61	74	(circa)180	348
Genoa	1,574	1,079	1,338	2,001	2,729	2,142	10,863
Naples	...	752	675	621	1,050	329	3,427
Total	93,687	102,316	78,996	123,729	136,354	177,354	712,436

II. Figures from Ports of Embarkation for Emigrants from Hungary.

Port of Embarkation	Average 1886–1890	Average 1891–1895	Average 1896–1900	Average 1901–1905	1906	1907
German ports	22,074	15,724	23,212	74,546	100,464	112,788
Antwerp	1,187 *	5,213	5,872	13,774	13,831	17,293
Dutch ports	954 *	3,441	2,140	6,835	6,593	13,799
Italian ports	1,508 *	628	832	287	375	155
Liverpool	..	..	..	1,957	542	1,963
Havre	..	..	..	1,020	3,412	9,523
Fiume	..	..	..	11,595	49,332 †	47,620
Trieste	..	..	..	173	3,621	6,028
Total	25,723 *	25,006	32,056	110,187	178,170	209,169

* Average of two years.

† Foreigners [i.e. non-Hungarians] included.

Year Book, 1907, page 65.

III. Figures from German Ports for Emigrants from Hungary.—By Destinations

Destination	Average 1896–1900	Average 1901–1905	1906	1907
Great Britain........	64	133	25	11
United States........	22,967	73,066	98,537	111,634
British N. A.........	101	652	227	302
Brazil.............	14	24	2	3
Argentina...........	9	610	1,660	836
Africa.............	50	58	1	1
Total	23,205	74,543	100,452	112,787

Year Book, 1907, page 65.

IV. Total Oversea Emigration from Hungary by Years as Reported from Ports of Embarkation

Year	Number
1896................................	24,846
1897................................	14,310
1898................................	22,965
1899................................	43,394
1900................................	54,767
1901................................	71,474
1902................................	91,762
1903................................	119,944
1904................................	97,340
1905................................	170,430
1906................................	178,170
1907................................	209,169
Total...........................	1,098,571

Year Book, 1907, page 65.

The Hamburg authorities give figures showing the numbers embarking for America direct and *via* England. In 1882 the figures were respectively 9,257 and 6,757, while in 1901 with 12,493 going direct across the ocean, only 26 were going *via* England.*

III. THE CENSUS

Important information can be deduced from the Austrian and Hungarian census returns. By comparing the population at a given date with that of a previous date plus the excess of births over deaths during the intervening period there can be found the loss or gain which is to be attributed to migration—

* Thirring: "Die Auswanderung aus Ungarn," page 25.

that is, to the excess of emigration over immigration or the reverse. The difficulties in using this information (apart from complications of detail, as for instance the presence of bodies of soldiers) are three. First, if there has been a loss of population no indication is given as to where the missing population has gone. It may be in South America or it may be just over the boundary. Second, only net results are shown, so that any influx of immigrants (as for instance the considerable immigration of Italians into Austria) will neutralize and hide a corresponding number of emigrants. Third, internal migrations may confuse the significance of the net results. For instance, a rural district might show a loss of population and a city district show a gain and yet the city might have been sending emigrants out of the country (though fewer than were coming in to it from elsewhere), while the country might have sent none abroad in spite of its diminished population. While this is not a very likely supposition, the fact that there is no way of controlling such facts is a serious defect in this method as a means of studying emigration. Some data obtained in this way will be found for Austria on page 48. For Hungary see page 104.

The corresponding figures for Croatia-Slavonia are given in Appendix XIII, page 453.

It is interesting to notice how the loss of population in Hungary differs from the numbers of emigrants registered as embarking. See Thirring, "Die Auswanderung aus Ungarn," pages 19 and 11.

PERIOD	EMBARKATIONS OF HUNGARIAN SUBJECTS	DECREASE OF POPULATION OF HUNGARY BY EXCESS OF EMIGRATION OVER IMMIGRATION
1881–1890	186,822	−195,209
1891–1900	285,317	−184,766
Total	472,139	−379,975

In the first decade more are lacking than the transatlantic movement accounts for, i. e., many emigrated elsewhere than to America; in the second period on the contrary, more are counted as embarking than the net loss of population allows for, which must mean that many returned and many embarked more than once.

IV. SPECIAL INQUIRIES AS TO EMIGRATION AT THE POINT OF ORIGIN

For Austria in general I have found no special data of this sort, except the figures for Carniola (so far as I know unpublished) which are given in Appendix XII.

For Hungary the situation is quite different since here there are two special independent sources of statistics as to emigrants; namely, reports of passes issued, and reports from local authorities as to those known to have emigrated from the place. As the year 1904 marks a change of law which affected these immigration statistics, it will be well to first consider data collected previous to that time.

HUNGARY; BEFORE AUGUST, 1904
(1) *Statistics of Passes*

Since up to August, 1904, passes were to be had only from the Ministry of the Interior at considerable expense of time and money, emigrants as a matter of practice very generally took their chances and emigrated without the required papers. One hears of men satisfying the request of German officials for papers with any sort of Magyar documents that they might happen to have, all being alike unintelligible.

The data drawn from passes were unreliable both because many thus went without them and also because men who never emigrated often procured passes, expecting to emigrate or on the chance of wanting to do so suddenly.

(2) *Reports from Local Authorities*

From 1899 on, the local authorities (the town clerk, or in the cities, the burgomaster) were required to fill out reports for all persons emigrating whether with or without a passport. These were quite full as to the points to be covered but failed to cover nearly all who actually emigrated. For instance in 1903 the figures for passports, incomplete as these were as a measure of emigration, proved to be larger by over a third than the figures for those reported as emigrating *with or without passports*.

Thirring (pages 19–20) gives the following figures showing how far both sets of Hungarian figures fall below those of the ports of embarkation:

YEAR	FIGURES OF EUROPEAN PORTS OF EMBARKA-TION	HUNGARIAN FIGURES	
		Passes to America	Oversea emigrants
1899	43,393	36,431	26,515
1900	54,767	44,105	31,092
1901	70,941	55,724	45,196
1902	91,762	77,249	56,346

HUNGARY SINCE AUGUST, 1904
(1) *Statistics of Passes*

In August, 1904, a change of law went into effect. Instead of passes being issued only by the Ministry of the Interior they were now to be issued in cities by police authorities, elsewhere by a county official, and were made procurable on written application at a cost of only one crown or about twenty cents. I was told that under the new order few went without passes, and that those going *via* Fiume all procured them, since the officers of the recently established Cunard service from that port absolutely required these papers.

(2) *Reports from Local Authorities*

The new legislation requires reports from the local authorities as to (a) those who have gone without passes and (b) those who have returned. It may be practicable to procure this information in small places where everyone's affairs are known, but in a city it is impossible to keep track of everyone in spite of the elaborate Hungarian system of police registry, which obliges weary travelers to report their arrival often before they have had time to wash their hands or even get off their gloves. An emigrant from a city, or one who leaves a village home and returns, as many are said to do, to Budapest, is likely to escape notice and in so far to invalidate the returns.

PUBLICATION OF HUNGARIAN DATA

Since January, 1905, the official monthly publication of the Central Statistical Commission has been printing all these various data as they come in, and the Hungarian statistical year books also give them in great fullness.

The last year book that I have seen contains among others the following data, all relating to 1907:

I. TOTAL EMIGRATION FOR 1907 FROM HUNGARY PROPER AND FROM CROATIA-SLAVONIA.

A. By Sex

	FROM HUNGARY PROPER	FROM CROATIA-SLAVONIA
Men	119,712	21,265
Women	47,777	4,228
Total	167,489	25,493
Per 1000 of population	9.3	9.8

B. By Language

Magyar	57,974	765
German	35,721	1,890
Slovak	32,439	298
Roumanian	26,481	10
Ruthenian	4,939	149
Croatian	1,128	15,461
Servian	7,020	6,494
Other	1,787	426

C. By Destination

America	149,372	22,828
Germany	6,644	710
Roumania	7,740	50
Other Balkan States	794	660
Other European States	1,767	1,228
Other parts of the world	1,172	17

Hungarian statistical year book, 1907, page 66.

These data are also given in full by counties and cities.

II. HEADS OF FAMILIES OR PERSONS EMIGRATING INDEPENDENTLY

A. By Age

EMIGRATING TO AMERICA

AGE	FROM HUNGARY PROPER	FROM CROATIA-SLAVONIA
Under 20	29,300	6,021
20–29	47,868	7,300
30–39	32,016	5,039
40–49	15,285	2,708
Over 50	1,928	390
	126,397	21,458

B. By Occupation

OCCUPATION	FROM HUNGARY PROPER		FROM CROATIA-SLAVONIA
	Emigrants to America	Slovak Emigrants (to all Destinations)	Emigrants to America
Agriculture Farmers*	12,345 ⎫	4,587 ⎫	12,308 ⎫
Laborers and servants	71,789 ⎬ 84,134	12,747 ⎬ 17,334	6,971 ⎬ 19,279
Miners	805 ⎭	386 ⎭	7 ⎭
Industrial employers	2,989	561	349
Commercial employers	283	51	19
Employed in commerce and transportation	14,964	2,483	1,201
Intellectual professions	369	24	35
Laborers	14,952	4,839	259
Domestic service	6,284	1,822	160
Other	1,617	415	149
Total	126,397	27,915	21,458

Hungarian statistical year book, 1907, pages 68 and 69.

Figures are also given by religious denominations and by months.

* The French term is *Production du Sol (Patrrons)*.

III. Returned Emigrants

	To Hungary Proper	To Croatia-Slavonia

A. By Sex

Men	37,721	7,296
Women	5,807	412
Total	43,528	7,708
Per 1000 of population	1.4	3.0

B. By Language

Magyars	14,730	136
Germans	6,226	315
Slovaks	11,281	50
Roumanians	6,842	1
Ruthenians	2,336	35
Croatians	345	5,100
Servians	1,270	2,000
Other	498	71
	43,528	7,708

C. By Country whence Returned

From America	40,483	6,692
Other	3,045	1,016

Hungarian statistical year book, 1907, page 72.

These data are also given by counties and cities, and in another table ages, occupations, and religion are given by nationalities.

IV. Data as to Passports

	Hungary Proper	Croatia-Slavonia
Total passports	237,607	49,461
" passports for emigration	178,299	47,534
" persons thereby authorized to travel	301,401	56,599
Total persons thereby authorized to emigrate to America	198,886	42,763

Hungarian statistical year book, 1907, page 77.

These figures are also given by counties and cities.

V. OTHER SOURCES

An additional source of information are the data furnished by the Cunard Line as to passengers going and returning in its Fiume vessels.

The figures as to persons naturalized or renouncing allegiance (*pertes de nationalité*) are also published, but in 1907 the cases of loss of nationality ascribed to America are three! The corresponding Austrian figures are equally unenlightening.

In addition to strictly statistical material Consular Reports sometimes supply valuable material.

The *Statistische Monatsschrift* publishes a continuous series of reports on emigration, which so far as America is concerned are largely a reproduction or working over of American statistics, of the data from the ports of embarkation and so forth. Occasionally, however, they contain valuable additional material. A complete list of these articles will be found in the Bibliography under *Statistische Monatsschrift*.

For Carniola and Croatia further statistical data, besides that in the text, will be found in Appendix XII and Appendix XIII respectively.

VI

SOME BOHEMIAN NURSERY RHYMES

I

(To be said pointing to the eyes, cheeks, etc., with appropriate pantomime.)

"Here are two little candles, [*eyes*]
"Here are two little cushions, [*cheeks*]
"Here is the pulpit,
"Here is the priest,
"Here is the little grave,
"Here is the little bell, ting a ling a ling."

II

"The little mouse was cooking porridge, [*to be said tickling the palm of the child's hand*]
"In an iron sauce pan;
"When it was done,
"She gave it around;
"To this one she gave it with a little spoon [*counting on the fingers and toes*]
"To this one she gave it with a little fork,
"To this one she gave it with a little stirrer,
"To this one she gave it with a little ladle,
"And to this one she did not give any,
"And she ran and she ran to camp [*running the fingers over the child's side and tickling*]
"For the sack of ginger
"Till she got here" [*tickling under the arm*].

III

"There was a little house,
"In the little house was a little table,
"On the little table a little dish,
"In the little dish a little water,
"In the little water a little fish.
"Where is the little fish?
"Pussy ate it.
"Where is pussy?
"She ran into the woods.
"Where are the woods?
"They are burned to dust.
"Where is the dust?
"The water carried it away.
"Where is the water?
"The cattle drank it up.
"Where are the cattle?
"The masters ate them.
"Where are the masters?
"They lie in the churchyard."

The first two of these jingles are translated from an oral version given me in New York.

Further Bohemian nursery rhymes may be found in the little Slabikař (or primer), with illustrations by the well known Bohemian artist Aleš, which is used by many Bohemian-American classes. (See Bibliography under Frumar.)

VII

SLOVAK POPULATION

I borrow the following data from Mr. Seton-Watson's "Racial Problems in Hungary," pages 11–12.

"The Slovaks form an overwhelming majority of the population in seven counties:

	SLOVAKS	PERCENTAGE OF SLOVAKS	PERCENTAGE OF MAGYARS
Arva	80,456	94.7	1.7
Trencsén	265,838	92.8	2.8
Liptó	75,739	92.5	3.3
Zólyom	110,633	89.4	7.2
Turócz	38,218	73.6	4.2
Nyitra	312,167	73.1	18.8
Sáros	114,132	66.1	6.1

"In this territory, which covers an area of 22,380 square kilometers, there are thus 997,183 Slovaks, side by side with 114,310 Magyars and 71,497 Germans. Of these latter races, however, the majority live upon the racial frontier, and thus the redistribution of the counties on a racial basis would leave a million Slovaks faced by a minority of 72,993 Magyars and Germans (seven per cent).

"In five other counties the Slovaks form over one-third of the population:

Szepes	99,240	58.2
Bars	94,777	57.5
Pozsony or Pressburg	153,466	51.1
Gömör	74,417	40.6
Hont	45,173	39.5

"In these counties there are no fewer than 347,421 Magyars and 60,932 Germans; but as all these counties are situated upon the linguistic frontier, redistribution would in their case also bring about a separation of the two races, and merely leave small German minorities in the counties of Szepes and Bars.

"There are also substantial Slovak minorities in the counties of Zemplén (106,064, or 32.4 per cent), Ung (42,582, or 28.1 per cent), Nógrád (64,083, or 26.9 per cent) and Abauj-Torna (35,809, or 22.9 per cent). On the west, the Slovaks extend into Moravia, from the neighborhood of Hodonin (Göding) almost as far as Kremsier, and in recent years this tiny territory has become a focus of Slovak national life, where the forces repressed in Hungary by the reactionary policy of the Magyars are able to expand freely. On the east the Slovaks are bounded by the Ruthenes; but the racial frontier has, during the past generation, moved slowly but steadily eastwards, at the expense of the latter race, which allows itself to be assimilated more easily than either the Slovaks or the Roumanians.

"In addition to the main Slovak districts, there are various racial islets in the neighborhood of Budapest, Komárom (Komorn) and Gödöllö, and in the rich plains of the Banat and the Bácska, near Nagy Becskerek and Neusatz (Ujvidék). The county of Pest contains 33,299 Slovaks, in addition to 24,726 in the capital itself: the county of Békés, 64,343 (or 23.2 per cent); Bács, 28,317; Csanád, 17,239; and Torontál, 14,761. Despite their isolation these little colonies are strongly Slovak in feeling, and being more prosperous and independent than their northern kinsmen, have succeeded in returning a Slovak member of Parliament (in Kölpény, county of Bács-Bodrog)."

See also Professor Niederle's *Národopisná Mapa Uherských*

Slováků. (Ethnographical Map of the Hungarian Slovaks on the basis of the census of 1900.) For the ethnography of Hungary see also above, page 31; Map III, page 32; and page 86.

VIII

STUDIES OF SLOVAK EMIGRATION

Besides the official statistics there are two studies of Hungarian emigration of some importance in Magyar. One is by Dr. Gustav Thirring, "A Magyarországi Kivándorlás és A Külföldi Magyarsag," Pp. x, 366; tables, charts and maps. Kilian, Budapest, 1904. A review of Thirring's book appeared in Társadalompolitikai Közlemények (Socialpolitische Mittheilungen) 1, 2. Budapest, 1904.

The gist of Dr. Thirring's article also appeared in German as "Die Auswanderung aus Ungarn; Beiträge zur Statistik und topographischen Verteilung der Auswanderung" in the *Bulletin de la Société Hongroise de Géographie*, Vol. xxx, 1902 (Also separately printed).

The other is by Mr. Lorant Hegedüs, "A Magyarok Kivándorlása Amerikába. Az Amerikai Magyar Telepek—A Felvidek Nyomora— Kivándorlás es Bevándorlás Szabalyozasa." (The Emigration of Hungarians to America—The American-Hungarian settlements—The Misery of Upper Hungary—The Regulation of Emigration and Immigration). Pp. 102, Budapest, 1899. Reprinted from the Budapest *Szemle* (Review). Mr. Hegedüs visited Magyar and other Hungarian colonies in America. Although I do not read Magyar, by having this and the preceding book translated to me I was able to make some use of them.

In Slovak is Dr. Emil Stodola's "Prispevok ku Statistike Slovenska" (Contributions to Slovak Statistics). Pp. 31. Turčiansky Sv. Martin, 1902. (Part IV, Emigration to America, pp. 14–21.) Useful also are Dr. Stodola's articles in *Die Politik* of Prague under dates June 18, 20 and 21, 1902. Another source is a manuscript account of Slovak emigration, kindly prepared for me by Mr. Miloslav Rybák, mining engineer.

IX

SLOVAK MEMORIALS PUBLISHED IN AMERICA

The following protests as to Hungarian policy have been published by Slovaks in the United States.

"Memorial presented by the Roman Catholic priests of Slovak nationality to their Eminences the Cardinal Archbishop, Archbishops and Bishops of the United States." Pp. 6. Wilkes-Barre, Dec. 1, 1902. (Signed by twenty-nine priests).

"Memorial addressed by American citizens of Slovak birth to the Hungarian members of the Interparliamentary Peace Congress held in the city of St Louis, Mo., September, 1904." Printed in English, French and Magyar, and signed by six presidents of Slovak societies (representing a combined membership of 65,000), and by six editors.

"Hungary Exposed." No date, author, nor place of publication is given. This is the republication in Magyar, with an English translation and an introduction, of "Ministerial Communication No. 393. Directed, Feb. 4 of the current year, by the Hungarian Minister of Religion and Instruction to the Cardinal Prince Primate, Archbishop of Esztergom in reference to the Spiritual Care of Hungarians who have emigrated to America." The complaint is that this secret order recommended that the priesthood in America be used for purposes of Magyarization and espionage, and that newspapers are supported to the same end.

X

A CASE OF HUNGARIAN POLITICAL PERSECUTION

Some of the grounds on which three young Slovak theological students were expelled from a Hungarian Catholic College in Vicuna in 1906 are grotesque to the point of the incredible. It was said that they (a) "formed a special group in which they aired their favorite views and drew suspicion on themselves by their somewhat retiring manners;" (b) that they nevertheless propagated Slovak national ideas, and that one of them admitted this, so that inquiry was unnecessary, though it was actually held; further (c) that they were in direct intercourse with two Slovak nationalists "which is in itself a sufficient reason for expulsion from an institute which aims at training patriotic pupils"; (d) "though in the institution every foreign (sic) language is forbidden, they smuggled in Mr. S. and talked Slovak with him." The students were not heard in defence. One of them whose Rector spoke of his *mores optimes et pietatem insignem* is now a priest in America. See Seton-Watson, pages 213–4.

Mr. Rovnianek, the Pittsburgh banker, came to America in a similar way, having been expelled from a seminary, as I have been told, because a Slovak book was found in his trunk.

XI

A RUTHENIAN POET IN CANADA

A series of articles called "Five Days in Galicia," by E. W. Thomson, appeared in the *Boston Transcript*, the first one under date of Oct. 17, 1905. The following passage seems worth quoting:

"How the Galicians, whether they be German, Polish, or Russian, feel toward their new country may best be told by their own poet Edmonton and the surrounding region know him only as Michael Gowda, interpreter to the Bellamy Agricultural Implement Company, and a very keen, clever stump speaker at election times. He was a school teacher in Galicia, and has been out here, after escaping from the Austrian army, some eight years. Michael has translated "Snowbound" and twenty more of Whittier's poems into Russian verse. He is engaged on an extensive translation, into English prose, of the popular poetry of his Slav countrymen. Moreover, he is, unless I mistake, a genuine poet himself. Here is a rough versification, made by myself, from his prose English translation of his poem to Canada.:

To Canada

O free and fresh—home Canada! can we,
    Born far o'er seas, call thee our country dear?
I know not whence nor how that right may be
    Attained through sharing blessings year by year.

We were not reared within thy broad domains,
    Our father's graves and corpses lie afar,
They did not fall for freedom on thy plains,
    Nor we pour out our blood beneath thy star.

Yet we have liberty from sea to sea,
    Frankly and true you gave us manhood's share,
We who, like wandering birds, flew hopefully
    To gather grain upon thy acres fair.

From ancient worlds by Wrong opprest we swarmed
    Many as ants, to scatter on thy land;
Each to the place you gave, aided, unharmed,
    And here we fear not kings nor nobles grand.

And are you not, O Canada, our own?
    Nay, we are still but holders of thy soil,
We have not bought by sacrifice and groan
    The right to boast the country where we toil.

But, Canada, in Liberty we work till death,
    Our children shall be free to call thee theirs,
Their own dear land, where, gladly drawing breath,
    Their parents found safe graves, and left strong heirs

To Homes and native freedom, and the heart
    To live, and strive, and die if need there be,
In standing manfully by Honor's part
    To save the country that has made us free.

They shall as brothers be to all the rest,
    Unshamed to own the blood from which they sprang,
True to their Father's Church, and His behest
    For whom the bells of yester Christmas rang.

XII

EMIGRATION FROM CARNIOLA TO AMERICA.

Data from inquiry carried on through the post office
by the Governor of Carniola since 1893

I. EMIGRATION, BY DESTINATIONS, 1893-1904

YEAR	EMIGRANTS TO			
	North America	Brazil	South America	Total Emigration to America
1893 (last half).......	414	3	1	418
1894.................	203	7	..	210
1895.................	1145	60	118	1329
1896.................	1625	832	441	2898
1897.................	978	96	44	1118
1898.................	1674	17	..	1691
1899.................	3287	6	38	3331
1900.................	2854	2	1	2857
1901.................	2189	..	6	2195
1902.................	5119	..	..	5119
1903.................	6511	1	..	6512
1904.................	2883	..	..	2883
Total (11½) years).	28,882	1024	649	30,561

II. NUMBER OF MARRIED AND SINGLE MEN, WOMEN AND CHILDREN EMIGRATING, 1893-1904

YEAR	SINGLE	MARRIED	WIVES	CHILDREN	OTHER MEMBERS OF HOUSEHOLD (*Angehörige*)
1893 (last half).	218	140	13	47	..
1894..........	118	61	2	25	4
1895..........	726	426	36	121	20
1896..........	1307	819	187	544	41
1897..........	563	336	36	181	2
1898..........	1039	532	15	101	4
1899..........	1946	1148	63	173	1
1900..........	1665	989	24	174	5
1901..........	1383	686	27	98	1
1902..........	3226	1559	63	256	15
1903..........	4184	1864	83	360	21
1904..........	1970	662	42	200	9
Total (11½ years)	18,345	9222	591	2280	123

III. Causes of Emigration and Disposition of Property

YEAR	PROPERTY		CAUSE OF EMIGRATION			
	Sold	Not sold	Hope to earn more	En-cum-bered prop-erty	Fear of army service	Other
1893 (last half)	10	88	374	12	1	31
1894..............	..	41	143	11	0	56
1895..............	11	279	891	86	2	350
1896..............	19	563	1978	23	1	896
1897..............	12	282	713	24	0	381
1898..............	5	431	1292	58	0	341
1899..............	15	920	2766	51	2	512
1900..............	10	582	2466	50	2	339
1901..............	12	457	1920	32	6	237
1902..............	19	1181	4513	63	9	534
1903..............	22	698	6067	52	1	392
1904..............	10	477	2443	23	3	414
Total (11½ years).....	145	5999	25,566	485	27	4483

XIII

EMIGRATION FROM CROATIA-SLAVONIA

I. Emigration to North America from Croatia-Slavonia, By Counties and Municipalities

COUNTY	1899	1900	1901	1902	1903	1907*
Lika-Krbava.....	46	37	153	102	407	2439
Modruš-Fiume....	1300	1742	2563	3804	3787	3039
Agram	1453	1108	2850	4040	5167	5616
Varasdin	3	1	78	115	199	7658
Bjelovar Križevci.	78	207	767	1051	1333	3389
Požega	37	55	100	342	574	1551
Virovitica........	1	2	6	17	123	2424
Syrmium	5	85	196	350	290	2285
Municipality						
Agram	..	11	3	4	7	121
Varasdin.........	..	..	1	..	17	27
Osiek	..	..	..	..	3	143
Zemun	..	..	..	8	..	136
Total for Croatia-Slavonia	2923	3248	6717	9833	11907	22,828

* The figures for 1907 are from the Hungarian statistical year book, 1907, page 65.

II. Croatia-Slavonia; Net Loss and Gain by Emigration and Immigration

County	1881–1890		1891–1900		For the Period	
	Absolute	Per cent	Absolute	Per cent	Absolute	Per cent
Lika-Krbava........	—15,365	—8.8	—12,901	—6.7	—28,266	—16.2
Modruš-Fiume......	—15,633	—7.7	—18,037	—8.2	—33,670	—16.6
Agram.............	—10,860	—2.8	—15,164	—3.9	—26,024	—6.6
Varasdin	—7,427	—3.2	—14,112	—5.5	—21,539	—9.4
Bjelovar Križevci..	+18,130	+8.3	+7,347	+2.8	+25,477	+11.6
Požega............	+15,279	+9.1	+9,031	+5.1	+24,310	+14.6
Virovitica.........	+11,949	+7.2	+1,459	+0.7	+13,408	+8.4
Syrmium...........	+14,029	+4.7	+5,230	+1.5	+19,259	+6.5
All Croatia-Slavonia......	+10,102	+0.5	—37,147	—1.7	—27,045	—1.5
Municipality						
Agram	+7,911	+27.9	+18,030	+18.1	+25,941	+91.4
Osiek	+1,896	+10.4	+33,895	+19.7	+5,791	+31.8
Total Population						
Hungary...........	—215,118	—1.6	—169,544	—1.1	—384,662	—2.8
Croatia-Slavonia....	+19,909	+1.0	—15,222	—0.7	+4,687	+0.2
Together...........	—195,209	—1.2	—184,766	—1.1	—379,975	—2.4

Thirring, "Auswanderung aus Ungarn," pages 9–11.

III. Emigration from Croatia-Slavonia to North America During the Four Years 1900–1903.

A. All Emigrants.   Total, 31,705

By Sex:
Male........................28,912
Female......................2,793

    Total...................31,705

By Language:
Croatian or Servian........30,339
Bohemian...................364
Magyar.....................297
German.....................583
Other, or Unknown..........122

                           31,705

By Religion:
Roman Catholic.............21,358
Greek Catholic.............499
Greek-Oriental.............9,584
Lutheran...................220
Reformed...................18
Israelite..................25
Other, or Unknown..........1

                           31,705

By Months:
January....................2769
February...................4073
March......................5653
April......................3632
May........................2546
June.......................1584
July.......................1490
August.....................2736
September..................2663
October....................1821
November...................1515
December...................1223

                           31,705

B. Persons Emigrating as Heads of Families or Independently.

Total, 30,682. Of these, 540 were heads of families accompanied by others.

By Sex:

Male.. 28,377
Female...................................... 2,305

    Total.................................. 30,682

By Age:

15 years and less........................... 401
15–20 years 6895
20–25   " 4870
25–30   " 5936
30–40   " 8348
40–50   " 3317
50–60   " 419
60   " 32
Unknown..................................... 464

    Total.................................. 30,682

By Occupation:

Intellectual vocations...................... 30
Agriculture and production of raw material .. 22,741
Industry.................................... 1,328
Commerce and transportation 98
Day labor not further specified 6,111
Other....................................... 374

    Total.................................. 30,682

By Property:

With property............................... 10,590
No property................................. 20,092

    Total.................................. 30,682

C. Persons Accompanying Head of Family. (*Familien Mitglieder*.) Total 1023

Over 12 years:

Male.. 194
Female...................................... 188

    Total.................................. 382

Under 12 years:

Male.. 341
Female...................................... 300

    Total.................................. 641

Grand Total, 1023

These data with the exception of those for 1907 in Table I and the whole of Table II were given me in manuscript by the kindness of the statistical authorities in Agram. For further Croatian statistics see Appendix V, pages 441–443.

XIV

BOHEMIAN AND POLISH LITERATURE OF AMERICAN SETTLEMENT

(1) BOHEMIAN

The Bohemian Literary Society, I believe, subsidized an attempt of a Mr. Habernicht to write the history of Bohemians in America, and two or three parts, one on Texas, which I have used, one on Missouri, which I have never been able to secure, were published in Bohemian in St. Louis, but the undertaking appears to have fallen through.

Mr. Thomas Čapek's "Památky Českých Emigrantů v Americe" (revised edition, Omaha, 1907), is mainly antiquarian.

Much material is in fugitive form,—pamphlets, articles, almanacs, memorial and occasional publications, and so forth. Of these I may mention the following.

"Česka Osada a její Spolkový Život v Cleveland, Ohio," is an illustrated history of Bohemians in Cleveland prepared for the Prague Ethnographical Exposition of 1895 and published by the Volnost press in Cleveland. Pp. 192.

" Památník Ceských Evanjelických Církví Spojených Státech"; this is a memorial of Bohemian Protestant churches in the United States, including an account of all Bohemian congregations of the following denominations, Presbyterian, Independent, Reformed, Congregational. Methodist and Baptist, existing in the year 1900; edited by V. Šiller, V. Prucha and R. M. De Castello, printed by the Krestansky Posel in Chicago, and liberally illustrated with cuts of churches, ministers and so on. Pp. 290.

"Krátké Dějiny a Seznam Česko-Katolických Osad ve Spoj. Státech Amerických" is a brief history and register of Bohemian Catholic colonies in the United States, in honor of the twenty-fifth jubilee of the Very Rev. Joseph Hessoun, by Rev. P. A. P. Houšt. St. Louis, 1890. Pp. viii, 552. Illustrated.

"Památnik 50ti Leteho Jubilea Č. S. P. S.; 1854–1894"; a memorial of the fiftieth jubilee of the Chekho-Slavonic Benevolent Society. Illustrated.

"Dějiny Česko-Narodniho Hrbitova v Chicago, Ill., etc." A history of the Bohemian National Cemetery in Chicago from its founding in 1877 to its 25th anniversary in 1902, by Frank Zdrubek. Geringer, Chicago. Pp. 143.

"Česke Chicago, Adresar Ceských Obchodníků, Živnostníků a Spolků." Bohemian Chicago, a directory of Bohemian tradesmen, business men and associations, including a short history of Bohemian Chicago; published by the Narodna Tiskarna (National Press,) Chicago, 1900. Pp. 252.

"Katolík Česko-Americký Kalendár," published by the Bohemian Benedictine press, 616 Allport St., Chicago.

"Almanach Česko-Slovanského Lidu v New Yorku a Okolí." (Almanac of the Bohemian-Slavonic people in New York and environs.) Published yearly by the Česka Tiskarna, 312 W. 71st St., New York City.

"The Catholic Bohemians of the United States," Rev. Valentine Kohlbeck in the *Champlain Educator*, xxv, pages 36–54; (Jan.–Mar. 1906).

Scattered material may also be found in the *Bohemian Voice*, a short-lived paper published in English for a short time with the hope of informing Americans about their Bohemian neighbors.

(2) POLISH

Father X. W. Kruszka, of Ripon, Wisconsin, has written a "Historya Polska w Ameryce" ("History of Poles in America"), in eight small volumes, published in Milwaukee, the first in 1905, the eighth in 1906, and illustrated with cuts, chiefly of buildings and of Polish priests and leaders.

In the Lemberg Magazine *Lud*, xi, pages 248–269 (Oct. 1905) appeared an article "Ludność Polska w Stanach Zjednoczonych Ameryki Polnocnej" by Dr. Michal Janik, based on two trips to America and containing references to several Polish accounts of Poles in America. I have an English manuscript translation of this article.

"Polskie Kolonie w Stanach Zjedn. poln. Ameryki e ich Krotkie Dzieje" ("Polish Colonies in the United States and a Short History of Them"), appeared in the Catholic Polish Calendar for 1895, published at 141 and 143 W. Division St., Chicago.

Charles Kraitser's "The Poles in the United States of America, Preceded by the Earliest History of the Slavonians and by the History of Poland" (Philadelphia, 1837, pp. 196) is a disappointing little volume. The discussion of Poles in the United States takes up only the last four pages, and consists of the text of a Polish memorial to Congress asking for a grant of land, of the act granting the land, and of complaints of the way in which the Polish exiles had been treated by Gallatin and others.

XV

CENSUS DATA TO 1880 WITH A CRITICAL CONSIDERATION OF THE USE OF THE CENSUS FOR THE PURPOSES OF THIS STUDY

For statistical data for the period, 1850–1880, we have nothing better than the census figures presented graphically in Chart I. Unfortunately the use of the census figures as a source of information as to Slavic population in the United States is subject to grave drawbacks. For the census does not deal with the question of nationality, but of nativity only, and its list of countries of birth is both incomplete and changing.

In 1850, of the countries with which we are concerned, Austria and Russia alone were given. In 1860 Poland was added, though Poland was and is divided among the three neighboring countries, Germany, Russia and Austria, and is therefore without claim to be considered at present as an independent country.

In 1870 Bohemia and Hungary were added to the census list, leaving Austria to mean Austria apart from Hungary and minus two of its seventeen *Länder*, viz. Galicia (or Austrian Poland) and Bohemia. These changes not only make comparisons impossible, but cause unavoidable pitfalls in getting the facts. Many natives of Bohemia would doubtless say, quite correctly, that they were born in Austria; many natives of Poland that they were born in Russia, Germany or Austria as the case might be; while others would reply, as the census plan intended that they should, more specifically. Natives of Moravia, Bohemia's sister province, all appear as Austrians, though to all intents and purposes they make one group with the Bohemians, a group perhaps as homogeneous in blood, speech, feeling and tradition as the Poles. In Texas, for instance, where the "Bohemians" are mostly from Moravia, the importance of the group is hidden entirely by the registration of all Moravians as natives of Austria in one group with Austrian Germans, Jews, Slovenians, Tyrolese Italians, and so on.

On the other hand it is easy to speak as if "natives of Hungary" were synonymous with Hungarians, "natives of Poland" with Poles, and so on. As a matter of fact this is of course far from being the case. In 1905, for instance, the immigration figures show Hungarians (Magyars) making only a little over a quarter of the immigrants from Hungary, while Russians are under two per cent of the immigrants from the Russian empire and Finland. The Jews especially are a complicating factor, presenting as they do characteristics and problems in sharp contrast with those of other immigrants, but remaining indistinguishable, so far as the census data go, from other persons born in the same country. This difficulty especially affects the Polish data. In 1905 there entered at our ports 92,388 Jews from Russia and 11,114 Jews from Austria; those who came from the Polish provinces of Russia and Austria (that is, doubtless the greater part of them), appear in the census simply as "natives of Poland" and quite distort the facts. Especially as regards concentration in cities the Polish Jews make the census figures for "natives of Poland" almost meaningless as regards Poles.

XVI

FATHER KRUSZKA'S LIST OF THE FOUNDING OF POLISH PARISHES PREVIOUS TO 1880

The first time a state appears in the list it is in italics.

YEAR OF
FOUNDING

1855. Panna Marya (*Texas*).

1856. Bandera, San Antonio, St. Jadwiga, Meyersville, Yorktown (Texas).

1857. Parisville (*Michigan*).

1858. Polonia (*Wisconsin*).

1863. First Milwaukee (Wisconsin).

1864. Pine Creek (Wisconsin).

1866. Washington, Krakow, Clover Bottom, Union (*Missouri*).

1868. Northeim (Wisconsin).

1869. First Chicago (*Illinois*).

1870. Bluff, New Waverly (Texas); Manitowoc (Wisconsin); Shamokin (*Pennsylvania*).

1871. Plantersville, Cottage Hall (Texas); Bay City (Michigan); Second Milwaukee, Hull (Wisconsin); Otis (*Indiana*).

1872. Marlin, Flatonia (Texas); first Detroit (Michigan); Cincinnati (*Ohio*).

1873. Bremond, Huntsville (Texas); first Grand Rapids (Michigan); first Berlin (Wisconsin); second and third Chicago (Illinois); Shenandoah (Pennsylvania); New York, first Buffalo, Dunkirk (*New York*); Berea (Ohio); Winona, Delano, Faribault (*Minnesota*).

1874. La Salle (Illinois).
1875. Brenham (Texas); Manistee (Michigan); Beaver
Dam, Princeton, Independence, North Creek
(Wisconsin); St. Joseph (Missouri); Radom (Illinois); Nanticoke, Excelsior, Blossburg, Pittsburg (Pennsylvania); Jeffersonville, Lanesville
(Indiana); Brooklyn (New York); first Toledo,
first Cleveland (Ohio).
1876. Czestochowa, Anderson (Texas); Poznán (Michigan);
Stevens Point, Poniatowski (Wisconsin); Brim-
field (Illinois); first South Bend (Indiana); second
Toledo (Ohio); N. Poznán (*Nebraska*).
1877. First Mt. Carmel (Pennsylvania).
1878. Krok (Wisconsin); first St. Louis (Missouri).

Kruszka, X. W. "Historya Polska w Ameryce," Milwaukee,
1905; II, pages 6, 7.

XVII

SLAVIC IMMIGRATION BY NATIONALITIES SINCE 1899

These figures are based on those in the Annual Reports of
the Commissioner General of Immigration and in the Monthly
Immigration Bulletins.

I. Total Slavic Immigration to the United States for the Decade 1899–1908

A. By Countries of Last Previous Residence

Country	Numbers	Per cent of total Slavic Im-migration for the Period
Austria-Hungary................	1,162,124	69.0
Russian Empire.................	424,966	25.0
German Empire.................	33,427	2.0
Bulgaria, Servia and Montenegro ..	32,396	2.0
Turkey in Europe..............	19,785	1.0
Other........................	14,501	1.0
Total.....................	1,687,199	100.0

B. By Nationality

NATIONALITY	NUMBERS	PER CENT OF TOTAL SLAVIC IMMIGRATION FOR THE PERIOD
Polish..........................	743,151	44.0
Slovak.........................	322,525	19.0
Croatian and Slovenian.........	275,800	16.0
Ruthenian....................	103,660	6.0
Bohemian and Moravian	84,877	5.0
Bulgarian, Servian and Montenegrin	76,047	4.5
Russian......................	56,242	3.0
Dalmatian, Bosnian and Herzegovinian...................	24,897	1.0
Total......................	1,687,199	100.0

II. IMMIGRATION TO THE UNITED STATES FROM THE FIVE MAIN SOURCES OF SLAVIC EMIGRANTS DURING THE DECADE 1899–1908

COUNTRY	TOTAL IMMIGRATION FROM SPECIFIED COUNTRY	SLAVIC IMMIGRATION FROM SPECIFIED COUNTRY	SLAVIC PERCENTAGE OF TOTAL IMMIGRATION FROM SPECIFIED COUNTRY
Austria-Hungary.........	1,893,676	1,162,124	61.0
Bulgaria, Servia and Montenegro	33,649	32,396	96.0
German Empire.........	320,658	33,427	10.0
Russian Empire.........	1,441,823	424,966	33.0
Turkey in Europe........	52,921	19,785	37.0
Total................	3,742,727	1,672,698	..

III. SLAVIC IMMIGRATION BY NATIONALITIES

YEAR	BOHEMIAN AND MORAVIAN	BULGARIAN, SERVIAN AND MONTENEGRIN	CROATIAN AND SLOVENIAN	DALMATIAN, BOSNIAN AND HERZEGOVINIAN	POLISH	RUSSIAN	RUTHENIAN	SLOVAK
1899	2,526	94	8,632	367	28,446	1,774	1,400	15,838
1900	3,060	204	17,184	675	46,938	1,200	2,832	29,243
1901	3,766	611	17,928	732	43,617	672	5,288	29,343
1902	5,590	1,291	30,233	1,904	69,620	1,551	7,533	36,934
1903	9,591	6,479	32,907	1,736	82,343	3,608	9,843	34,427
1904	11,911	4,577	21,242	2,036	67,757	3,961	9,592	27,940
1905	11,757	5,823	35,104	2,639	102,437	3,746	14,473	52,368
1906	12,958	11,548	44,272	4,568	95,835	5,814	16,257	38,221
1907	13,554	27,174	47,826	7,393	138,033	16,807	24,081	42,041
1908	10,164	18,246	20,472	3,747	68,105	17,111	12,361	16,170
1909	6,850	6,214	20,181	1,888	77,565	10,038	15,808	22,586

XVIII

SLAVIC ALIENS, ADMITTED AND DEPARTED, 1908–1909

RACES	JULY, 1908, TO MAY, 1909, INCLUSIVE		
	Admitted	Departed	Increase (+) or decrease (−)
Bohemian and Moravian	6,738	1,102	+ 5,636
Bulgarian, Servian, Montenegrin	6,934	3,352	+ 3,582
Croatian and Slovenian	22,284	11,120	+ 11,164
Dalmatian, Bosnian, Herzego-vinian	1,889	715	+ 1,174
Polish	74,524	25,204	+ 49,320
Russian.....................	9,522	6,099	+ 3,423
Ruthenian	16,237	1,959	+ 14,278
Slovak.....................	26,560	‾10,224	+ 16,336

For these figures see Monthly Immigration Bulletins.

XIX

IMMIGRANT ARRIVALS WHO HAVE BEEN IN THE UNITED STATES BEFORE

These figures, drawn from Table III of the Annual Report of the Commission General of Immigration, cover the fifteen immigrant groups which were the largest in 1906 and also the four additional Slavic groups which do not come within this list. Slavic groups are in italics; the rank of groups as regards total numbers in 1906 is indicated by numbers in parentheses. The same figures for 1900 are given in a second column.

PERCENTAGE OF IMMIGRANT ALIEN ARRIVALS WHO HAVE BEEN IN THE UNITED STATES BEFORE

NATIONALITY	1906	1900
(7) English..............................	27.3	30.6
(10) Irish.................................	21.4	16.9
(13) Scotch..............................	20.3	35.6
(11) *Slovaks*.............................	18.5	16.0
(5) Scandinavians........................	16.7	18.9
(6) North Italians	14.4	16.3
(4) Germans.............................	13.2	12.2
(1) South Italians........................	13.0	11.2
(8) *Croatians and Slovenians*..............	12.6	9.8
(9) Magyars.............................	9.8	12.1
(14) *Ruthenians*...........................	9.7	8.5
(3) *Poles*................................	5.9	4.9
(12) Greeks...............................	5.6	8.9
Dalmatians, Bosnians and Herzegovinians	4.7	9.0
Russians...............................	4.5	2.6
Bulgarians, Servians and Montenegrins..	3.5	7.8
Bohemians and Moravians.............	3.4	5.4
(15) Lithuanians...........................	2.8	1.3
(2) Hebrews.............................	1.7	1.9
All immigrants....................	17.4	11.6

XX

WAGES OF UNSKILLED LABORERS

Data as to the wages of Slavic laborers are given in Mr. F. J. Sheridan's article "Italian, Slavic and Hungarian Unskilled Immigrants in the United States," U. S. Bulletin of Labor, No. 72, Sept., 1907, pp. 427 and 428.

The following table, showing as it does higher rates for Slavs and Hungarians than for Italians, is of interest.

NUMBER AND PER CENT OF ITALIAN, SLAVIC AND HUNGARIAN, UNSKILLED LABORERS SENT OUT BY NEW YORK EMPLOYMENT AGENCIES, RECEIVING SPECIFIED RATES OF WAGES PER HOUR

I a. Slavs and Hungarians—Northern States.

WAGE GROUP	LABORERS RECEIVING EACH RATE OF WAGES		AVERAGE RATE OF WAGES PER DAY OF 10 HOURS FOR EACH GROUP	TOTAL LABORERS IN EACH GROUP	
	Number	Rate Per Hour		Number	Per cent
Under $0.130 per hour ..	62	$0.1250	$1.25	62	4.77 ⎫
$0.130 or under $0.150 per hour.............	22	.1300			⎪
	92	.1350	1.37	191	14.69 ⎬ 74.92
	51	.1400			⎪
	26	.1450			⎪
$0.150 per hour.........	721	.1500	1.50	721	55.46 ⎭
$0.155 or under $0.175 per hour.............	10	.1550			
	27	.1600			
	15	.1650	1.63	72	5.54
	9	.1667			
	11	.1700			
$0.175 or over per hour...	199	.1750			
	27	.1800	1.78	254	19.54
	10	.1900			
	18	.2000			
Total............	1,300	.1531	1.53	1,300	100.00

I b.   Italians—Northern States.

WAGE GROUP	Number	Rate Per Hour	Avg	Number	Per cent
Under $0.130 per hour ..	5	$0.1200	$1.25	805	5.93 ⎫
	800	.1250			⎪
$0.130 or under $0.150 per hour.............	1,346	.1300			⎪
	1,056	.1350	1.36	4,056	29.87 ⎬ 92.33
	1,309	.1400			⎪
	345	.1450			⎪
$0.150 per hour.........	7,675	.1500	1.50	7,675	56.53 ⎭
$0.155 or under $0.175 per hour.............	72	.1550			
	329	.1600			
	4	.1610	1.61	639	4.71
	143	.1650			
	87	.1660			
	4	.1700			
$0.175 or over per hour..	327	.1750			
	51	.1780			
	14	.1850	1.76	402	2.96
	8	.1875			
	2	.1945			
Total............	13,577	.1455	1.46	13,577	100.00

II *a*. Slavs and Hungarians—Southern States.

Under $0.130 per hour..	16	$0.1042	$1.21	349	19.40	
	84	.1137				
	234	.1250				
$0.130 or under $0.150 per hour.............	15	.1273	1.34	582	32.35	82.38
	285	.1300				
	74	.1350				
	119	.1367				
	36	.1375				
	68	.1400				
$0.150 per hour.........	551	.1500	1.50	551	30.63	
$0.155 or under $0.175 per hour.............	262	.1600	1.60	262	14.56	
$0.175 or over per hour ..	51	.1750	1.79	55	3.06	
	4	.2000				
Total...........	1,799	.1414	1.41	1,799	100.00	

II *b*. Italians—Southern States.

Under $0.130 per hour ..	68	$0.1136	$1.22	286	10.40	
	14	.1166				
	14	.1200				
	164	.1250				
	26	.1272				96.19
	145	.1363				
$0.130 or under $0.150 per hour	124	.1375	1.37	305	11.09	
	36	.1400				
$0.150 per hour.........	2,055	.1500	1.50	2,055	74.70	
$0.155 or under $0.175 per hour.............	45	.1600	1.60	45	1.63	
$0.175 or over per hour .	60	.1750	1.75	60	2.18	
Total...........	2 751	.1464	1.46	2,751	100.00	

"It should be stated that the rates quoted cover 1905 and part of 1906, and therefore the advances in wage rates for laborers, especially in the North, on account of the demand that has taken place generally since that time, are not included in this presentation. In many cases there have been advances of 10 per cent or more." It is of interest to compare these wages with those quoted on page 56.

XXI

NATIONALITY OF MEN EMPLOYED BY AN-THRACITE AND BITUMINOUS COAL COMPANIES

The following data are from page 413 of Mr. Sheridan's article quoted in Appendix XX.

ANTHRACITE COAL EMPLOYES

"The nationality of the anthracite mine workers was secured in detail for the year 1905 by the bureau of industrial statistics of the State of Pennsylvania.

"In a total of 92,485 men employed by 116 companies out of a total of 140 the numbers were as follows:

NUMBER AND PER CENT OF EACH NATIONALITY WORKING FOR 116 ANTHRACITE COMPANIES OF PENNSYLVANIA IN 1905

[Compiled from the Report of the Secretary of Internal Affairs of Pennsylvania for 1905: Part III, Industrial Statistics, pages 458 and 459]

NATIONALITY	NUMBER	PER CENT OF TOTAL	NATIONALITY	NUMBER	PER CENT OF TOTAL
Slavic and Hungarian	36,049	39.0	English	2,497	2.7
Italian	3,975	4.3	Scotch	289	.3
American, mostly of			German	4,033	4.4
Slavic and other			Other nationalities	10,989	11.9
foreign parentage	25,905	28.0			
Irish	6,351	6.8	Total	92,485	100.0
Welsh	2,397	2.6			

BITUMINOUS COAL EMPLOYES

"In the bituminous coal-mining region of Pennsylvania 398 companies employing 55,583 men reported nationality in full detail as follows:

NUMBER AND PER CENT OF EACH NATIONALITY WORKING FOR 398 BITUMINOUS COMPANIES OF PENNSYLVANIA IN 1905

[Compiled from the Report of the Secretary of Internal Affairs of Pennsylvania for 1905: Part III, Industrial Statistics, page 475]

NATIONALITY	NUMBER	PER CENT OF TOTAL	NATIONALITY	NUMBER	PER CENT OF TOTAL
Slavic and Hungarian	21 708	39.0	Scotch	1,189	2.1
Italian	6,824	12.3	Welsh	313	.6
American, mostly of			German	1,721	3.1
Slavic and other			Eleven other nation-		
foreign parentage	17,347	31.2	alities	2,999	5.4
English	2,751	5.0			
Irish	731	1.3	Total	55,583	100.0

"It will thus be seen that the Slavic, Hungarian, and Italian races are numerically predominant in both the anthracite and bituminous coal fields of Pennsylvania.

"The Slavic races are also numerically strong in the iron and steel industries of Pennsylvania, while in the cotton, woolen, and textile industries their representation is small."

XXII

STATISTICS OF SLAVS IN AGRICULTURE

Map XI shows the distribution of Slavic farmers and farm laborers so far as this can be learned from the census data. By Slavic is here meant those whose parents were born in Austria, Bohemia, Hungary, Poland or Russia. These figures, while the best that are available, are a very imperfect source of information as to Slavic occupations, excluding Slavs of parent nativity other than those specified (for instance, Bulgarians), and including all others of the specified parent nativities, not only Slavs but non-Slavs, as for instance Polish and Russian Jews (to the small degree to which they are on farms), and Hungarians, Germans and other non-Slavic elements from the countries specified. Also the figures give no idea of the numbers of the families of farmers and farm laborers.

The difficulty with the mode of presentation followed on Map XI is that it exaggerates to the eye the numbers in large states like Texas, and underrates them in small states like Connecticut, but a presentation not of absolute numbers but in terms of density (proportion to area) or of percentage of population has its own drawbacks.

It may be of interest, however, to have the facts as to the per cent of the whole class of farmers and farm laborers whose parents were born in Austria, Bohemia, Hungary, Poland or Russia (i. e., persons having both parents born as specified or one parent born as specified and one native). The figures refer to males over ten, and are based on Table 41 of the volume on Occupations, Census of 1900. States with less than two hundred of the Slavic group are omitted.

I. Percentage of Total Farmers in Each State Whose Parents were Born in Specified Countries

South Dakota	11.06	Colorado	1.57
North Dakota	10.08	Michigan	1.25
Nebraska	6.42	Oregon	1.20
Wisconsin	5.25	New York	1.06
Connecticut	4.90	California	.61
Minnesota	4.65	Illinois	.48
Kansas	3.12	Maryland	.39
Massachusetts	3.03	Pennsylvania	.37
New Jersey	2.51	Missouri	.28
Oklahoma	2.48	Indiana	.27
Washington	1.97	Ohio	.24
Texas	1.93	Arkansas	.16
Iowa	1.65	Virginia	.08

United States....... 1.12
Including females. 1.07

The following table gives the totals for the United States for each country of birth and each kind of agricultural pursuit separately.

II. Males Ten Years of Age and Over of Specified Parent Nativity Gainfully Employed as Specified

	Austria	Bohemia	Hungary	Poland	Russia	Together
Agricultural laborers	6,134	13,356	1,494	12,514	9,539	43,037
Farmers, planters and overseers........	9,086	23,058	1,502	11,872	13,390	58,908
All others in agricultural pursuits	884	443	231	1,100	832	3,490
Total in agricultural pursuits........	16,104	36,857	3,227	25,486	23,761	105,435

Cf. Table lxxvi. Census of 1900. Volume on Occupations.

It is interesting to note that in every case except that of Poland, farmers are more numerous than farm laborers.

It is also interesting to compare different nationalities as regards the proportions occupied in agriculture, as shown in the next table.

III. Number Occupied in Agriculture per Thousand Males of Specified Parentage Engaged in Gainful Occupations

(Slavic Groups are in Italics)

Birthplace of parents:

Hungary.................................. 35
Italy..................................... 62
Austria.................................. 96
Russia...................................116*
Poland...................................122*
Ireland...................................155
Canada (French)...........................168
Scotland..................................212
England and Wales.........................225
France....................................248
Canada (English)..........................264
Germany...................................281
Sweden....................................328
Bohemia.................................354
Switzerland...............................396
Denmark...................................444
Norway....................................546

* For Poles and Russians these figures are unfortunately rendered almost meaningless by the presence of the large Hebrew group from Poland and Russia.

XXIII

MONEY ORDERS TO EUROPE

Besides the statements as to remittances given in the various chapters of Part I the following data are submitted, taken from pages 479-480 of Mr. Sheridan's article quoted in Appendix XX.

I. International Money Orders Issued in the United States and Sent to Italy and the Slavic Countries for Each Calendar Year from 1900 to 1906

[Figures relating to money orders are from the annual reports of the transactions of the New York post-office. The amounts are those sent from all post-offices in the United States]

YEAR ENDED DECEMBER 31—	MONEY ORDERS SENT TO ITALY, AUSTRIA-HUNGARY, AND RUSSIA		MONEY ORDERS SENT TO OTHER COUNTRIES	
	Number	Amount	Number	Amount
1900........	163,691	$3,845,251.14	840,416	$11,857,176.71
1901........	263,599	6,251,887.64	901,039	12,742,945.59
1902........	395,644	10,464,447.48	1,014,904	14,599,437.34
1903........	594,565	17,385,759.72	1,144,121	16,882,454.90
1904........	700,611	18,997,965.90	1,204,861	17,722,935.48
1905........	966,718	26,014,022.06	1,356,859	20,167,420.66
1906........	1,179,805	36,798,561.92	1,577,652	25,636,781.02
Total	4,264,633	$119,757,895.86	8,039,852	$119,609,151.70
Av. am't of each order......	....	$28.08	....	$14.88

YEAR ENDED DECEMBER 31—	AMOUNT OF MONEY ORDERS SENT TO ITALY	IMMI-GRANTS FROM ITALY	AMOUNT OF MONEY ORDERS SENT TO AUS-TRIA-HUNGARY AND RUSSIA	IMMIGRANTS FROM AUSTRIA-HUNGARY AND RUSSIA
1900........	$1,362,166.42	[a] 484,207	$2,483,084.72	[a] 1,401,689
1901........	1,905,611.75	135,996	4,346,275.89	198,647
1902........	3,607,795.61	178,375	6,856,651.87	279,336
1903........	7,729,257.86	230,622	9,656,501.86	342,104
1904........	8,780,255.81	193,296	10,217,710.09	322,297
1905........	11,092,446.60	221,479	14,921,575.46	460,590
1906........	16,239,134.40	273,120	20,559,427.52	480,803
Total	$50,716,668.45	1,717,095	$69,041,227.41	3,485,466

[a] Total number living in the United States, exclusive of Alaska and Hawaii, as reported by the census.

II. Amount of Money Orders Sent to Italy and to Austria-
Hungary and Russia per Immigrant for the Entire
Seven Years, 1900 to 1906

Country	Immi-grants, 1900 to 1906 (a)	Amount of Money Orders Sent	Amount Per Immi-grant
Italy..........................	1,717,095	$50,716,668.45	$29.54
Austria-Hungary and Russia ..	3,485,466	69,041,227.41	19.81

a Includes total living in the United States in 1900, together
with those arriving from 1901 to 1906.

"This table shows that for every man, woman, and child born
in Italy and living in or arriving in the United States, $29.54
was sent to Italy during the seven years 1900 to 1906, inclusive,
or $4.22 per year per person, and for immigrants from Austria-
Hungary and Russia in the same period $19.81 was sent to those
countries, or $2.83 per year per person."

III. Number and Amount (Total and Average) of Money
Orders Sent to Italy, Hungary, Austria, and Russia
During the Seven Years Ending December 31, 1906

Country	Number of Orders Sent	Amount of Money Orders	Aver-age Amount of Order
Italy..........................	1,314,350	$50,716,668.45	$38.59
Hungary.....................	709,700	22,917,566.01	32.29
Austria......................	892,965	22,452,492.27	25.14
Russia.......................	1,347,618	23,671,169.13	17.57

IV. Average Amount of Each Money Order Sent to Principal Countries in 1906

Country	Average Amount of Each Order Sent	Country	Average Amount of Each Order Sent
Italy..............	$40.51	Germany.........	$14.96
Hungary..........	35.21	Sweden..........	20.60
Austria...........	28.80	Norway..........	22.89
Russia...........	19.19	Greece..........	42.52
Great Britain......	13.28		

"The total amount of money orders sent in 1906 to all countries was $62,435,342.94, and of this the amount sent to Italy and the Slavic countries was $36,798,561.92, or 58.9 per cent of the total, while the number of orders sent was but 42.8 per cent of the whole number. During the seven years there was sent to Italy 30.8 per cent of the number of orders and 42.3 per cent of the total amount of money sent to Austria, Hungary, Russia, and Italy combined, while the Italians constituted but 33 per cent of the total number of immigrants from the four countries.

"It is probable that the reason for this is that a greater number of immigrants from the Slavic countries brought their families to the United States than did the Italians. The remittances through the post-offices are but a small proportion of the total amount transmitted and carried over in person. Large amounts of which there are no records are sent over through the Italian bankers, and also by bankers of other nationalities.

"The amount of money transmitted in the ordinary course of business must be allowed for and this would reduce in so far the amount of the remittances really representing the sendings of immigrants."

XXIV

POLISH FARMERS

Compare with the account in the text the following passage from an article in the Boston *Evening Transcript*, August 4, 1909, called "Absorbing the Alien; Hadley as a New England in Microcosm":

"The Polish people possess qualities of value to any town. They are not transient squatters, but come with the expectation, hope and purpose of making permanent homes. Their industry and thrift are shown in their success with farms given up by the natives. Every member of a Polish family helps in the work of cultivation. It is the pioneer stage with these people, and women and children share in the toil of the father.

"Their dealings in a business way amongst themselves and with their neighbors are characterized by shrewdness and caution. They are both thrifty and honest. Obligations are paid promptly. A physician who has a large practice among these people says that his fee is paid on the spot, or if there is no money on hand, within twenty-four hours. This is in striking contrast with the practice in many American homes, where the doctor's account is usually settled last. But if the medical man's attendance does not, after a few visits, result in improvement, another physician is called in or the patient may be left to die or recover as nature may decree. The same keen sense of money value is seen in the experience of evening schools. Those in charge find that they must make it clear that the studies and instruction possess direct pecuniary advantage and give definite training for wage earning or the attendance falls off rapidly.

"It must be acknowledged that the customs and manners of the Poles are crude and in many ways repugnant to American ideas, but their standards of morality are, on the whole, commendable. An evidence of this is found in their comparatively low death rate as shown in the study of various nationalities in Manhattan for the year 1906. The greatest mortality is from children's diseases and doubtless results from the ignorance of parents. The stock is characterized by a vigor and vitality that must be conditioned on right living. The family is regarded with respect and reverence.

"In mental quality the Pole shows his ability to cope with his Yankee neighbor in the market place. His readiness in mastering the art of farming speaks well for his quickness of observation and his power to apply information and adjust himself to new conditions. The children are faithful in attendance on school in the grades and often distinguish themselves by their fine standing. Few if any have, so far, entered Hopkins Academy, the secondary school of the town. There is a strong disposition to put the boys and girls to work when the State's requirements for schooling have been met, but this policy is based not so much on lack of interest in education, as it is on the wish to add to the income of the family. As the Poles gain in material prosperity there is every reason to expect that they will seek larger educational advantages for their children and the record of many of these in the lower grades augurs well for their success in the high school."

XXV

CENSUS DATA AS TO INTERMARRIAGE

(Vol. I, 1900, pages cxc, cxci, cxcii, and Table 56)

I. Native White Persons of Foreign Parentage

Specified Country	Both Parents Born as Specified	One Parent Born as Specified and One Parent Native
Austria............	133,774	26,281
Bohemia...........	168,449	31,362
Hungary...........	66,727	6,031
Poland............	290,912	19,006
Russia............	247,672	15,241

II. White Persons [Native and Foreign Born] of Foreign Parentage

Specified Country	Both Parents Born as Specified	One Parent Born as Specified and One Parent Native
	Per cent	Per cent
Austria.................	93.9	6.1
Bohemia................	91.2	8.8
Hungary................	97.2	2.8
Poland.................	97.2	2.8
Russia.................	97.8	2.2

III. White Persons Having Fathers Born as Specified

Specified Country	Mothers also Born as Specified	Mothers Born in Other Foreign Countries	Mothers Native	Total
	Per cent	Per cent	Per cent	Per cent
Austria............	89.3	6.4	4.3	100
Bohemia...........	92.0	2.1	5.9	100
Hungary...........	93.3	4.5	2.2	100
Poland............	94.9	2.9	2.2	100
Russia............	94.0	4.2	1.8	100

IV. White Persons Having Mothers Born as Specified

Specified Country	Fathers Born as Specified	Fathers Born in Other Foreign Countries	Fathers Native	Total
Austria............	92.5	6.0	1.5	100
Bohemia...........	93.3	3.6	3.1	100
Hungary...........	95.6	3.9	0.5	100
Poland	97.8	1.7	0.5	100
Russia............	97.1	2.5	0.4	100

V. Persons of Mixed Foreign Parentage Classified According to Combinations of Parentage

(Census, Table 56.)

Father Born in	Mother Born in		Father Born in	Mother Born in	
Austria......	Bohemia	1,741	Hungary	Italy	39
Austria......	Canada (Eng.)	269	Hungary	Norway	17
Austria......	Canada (Fr.)	62	Hungary	Poland	427
Austria......	Denmark	34	Hungary	Russia	346
Austria......	England	880	Hungary	Scotland	23
Austria......	France	503	Hungary	Sweden	46
Austria......	Germany	14,938	Hungary	Switzerland	114
Austria......	Hungary	2,534	Hungary	Wales	17
Austria......	Ireland	1,095	Hungary	Other countries	116
Austria......	Italy	517	Poland......	Austria	1,617
Austria......	Norway	72	Poland......	Bohemia	771
Austria......	Poland	1,153	Poland......	Canada (Eng.)	190
Austria......	Russia	3,140	Poland......	Canada (Fr.)	56
Austria......	Scotland	122	Poland......	Denmark	18
Austria......	Sweden	178	Poland......	England	1,039
Austria......	Switzerland	802	Poland......	France	196
Austria......	Wales	37	Poland......	Germany	11,164
Austria......	Other countries	1,023	Poland......	Hungary	977
Bohemia	Austria	1,676	Poland......	Ireland	331
Bohemia	Canada (Eng.)	154	Poland......	Italy	336
Bohemia	Canada (Fr.)	33	Poland......	Norway	41
Bohemia	Denmark	22	Poland......	Russia	2,633
Bohemia	England	89	Poland......	Scotland	67
Bohemia	France	68	Poland......	Sweden	141
Bohemia	Germany	4,024	Poland......	Switzerland	115
Bohemia	Hungary	455	Poland......	Wales	18
Bohemia	Ireland	132	Poland......	Other countries	457
Bohemia	Italy	11	Russia.......	Austria	5,163
Bohemia	Norway	22	Russia.......	Bohemia	191
Bohemia	Poland	294	Russia.......	Canada (Eng.)	190
Bohemia	Russia	166	Russia.......	Canada (Fr.)	22
Bohemia	Scotland	21	Russia.......	Denmark	65
Bohemia	Sweden	35	Russia.......	England	2,279
Bohemia	Switzerland	103	Russia.......	France	395
Bohemia	Wales	..	Russia.......	Germany	13,907
Bohemia	Other countries	223	Russia.......	Hungary	1,414
Hungary. ...	Austria	1,219	Russia.......	Ireland	418
Hungary	Bohemia	728	Russia.......	Italy	24
Hungary	Canada (Eng.)	34	Russia.......	Norway	101
Hungary	Canada (Fr.)	8	Russia.......	Poland	3,506
Hungary	Denmark	11	Russia.......	Scotland	87
Hungary	England	274	Russia.......	Sweden	512
Hungary	France	123	Russia.......	Switzerland	211
Hungary	Germany	6,186	Russia.......	Wales	14
Hungary	Ireland	310	Russia.......	Other countries	1,662

XXVI

A POLISH CRITICISM OF CHURCH SCHOOLS

An article in the Milwaukee *Press* (*Prasa*), after noting that in a competition among Polish pupils in writing reportorial articles, "All those whose work was below the required percentage were born and educated in this country," while the successful competitors were educated in Europe, asks why this was so:

"Why, then, are they such poor writers?" To its own query it then replies as follows.

"Because of the poor and faulty educational facilities. Being mostly orthodox Catholics, Polish parents are compelled to send their children to Polish parochial schools. All other schools, especially the public schools, are denounced from the pulpit and in the so-called 'church press' as 'unchristian, pagan and demoralizing institutions.' Parents sending their children to any other but the parochial school are denounced, threatened, ostracized, even expelled from the church, and their children are persecuted.

"With the exception of those where the priest himself is a sincere educator, the parochial schools are poor, many of them very poor, educational institutions. Reading, writing, arithmetic, geography and history are taught in many of them rather superficially. On the other hand many hours every day are spent for reciting catechism and church formulas, which is called 'teaching religion,' but it is far from being really religion.

"The result of such poor system of teaching is that the Polish children, after spending six or seven years in the parochial school, can hardly pass an examination for the fifth grade in the public schools—if they want to continue their education in the public school.

"The rule in most of the parishes is that the child shall not leave the parochial school until after first communion: and no child is accepted to first communion until after being thirteen years of age. It very often happens that a brighter child finishes all the grades in the parochial school at the end of its eleventh or twelfth year. But it is not allowed to leave the parochial school until it is over thirteen years of age. It is required to stay in the parochial school and waste one or two years doing nothing.

"Now a child being thirteen years of age, and graduating only into the fifth, or even sixth grade, has three or four more years to study in order to graduate from the public school. Therefore the child that attends a parochial school must study in the common school until it gets to be sixteen or seventeen, sometimes even eighteen years of age; while the child that attends the public school finishes the same studies when it is about fourteen years of age.

"In some parishes, so-called 'high schools' are established for those who have graduated from the parochial school. Not much of importance is taught in these so-called 'high schools,' their main object being to keep the children away from the public school.

"You will, please, remember that half of the Polish population here still belong to the 'workingman's class,' and that Polish families are quite large. Therefore very few Polish parents can afford to send all their children to school after the fourteenth year.

"So you can see where the fault is: not with the Polish people, but with the church authorities, who by such queer means compel the people to keep their children in ignorance.

"The Polish people realize this more and more. They demand better parochial schools, but their demands are ignored.

"Driven to desperation by the purposely poor parochial system, they do not mind any more threats, ridicule and persecution; they see that their first duty towards their children is good schooling. And were the public school authorities not so slow in adding the Polish language to their curriculum in the Polish districts, half of the Polish children would be now in the public schools.

"Of course, the church authorities will deny that the system of teaching in the parochial schools is faulty. But you cannot deny facts and results."

The view of a Ruthenian priest may be worth quoting:

"Education, the school alone, can help. But success can be neither quick nor easy. My people distrust these schools, teaching their children in a language that they cannot understand themselves. Their whole history prepares them to suspect ulterior purposes. Perhaps, too, they have sometimes seen political influences at work in public schools. They have most confidence in parochial schools, but as supplementary to the public schools, not as a substitute."

XXVII

PERCENTAGE OF ILLITERACY AMONG IMMIGRANTS 14 YEARS OF AGE AND OVER FOR THE YEAR ENDED JUNE 30, 1900

(Slavic groups are in Italics)

(41) Turkish...............................78.7
(40) Portuguese.............................60.0
(39) Syrian................................56.4
(38) Italian (Southern).....................54.5
(37) Filipinos.............................50.0
(36) *Ruthenian (Russniak)*.................49.0
(35) Pacific Islanders......................41.0
(34) Mexican..............................38.3
(33) *Croatian* and *Slovenian*.............37.4
(32) *Bulgarian, Servian* and *Montenegrin*..35.9
(31) *Dalmatian, Bosnian* and *Herzegovinian*..32.9
(30) Lithuanian...........................32.1
(29) *Polish*.............................31.6
(28) *Russian*............................28.8
(27) *Slovak*.............................28.0
(26) Roumanian............................25.1
(25) Armenian.............................24.4
(24) African (black)......................23.9
(23) Spanish American.....................22.8
(22) Hebrew..............................22.8
(21) Korean..............................22.5
(20) Greek...............................17.5
(19) Magyar..............................16.9
(18) Italian (Northern)...................11.8
(17) Dutch and Flemish.....................9.9
(16) Japanese.............................8.9
(15) Not specified.........................7.9
(14) Cuban................................6.9
(13) German...............................5.8
(12) West Indian..........................5.4
(11) Spanish..............................5.0
(10) French...............................4.1
(9) Welsh................................3.7
(8) Irish................................3.2
(7) *Bohemian* and *Moravian*.............3.0
(6) Finnish..............................2.7
(5) Scotch...............................2.1
(4) English..............................2.0
(3) Hawaiian.............................1.9
(2) Chinese..............................1.4
(1) Scandinavian.........................0.8

Total..................................24.2

Industrial Commission, Vol. XV, pages 282-3.

BIBLIOGRAPHY

This list of titles, while not confined to works mentioned in the text, or even to those consulted, is of course in no sense exhaustive.

BIBLIOGRAPHY

Abbott, Dr. Edith: The Wages of Unskilled Labor in the United States, 1850–1900. *Journal of Political Economy,* 13: 321–367 (June, 1905).
Women in Industry; a Study in American Economic History. Pp. xxi, 408. Appleton, 1910.

Abbott, Ernest Hamlin: America's Welcome to the Immigrant. Ill. *Outlook,* 72: 257–264 (Oct. 4, 1902).

Abbott, Grace: The Bulgarians of Chicago. *Charities and the Commons,* 30: 650–660 (Jan. 9, 1909).

Absorbing the Alien. Hadley as a New England in Microcosm. Boston *Evening Transcript,* Aug. 4, 1909.

Accidents. See Eastman.

Adams, Samuel Hopkins: Pittsburgh's Foregone Asset, the Public Health. *Charities and the Commons,* 21: 940–950 (Feb. 6, 1909).

Addams, Jane: Newer Ideals of Peace. Pp. xviii, 243. Macmillan 1904.

Aeltere und neuere Magyarisirungs-Versuche in Ungarn mit besonderer Rücksicht auf die Slovaken. Urbánck, Prague, 1876. Pp. 113.

Agriculture: For conditions in U. S., see Farming, Bohemians in U. S.; Poles on Farms. See also Austria-Hungary and the Balkan States; Buchenberger; Galicia; Oesterreichisches Staatswörterbuch; Pratt; Schilder; Schullern-Schrattenhofen.

Ainsworth, F. H.: Are We Shouldering Europe's Burden? *Charities,* 12: 134–135 (Feb. 6, 1904).

Albania. See Durham.

Alden, Percy, Ed.: Hungary of Today: By Members of the Hungarian Government, etc. Ill. Pp. xii, 415. New York, 1909.

Alexander, William: Picturesque Representations of the Dress and Manners of the Austrians. Illustrated by fifty colored engravings with descriptions. London, 1814. (These are the same plates, in inferior form, as those in Moleville's book.)

Allen, Joseph Henry: An Historical Sketch of the Unitarian Movement since the Reformation. "The Polish Brethren," Ch. iv, 73–97. New York, 1894.

Almanach Českoslovanského Lidu v New Yorku a Okolí. Ill. Vol. 1. Česka Tiskárna (Bohemian Press), 312 West 71st St., New York City.

The American Pioneer; a monthly periodical, devoted to the objects of the Logan Historical Society, or to collecting and publishing sketches relating to the early settlement and successive improvement of the country. (Letter from "Polonus" referring to John of Kolno, i, 399; reference to Sodowskys i, 119, and ii, 325.) Cincinnati, 1844, 1843. 2 vols.

Annuaire Statistique Hongrois. Traduction officielle. Office Central de Statistique du Royaume de Hongrie. Budapest. (Appears annually.)

Arden, Ivan: The Ruthenians in America. *Charities,* 13: 245–252 (Dec. 3, 1904).

Art. See Jurkovič; Švarc; Uprka.

Assimilation. See Addams; Boas; Lee; Tarde.

Auerbach, Bertrand: Les Races et les Nationalités en Autriche-Hongrie. Pp. 336. Maps. Alcan, 1898.

Austria. See Austria-Hungary and the Balkan States; Baedecker; Colquhoun; Diplomatic and Consular Reports; Drage; Leger (History of Austro-Hungary); Lévy; Merse; Oesterreichisch-Ungarische Monarchie in Wort und Bild; Oesterreichisches Staatswörterbuch; Palmer, E. H. E.; Partsch; Whitman. See also Austrian Statistics, Emigration from Austria-Hungary, and Hungary.

Austria-Hungary and the Balkan States. Maps. Royal (British) Commission on Labor. 1894. Vol. XI, pp. 225. [A treasury of information on economic and social conditions.]

Austrian Census of 1900. Die Summarischen Ergebnisse der Volkszählung; die Ergebnisse der Volkszählung vom 31 December, 1900, in den im Reichsrathe vertretenen Königreichen und Ländern, Heft I, *Oesterreichische Statistik;* herausgegbben von der K. K. Statischen Central Commission, lxxxiii, Vienna, 1902.

Austrian Statistics. See, beside above, Mittheilungen aus dem Gebiete der Statistik; Oesterreichisches Statistisches Handbuch; Statistisches Jahrbuch der Oesterreichischen Monarchie; Statistische Monatsschrift; Twardowski.

Baedecker, Karl: Austria, including Hungary, Transylvania, Dalmatia and Bosnia. Handbook for Travelers. Pp. 479. Maps. 1900.

Bailey, Alice Ward: A Bright Green Pole. *Outlook,* Feb. 6, 1904. (A story of a Polish house-maid in an American family.)

Bain, A. Nisbet: Cossack Fairy Tales and Folk-tales. Translated from the Ruthenian. Ill. Pp. 12, 290. London, 1894.

Balch, Emily G.: A By Election in Hungary; a Study of Political Crises. Springfield *Sunday Republican,* Oct. 22, 1905.

A Shepherd of Immigrants. *Charities*, 13: 193–4 (Dec., 1904).

Oesterreichische Fragen in Amerikanischer Beleuchtung. *Der Weg,* I, No. 24, pp. 3–5; No. 26, pp. 5–7. Vienna, 1906.

Review of Rauchberg's Der Nationale Besitzstand in Boehmen. *Political Science Quarterly*, 21: 155–8. 1906.

The Story of a Bohemian Pioneer. *The Chautauquan*, February, 1906, pp. 396–403. (Reprinted above, pages 343–348.)

A Week in Herzegovina and Bosnia. Bryn Mawr *Alumnæ Quarterly*, 2: 5–22. Ill. Oct., 1908. (Also printed in the *Wellesley College Magazine* for May, 1909.)

Ballagh, J. C.: White Servitude in the Colony of Virginia. Johns Hopkins University Studies in Historical and Political Science. 13: 99. 1895.

Benda, Wladyslaw T.: Tatra, a Mountain Region between Galicia and Hungary. *Century*, 72: 169–179 (June, 1906).

Life in a Polish Village. *Century*, 76: 323–332 (July, 1908).

Bibliographies. 'See Commons (Races and Immigrants in America); Edwards, R. H.; Library of Congress; Strong.

Bittner, Bartoš: Katechizmus Svobodomyslné Mladeže; to jest narys mravonky, založene na vědeckém nazoru světa pro školu i poučeni soukromé. (Catechism for freethinking young people; i. e., an outline of morals based on a scientific view of the world, for schools and private instruction.) Geringer, 150 W. 12th St., Chicago.

Blackwell, Emily Stone: Columbia. (Translation from Hurban-Vajansky's Slovak poem.) *Springfield Republican*, Jan. 14, 1908.

Blaxter, H. V.: The Aldermen and Their Courts. *Charities and the Commons*, 21: 851–858 (Feb. 6, 1909).

Boas, Franz: Race Problem in America. *Science*, 29 839–849. 1909.

Boeckh, Richard: Die Statistische Bedeutung der Volkssprache als Kennzeichen der Nationalität. Berlin, 1866.

The Determination of Racial Stock among American Immigrants. Quarterly Publications of American Statistical Association, Dec., 1906. Pp. 199–221.

Bohemia. See Balch; Bowring; Guide to the Bohemian Section, London, 1906; Leger; Lutzow; Rauchberg.

Bohemia, Emigration from. See Consular Officers of the U. S., Reports of; Jonas.

Bohemian National Hymn. (Translated.) *Charities*, 13: 205 (1904).

Bohemian Settlements in Kewaunee County, MSS. in possession of State Historical Society of Wisconsin.

Bohemian Voice. Vols. 1 and 2. Omaha, Neb., 1892 and 1893.

Bohemians in the United States. For a list of authorities on Bohemian settlement in the United States see Appendix xiv, page 456. The authorities listed in this appendix do not for the most part appèar in this Bibliography.

See also Almanach Československého Lidu v New Yorku a Okolí; The Bohemian Settlements in Kewaunee County; Bruemmer; Čapek; České Chicago; Habernicht; Hrbek; Humpal-Zeman; Katolík; Masaryk; Mashek; Náprstek; Riis; Robins; Rosicky; Vlach; Zdrůbek (History of Bohemian National Cemetery in Chicago).

Bosnia and Herzegovina. See Balch; Coffin; Evans; Henderson; Hutchinson; Munro; Peez; Revel.

Bovill, W. B. F.: Hungary and the Hungarians. Ill. New York, 1908.

Bowring, Sir John: Poetry of the Magyars. Preceded by a sketch of the language and literature of Hungary and Transylvania. 1830.
Servian Popular Poetry. London, 1827.
Specimens of the Russian Poets; with remarks and biographical notices. 2 vols. London, 1821.
Wybor Poezyi Polskiey. Specimens of the Polish poets with notes and observations on the literature of Poland. London, 1827.
Wybor z Básnictiwi Českého. Cheskian Anthology; being a history of the poetical literature of Bohemia, with translated specimens. London, 1832.

Brandes: Impressions of Poland. 1888.

Browning, Ellen H.: A Girl's Wanderings in Hungary. Ill. Longmans, 1896. (Chapter XVII contains a slight description of Slovak character and wedding customs.)

Bruemmer, Louis: Manuscript in regard to Bohemian settlement in Wisconsin in library of Historical Society of Wisconsin.

Buchenberger: Oesterreichische Agrarpolitik seit der Grundentlastung. Zft. f. d. Gesammt-Staatswissenschaften, pp. 577–93. 1899.

Building, Loan and Homestead Associations of the State of Illinois, Thirteenth Annual Report of the Auditor of. 1904.

Bukowina. See Jandaurek; Kaindl; Mittheilungen des Statistischen Landesamtes; Protokolle der Auswanderungs-Conferenzen; Vertheilung des Grundbesitzes in der Bukowina.

Bulgaria. See Dicey.

Bulgarians. See Abbott, Grace; Sonnichsen.

Butler, Elizabeth Beardsley: Women and the Trades. Charities Publication Committee, New York, 1910.

Buzek, Dr. Josef: Das Auswanderungsproblem und die Regelung des Auswanderungswesens in Oesterreich. Zft. für Volkswirtschaft, Socialpolitik und Verwaltung. 10: 441–511, 553–595. 1901.
Der Einfluss der Ernten, respective der Getreidepreise auf die Bevölkerungsbewegung in Galizien in den Jahren 1878–98. Statistische Monatsschrift, N. F. 6; 167–216. 1901.

Die Ueberseeische Oesterreichische Wanderung in den Jahren 1896 bis 1898. *Ibid.*, N. F. 6: 72–105. 1900.

Byington, Margaret F.: Homestead, A Steel Town and its People. *Charities and the Commons*, 21: 613–628 (Jan. 8, 1909).
Households Builded upon Steel. *Ibid.*, 1073–1104 (Mar. 6, 1909).
The Mill Town Courts and their Lodgers. *Ibid.*, 913–922 (Feb. 6, 1909).

Čapek, Tomaš: Památky Českých Emigrantů v Americe; Příspěvek k dějinam česko-amerického vystěhovalectvi. (Memorials of Bohemian Emigrants in America: A Contribution to the history of Bohemian-American Emigration.) Second revised edition, pp. 112. Ill. Narodni Tiskárny Press, Omaha, Nebraska, 1907.
The Slovaks of Hungary. Slavs and Pan Slavism. Pp. xvi, 214. Maps. Ill. New York, 1906.
Čechen in Preussisch-Oberschlesien, Die. Stimme eines Rufenden aus Preussisch-Oberschlesien. Von einem Slaven. Pp. 18. Urbánek, Prag, 1875.
České Chicago: Adresař Českých Obchodníků a Spolků. (Bohemian Chicago: Directory of Bohemian business men and societies.) Narodni Tiskárny Press, 700–704 Loomis St., Chicago, 1900.
Churches. See Dabovich; Grose; McLanahan; Official Catholic Directory; Shipman. See also Religious Aspect of Immigration.
Cigar Making. See Riis; Robins.
Claghorn, Kate Holladay: Changing Character of Immigration. Ill. *World's Work*, 1: 381–387 (1900–1901).
Immigration and Dependence. *Charities*, 12: 135–137 (Feb. 6, 1904).
Immigration in its Relation to Pauperism. Annals of American Academy of Political and Social Science, 24: 207–220 (July, 1904).
Our Immigrants and Ourselves. *Atlantic*, 36: 535–548 (1900).
Slavs, Magyars and Some Others in the New Immigration. *Charities*, 13: 199–205 (Dec. 3, 1904).
Coffin, M. C.: Where East meets West: Visit to Picturesque Dalmatia, Montenegro and Bosnia. Ill. *National Geographic Magazine*, 19: 309–344 (May, 1908).
Colquhoun, A. R. and Mrs. E.: The Whirlpool of Europe; Austria, Hungary and the Habsburgs. Ill. Pp. 349. 1907.
Coman, Katharine: The Industrial History of the United States. Pp. xiii, 343, xxiv. Macmillan, 1907.
Comenius, Johann Amos: The Labyrinth of the World and the Paradise of the Heart. Edited and translated by Count Lutzow. Pp. 347. London, 1901.
Commission on Immigration of New York State, appointed pursuant to the provisions of Chapter 210 of the laws

of 1909. Report transmitted to the legislature April 5, 1909. Pp. xiv, 252.

Commons, J. R.: Immigration and its Economic Effects. Industrial Commission, Vol. 15: 293–743. 1901.
Immigration and Labor Problems. (In La Follette, Robert M. *ed.* The Making of America, Vol. 8: 236–261. Chicago, 1906.)
Races and Immigrants in America. Ill. Macmillan, 1907.
Slavs in the Bituminous Mines of Illinois. *Charities,* 13: 227–229 (Dec. 3, 1904).
Trade Unionism and Labor Problems, xiv, 628. Ginn & Co., 1905.
Wage Earners of Pittsburgh. *Charities and the Commons,* 21: 1051–1066 (Mar. 6, 1909).

Communal Household. See Zadruga.

Consular Officers of the U. S., Reports of:
Emigration and Immigration. 49th Congress, 2nd Session, House of Representatives, Ex. Doc. 157, 1887. Pp. iv, 748. (See index under Austria-Hungary, Russia.)
Jonas, Charles: Emigration from Bohemia, 491–493. Bohemian and Hungarian Emigration to the United States, 493–494; in U. S. Consular Reports, xxxii, No. 114. (1890.)
Consular Reports, Special. Emigration to the United States. Vol. 30, 1904. Pp. xv, 210. Austria-Hungary, 1–15; Russia, 104–111.

Connor, Ralph: The Foreigner, A Tale of Saskatchewan. Pp. 384. New York, 1909. (A Story of Slavs, especially Ruthenians, in Western Canada.)

Conway, J.: Catholic Education in the United States. (Quoted by Kruszka.)

Costume. See Alexander; Ferrario; Moleville.

Croatia. See Evans; Koch; Kovačevič; Die Königreiche Kroatien und Slavonien; Monatliche Statistische Mittheilungen (Agram); Viestnik; Volkszählung vom 31 Dezember, 1900, in den Königreichen Kroatien und Slavonien; Zadruga; Zoričič.

Crowell, F. Elizabeth: Housing Situation in Pittsburgh. *Charities and the Commons,* 21: 871–881 (Feb. 6, 1909).
Painter's Row. *Ibid.,* 897–910.

Crowell, Katharine B.: Coming Americans. Willett Press, New York.

Curtin, Jeremiah: Myths and Folk-tales of the Russians, Western Slavs and Magyars. Pp. xxv, 555. Boston, 1890.

Czerwinski, Albert: Geschichte der Tanzkunst bei den cultivierten Völkern von den ersten Anfängen bis auf der gegenwärtigen Zeit. Pp. viii, 264, Leipzig, 1862.

Dabovich, Rev. Sebastian: The Holy Orthodox Church or the Ritual, Services and Sacraments of the Eastern Apostolic (Greek Russian) Church. Pp. 85. Wilkesbarre, Pa., 1898.

Dalmatia. See Coffin; Diehl; Evans; Holbach; Munro; Peixotto; Smythe; Wilkinson; Wingfield.

Dances. See Czerwinski; Waldau.

Daszynska-Golinska, Dr. Zofia: Neuere Literatur über Galizisches Agrarwesen. Sozial-Wirtschaftliche Dorfmonographien. Archiv für Social wissenschaft und Socialpolitik, 20: 720–733, 1904.

Deniker, Joseph: The Races of Man; an outline of Anthropology and Ethnography. Ill. Pp. xxiii, 611. Scott, London, 1901.

Devine, Edward T.: Immigration as a Relief Problem. *Charities*, 12: 129–133 (Feb. 6, 1904). The Pittsburgh Survey. *Charities and the Commons*, 21: 1035. (Mar. 6, 1909.)

Dicey, Edward: History of the Peasant State. London, 1894.

Diehl, C.: En Méditerranée. 1901. (Contains *Les Souvenirs de la France en Dalmatie*.)

Diplomatic and Consular Reports (British). Finances and General Economic Conditions of Austria-Hungary for the years 1900–1904. No. 3343. Annual Series. Pp. 134. April, 1905.

Dixon, Charlton: Slovak Grammar for English Speaking Students. Second Edition, pp. 134. Rovnianek, Pittsburgh, 1904.

Donaldson, Th.: The Public Domain. Gov. Printing Office, 1884. (See p. 212 for Congressional grant to Polish exiles.)

Dowie, Menie Muriel: A Girl in the Karpathian Mountains. London, 1891. (Also published under the author's married name of Mrs. Norman.)

Drage, Geoffrey: Austria-Hungary. Pp. xvii, 846. Dutton, 1909.

Durham, Mary Edith: The Burden of the Balkans. Pp. xii, 331. Ill. London, 1905. High Albania. Pp. xii, 352. Ill. London, 1909. Through the Lands of the Serb. Pp. xi, 345. Ill. London, 1904.

Eastman, Crystal: One Year's Work Accidents and Their Cost. I. Why Industrial Accidents Happen. II. What happens after the Accident. *Charities and the Commons*, 21: 1143–1174 (Mar. 6, 1909). The Temper of the Workers under Trial. *Ibid.*, 561–570. Work-Accidents and the Law. Charities Publication Committee, 1910.

Edmonds, J. M.: An Introduction to Comparative Philology for Classical Students. Pp. vi, 235. Cambridge University Press, 1906.

Edwards, Charles E.: Protestantism in Poland, a Brief Study of its History as an Encouragement to Mission Work among the Poles. Westminster Press, Phila., 1901.

Edwards, Richard Henry: Immigration. Studies in American Social Conditions, No. 3. (An outline and references for study.) Pp. 32. Madison, Wisconsin. Jan., 1909.

Elkinton, Joseph: The Doukhobors. *Charities*, 13: 252–256 (Dec. 3, 1904).

Emigration from Austria-Hungary. See Buzek; Consular Officers; Drage; Graetz; Hegedüs; Levay; Mischler; Schwegel; Statistische Monatsschrift; Stodola; Thirring; Vay de Vaya and Luskod. See also Appendix viii, p. 447.

Ethnology. See Boeckh; Čapek (The Slovaks of Hungary); Deniker; Ficker; Komarow; Lévy; Niederle; Rauchberg (Die Bevölkerung Oesterreichs); Ripley; Slawen.

Evans, Arthur John: Illyrian Letters; a selection of correspondence from Bosnia, Herzegovina, Montenegro, Albania, Dalmatia, Croatia and Slavonia, addressed to the Manchester Guardian, 1877. Pp. xxi, 255. Maps. Longmans, 1878.

Through Bosnia and the Herzegovina on foot during the Insurrection, August and September, 1875; with an historical review of Bosnia and a glimpse of the Croats, Slavonians, and the ancient Republic of Ragusa. Ill. Longmans, 1876.

Family Life. See Byington; Garret; McDowell; Sayles; White.

Farming. See Hening; Horton; Smalley. See also Bohemians in the U. S., Poles on Farms, and, for conditions in Austria-Hungary, see Agriculture.

Faust, Albert Bernhardt: The German Element in the United States; with special reference to its political, moral, social and educational influence. 2 vols. Ill. Houghton, Mifflin, 1909. (For Moravian Brethren see Index.)

Fehlinger H.: Die Oesterreicher in den Vereinigten Staaten von Amerika. Statistische Monatsschrift, 1907.

Ferrario, Giulio: Il Costume Antico e Moderno, etc. Folio. Plates, Milan, 1829. See Index, Vol. XVIII, under Austria, Croatia, Polacchi, Polonia, Russi, Russia, Russinie o Russniachi, Slavinzi, Slavi, Slavoni o Schiavoni, Ungherese, Ungheria.

Ficker, Adolf: Ethnographische Karte der Oest.-Ung. Monarchie. Nach Frhr. v. Czoernig's Karte in 4 Blätter, reducirt in 1 Blatt. Mit erklärendem Text. Vienna, 1870.

Die Volkerstämme der Oes.-Ung. Monarchie, ihre Gebiete, Gränzen und Inseln. Historisch-geographisch und statistisch dargestellt; mit 4 Karten. Mittheilungen aus dem Gebiete der Statistik, Vol. xv, 1869.

Fiction. See Bailey; Connor; Foster; Franzos; Freytag; Gerard; Gogol; Harriman; Jirasek; Johnson; Mikszath; Nemec; Neruda; Orczy; Przewa-Tetmajer; Reuter; Ritter; Sandor-Gjalski; Sienkiewycz; Steiner.

First Catholic Slovak Union of U. S. A., Constitution and By-laws; under the patronage of the Virgin Mary, Patroness of Hungary; amended at the XII Convention held in 1906, at McKeesport. Organized in 1890 at Cleveland, Ohio. Pp. 99. (In English and Slovak.)

Fitch, John A.: Some Pittsburgh Steel Workers. *Charities and the Commons*, 21: 553–560 (Jan. 2, 1909). The Steel Industry and the Labor Problem. *Ibid.*, 1079–1092 (Mar. 6, 1909).

Fleming, W. L.: Immigration to the Southern States. *Political Science Quarterly*, 20: 276–297 (1905).

Folk-Lore. See Curtin; Krauss; Mijatovich; Mijatovics; Wissenschaftliche Mittheilungen aus Bosnien und der Hercegovina.

Foster, Maximilian: The Citizen. *Everybodys*, Nov. 1909, pp. 625–640.

Franzos, Carl Emil: Aus Halb-Asien; Culturbilder aus Galizien, der Bukowina, Süd Russland und Rumänien. Second Edition, 1878.
For the Right. Translated by J. Sutter, N. Y. 1888.
The Jews of Barnow. (8 Stories.) Translated from the German by M. W. Macdowall. (With a preface by Barnes Phillip.) Pp. xxii, 21, 334. Appleton, 1883.
Vom Don zur Donau; neue Kulturbilder aus Halb Asien. *Contents:* Markttag in Barnow. Die Gezwungenen. Mein Onkel Bernhard. Martin der Rubel. Die Literatur der Kleinrussen. Das Volkslied der Kleinrussen. Toras Szewczenko. Thodika. Rumänische Sprichwörter. Aus Pest's Verbrecherhöhlen. Der Ahnherr des Messias. Die Cultur Entwicklung in Halb-Asien. Revised edition, 2 vols. Berlin, 1898.

Free-thinkers. See Almanach Československého Lidu v New Yorku a Okolí; Bittner; Pohřebni Řeci (Funeral Speeches); Špera; Zdrůbek.

Freytag: Debit and Credit. (A German youth in Poland at the time of the insurrection.)

Frumar, Adolph and Jursa, Jan: Slabikař pro Školy Obecné. (Primer for Public Schools.) Ill. by M. Aleš. Cisařský Královský Školni Knihosklad. Prague, 1902.

Furdek, Rev. Stephen: Jednota; Katolícky Kalendár, pp. 196. Ill. 1907. (Contains a list of Catholic Slovak colonies and priests in the United States.)
Život Slovakov v Amerike. (Life of Slovaks in America.) In Tovaryšstvo, Vol. iii (1890). Ruzomberok, Hungary.

Galicia. See Daszynska-Golinska; Dowie; Franzos; Gerard; Jandaurek; Pennell; Pilat; Statistische Mittheilungen über die Verhältnisse Galiziens; Thomson. See also Agriculture; Bukowina; Ruthenians.

Garret, Laura B.: Notes on the Poles in Baltimore. *Charities*, 13: 235–239 (Dec. 3, 1904).

Gerard, Dorothea: (Madame Longard de Longarde)
An Impossible Idyll. (Story of an English family in Galicia.)
Orthodox. Tauchnitz, 1891. (Story of Galician Jews.) This and the following novel give highly interesting pictures of Ruthenian life, especially in priestly families.

The Supreme Crime. Tauchnitz, 1901.

The Wrong Man. Appleton, 1896.

Gibbons, William Frithey: The Adopted Home of the Hun:
A Social Study in Pennsylvania. *American Magazine
of Civics*, Sept., 1895, pp. 315-323.

Gogol, Nicolai Vasilievitch: Evenings in Little Russia. Trans.
by E. W. Underwood and W. H. Cline. Pp. xxiii,
153. Lord, Evanston, 1903. (Contains. beside preface,
The Fair of Sorotchinetz; An Evening in May; Mid-
Summer Evening.)

St. John's Eve. Trans. by J. H. Hapgood. Pp. 383.
Crowell, 1886. (Contains, beside introduction, St.
John's Eve,—same tale as Mid-Summer Evening in
preceding volume; Old Fashioned Farmers; The
Tale of How Ivan Ivanovitch quarrelled with Ivan
Nikiforovitch; The Portrait; The Cloak.)

Evening on the Farm near the Dikanka. (This is another
translation of the same or part of the same set of
poetical fales full of. the superstition and passion of
the Little Russian peasant.)

Taras Bulba. Trans. by Isabel F. Hapgood. Pp. 295.
Crowell, 1886. (A brilliant sketch of Cossack life
among the Little Russians of old.)

Graetz, Dr. Victor: Ueber die Auswanderungsfrage in Oesterreich. *Volkswirtschaftlichen Wochenschrift*, Feb. 23,
1905. (Also separately printed. Pp. 26.)

Gregory, John G.: Foreign Immigration to Wisconsin. Proceedings State Historical Society of Wisconsin, 1901,
pp. 137-143. 1902.

Grose, Howard B.: Aliens or Americans? With Introduction
by Josiah Strong. Young People's Missionary Movement. Pp. 337. New York, 1906. (In series of
Forward Mission Study Courses of Am. Baptist Home
Missionary Society.)

Guide to the Bohemian Section and to the Kingdom of Bohemia.
Bohemian Section at the Austrian Exhibition, Earl's
Court, London, 1906. Pp. 224. Ill. Maps. Wiesner,
Prague, 1906. (Contains a brief bibliography of
English works relating to Bohemia.)

Habernicht: Dějiny Čechů Amerických, Dil třeti; Stát Texas.
(History of American Chekhs; Third Part; the State
of Texas.) Copyrighted by the Bohemian Literary
Society, 1904. Pp. 129. Ill. See Appendix xiv, page
456, for further reference to this publication.

Hall, Prescott F.: Immigration and its Effects upon the United
States. Holt, 1906.

Harriman, Karl Edwin: The Home Builders. Pp. 329, London.
(Stories of Polish-Americans.)

Hegedüs, Lorant: A Magyarok . Kivándorlása Amerikába. Az
Amerikai Magyar Telepek—A Felvidek Nyomora—
Kivándorlás es Bevándorlás Szabalyozasa. (The Emi-
gration of Hungarians to America—The American-

Hungarian settlements—The Misery of Upper Hungary —The Regulation of Emigration and Immigration.) Pp. 102, Budapest, 1899. Reprinted from the Budapest *Szemle* (Review).

Henderson, Major Percy E.: A British Officer in the Balkans. The account of a journey through Dalmatia, Montenegro, Turkey in Austria (*sic*), Magyarland, Bosnia and Herzegovina. Pp. 302. Ill. Lippincott, 1906.

Herder, Johann Gottfried von: Outlines of a Philosophy of a History of Mankind. Trans. from the German by Churchill. Pp. xvi, 632. London, 1800.

Herzegovina. See Bosnia and Herzegovina.

Holbach, Mrs. M. M.: Dalmatia, the Land where East meets West. Ill. London, 1908.

Holt, Hamilton, editor: The Life Stories of Undistinguished Americans as told by Themselves. With an Introduction by Edwin E. Slosson. Chapter II, Life Story of a Polish Sweatshop Girl. Pott, N. Y., 1906.

Housing. See Byington; Crowell.

Hrbek, Sarah: Bohemian Citizens have done much for Cedar Rapids. *Cedar Rapids Republican*, Semi-Centennial Magazine edition. June 10, 1906.

Hruszewski, Michael: Geschichte des Ukrainischen (Ruthenischen) Volkes. Vol. 1, Leipzig, 1906.
Die Klein Russen. (In Melnik, J. ed. : Russen und Russland.)

Humpal-Zeman, Josefa: Bohemia: A Stir of its Social Conscience. *The Commons*, July, 1904.
The Bohemian People in Chicago. (In Hull House Maps and Papers. Pp. viii, 230. Crowell, 1895.) Chapter vi, 115–131.
Bohemian Settlements in the United States. Industrial Commission, vol. 15, pp. 507–510. 1901.

Hungarian Emigration. *American Monthly Review of Reviews*, 33 : 354–6. 1906.

Hungarians. See Hungary.

Hungarian Statistical Year Book. See Annuaire Statistique Hongrois.

Hungary. See Alden; Balch (A By Election); Bovill; Bowring; Browning; Consular Reports; Irby; Pink; Recouly; Seton-Watson. See also Slovaks.

Hungary, Emigration From. See Emigration from Austria-Hungary.

Hurban-Vajanský: See Vajanský.

Hutchinson, Frances H.: Motoring in the Balkans along the Highways of Dalmatia, Montenegro, the Herzegovina and Bosnia. Ill. Pp. xiii, 341. McClurg, 1909.

Illegitimacy. See Spann.

Immigrants' Guides. See Immigration Department, Y. M. C. A.; Roberts; Rosicky; Severance; Šusteršič.

Immigration. See Emigration.

Immigration Commission, Federal, created under section 39 of the Immigration Act of Feb. 20, 1907. Hearing Jan. 18, 1908, in relation to Section 42 of Immigration Act.

Statement relative to the work and expenditures of the Immigration Commission. House of Representatives, 60th Congress, 2nd Session, Document No. 1489, pp. 44. Washington, 1909.

Steerage Conditions, Partial Report on. 61st Congress, 2nd Session, Senate Document No. 206. Pp. 46. Washington, 1909.

Importing Women for Immoral Purposes. Report from the Immigration Commission, transmitting in response to Senate Resolution No. 36 by Senator Lodge a partial report to Congress on the Importation and Harboring of Women for Immoral Purposes. 61st Congress, 2nd Session, Senate Document No. 196. Pp. 61. Washington, 1909.

Immigration Department, International Committee of Young Men's Christian Association. The Country to Which You Go. Pp. 12. How to Become a Citizen of the United States. Pp. 10. (For these and various other pamphlet publications address Dr. Peter Roberts, 124 E. 28th St., N. Y.)

Immigration, Commissioner General (Federal) of. Annual Reports. 1895 (J. H. Senner); 1896 and 1897 (Herman Stump); 1898, 1899, 1900 and 1901 (T. V. Powderly); 1902, 1903, 1904, 1905, 1906, 1907 (F. P. Sargent); 1908 (A. Warner Parker, Acting Com. Gen.); 1909 (Daniel O'Keefe).

Immigration Statistics, United States, 1820–1892. Treasury Department. Arrivals of Alien Passengers and Immigrants in the United States from 1820 to 1892. Prepared by the Bureau of Statistics. (Portion of Quarterly Report No. 2, Series 1892–93.) Pp. 151. Washington, 1893.

Immigration, Superintendent (Federal) of. Annual Reports. 1892 (W. D. Owen), 1893 (Herman Stump), 1894 (J. H. Senner).

Industrial Commission, vol. 15. Reports on Immigration. Pp. cxxvi, 840. 1901. (An invaluable storehouse of information; the rest of the volume is separately paged and is on a different subject.)

Industrial Commission, vol. 17. 1901. Labor Organizations, Labor Disputes, and Arbitration and Railway Labor. (Consult index under *Foreigners* and *Immigration*.)

Irby, Miss: Across the Carpathians.

Jandaurek, Julius: Das Königreich Galizien und Lodomerien und das Herzogthum Bukowina. Ill. Pp. 202. Graeser, Vienna, 1884.

Janik, Michal: Ludność Polska w Stanach Zjednoczonych Ameryki Polnocnej. (The Polish People in the United States of North America.) Lud, 11, 248–269. Lemberg, 1905.

Jirasek, A.: Chodische Freiheits Kämpfer. Translated into German by B. Lepař. Otto, Prague, 1904. (An historical novel of a Bohemian peasant revolt.)

Johnson, Emily S.: Landless Men. *Atlantic*, 99: 335–345 (March 1907).
Ticket for Ona. *Atlantic*, 101: 106–113 (Jan., 1908).
Wife from Vienna. *Atlantic*, 97: 17–25 (Jan., 1906).
Wocel's Daughter. *Atlantic*, 97: 797–808 (June, 1906).
The Younger Generation. *American Magazine*, 62 : 465–477 (September, 1906). (Delightful stories of Pennsylvania mining folk.)

Jonas, Charles: Bohemian Made Easy: A Practical Bohemian Course for English-speaking People. Second edition. Pp. 294. Slavic Press, Racine, Wisconsin, 1900. See also Consular Officers.

Jurkovič, Dušan: Slovak Popular Art. In Seton-Watson. Racial Problems in Hungary, 352–362.

Kaindl, R. F.: Geschichte der Bukowina von der ältesten Zeiten bis zur Gegenwart unter besonderer Berücksichtigung der Kulturverhältnisse. Ill. Pp. 232. Pardini. Czernowitz, 1904.

Kálal, Karl: O Působení Židů na Slovensku. (Of the Influence of the Jews among the Slovaks.) *Osvěta*, 30: 197–202, 303–313. 1900.
Působení Židů mezi Uherskými Rusy. (Influence of the Jews among the Hungarian Russians [sc. Ruthenians]) *Osvěta*, 30: 402–405. 1900.
Na Krasnem Slovensku. Pp. 110. Ill. Vilimek, Prague (no date).

Kapp, Friedrich: Aus und über Amerika. (Includes Zur Auswanderungsfrage.) Berlin, 1876.
European Emigration to the United States. A paper read before the Am. Soc. Science Ass'n. Oct., 1869. Pp. 29. New York, 1869.
Immigration and the Commissioners of Emigration of the State of New York. Ill. Pp. 241. New York, 1870.

Katolík; Česko-Americký Kalendář (The Catholic; Bohemian-American Calendar). Vol. 12, 1907. Ill. Bohemian Benedictine Press, 696 Allport St., Chicago.

Kaupas: The Lithuanians in America. *Charities*, 13: 231–235 (Dec. 3, 1904).

Kelley, Florence: Factory Inspection in Pittsburgh. *Charities and the Commons*, 21: 1105–1116 (Mar. 6, 1909).

Kellogg, P. U.: The McKee's Rocks Strike. *The Survey*, 22: 656–666 (Aug. 7, 1909).

Kellor, Frances A.: Immigration and Household Labor. A

Study of Social Conditions. *Charities*, 12: 151–152 (Feb. 6, 1904).

Protection of Immigrant Women. *Atlantic*, 101: 246–255. 1908.

Koch, Felix J.: In Quaint, Curious Croatia. *National Geographic Magazine*, 19 : 809–832. Ill. 1908.

Kohlbeck, Rev. Valentine: The Catholic Bohemians of the United States. *Champlain Educator*, 25: 36–54 (Jan.–Mar., 1906).

Kollár, Jan: Ueber die Literarische Wechselseitigkeit zwischen den verschiedenen Stämmen und Mundarten der Slawischen Nation. 2nd edition, Leipzig, 1844.

Komarow: Karta Slavjanskich Narodnostej (Chart of Slavic Nations). St. Petersburg, 1890. (Quoted in article "Slawen" in Meyer's Conversations Lexicon.)

Königreiche Kroatien und Slavonien auf der Milleniums— Landesausstellung des Königreichs Ungarn in Budapest, 1896. Pp. vii, 258. Agram, 1896.

Koukol, Alois B.: A Slav's a Man for A' That. *Charities and the Commons*, 21: 589–598 (Jan. 2, 1909).

Kovačevič, Dr. Milan: Die Auswanderung. *Agramer Tagblatt*, April 18, 19, 20, 1905. (See also an article under the same title under date of April 26.)

Kraitser, Charles: The Poles in the United States of America, preceded by the Earliest History of the Slavonians and by the History of Poland. Pp. 196. Philadelphia, 1907.

Krasinska, Françoise, Countess: The Journal of Countess Françoise Krasinska, great grandmother of Victor Emmanuel. Translated from the Polish by Kasimir Dziekonska. Pp. 182. Port. McClurg, Chicago, 1899. (A charming diary of a little Polish noblewoman toward the end of the 18th century.)

Krasinski, H.: The Cossacks of the Ukraine, comprising biographical notices of the most celebrated chiefs or atamans, including Chmielnicki, Stenko Razin, Mazeppa, Sava, Zelezniak, Gonta, Pugatchef, and a description of the Ukraine.

Krasinski, Count Valerian Skorobahaty: Historical Sketch of the Rise, Progress and Decline of the Reformation in Poland, and of the Influence which the Scriptural Doctrines have exercised on the Country in literary, Moral and Political Respects. 2 vols. London, 1838.

Montenegro and the Slavonians of Turkey. London, 1853.

Sketch of the Religious History of the Slavonic nations; being a second edition of his lectures on this subject, revised and enlarged. Edinburgh, 1851.

Pan Slavismus und Germanismus.

Krauss, Dr. Friedrich Salomon: Sagen und Märchen der Süd-Slaven, zum grossen Teil aus ungedruckten Quellen. Pp. lii, 430. Leipzig, 1883.

Sitte und Brauch der Süd-Slaven; nach heimischen gedruckten und ungedruckten Quellen. Pp. xxvi, 681. Vienna, 1885.

Slavische Volksforschungen; Abhandlungen über Glauben, Gewohnheitsrechte, Sitten, Braüche und die Guslarenlieder der Süd Slaven, vorwiegend auf Grund eigener Erhebungen. Leipzig, 1908.
Volksglaube und religiöser Brauch der Süd Slaven. Pp. xvi, 176. 1890.

Kruszka, X. Waclaw: Historya Polska w Ameryce; Poczatek, Wzrost i Rozwoj Osad Polskich w Polnocnej Ameryce w Stanach Zjednoczonychi Kanadzie. (Polish History in America; origin, growth and distribution of Polish colonies in United States and Canada.) Eight 12mo volumes, 1905–1906. Milwaukee, Kuryer Press.

Kucera, Magdalena: The Slavic Races in Cleveland. *Charities*, 13: 377–378. 1904.

Labor, U. S. Department of. Charts Exhibited at the Pan-American Exposition. (Chart III, showing relative real wages—wages measured by wholesale price, 1840–1899.) Bulletin No. 38. (Jan., 1902.)

Labor Organization and Immigrants. See Commons; Fitch; Industrial Commission, vols. xv and xvii; Kellogg; Mitchell; Ripley; Roberts; Smith; Stewart; Warne; Wing; Wright.

Language. See Boeckh; Die Statistische Bedeutung, etc.; Dixon; Edmonds; Jones; Mametej; Ruthenian-American Vocabulary; Safařik; Slavonian-English and English-Slavonian Dictionary; Slovak American Interpreter.

Lee, Joseph: Assimilation and Nationality. *Charities and the Commons*, 19: 1453–1455. 1908.

Leger, Louis Paul Marie: Cyrille et Methode: Etude Historique sur la Conversion des Slaves au Christianisme. Pp. xxv, 230. Paris, 1868.
Etudes Slaves. Voyages et Littérature. Pp. viii, 347. Paris, 1875.
A History of Austro-Hungary from the earliest times to the year 1889. Translated from the French by Mrs. Birkbeck Hill with a preface by Edward A. Freeman. Pp. xxxiv, 672. Map. Putnam, 1889.
Le Monde Slave. Pp. xxii, 344. 2nd edition. Paris, 1897.
Nouvelles Etudes Slaves. Histoire et Littérature. Pp. iii, 406. Paris, 1880.
Recueil de Contes Populaires Slaves. Traduits sur les textes originaux. Pp. xiv, 266. Paris, 1882.
Russes et Slaves. Etudes politiques et littéraires. Ie Série; II Série; III Série.
La Save, le Danube et le Balkan. Voyage chez les Slovènes, les Croates, les Serbes et les Bulgares. Pp. x, 279. 2nd edition. Paris, 1889.
Souvenirs d'un Slavophile. Pp. 314. Paris, 1905.

Legislation as to Emigration. See Levay; Whelpley.

Levay, Baron Louis de, Royal Commissioner of Emigration: The Hungarian Emigration Law. *North American,* 182: 115–122. 1906.

Lévy, Daniel: L'Autriche-Hongrie; Ses Institutions et ses Nationalités. Paris, 1871.

Library of Congress: A List of books (with references to periodicals) on Immigration. Compiled under the direction of Appleton Prentiss Clark Griffin, Chief Bibliographer. Third issue with additions. Pp. 157. Government Printing Office, Washington, 1907.

Lichard, Milan and Kolísek, Rev. Alois: Slovak Popular Melodies. (In Seton-Watson's Racial Problems in Hungary, 372–391.)

Life Story of a Hungarian Peon. *Independent,* 63: 557–564. 1907.

Literature. See Bowring; Comenius; Kollár; Mijatovics; Morfill; Murko; Šafařik; Lutzow; Škultéty; Talvi; Wratislaw. See titles in Seton-Watson's bibliography, Racial Problems in Hungary, p. 528.

Lithuanians. See Kaupas.

Little Russians. See Ruthenians.

Lovejoy, Owen R.: The Slav Child: A National Asset or a Liability. *Charities,* 14: 882–884 (July, 1905).

Loydold, L.: Die Ein- und Auswanderung durch den Hafen von New York im I Semester, 1908. *Statistische Monatsschrift,* N. F. Pp. 13: 637–666. 1908.

Lutzow, Count F. N. H. V.: Bohemia; an historical sketch. Pp. xviii, 438. Maps. London, 1896.

A History of Bohemian Literature. Pp. xii, 425. Appleton, 1899.

Lectures on the Historians of Bohemia. Ilchester Lectures for 1904. Pp. vii, 120. London, 1908.

The Life and Times of Master John Hus. Pp. xi, 398. Ill. Dent, 1909.

The Story of Prague. Pp. xix, 206. Ill. London, 1902.

McDowell, Mary E.: The Struggle in the Family Life. *Charities,* 13: 196–7 (Dec. 3, 1904).

McLanahan, Samuel: Our People of Foreign Speech. A handbook distinguishing and describing those in the United States whose native tongue is other than English, with particular reference to religious work among them. Pp. 105. Maps. Revell, 1904.

Magyars. See Hungarians.

Mailáth, Joseph: Studien über die Landarbeiterfrage in Ungarn. Wiener Staatswissenschaftliche Studien, Vol. vi, Heft II. Map. Deuticke, 1905.

Die Magyarische Staatsidee, Kirche und Nationalitäten in Ungarn. Geschildirt von einem Slovaken. Pp. 56. Prague, 1887.

Mamatej, Albert: Nový [Americký Tlumač. (New American Interpreter) [Slovak]. Pp. 291. Rovnianek, Pittsburgh.

Masaryk, Dr. Alice G.: The Bohemians in Chicago. *Charities,* 13: 206–210 (Dec. 3, 1904).

Mashek, Nan: Bohemian Farmers in Wisconsin. *Charities,* 13: 211–215 (Dec. 3, 1904).

Maurice, C. Edmund: The Revolutionary Movement of 1848–9 in Italy, Austria-Hungary and Germany, with some examination of the previous thirty-three years. Pp. xxiv, 515. Ill. London, 1887.

Mayo-Smith, Richmond: Theories of Mixtures of Races and Nationalities. *Yale Review,* Vol. 3.

Mayr, H. V.: Statistiche Monatsschrift, 1897.

Meinzingen, Dr. Franz von: Die Binnenlandische Wanderung und ihre Rückwirkung auf die Umgangssprache nach der letzten Volkszählung. N. F. vii : 693–729.
Statistische Monatsschrift, 1902.
Die Wanderbewegung auf Grund der Gebürtigkeitsdaten der Volkszählung vom 31 December, 1900. *Ibid.,* 1903.

Merse, Max: L'Autriche à l'Aube du XX Siècle. Preface de M. d'Estournelle de Constant. Pp. vii, 175. Paris, 1904.

Mijatovich, Chedomil: Servia and the Servians. Boston, 1908. (A story of Magyars and Slovaks in Hungary.)

Mijatovics, Elodie Lawton: The History of Modern Serbia. Pp. xiv, 272. London, 1872.
Serbian Folklore. Popular tales selected and translated . . . . edited with an introduction by the Rev. W. Denton. Pp. vi, 316. London, 1874.
Kossovo. Serbian national songs about the battle of Kossovo in one poem. Tr. London, 1881.

Mikszath, Kalman: St. Peter's Umbrella. Translated from the Hungarian by B. W. Worswick, with Introduction by R. Nisbet Bain. Pp. xii, 289. 1901.

Miners. See Commons; Roberts; Warne.

Mischler, E.: Die Auswanderung aus Oesterreich-Ungarn. *Sozialpolitisches Centralblatt.* Aug. 1, 1872.

Mišik, Štefan: Kostol a Fara v Hnilci, Kratka Monografia. (Church and parish in Hnilec; a brief monograph). Turc. Sv. Marten. 1895.

Mitchell, John: Organized Labor. Its Problem, Purposes, and Ideals, and the Present and Future of American Wage Earners. Chap. XXI, The Immigrant and the Living Wage. Pp. xii, 436. Ill. Phila., 1903.

Mittheilungen aus dem Gebiete der Statistik. Herausgegeben von der K. K. Statistischen Central Commission. Vienna, 1852–1874.

Mittheilungen des Statistischen Landesamtes des Herzogthums Bukowina. Edited by Anton Zachar. Czernowitz.

Moleville, M. Bertrand de: Translated by R. C. Dallas. The Costume of the Hereditary States of the House of Austria, Displayed in fifty colored engravings, with Descriptions and an Introduction. London, 1804.

Monatliche Statistische Mittheilungen herausgegeben vom Königl. Stat. Landesamte in Zagreb. (In German and Croatian.)

Montenegro. See Coffin; Krasinski (Montenegro and the Slavonians of Turkey); Revel; Wilkinson.

Moore, Henry Hoyt: The Black Dirt People, *The Outlook*, 93: 949–957 (Dec. 25, 1909).

Morfill, W. R.: History of Poland. (The Story of the Nations Series.) New York, 1893. The Dawn of European Literature. Slavonic Literature. Pp. viii, 264. S. P. C. K. London, 1883. Slavonic Literature. S. P. C. K. London, 1883.

Munro, A.: Rambles and Studies in Bosnia-Herzegovina and Dalmatia, with an account of the proceedings of the Congress of Archeologists and Anthropologists held in Aug., 1894. Ill. Edinburgh, 1895.

Murko, Matthias: Deutsche Einflüsse auf die Anfänge der Slavischen Romantik. Graz, 1897.

Music. See under Lichard. A bibliography of Bohemian, Moravian and Slavak composers and folksongs will be found in Seton-Watson's Racial Problems in Hungary. Pp. 526, sq.

Nagel, Dr. Emil: See Statistische Monatsschrift, 1883, 1884, 1885.

Náprstek, Vojta: Pametni Listék. Pp. 18. Ill. Prague, 1894.

National Civic Federation. Facts about Immigration: being the Report of the proceedings of Conferences on Immigration held in New York City, Sept. 24 and Dec. 12, 1906, by the Immigration Department of the National Civic Federation; containing also a description of the work of the Immigration Department and a brief summary of the objects of the National Civic Federation. Pp. 151. Jan., 1907.

National Slavonic Society of the U. S. A. Constitution and By-Laws. Organized Feb. 16, 1890, revised and adopted at the Convention held at Connellsville and New Haven, Pa. . . . 1906. (In English and Slovak.) Pp. 185. Press of P. V. Rovnianek & Co. Pittsburgh, 1906.

Nemec, Božena: The Grandmother, A Story of Country Life in Bohemia. Translated from the Bohemian with a biographical sketch of the author, by Frances Gregor, B. L. Pp. 352. McClurg, 1892. (A little Bohemian Classic. A charming story of Bohemian country life.)

Neruda, Jan: Kleinseitner Geschichte. Trans. by Franz Jurenka. Reklam, Leipzig. (Charming stories of Prague life. A Bohemian classic.)

Niederle, Dr. Lubor: Národopisná Mapa Uperských Slováků na Základě Sčitání Lidu z Roku 1900. (Ethnographical Chart of the Hungarian Slovaks on the basis of the Census of 1900.) Pp. 208. Maps. Wiesner, Prague, 1903.

Norton, Eliot: The Need of a General Plan for settling Immigrants Outside the Great Cities. *Charities*, 12: 152–154 (Feb. 6, 1904).

Oesterreichisches Statistisches Handbuch. 1882 (?)–1907. K. K. Statist. Zentral Kommission. Vol. 26, 1907. For earlier years see Statistisches Jahrbuch der Oesterreichischen Monarchie.

Oesterreichisches Staatswörterbuch. Ulrich und Mischler. See articles on Agrarverfassung Ausgedinge, and other subjects.

Oesterreichisch-Ungarische Monarchie in Wort und Bild; Auf Anregung und unter Mitwirkung des Kronprinzen Erzherzog Rudolf. 25 vols. Ill. Vienna, 1886.

Official Catholic Directory. Wiltzius Co., Milwaukee.

Orczy, Baroness: A Son of the Soil. (A story of Magyar life.)

Osada, Stanislaw: Historya Zwiazku Narodwego Polskiego i Rozwoj Ruchu Narodowego Polskiego w Ameryce Polnocny. (History of the Polish National Alliance and Development of the Polish National Movement in North America.) Pp. 747. Ill. Press of the Polish National Alliance, Chicago, 1905.

Palmer, E. H. E.: Austro-Hungarian Life in Town and Country. Ill. New York, 1903.

Palmer, Frances E.: Russian Life in Town and Country. Pp. 11, 320. Ill. Putnam, 1901.

Panslavism. See Čapek (The Slovaks of Hungary. Chaps. ii and iv); Colquhoun (Chap. xiii); Drage (Austria-Hungary, pp. 543, 548–559); Kollár; Krasinski (Pan Slavismus und Germanismus, Sketch of Religious History of the Slavonic Nations); Leger (Etudes Slaves, Le Monde Slave, Nouvelles Etudes Slaves (Russes et Slaves Series I); "Panslawismus" (Article in Meyer's Conversations Lexicon); Stead, Wm.; Seton-Watson.

Partsch, Joseph: Central Europe. Pp. xiv, 358. Maps. Ill. Appleton, 1903.

Peasant. See Austria-Hungary and the Balkan States; Buchenberger; Galicia; Mailáth Oesterreichisches Staatswörterbuch; Pratt; Schullern-Schrattenhofen. See also Agriculture.

Pflügl, Richard v.: See Statistische Monatsschrift, 1903, 1905, 1906, 1909.

Peez, Carl: Mostar und sein Culturkreis; ein Städtebild aus der Herzegovina. Pp. 13, 245. Ill. Leipzig.

Peixotto, Ernest C.: Impressions of Dalmatia. *Scribner's*, 40: 1–18 (1906).

Pennell, Joseph: The Jew at Home. Ill. Pp. 105. Appleton, 1892. (A one-sided and very unfavorable account of the Polish and Russian Jews and of Jewish towns in Galicia.)

Philology. See Language.

Pilat, Dr. Th.: Die Auswanderung aus den Podolischen Bezirken nach Russland im Jahre 1892. Statistische Monatsschrift. Pp. xix, 61–87 (1893).

Pink, Luis H.: The Magyar in New York. *Charities*, 13: 262–263 (Dec. 3, 1904).

Pohřebni Reči nad rakvi a u hrobu pro veškeré Damské Spolky. (Funeral Speeches over the coffin and at the grave, for Ladies' Societies.) Pp. 36. Geringer, 150 W. 12th St., Chicago.

Poland. See Brandes; Krasinska; Krasinski; Morfill; Sienkiewycz. See also Galicia.

Die Polen in Rheinisch-Westfälischen Kohlenbezirk. Alldeutscher Verband. Munich, 1902. (Interesting on the question of assimilation.)

Poles on Farms. See Kruszka; Moore; Sanford; Titus; Tomkiewicz; Tyler (articles in Boston *Daily Globe* (June 29, 1902), Springfield *Sunday Union* (Jan. 7, 1906), New York *Herald* (Jan. 14, 1906), Boston *Evening Transcript* (May 8, 1909, and Aug. 4, 1909). See also under Farming. For conditions in Austria-Hungary see Agriculture.

Poles in the United States. Besides above references on Poles on Farms, see *The American Pioneer;* Bailey; Ballagh; Conway; Donaldson; Garret; Harriman; Janik; Kraitser; Kruszka; Osada; Polish Exiles; Polskie Colonie; Proper; Roosevelt; Sanford; Tomkiewicz. See also above, Appendix xiv (1), page 457.

Polish Exiles. *New England Magazine*, 8: 33–40 (Jan., 1835). See also series of four sonnets called "Slavonia" by J. G. Percival; two based on quotations from Russian, one from Polish, one from Bohemian, *ibid.*, pp. 88–90.

Polish Religious History. See Allen; Edwards; Krasinski.

Polskie Kolonie w Stanach Zjedn. Poln. Ameryki i ich krótkie Dzieje. (Polish Colonies in U. S. A. and a brief history of them.) Pp. 226-247, Kalendarz Katolicki na Rok Zwyczajny 1895. Press of Ludi Polskiego w Ameryce. 141-143 West Division St., Chicago.

Pratt, E. A.: Organization of Agriculture. New York, 1904.

Probst, Dr. Friedrich: See under *Statistische Monatsschrift*, 1892 and 1893.

Prochazka, Karel: Kolarovicti Dratenici; Narodopisna Studie. (The Tinkers of Kolarovice; an ethnographical Study.) Pp. 96. Ill. Cyrillo-Methodius Publishing House, Prague.

Proper, Edward Emberson: Colonial Immigration Laws. Columbia University Studies in History, Economics and Public Law, xii. Pp. vi, 91 (1900).

Protokolle der in der Zeit vom 9 März bis 7 December 1900, bei K. K. Landesregierung in Czernowitz abgehaltenen Auswanderungs-Conferenzen. Pp. 148. Czernowitz, 1901. The same for the Conferences of April 20 to May 10, 1901. Pp. 164.

Przewa-Tetmajer, Kazimierz. Aus der Tatra. Translated by Immendorf, J. von. Pp. 259. Marchlewski. Munich. 1903. (In Internationale Novellen Bibliothek.)

Radič, Stjepan: Moderna Kolonizacija i Slaveni. Maps. Pp. vi, 374. Matica Hrvatska, Agram, 1904.

Rambaud: L'Ukraïne et ses Chansons Historiques. *Revue des Deux Mondes*, 1877.

Rauchberg, Dr. Heinrich: Die Bevölkerung Oesterreichs auf Grund der Ergebnisse der Volkszählung vom 31 Dec., 1890. Vienna, 1895.

Der Nationale Besitzstand in Böhmen. Leipzig, 1905. 3 vols. Reviewed by E. G. Balch in the *Political Science Quarterly*, 21 : 155–8 (1906).

Recouly, Raymond: Le Pays Magyar. Alcan, 1903.

Religious Aspects of Immigration. See Crowell, K. B.; Edwards; Grose; McLanahan; Roberts; Steiner; Strong. See also Churches.

Reuter, Fritz: Ut Mine Stromtid (Translated as "Seed Time and Harvest," or "An Old Story of my Farming Days.")

Revel, H. A.: Aus den schwarzen Bergen, novellen aus Herzegovina und Montenegro. Pp. 173. Stuttgart, 1904.

Riis, Jacob: How the Other Half Lives. Pp. xvi, 304. Scribner's, 1890. (Chap. XII. The Bohemians—Tenement House Cigar Making.)

Ripley, Wm. Z.: Race Factors in Labor Unions. *Atlantic*, 93 : 299–308. 1904.

Races in the United States. *Atlantic*, 102 : 745–759. 1908.

Races of Europe. 2 vols.

Ritter, William: Fillette Slovaque. Paris, 1903.

Roberts, Peter: Anthracite Coal Communities; a Study of the Demography, the Social, Educational and Moral Life of the Anthracite Regions. Pp. xiii, 378. New York, 1904.

The Anthracite Coal Industry, with Introduction by Professor W. G. Sumner. Pp. 261. Macmillan, 1901.

English for Coming Americans; a rational system for teaching English to Foreigners. Pp. 82. New York, 1909.

Heeding the Call of a Million Men. The Young Men's Christian Association at work for Emigrants and Immigrants. Paper presented at the World's Conference of Young Men's Christian Associations. Barmen-Elberfeld, Germany, 1909. Pp. 30. Published by Industrial Department of International Committee of Y. M. C. Associations. 124 East 28th St., New York City.

The Sclavs in the Anthracite Coal Communities. *Charities*, 13 : 215–222 (Dec. 3, 1904).

Robins, Dr. Jane E.: The Bohemian Women in New York. I. Their Work as Cigar-makers. II. Home work among them. *Charities*, 13 : 195–196 (Dec. 3 ,1904).

Romanczuk, Julian: Die Ruthenen und ihre Gegner in Galizien. Pp. 40. Stern, Vienna, 1902.

Roosevelt, Th.: Winning of the West. (Reference to Sodowsky, i, 164; see also index.)

Rosický, Jan: Jak je v Americe; pro poučeni nově do Ameriky přijetých krajinů ze své zkušenosti 45-letiho pobytu v Amerike a 30-letiho působeni žurnalictickeho napsal Jan Rosický řidící rolnického Časopisu "Hospodař". (How it is in America; written for the information of fellow countrymen newly come to America, by Jan Rosický, managing editor of the agricultural paper Hospodar, from the experience of his 45 years' stay in America and 30 years' journalistic activity.) Pp. 48. Ill. Narodni Tiskarny (National Press) Omaha, 1906.

Rovnianek, P. V.: The Slovaks in America. *Charities,* 13: 239–245 (Dec. 3, 1904).

Royal (British) Commission on Labor. See Austria-Hungary and the Balkan States.

Ruthenian-American Vocabulary and Phrase Book. (The title of the original is in Ruthenian.) Pp. 112. Svoboda Press, Scranton, Pa.

Russia Emigration from; Consular Officers. See Consular Reports

Ruthenians. See Arden; Connor; Franzos; Hruszewski; Rambaud; Romanczuk; Ruthenische Revue; Sembratowycz; Thomson. See also Galicia.

Ruthenische. Halbmonatsschrift; Editors Basil R. v. Jaworskyj, Dr. Andreas Kos, Roman Sembratowycz. Vol. 1, 1903.

Rybák, Miloslav: The Slovak Emigration. (Unprinted MSS., 33 pp.)

Šafařík, P. J.: Geschichte der Slawischen Sprache und Literatur nach allen Mundarten. Tempsky, Prague, 1869.

Sandor-Gjalski: Erzählungen. Trans. from the Croatian by Ida Fürst. Pp. 96. Reklam, Leipzig. (Stories of Croatian Life.)

Sanford, Albert Hart: The Polish People of Portage County. Proceedings of the State Historical Society of Wisconsin at its 55th Annual Meeting. Pp. 259–288. Ill. Madison, 1908. (This article was unfortunately unknown to me when writing of this Polish settlement. See above, page 230.)

Sanitation. See Adams, S.; Wing, F.

Sasinek, Franz V.: Die Slovaken; eine Ethnographische Skizze. Second revised edition. Pp. 50, Prague, 1875.

Sayles, Mary Buell: Housing and Social Conditions in a Slavic Neighborhood. *Charities,* 13: 257–262 (Dec. 3, 1904).

Schilder, Sigmund: Agrarische Bevölkerung und Staatseinnahmen in Oesterreich. Pp. viii, 170. Vienna, 1906.

Schimmer: See Statistische Monatsschrift, 1886, 1887.

Schmid: See Statistische Monatsschrift, 1888, 1890.

Schullern-Schrattenhofen, Dr. Hermann: Die Oesterreichische Landwirthschaft in ihren socialen Bezielungen. In Sociale Verwaltung in Oesterreich am Ende des 19 Jahrhunderts. Band I, Heft V. Pp. 1–40. Vienna, 1900.

Schwegel, Dr. H. (Vice consul for Austria-Hungary in Chicago): Die Einwanderung in die Vereinigten Staaten von Amerika, mit besonderer Rücksicht auf die Oesterreichisch-Ungarische Auswanderung. *Zeitschrift für Volkswirtschaft, Social Politik nnd Verwaltung.* 13: 160–207 (1904).

"Scotus Viator." See Seton-Watson.

Sembratowycz, Roman: Das Zarentum im Kampfe mit der Zivilisation. Pp. 56. Stern, Vienna, 1905.

Seton-Watson, R. W. ("Scotus Viator"): Racial Problems in Hungary. Pp. xxvii, 540. Plates. Constable, London, 1908.

Servia. See Bowring; Durham; Mijatovich; Mijatovics.

Severance, Mary F.: A Guide to American Citizenship. Pp. 48. 1909. (Published in various languages.)

Sheridan, Frank J.: Italian, Slavic and Hungarian Unskilled Immigrant Laborers in the United States. U. S. Bulletin of Labor, No. 72. Pp. 403–486. Sept., 1907.

Shipman, Andrew J.: Our Russian Catholics: the Greek Ruthenian Church in America. Part I: The Greek Church and the Union, 251–260. Part II: The Greek Catholic Church of Today, 430–452. Part III: The Greek Catholics in the United States, 570–579 and 663–673. *The Messenger,* vol. 13, 1904. Messenger Office, 27–29 West 16th St., New York.

Sienkiewycz, Henryk: With Fire and Sword. An historical novel of Poland and Russia. Translated from the Polish by Jeremiah Curtin. Boston, 1890.
The Deluge. An historical novel of Poland, Sweden and Russia. Translated by Jeremiah Curtin. 2 vols. Boston, 1891.
Pan Michael. An historical novel of Poland, the Ukraine and Turkey. Trans. by Jeremiah Curtin, Boston, 1896. (These three novels in this order are the famous "trilogy.")
After Bread. A Story of Polish Emigrant life to America. Trans. by Vatslaf A. Hlasko and Th. N. Bullick. Pp. 165, 59. (The author, perhaps influenced by the opinions prevailing in conservative and agrarian Polish circles, pictures Polish immigrants who perish miserably in America.) Fenno, N. Y., 1897.
On the Field of Glory. An historical novel of the time of King John Sobieski. Trans. by Jeremiah Curtin, Boston, 1896.
Hania (and other stories). Trans. by Jeremiah Curtin, Boston, 1900.
Knights of the Cross. (A story of the struggle of Poland

506   BIBLIOGRAPHY

against the Teutonic Knights.)   Trans. by Jeremiah
    Curtin, Boston, 1900.
Sielanka, a Forest Picture, and other stories.   Trans.
    by Jeremiah Curtin, Boston, 1898.
Yanko the Musician and other Stories.   Trans. by Jeremiah
    Curtin,   Boston, 1893.   (All the stories in this collec-
    tion besides others, are also contained in "Sielanka."
Škultéty,   Jozef: Venec   Slovenských   národných   piesní.
    (Anthology of Slovak national songs.)   Pp. 288.   Turc
    St. Martine, 1897.
Slavic Alliance in Cleveland.   Short account of the history, its
    founding, its function and aims.   (Title translated,
    published in various Slavic languages.)   Cleveland,
    1904.
Die Slaven und die Nationalitätenfrage; Gedankenskizze von
    einen Slovaken.   Pp. 40.   Prag, 1881.
Slavonian-English and English-Slavonian Pocket Dictionary.
    (Slavonian here means Slovak.)   Pp. 116.   Emil
    Nyitray, 77 First Ave., N. Y.
Slavonic (sc. Slovak) Evangelical Union of America, Incorporation
    and Bylaws of.   (In English and Slovak.)   Pp. 72.
    Press of Slovenska Pravda,   19 Main St. Freeland, Pa.,
    1903.
Slawen, article in Meyer's Conversations Lexicon.
Slovak American Interpreter.   Nový Anglický Tlumočnik pre
    Slovakov v Amerike.   5th edition.   Pp. 108.   Press
    of Slovak v Amerike, 198 East 10th St., N. Y.   1904.
Slovaks.   See Aeltere und Neuere Magyarisierungs Versuche
    in Ungarn; Balch (A By Election); Browning; Capek;
    Hegedüs; Irby; Jurkovič; Kálal; Lichard; Die Magyar-
    ische Staatsidee; Mišik; Niederle; Ritter; Rybák;
    Sasinek; Seton-Watson; Die Slaven und die Nation-
    alitäten frage;   Stodola;   Die Unterdrückung der
    Slovaken; Úprka; Vajanský.   See also Emigration
    from Austria-Hungary.
Slovaks in the United States.   First Catholic Slovak Union of
    U. S. A.;   Furdek;   National Slavonic Society of the
    U. S. A.;   Rovnianek.
Smalley, E. V.:   The Isolation of Life on the Prairie Farm.
    Atlantic Monthly, 72: 378–382 (1893).
Smith, Rufus D.:   Some Phases of the McKee's Rocks Strike.
    Survey, 23: 38–45 (Oct. 2, 1909).
Smythe, E. A., Viscountess Strangeford: Eastern Shores of the
    Adriatic.   1864.
Somogyi, Mano: A Hazai Vándoripar és Vandorkereskedés
    (Wandering Dealers and Workers).   Pp. 61.   Buda-
    pest, 1905.
Sonnichsen, Albert: Confessions of a Macedonian Bandit.
    Pp. 268, Ill.   Duffield, 1909.
Spann, Dr. Othmar: Die Unehelichkeit in Oesterreich nach
    Volkstämmen und ihre Entwiklung im letzten Jahr-
    zehnt.   Statistische Monatsschrift.   N. F. 14: 120–122
    (1909).

Špera, Josef: Maly Katechismus v Otázkách a Odpovědích pro česko-americke Školy dle Katechismu Patera Cipína (Little Catechism in Questions and Answers for Bohemian-American schools after the catechism of Cipina). Pp. 8o. Geringer, 150 W. 12th St., Chicago.

Statistische Mittheilungen über die Verhältnisse Galiziens. Edited by Dr. Th. Pilat. Statistisches Bureau des Galizisches Landes-Ausschuss. Lemberg.

Statistische Monatsschrift. Herausgegeben vom Bureau der K. K. Statistischen Central Commission. 1875. In this official statistical monthly have appeared a series of papers on Austrian emigration, as follows:
Schimmer, G.: Auswanderung Oesterreichs 1876. iii, 523–4. 1877. Auswanderung Oesterreichs im jahre 1877. v, 27. 1879. Auswanderung nach den Vereinigten Staaten von Nord America. v, 423–4. 1879. Auswanderung Oesterreichs im Jahre 1878. vi, 32. 1880. Auswanderung aus Oesterreich, im Jahre 1879. vii, 129–130. 1881. Auswanderung Oesterreichs, im Jahre 1880. viii, 138–9. 1882. Auswanderung Oesterreichische, im Jahre 1881. viii, 595–6. 1882.
Nagel, Dr. Emil: Auswanderung aus Ungarn. ix, 509. 1883. Oesterreichs Auswanderung im Jahre 1882. x, 141–2. 1884. Auswanderung Oesterreichs im Jahre 1883. xi, 40–41. 1885.
Schimmer: Auswanderung aus Oesterreich im Jahre 1884. xii, 34–6. 1886. Auswanderung aus Oesterreich im Jahre 1885. xiii, 132–4. 1887.
Schmid: Auswanderung, die überseeische oesterreichische im Jahre 1886. xiv, 39–42. 1888. Auswanderung, die überseeische oesterreichische in den jahren 1887 und 1888. xvi, 149–164. 1890.
Probst, Dr. Friedrich: Auswanderung, die überseeische oesterreichische insbesondere in den Jahren 1889 und 1890. xviii, 1–25. 1892. Auswanderung, die überseeische oesterreichische im Jahre 1891. xix, 379–388. 1893.
Pilat, Prof. Dr. Th.: Auswanderung, die, aus den podolischen Bezirken nach Russland xix, 61–87, 1893.
Mayr, H. v.: Die überseeische oesterreichische Wanderung, 1892–1895. N. F. ii, 580–601, 1897.
Buzek: Die überseeische oesterreichische Wanderung in den Jahren 1896 bis 1898. N. F. v, 72–105, 1900.
Meinzingen, Dr. Franz von: Die binnenländische Wanderung und ihre Rückwirkung auf die Umgangssprache nach der letzten Volkszählung. N. F. vii, 693–729, 1902.
Pflügl, Richard v.: Die überseeische oesterreichische Wanderung in den Jahren 1899–1901. N. F. viii, 496–532, 1903.
Meinzingen, Franz v.: Die Wanderbewegung auf Grund der Gebürtigkeitsdaten der Volkszählung vom 31 Dezember, 1900. N. F. viii, 133–161, 1903.
Pflügl, Richard von: Die überseeische oesterreichische Wanderung in den Jahren 1902 und 1903. N. F. x, 344–407, 1905. Die überseeische oesterreiche Wan-

derung in den Jahren 1904 und 1905 und die Ein-
wanderungsverhältnisse in den Wichtigsten über-
seeischen Staaten in diesen Jahren. N. F. xi, 495–509,
573–629, 1906.

Fehlinger, H.: Die Oesterreicher in den Vereinigten Staaten
von Amerika. N. F. xii, 172–5, 1907.

Loydold, L.: Die Ein- und Auswanderung durch den Hafen
von New York im I Semester 1908. N. F. xiii,
637–666, 1908.

Pflügl, Richard v.: Die überseeische oesterreichische
Wanderung in den Jahren 1906 und 1907 sowie die
Einwanderungs und sonstige Verhältnisse in den
wichtigsten Einwanderungs Staaten. N. F. xiv,
239–256, 308–324, 355–384, 408–440, 1909.

Statistisches Jahrbuch der Oesterreichischen Monarchie (continued by Oesterreichisches Statistisches Handbuch).

Statistikai Havi Közlemények (Monthly Statistical Publications).
Edited and Published by the Royal Central Statistical
Commission. Budapest.

Stead, W. T.: The Arrival of the Slav. *Contemporary Review*,
1909.

Steerage. See Immigration Commission, Steerage Conditions;
Kapp; Vay de Vaya and Luskod.

Steiner, Edward A.: The Immigrant Tide, its Ebb and Flow.
Ill. Pp. 370. N. Y., 1909.
The Mediator: A tale of the Old World and the New.
Revell, 356, 1907. (A picture of Ghetto Life.)
On the Trail of the Immigrant. Ill. Revell, 1906.

Stewart, Ethelbert: Influence of Trade Unions on Immigrants.
In La Follette, Robert M. *ed.* The Making of America,
vol. 8. Pp. 226–235, Chicago.

Stodola, Dr. Emil: "Prispevok ku Statistike Slovenska"
(Contributions to Slovak Statistics). Pp. 31. Turčiansky Sv. Martin, 1902. Part iv, Emigration to
America, pp. 14–21.
Die Auswanderung der Slovaken nach Amerika. Articles
on Slovak Emigration in *Die Politik* of Prague (June
18, 20, 21, 1902).

Strong, Josiah (Editor): Immigration. Facts of Immigration; The Immigrant and the City; Exclusion Laws;
The Church and the Foreigner. (Part of The Gospel
of the Kingdom, a course of Study for men and women
on Living Social Problems in the Light of the Gospel
of Jesus Christ.) Published monthly by the American
Institute of Social Service. Bible House, Astor Place,
N. Y. Pp. 65–72. (June, 1909).

Šuteršič, Rev. F. S.: Poduk Rojakom Slovencem. Ki se
hočejo naseliti v Amerik. (A Guide for Slovenians.)
Amerikanski Slovenic Press. Joliet, Ill., 1903.

Svarc, V.: The Culture which the Slav Offers America; the
Handicraft and Industrial Exhibition conducted by
the Slavic Alliance of Cleveland. *Charities*, 14: 875–
881 (July 1, 1905).

Talvi [(Mrs. Robinson born Thérèse von Jacobi): Historical View of the Languages and Literature of the Slavic Nations, with a sketch of their Popular Poetry; with a preface by Edward Robinson, D.D., LL.D. Pp. ix, 412. Putnam, 1850.

Tarde, Gabriel: The Laws of Imitation. Translated by Elsie Clews Parsons, with an Introduction by Franklin H. Giddings. Pp. xxiv, 404. Holt, 1903.

Taxation. See Diplomatic and Consular Service; Drage; Twardowski.

Thirring, Gustav: Die Auswanderung aus Ungarn; Beiträge zur Statistik und topographischen Verteilung der Auswanderung. Bulletin de La Société Hongroise de Géographie. Vol. xxx, 1902 (also separately printed, pp. 29). This is practically the gist of the following Magyar work.
A Magyarországi Kivándorlás és A Külföldi Magyarsag. Pp. x, 366; tables, charts and maps. Kilian, Budapest, 1904. Reviewed in Tarsadalompolitikai Közlemények (Social-politische Mittheilungen) by Bányász László.

Thomson, E. W.: Five Days in Galicia. (A series of articles in the Boston *Evening Transcript*, the first of them under date of Oct. 17, 1905, describing Ruthenian settlers in Canada).

Titus, Edward Kirk: The Pole in the Land of the Puritan. *New England Magazine*, N. S. Pp. xxix, 162–166 (Oct., 1903).

Tomkiewicz, J. W. S.: Polanders in Wisconsin. Proceedings State Historical Society of Wisconsin, 1901. Pp. 148–152, 1902.

Travels. See Durham; Evans; Henderson; Hutchinson; Irby. See also Albania; Dalmatia; Hungary; Servia.

Twardowski, Dr. J. v.: Statistische Daten über Oesterreich. Pp. 125. Leipzig, 1902.

Tyler, Elizabeth S.: The Poles in the Connecticut Valley. *Smith College Monthly*, 16 : 579–586 (June, 1909).

Umlauft, Friedrich: A. Hartleben's kleines statistisches Taschenbuch über alle Länder der Erde. Vienna, 1905.

Uprka, Joža: Vybor jeho Praci (Selections from his work). (This work contains 39 large and very fine reproductions in color and one etching from Uprka's pictures of the Slovaks of Moravia. Accompanying text [in Bohemian, French or German] by Joseph Klvaňa and V. Mrštik. The Bohemian text has extra illustrations in black and white and in color.) Published in two parts by "Unie," sold by B. Koči, Frantiskovo Nab. 14, Prague (1901).

United States Census.

Unterdrückung der Slovaken durch die Magyaren. Pp 76, Prague, 1903.

Vajanský, Svetozár Hurban: Slovak Popular Poetry. In Seton-Watson, Racial Problems in Hungary, pp. 362–372.

Vay de Vaya and Luskod: To America in an Emigrant Ship. *Living Age,* 252 : 173–182 (1907). (From the Monthly Review.) An account by a Hungarian chaplain of the voyage from Fiume to New York and of Hungarian causes of emigration.

Vertheilung des Grundbesitzes in der Bukowina. *Statistische Monatsschrift,* N. F. Vol. xvii, pp. 642–5 (1902).

Verwyst, Rev. P. C.: Life and Labors of Rt. Rev. Frederic Baraga, first bishop of Marquette, Michigan. To which are added short sketches of the Aims and Labors of other Indian Missionaries of the Northwest. Wiltzius, Milwaukee, 1900.

Viestnik, Kr. Zemaljskoga Statističkoga Ureda v Zagrebu. (Statistical publications of the royal statistical Bureau in Agram.)

Vlach, J. J.: Our Bohemian Population. Proceedings State Historical Society of Wisconsin, 1901. Pp. 159–162, 1902.

Volkszählung vom 31. Dezember, 1900, in den Königreichen Kroatien und Slavonien: Hauptergebnisse nach Verwaltungs-Gemeinden, herausgegeben vom Kg. Stat. Landesamte in Zagreb. (In German and Croatian.) Pp. 34. Agram, 1902. The same, Hauptergebnisse nach Wohnorten (in German and Croatian). Pp. 360.

Wages. See Abbott; Commons; Fitch; Labor, Dept. of; Sheridan.

Waldau, Alfred: Böhmische Nationaltänzen. 2 vols. Prague, 1860.

Wandering Trades, Slovak. See Prochazka; Somogyi; Kálal.

Warne, F. J.: The Coal-mine Workers: A Study in Labor Organization. Pp. 252. Longmans, 1905.

The Slav Invasion and the Mine Workers; a study in Immigration. Pp. 211. Lippincott, 1904.

Some Industrial Effects of Slav Immigration. *Charities,* 13 : 223–226 (Dec. 3, 1904).

The Union Movement among Coal-mine Workers. Bulletin of U. S. Bureau of Labor, No. 51. Pp. 380–414. (Mar., 1904.)

Watchorn, R.: Gateway of the Nation. *Outlook,* 87 : 897–912 (1904).

Whelpley, F. D.: Control of Emigration in Europe. *North American Review,* 180 : 856–867 (June, 1905).

White, Elizabeth T.: Investigation of Slavic Conditions in Jersey City. Printed for Whittier House [a Jersey City Settlement], 1907.

Whitman, S.: The Realm of the Habsburgs. London, 1893.

Wilkinson, J. G.: Dalmatia and Montenegro. 2 vols. London, 1848.

Wing, Frank E.: Thirty-five Years of Typhoid. *Charities and the Commons,* 21 : 923–937 (Feb. 6, 1909).

Wing, M. T. C.: The Flag at McKee's Rocks. *Survey,* 23 : 45–46 (Oct. 2, 1909).

Wingfield, W. F.: A Tour in Dalmatia, Albania, and Montenegro, with a Sketch of the Republic of Ragusa. London, 1859.

Wissenschaftliche Mittheilungen aus Bosnien und der Herzegovina. Gerold's Sohn, Vienna.

Women Immigrants. See Abbott; Butler; Immigration Commission; Kellor.

Wratislaw, Albert Henry: Lýra Českoslovanska. Bohemian folk songs, ancient and modern, translated from the original Slavonic, with an introductory essay. London, 1849.

Native Literature of Bohemia in the 14th Century. Four lectures on the Ilchester Foundation, 1878.

Wright, Carroll D.: Influence of Trade Unions on Immigrants. Bulletin of U. S. Bureau of Labor, No. 56, pp. 1–8 (Jan., 1905).

Zadruga. (The titles under this head are not listed separately under authors' names.)

Bogisič, Dr. V.: Zbornik Sadašnjih Pravnih Običaja u Južnih Slovena (Collection of present customary laws among the South Slavs), Agram, 1874.

Demelič, F.: "Le Droit Coutumier des Slavs Méridionaux" d'après les recherches de M. V. Bogisitsch, Paris, 1877. De La Forme dite *Inokosna* de la Famille Rurale chez les Serbes et les Croates, Paris, 1884.

Cuculič, Milorad v.: Studija o Zadružnom Zakonu. (A study of the Zadruga law.) Agram, 1884 and 1885.

Halladi, Franz: A German translation of the Croatian law as to land-holding associations (Grundgenossenschaften). Hardtmann, Vienna.

Ivič: Die Hauscommunionen. Semlin, 1874.

Janovič & Gruič: Slavs du Sud. Paris, 1853. Pp. 104-5.

Laveleye, Émile de: De la Propriété et ses Formes Primitives (translated into German by Karl Bücher as Das Ureigenthum. 1879).

Maine, Sir Henry Sumner: Ancient Law. Village Communities in the East and West.

Peisker: Die Serbische Zadruga.

Popovič: Recht und Gericht in Montenegro. Agram, 1877. (Pp. 32-50.)

Spevac, Dr. J.: O Jurističnoj Naravi Zadruge. (On the juridical character of the Zadruga.) Agram, 1884.

v. Tkalec: Das Staatsrecht des Fürstenthums Serbiens, Leipzig, 1858. (Pp. 60-66.)

Turner: Slavisches Familienrecht. Strassburg, 1874. (For Zadruga see pp. 2, 11, 15, 50.)

Utješenovič: Die Hauscommunion der Südslawen. Vienna, 1859.

Vojnovič, Dr. K. v.: Seoska Obitelj Kod Hrvata i Srba. (The Peasant Family among Croatians and Servians.) Agram, 1885.

Vrbanič, Dr. F.: Rad Hrvatskoga Zakonarstva na Polja Uprave od g. 1861. (Croatian Administrative Legislation since 1861.) Agram, 1893. (Said to contain an especially instructive passage on Croatian Zadruga legislation.)

Zoričič, M.: Die bäuerliche Haus-Communion. (See below.)

Zdrůbek, Frank B.: Dějiny Česko-Národního Hřbitova v Chicagu, Illinois, od jeho Založeni 1877 do jeho 25-letí jubilejní slavnosti 1902. Ill. Pp. 144. Geringer, Chicago. Pohřebni Řeci s přidanim řeci při pojmenování dítek, řeč kmotra, a poděkování otce. (Funeral addresses with additional speeches for use at the naming of children, speech of the sponsors and thanks of the father.) Pp. 56. Geringer, Chicago.

Zoričič, Milovan: Demographische Arbeiten in den Königreichen Kroatien und Slavonien. Pp. 70. Agram, 1887.
Die bäuerliche Haus-Communion in den Königreichen Kroatien u. Slavonien. VIII International Congress for Hygiene and Demography. Budapest, 1894. Pp. 21. Separately printed, Budapest, 1897.
Naši izseljenici u sjedinj. državama Američkim. (Our Emigrants to the U. S. A.) Viestnik kr. Zemaljskoga Statističkoga Ureda u Zagrebu. 2 : 108, 1900. (This appears to be mainly if not wholly based on American material.)
Statistische Skizze der Königreiche Kroatien und Slavonien. Pp. 170. Agram, 1885.

INDEX

INDEX